MONOGRAPHS OF
THE MEDIAEVAL ACADEMY
OF AMERICA
No. 4

ACADEMY PUBLICATIONS

No. 1, *A Concordance of Boethius*, by LANE COOPER

No. 2, *A Concordance to the Historia Ecclesiastica of Bede*, by P. F. JONES

No. 3, *A Survey of the Manuscripts of Tours*, by E. K. RAND, two volumes, text and plates

No. 4, *Lupus of Ferrières as Scribe and Text Critic*, by C. H. BEESON, with a fascimile of *MS. Harley 2736*

No. 5, *Genoese Shipping in the Twelfth and Thirteenth Centuries*, by E. H. BYRNE, (*Monograph No. 1*)

No. 6, *Greek and Syrian Miniatures in Jerusalem*, by W. H. P. HATCH, with reproductions

No. 7, *Harūnū'l-Rashīd and Charles the Great*, by F. W. BUCKLER, (*Monograph No. 2*)

No. 8, *Alien Merchants in England, 1350 to 1377*, by ALICE BEARDWOOD (*Monograph No. 3*)

No. 9, *A Concordance of Prudentius*, by R. J. DEFERRARI and J. M. CAMPBELL

No. 10, *The Script of Cologne from Hildebald to Hermann*, by L. W. JONES, text and plates

No. 11, *Feudal Monarchy in the Latin Kingdom of Jerusalem, 1100–1291*, by J. L. LA MONTE (*Monograph No. 4*)

No. 12, *Alexander's Gate, Gog and Magog, and the Inclosed Nations*, by A. R. ANDERSON (*Monograph No. 5*)

FEUDAL MONARCHY IN THE LATIN KINGDOM OF JERUSALEM 1100 TO 1291

JOHN L. LA MONTE

Assistant Professor of History
The University of Cincinnati

THE MEDIAEVAL ACADEMY OF AMERICA

CAMBRIDGE, MASSACHUSETTS

1932

KRAUS REPRINT CO.
New York
1970

The publication of this book was made possible by a fund granted the Academy by the Carnegie Corporation of New York

Reprinted with the permission of the original publisher
KRAUS REPRINT CO.
A U.S. Division of Kraus-Thomson Organization Limited

DEDICATED TO

CHARLES L. LA MONTE

MY FATHER

CHARLES H. HASKINS

MY MASTER

PREFACE

THE Latin kingdom of Jerusalem, as a typical feudal state, has long been studied by scholars interested in feudal institutions, who have discerned in the *Assises de Jérusalem* as clear a picture of the workings of feudal government as it is possible to find anywhere. Even though the kingdom of Jerusalem has never enjoyed the vogue accorded the crusades themselves, it has not been without its historians from the time of William of Tyre to the present. Students of legal history have explored the *Assises*, economic historians have studied the trade relations of the western commercial cities with the ports of the Latin states, and the general history of the crusading principalities, especially with emphasis on their relations with their Moslem neighbors, has been written. The *Geschichte des Königreichs Jerusalem* of Reinhold Röhricht stands out as the monumental study of the crusading states and provides an invaluable basis on which any more specialized treatises may be reared. The renaissance of crusading studies which is connected with the names of Von Seybel, Röhricht, and Hagenmeyer in Germany, Riant, Mas Latrie, Rey, and Delaville Le Roulx in France, Stevenson and Kingsford in England, and Munro in America, has made the crusades and the Latin states comparatively familiar fields of mediaeval history. None the less the only study hitherto made on the institutions of the kingdom of Jerusalem, that of Gaston Dodu, *Histoire des Institutions Monarchiques dans le Royaume Latin de Jérusalem* (Paris; Hachette, 1894), was written before much of the best work had been done and suffered from the consequent drawbacks. Dodu was particularly unfortunate in having written before Röhricht's *Regesta Regni Hierusalimitani* had appeared, the indispensible guide to the documentary sources of the kingdom. Dodu bases his view of the monarchical institutions of Jerusalem upon the *Assises* and upon the chroniclers, especially William of Tyre, making but slight use of the documentary materials. In the present reconsideration of the institutions of Jerusalem I have relied essentially upon documents, which afforded materials in some

vii

cases confirming, in others, I think, disproving the conclusions reached by Dodu.

Further, this study differs essentially from that of Dodu in the materials selected to illustrate the *Assises*. In searching for historical data to confirm the provisions of the *Assises*, Dodu drew most of his illustrations from the history of William of Tyre, which chronicles the Outremer States from their founding to 1184, and from the other chroniclers of the first crusade. Grandclaude, however, has conclusively established that the oldest of the books which make up the *Assises* dates from the last decade of the twelfth century or the first of the thirteenth, and that the institutions which are reflected in the majority of the books of the *Assises* are not those of the early kingdom of Jerusalem but those of the so-called 'second kingdom' of the thirteenth century. Thus the historical facts which really illustrate the statements of the *Assises* must be drawn not, as Dodu did, from the twelfth century historians, but from the chroniclers of the thirteenth century,—from the *Gestes des Chiprois*, and the continuators of William of Tyre. To cite but a single example of the distorted perspective which Dodu gives, the account of the relations of the kings with the patriarchs given in the *Institutions Monarchiques* is the story of the rivalry and hostility which marked the first decades of the kingdom, the struggles of Baldwin I and II with the patriarchs Daimbert, Evremar, Arnulf, and Stephen; Dodu takes no account of the friendly and peaceful relations which prevailed throughout the later years of the kingdom.

This volume seeks to study as a whole the monarchical institutions of the kingdom of Jerusalem. The first section of the work is devoted to a study of the chief constitutional developments within the kingdom, traced chronologically. The history of the kingdom is divided arbitrarily into three periods:—the first kingdom from 1100 to 1174; the years of transition from 1174 to 1210; and the second kingdom from 1210 to 1291. In the first two periods the historical background for the *Assises* is sketched; the third shows how the laws were applied to the actual constitutional history of the state. Following this historical section come, in the second division of the book, chapters devoted to certain of the more important aspects of the administration:—the courts, high and low; the chancery and the grand officers; the military establishment; and the administration of

finance. The third section of the book shows the relations of the
Jerusalemite monarchs to some of their contemporaries:—their
vassals, the counts of Tripoli and Edessa, and the princes of Antioch;
their overlord, the Pope; the patriarchs; the Orders of the Hospitallers, Templars, and Teutonic Knights; and the Italian and
Provençal communes which established colonies in the ports of
Outremer and played such important rôles in the political and economic life of the crusading principalities. In each case we have
sought to show whether the group or institution under consideration
helped or hindered the monarchy, and to emphasize the significance
of the relationship to the kingdom of Jerusalem. The author hopes
that in the section devoted to the institution he has brought to
light some new facts concerning the administration of the kingdom,
but the real purpose of the work is not so much to bring out facts
hitherto unknown as to focus into a single study the various phases
of the institutional development and organization of the kingdom.
Much of the material covered in this volume is not new, but it is so
scattered that a single treatise which aims to cover the entire field
should not be out of place.

The scope of the work has been strictly limited. The kingship
is the center around which the work was built. The relations with
the Arab states, the social organization of the Frankish and native
populations, and the intellectual history of the crusading states
have been purposely omitted. The present volume does not approxi-
mate the scope of Prutz's *Kulturgeschichte der Kreuzzüge;* social
history will have to be sought in Rey's *Colonies Franques*, commercial history in Heyd's *Histoire du Commerce du Levant,* the wars and
campaigns against the Saracens in Röhricht's *Geschichte.* While
all of these subjects are of vital importance to a rounded view of Outremer civilization, they do not belong in a study which is confessedly
constitutional and institutional. Not even all the institutions have
been discussed; private law has been slighted save as it affected public, the ecclesiastical hierarchy and organization has been considered only as it was related to the monarchy; the institutions of
the kingdom of Cyprus have been reserved for treatment in a separate volume.

The name, 'Latin Kingdom of Jerusalem,' as used in the title refers
to all the states which were under the overlordship of the king of Jeru-

salem. There is some confusion inevitably in the use of a title which may refer to two distinct things: the kingdom of Jerusalem in its larger sense is that referred to above, but in a lesser sense the kingdom of Jerusalem may refer only to the royal domain lands, excluding the counties of Edessa and Tripoli and the principality of Antioch. To avoid this confusion I have made use of the terms Outremer and principality of Jerusalem. But as Outremer properly includes the kingdom of Cyprus as well as Jerusalem, the use of this term has been limited. Unfortunately there is no convenient differentiating term for Jerusalem like the Ile de France for the French royal domain exclusive of the feudal dependencies of the French crown. For this reason I have fallen back on the use of the term *principality* where the sense might have been confused by the use of the more technically correct title of kingdom.

In the matter of the spelling of proper names, as there is no accepted rule for the standardization of medieval names, an arbitrary method has been followed throughout this work, names having a clear English equivalent have been given the English form (John, Ralph, Walter, William, instead of Jean, Johannes, Raoul, Gautier, Guilelmus, etc.); names which do not have ordinary English equivalents have been kept in the French form (Amaury, Foulque, Renaud). The use of *de* or *of* before the last name has been governed by attempting to use *de* where it is a family name (d'Ibelin, de Lusignan, de Gibelet), and *of* where the name is that of a place of which the individual was lord (of Beirut, of Jaffa, etc.); thus John d'Ibelin of Beirut, Hugh de Puiset of Jaffa. In a few cases, men well known under the modern vernacular form of their name have been allowed to appear under that form,—Jacques de Vitry, Dominico Michieli, Benedetta Zaccaria. Oriental names have followed accepted English transliterations,—though Colonel Lawrence's attitude has more than once commended itself throughout the process of standardizing proper names. In references in the notes to the works of writers where the name of the author is given as an abbreviation for the title of the work, the original spelling has been preserved, as Jacques d'Ibelin, which is merely a shortening of the title *Le Livre de Jacques d'Ibelin.* William of Tyre, Albert of Aix, and a few others are, however, so well known under the English forms of their names that these have been followed.

This volume is based upon a dissertation presented at Harvard University in 1928. Since then, further study, the opportunity for which was most generously made possible by the Social Science Research Council, which gave the author a travelling fellowship to visit the Near East and to spend a year in collecting materials for his projected history of Cyprus under the Lusignans, and the criticism kindly given by several scholars have led to a total revision of the original thesis. Only a few sections bear any marked resemblance to the manuscript in the Harvard University Library; one chapter of the original was published separately in the *Haskins Anniversary Essays*, others have been thrown out, several new ones added, and the whole has been broadened and completely rewritten.

In acknowledging the assistance and encouragement which I have received, thanks are due first of all to Professor Charles Homer Haskins, under whose guidance and direction the subject was originally approached, and who has followed the work with that unfailing interest which all who were privileged to work under him know so well and appreciate so deeply. Professor Robert P. Blake has been no less kind in encouraging the author at all stages of his work, in reading the manuscript, offering suggestions, and finally subjecting the completed work to an exhaustive editorial criticism. Among other scholars who have read some or all of the book and who have materially assisted the author with advice, for which thanks are rendered, may be mentioned: Professor Charles H. McIlwain and Dr Gaines Post of Harvard University; Professor Dana C. Munro of Princeton; Professor Max Handman of Michigan; Professors August C. Krey and Herbert Heaton of the University of Minnesota; and last but not least Professor Edgar H. McNeal of the Ohio State University, who first taught the author to love the Middle Ages and to seek therein his life work and enjoyment. I wish also to proffer my thanks to the Mediaeval Academy and Mr John Marshall, who have made possible and pleasurable the publication of the work. Lastly, for many hours of labor spent in correcting the manuscript, reading proof, and compiling the index, as well as for her lively interest and unfailing encouragement, I wish to express my appreciation to Katherine R. La Monte, my wife.

JOHN L. LA MONTE.

CINCINNATI, OHIO.

CONTENTS

APPENDICES

LIST OF ABBREVIATIONS

Employed to Designate Works Frequently Cited in the Notes

A.H.R.—*American Historical Review*, New York, 1895—

Abrégé—*Abrégé des Assises de la Cour des Bourgeois* in *Assises de Jérusalem*, vol. ii, 227–352.

Albert Aix—Albertus Aquensis, *Historia Hierosolymitana*, in *R. H. C. Occ.*, iv, 265–713.

Annales Terre Sainte—*Annales de Terre Sainte* edited by R. Röhricht, in *Archives de l'Orient Latin*, ii, B, 427–61.

Archives—*Archives de l'Orient Latin*, 2 vols: Paris: Société de l'Orient Latin, 1881–84.

Assises—*Les Assises de Jérusalem*, edited by Count Beugnot, *R. H. C. Lois*, 2 vols: Paris, 1841–43.

Assises d'Antioche—*Les Assises d'Antioche*, edited by P. Alishan, Venice; Société Mekhithariste, 1876.

Assises de Romanie—*Les Assises de Romanie*, edited by G. Recoura, Paris: Champion, 1930.

Assises Cour Bourg.—*Les Assises de la Cour des Bourgeois*, in *Assises*, ii, 3–226.

B. E. C.—*Bibliothèque de l'École des Chartes*, Paris, 1839—

Caffaro, *Annales*—Caffaro de Caschifelone, *Annales Ianuensis*, edited by L. T. Belgrano in *Fonti per la Storia d'Italia* (Turin, 1890), vol. xi. (The *Liberatio Civitatum Orientis* is published in the same volume, and the continuators of Caffaro in the *Annales Ianuensis* are found in the succeeding three volumes of the *Fonti*.)

Camera—M. Camera, *Memorie Storico-diplomatiche dell' antica Città e Ducato di Amalfi*, 2 vols, Salerno, 1876.

Chronologie—H. Hagenmeyer, 'Chronologie de la Première Croisade 1094–1100' and 'Chronologie du Royaume de Jérusalem 1100–1105', *R. O. L.*, vi–xii (1898–1911). The references are cited by the number in the *Chronologie*, the numbering running consecutively through the two series.

Clef Assises—*La Clef des Assises de la Haute Cour*, in *Assises*, i, 573–600.

D. L. *Archives*— J. Delaville Le Roulx, *Les Archives, la Bibliothèque et le Trésor de l'Ordre de St Jean de Jérusalem à Malte*, Paris: Bibliothèque des Écoles Françaises d'Athènes et de Rome, xxxii, 1883.

D. L. *Cartulaire*—J. Delaville Le Roulx, *Cartulaire Général de l'Ordre des Hospitaliers de St Jean de Jérusalem*, 4 vols, Paris, 1894–1904. (Cited by number of document, volume not indicated.)

Delaborde—H. F. Delaborde, *Chartes de la Terre Sainte provenant de l'Abbaye de Notre Dame de Josaphat*, Paris: *Bibliothèque des Écoles Françaises d'Athènes et de Rome*, xix, 1880.

Docs. Rel. Succ. Tr.—*Documents Relatifs à la Successibilité au Trône et à la Régence*, in *Assises*, ii, 397–422.

Docs. Inéd.—*Collection des Documents Inédits sur l'Histoire de la France*, Paris, 1835—

Dodu—G. Dodu, *Histoire des Institutions Monarchiques dans le Royaume Latin de Jérusalem*, Paris, 1894.

E. H. R.—*English Historical Review*, London, 1885—

Eracles—*Le Livre d'Eracles*, continuator of William of Tyre in Old French; edited in *R. H. C. Occ.*, vol. ii. (When citation to the Old French translation of William of Tyre has been made the references are to William Tyre, French text;—these occur in the vol. i of the *R. H. C. Occ.* below the Latin text of William. References to *Eracles* are always to the continuator in the second volume. References to *Rothelin Eracles* are to the so-called Rothelin manuscript of the work, edited at the end of the Académie edition.)

Ernoul—*La Chronique d'Ernoul*, edited by L. Mas Latrie, Paris, Société de l'Histoire de France, 1871.

Familles—DuCange, *Les Familles d'Outremer*, edited by E. G. Rey, Paris: *Docs. Inéd.*, 1869.

Fulcher—Fulcherius Carnotensis, *Historia Hierosolymitana*, edited by H. Hagenmeyer, Heidelberg, 1913.

Geoffrey le Tort—*Le Livre de Geoffrey le Tort* in *Assises*, i, 433—450.

Gestes—*Les Gestes des Chiprois*, edited by L. de Mas Latrie, in *R. H. C. Docs. Arm.*, ii, 651–872. (As the citations are made by paragraph and not by page, the references can be checked in the older edition of G. Raynaud (Paris, 1887). They are not the same, however, as the paragraph numbers in the edition by C. Kohler of the *Mémoires de Philippe de Novare* (Paris, *Classiques Français du Moyen Age*, 1913). Direct quotations follow the spelling of the edition in the *R. H. C.*).

Grandclaude—M. Grandclaude, *Étude Critique sur les Livres des Assises de Jérusalem*, Paris, 1923.

Heyd—W. Heyd, *Histoire du Commerce du Levant au Moyen Age*, translated by F. Raynaud, French edition, 2 vols, Leipzig: Harrassowitz, 1885–86; anastatic reprint, 1923.

Huillard Bréholles—Huillard Bréholles, *Historia Diplomatica Friderici Secundi*, 12 vols, Paris, 1852-61. (Vol. xii is the introduction and is sometimes cited as such.)

Ibelin—*Le Livre de Jean d'Ibelin* in *Assises*, i, 7-432.

Jacques d'Ibelin—*Le Livre de Jacques d'Ibelin* in *Assises*, i, 451-68.

Liber Jurium—*Liber Jurium Reipublicae Ianuensis*, edited by Ricotti, Turin: *Historiae Patriae Monumenta*, vii, ix; 1854.

Livre au Roi—*Le Livre au Roi* in *Assises*, i, 601-644.

Mas Latrie—L. de Mas Latrie, *Histoire de l'Île de Chypre sous le Règne des Princes de la Maison de Lusignan*, 3 vols, Paris, 1852-61. (Vol. i is a narrative history of Cyprus to 1291; vols ii and iii are documents.)

Méry—Méry, *Histoire analytique des actes et des deliberations . . . de la municipalité de Marseille*, vol. i, Marseilles, 1841.

M. G. H. Epis.—*Monumenta Germaniae Historica, Epistolae*, Berlin, 1883-94.

M. G. H. SS.—*Monumenta Germaniae Historica, Scriptores*, Hanover and Berlin, 1826-74.

Migne—Migne, *Patrologia Latina*, 221 vols, Paris, 1844-64.

Müller—G. Müller, *Documenti sulle relazioni delle citte Toscane coll'oriente cristiano e coi Turchi*, Florence, *Documenti degli Archivi Toscani*, iii, 1879.

Munro-Crusades—*The Crusades and other Historical Essays presented to D. C. Munro*, edited by L. J. Paetow, New York: Crofts, 1928.

Muratori—Muratori, *Rerum Italicarum Scriptores*, Milan, 1723-51.

Novare—Philippe de Novare, *Livre de forme de plait*, in *Assises*, i, 469-571.

P. P. T. S.—Palestine Pilgrims' Text Society publications, 13 vols, London, 1890-97.

Paoli— G. Paoli, *Codice Diplomatico del sacro militare ordine Gerosolimitano oggi di Malta*, 2 vols, Lucca, 1733. (All citations are to volume i.)

Prutz, *Kulturgeschichte*—H. Prutz, *Kulturgeschichte der Kreuzzüge*, Berlin, 1883.

R. H. C.—*Recueil des Historiens des Croisades*, 16 vols, Paris, Académie des Inscriptions, 1841-1906; subdivided into the following series:—

R. H. C. Occ.—*Historiens Occidentaux*, 5 vols., 1844-95.

R. H. C. Or.—*Historiens Orientaux*, 5 vols, 1872-1906.

R. H. C. Grec.—*Historiens Grecs*, 2 vols, 1875-81.

R. H. C. Docs. Arm.—*Documents Arméniens*, 2 vols, 1869-1906.

Assises—Lois, *Les Assises de Jérusalem*, 2 vols, 1841-43.

R. H. Fr.—*Recueil des Historiens de Gaul et de France*, 24 vols, Paris, Académie des Inscriptions, 1783-1904.

R. O. L.—*Revue de l'Orient Latin*, 12 vols, Paris, 1893–1911.

Regesta—R. Röhricht, *Regesta Regni Hierosolymitani*, Innsbruck, 1893; *Additamentum*, 1904. (Documents cited *a* are in the *Additamentum*.)

Rey, *Colonies*—E. G. Rey, *Les Colonies Franques de Syrie au XII et XIII Siècles*, Paris, 1883.

Röhricht—R. Röhricht, *Geschichte des Königreichs Jerusalem*, Innsbruck, 1898.

Rozière—E. de Rozière, *Cartulaire d l'Église du St Sépulcre de Jérusalem*, Paris, 1849.

Schlumberger, *Numismatique*—G. Schlumberger, *Numismatique de l'Orient Latin*, Paris, 1878; *Supplément*, 1882.

Soc. His. Fr.—*Société de l'histoire de la France*, Paris, 1835—

Strehlke—E. Strehlke, *Tabulae Ordinis Theutonici*, Berlin, 1869.

Tafel-Thomas—G. Tafel and G. M. Thomas, *Urkunden zur älteren Handels- und Staats-geschichte der Republik Venedig*, Vienna; *Fontes Rerum Austriacarum*, sect. II, vols, xii–xiv; 1858.

Usamah—P. K. Hitti, *An Arab-Syrian Gentleman and Warrior in the Period of the Crusades*, being a translation of the Memoirs of Usāmah ibn-Munquidh, New York; *Records of Civilization*, 1929.

William Tyre—Willermus archiepiscopus Tyrensis, *Historia Rerum in Partibus Transmarinis Gestarum*, in *R. H. C. Occ.*, vol. i.

INTRODUCTION

THE institutions of the Latin crusading states owe much of their interest to the geographical location of the states themselves. Stretched along the Levantine seaboard from the Taurus passes to the desert of Sinai in the first and second centuries of their existence, the Latin principalities formed a Christian wedge in the side of the Moslem world. They nestled into that meeting place of East and West which is the Near East, that land of color and squalor, where time is unimportant and even now the machine age progresses leisurely. Before the first century elapsed they had already begun to be dislodged from their precarious foothold on the Asian shore; after another century had passed they vanished, but they still existed in Cyprus,—that island which Richard of England had conquered almost by hazard on his way to Acre in 1192 and which was destined to be the eastern outpost of Latin Christianity for over two and a half centuries.

It is of course a misnomer to refer to the East as 'unchanging', for there is change everywhere, but the Levant and the Orient in general tend to retain their customs and institutions for a far longer period of time than does the West; even in our feverish modern age the eastern Mediterranean world retains much of its 'antique flavor'. The Chevrolet in which modern Syria rides must stop and wait for a caravan of camels and donkeys to pass; bales of goods, perhaps from France or the United States, are still unloaded from the ships in Tyre harbor by naked porters who wade out and carry them in to the beach on their heads.

The Levant has always been a meeting ground of East and West, of the old and the new. It takes what it will from the newer West and keeps what it desires from the older Orient. The crusaders, who went to the East with their ideas of western feudalism, had to adapt them to the conditions of the country with its Byzantino-Saracen background and its well-developed institutions. It was a hard task, for the crusaders were mostly French, and they clung to

xix

their own institutions and customs as far as they were able. The *Assises de la Haute Cour* are in essence French feudal law, and the feudal system of Jerusalem, if the feudal system be taken to mean only the relations between the land-holding nobility, was pure western feudalism which the crusaders had brought with them from their western homes. Once established it was preserved. The forces which affected feudalism in the West had but little effect on the slower moving East. For there is truth in the old assertion that in the feudal system of Jerusalem we find an almost ideal system of feudalism. Western institutions of the eleventh and twelfth centuries are transplanted into a semi-virgin field and are retained into a later age when the West itself had largely abandoned them. Professor C. H. McIlwain points out that to find the English constitutional ideals of the Middle Ages carried out to their ultimate realization we must study American, and not modern English, institutions. It might be said for feudalism that the best examples we have of French feudalism are in Jerusalem, Cyprus, and Achaia. The colonist carried with him from his native land his native ideal of the state and put it into effect as far as he was able in the land of his adoption.

But in their relations with the non-noble, non-Frankish classes of society, the crusading barons were constrained to adopt the customs of the people; the *Assises de la Cour des Bourgeois* are a fusion of eastern and western laws, based primarily on the old Roman law which, through the medium of the Syro-Roman law books, had become, in the centuries of Byzantine and Arab rule, the custom law of the country.

The Frankish nobility became only superficially orientalized. Although they adopted oriental dress, oriental manners, and an oriental mode of living, they never really acquired much of the oriental culture or *Weltanschauung*. The scientific learning of the Arabs found its way into Europe through Spain and Sicily, not through the Latin states. The court ceremonial and court officers of Jerusalem were western and feudal, not eastern. The vassal knelt to his lord, but there was none of the prostration before the divine monarch; seneschals and constables, not wazirs, advised the king.

The lower classes of society were oriental, and the institutions which affected them bear an eastern imprint. The financial system of the kingdom of Jerusalem was, as will be shown below, largely derived from the pre-existent Arabic system, and the lower administrative officials, of whom we know so little, bear Arabic or Greek titles. Just as William the Conqueror superimposed his Norman feudalism on the institutions of Anglo-Saxon England, so the crusading leaders erected their feudal institutions on the base of the Byzantino-Saracen. That fusion, however, which characterized the English and, to an even greater degree, the Norman-Sicilian systems, never came about in Jerusalem.

It is interesting to compare Jerusalem with Sicily.[1] Both countries had Byzantine and Saracen institutions; both were conquered by a few dominant warriors from the West who formed a small ruling class over a large native population. In both the conquest was accomplished under several leaders and almost without any single accepted chief. In both instances a northern feudal system was superposed on an oriental centralized administrative bureaucracy. Yet in Sicily it was the close-knit Norman, in Palestine the loose French system,—and the results were opposite. The princes of the house of Guiscard imposed their rule on their colleagues and vassals and became strong monarchs ruling by means of an effective centralized bureaucratic system of administration, taking from the former regime those institutions which had helped to build up a centralized power, and at the same time retained the elements of strength to be found in their own feudalism. The princes of Outremer, though they took over some of the old institutions, remained feudal lords, bound by their vassals and their dependence on the military support of the great feudatories. They attempted to assert themselves; the *Assise* of Amaury *sur la ligece* was a revolutionary *coup-d'état* which aimed at securing for the kings of Jerusalem all the advantages of the Norman reservation of fealty and the strength which the English Angevins enjoyed as a result of the writ *Praecipe*. But their attempt failed; the measure which sought to reduce the vassals to impotence recoiled on the kings; the in-

---

[1] The term Sicily denotes all the Norman states in south Italy—Apulia, Calabria, etc., as well as Sicily proper.

crease of power went to the *Haute Cour*, leaving the kings more than ever subject to the will of the baronage. Conditions within the kingdom forbade the king's exercise of undue power. The constant necessity for defense and the inability of the kings to take up arms against their vassals prevented absolutism from developing. Feudal barons everywhere strove to retain their privileges and immunities, and those of Jerusalem were rather more fortunate than their western contemporaries. The situation in Jerusalem, where the king was subject to the *Haute Cour*, was one which the English barons tried to establish when they forced Magna Carta on their reluctant monarch; it was the position they had enjoyed in the days of Stephen; it was that which was prevalent in France until Philip Augustus extended his strong rule over the provinces and brought his vassals to heel.

If a western cognate be sought for the feudal institutions of Outremer, especially for the position of the king, it is to be found in France in the late eleventh and twelfth centuries before the administrative reforms of Philip Augustus. Like the early Capetians, the kings of Jerusalem were semi-elective; in both states the hereditary principle gradually replaced the elective. In both, the monarchs were generally subject to the will of their vassals. Ivo of Chartres tells us in reference to the proposed marriage of Louis VI that it would have been 'annulled by the unanimous decision of the bishops and the great lords' and that the king therefore renounced the idea.[1] The position of the rulers of the mediaeval Spanish states is also somewhat similar to that of those of Jerusalem, and there is much in common between the *Cortes* and the *Haute Cour*.[2]

Generally speaking we may affirm that the king of Jerusalem was merely the most important feudal lord, *primus inter pares* in his

---

[1] Ivo of Chartres, *R. H. Fr.*, xv, 149. In making our comparisons with France great reliance has been placed on A. Luchaire, *Histoire des Institutions Monarchiques de la France* (2nd ed., 2 vols, Paris, 1891).

[2] I do not feel that J. Longnon, *Les Français d'Outremer au Moyen Age* (Paris: Perrin, 1929), p. 102, justifies his statement that the Frankish states of Syria more closely resemble the Norman colonies in Sicily than the Spanish states, unless he has reference to the part played in both by the French. The French settled in Syria and in Sicily as they did not in Spain, but I think there are closer resemblances between the Spanish and Outremer states than between Jerusalem and Sicily.

relationship to his vassals, and what powers he possessed were rather those of a feudal suzerain than of a monarch. His chief advantage, apart from the prestige of his title, was that he had no suzerain above him to whom he was obliged to defer. Ibelin says that the king can give lands in any manner he desires, as allod, frankalmoin, with or without service, for he has no suzerain whose rights must be respected, and that he can even give to the Church or to communes if he so desires, nor may his heirs legally recall or annul his acts.[1] But in all matters of policy, and in all matters which affected a liegeman in his honor, his life, or his fief, the king was bound by the decisions of his council. Above all he was subject to the laws. Fulcher of Chartres gives an ideal picture of the king of Jerusalem:

Rex etiam contra iussa non praeficitur. Nam iure et secundum Deum electus, benedictione authentica sanctificatur et consecratur. Qui cum suscepit regimen illud cum corona aurea, suscepit quoque iustitiae obtinendae onus honestum. Cui iure, sicut et episcopo de episcopatu, potest decenter obiici; bonum opus disiderat qui regnum disiderat. Quod si iure non regit, non rex est.[2]

The Middle Ages we concede were legally minded; the states of Outremer were legalistic enough and had their full quota of jurists. If we can trust the *Assises*, Jerusalem in the thirteenth century was a state which would have delighted old Sir Edward Coke and the common law judges who maintained the sovereignty of the law. But as law was custom and custom was formulated by the *Haute Cour*, the sovereignty, could such a thing be said to exist in the thirteenth century at all, lay in the council of the barons. Dodu has summarized the position of the king in regard to the court in a succinct sentence:

En effet le royaume de Jérusalem était un État aristocratique dans lequel la véritable souveraineté appartenait non pas au roi mais au corps de la

---

[1] Ibelin, cxli, 215–16: '*Car il est de sa seignorie soul seignor et chief, ne ne la tient d'aucun seignor que de Dieu.*' The kings of Cyprus had the right to abolish the distinction between noble and bourgeois lands and to permit the acquisition of noble lands by bourgeoisie. (*Abrégé Cour Bourg.*, xxiv, 255; Beugnot, *Assises*, ii, Introduction, p. 62.)

[2] Fulcher of Chartres, II, vi, 386–87.

noblesse, c'est-à-dire à l'ensemble des hommes d'armes devant au roi l'hommage et le service militaire à titre féodal.[1]

Viewed from this angle, Jerusalemite institutions show what the feudal institutions of western Europe might have been had not the royal power gained the upper hand and directed them into another channel. Besides this they did adopt some features of the earlier systems; they themselves transmitted to the West some few institutions and certain departures from the regular feudal regime which helped the more fortunate western monarchs establish their states.

To trace the influence of the institutions of one state upon another is, as Dr Haskins has pointed out, a dangerous field of speculation and one in which there are many hidden snares.[2] It is easy enough to see how France influenced Jerusalem, also where the Byzantino-Arabic financial system played a rôle, but it is harder to indicate where the institutions of Jerusalem affected those of the West. Stubbs finds in the election of the earl of Pembroke as regent for Henry III in 1216 a reflection of the eastern practice. 'The plan adopted', he says, 'was that which the vassals of the Frank kingdom in Palestine had used on such occasions.'[3] But we shall see that election was not always the rule in Jerusalem; that later the regent was the nearest male relative of the heir,—the Outremer practice thus conforms to the western. In one case an eastern practice seems to have been taken over by the West. This was when Charles I of Anjou-Sicily attempted to force the liegemen who held fiefs in Sicily to remain in residence in the newly conquered kingdom. Both Jerusalem and Sicily had to face the same problem: how could they keep in service French knights who, like Otho de la Roche of Athens, had wearied of their new surroundings and longed to return to their homes in France? The military needs of the kingdom required that a full military establishment be maintained,

[1] Dodu, p. 160.

[2] C. H. Haskins, 'England and Sicily in the Twelfth Century', *E. H. R.*, xxvi (1911), 433 *et seq.*, shows the pitfalls which await the rash speculator in the field of comparative institutions.

[3] Stubbs, *Constitutional History of England* (Oxford, 1875), ii, 20.

and consequently we find laws forbidding vassals to leave the
country for more than a year and a day, and providing that the fiefs
of any men who did remain away for longer than the permitted time
should be confiscated.[1]

Another contribution made by Jerusalem to western institutions
is the tax levied in Jerusalem in 1183, which introduced the precedent for the assessment by the possessor of the values on movable
goods, and provided the model which was followed in Henry II's
Saladin Tithe.[2]

It is hard to determine what was the influence of Jerusalemite
institutions because we cannot date many of them accurately. For
most of our information we are still dependent upon the *Assises*,
which are late. It would be of the greatest interest could we
ascertain whether the Jerusalemite practice of sending the viscount
into the ecclesiastical courts in cases of disputed jurisdiction had
aught to do with the attempts of the English and French kings to
check benefit of clergy. Had Jerusalem worked out this solution
of the problem before Henry II was wrestling with the *Constitutions
of Clarendon?* We only know that a century later they had done so,
but do not know how long it had been the practice when the *Assises
de la Cour des Bourgeois* were written. Though we cannot determine accurately how much the institutions of Jerusalem influenced
those of the western world, and in no case was the amount great, to
study the kingship in Jerusalem is none the less interesting and
profitable.

The history of the kingdom of Jerusalem exhibits two main ten-
dencies; and the constitutional history of the realm is, through lack
of pertinent evidence, largely concerned with two problems: first,
how the monarchy developed from the elective kingship founded by
the lords of the first crusade into the hereditary monarchy of the
thirteenth century; second, the relations of the king with the baronage. These two themes are inextricably interwoven; strangely

[1] L. Cadier, *Essai sur l'Administration du Royaume de Sicile sous Charles I et Charles II
d'Anjou (Écoles Françaises d'Athènes et de Rome*, lix, Paris, 1891), p. 18.
[2] See below chapter 8, p. 180.

enough the resultant struggle is not, as might be expected, whether the hereditary king controlled his barons or the barons controlled their elective king. The elective king, rather, struggled with his barons for control; later on, the hereditary monarch recognized the limitations placed upon him by the High Court and accepted the domination of the baronage.

The history of the kingdom can be divided for convenience into two periods: that of the 'first kingdom' of the twelfth century, from the first crusade and the founding of the state to the fall of Jerusalem and the destruction of the kingdom by Saladin together with the almost total anarchy which attended the third crusade; and that of the 'second kingdom' of the thirteenth century, from the reconstruction after the third crusade to the final loss of the continental realm with the fall of Acre in 1291. Where the exact division comes can only be fixed arbitrarily; for the purposes of this study we put it at 1210 when John de Brienne became king of Jerusalem. As with all arbitrary divisions of history, this break is hardly observable when considered in its immediate background and its results; only by viewing the history of the kingdom as a whole can we see any change. The year 1210 closes the period of transition which runs from the accession of Baldwin IV to that of John de Brienne; a period when the kingdom was menaced, when it tottered, fell, and was revived. It was a period when *sauve qui peut* was *de facto* the guiding maxim of the state; constitutional rules and principles were cast aside, the war and the necessity of defense overshadowed all else. An invalid king, a disputed succession, the absence of a male heir, factional strife among the barons, the overwhelming pressure of the Saracen invasion, the forces of the third crusade who brought with them further disagreement and strife, and the emergence of strong, natural leaders among the barons, all contributed to make this period one of anarchy and disturbance. It was an era of destruction, and the reconstruction which followed had to recognize the changes which had occurred. In the first kingdom the monarch, though elective, had asserted himself on occasion and enforced his will on the barons. There had been conquests and new lands to bestow, tribute had been coming into the royal coffers, the kings had been men of more than average ability. The king might owe his election to the barons, but once elected he exercised considerable authority. In the second kingdom the monarchs held their title by hereditary right; but the control of affairs had passed into the hands of the barons, and the kings reigned but did not rule. There was more than boasting in the claim of the Ibelin that his family has led the hosts of Cyprus more often than had that of the Lusignan. Until Peter I of Cyprus in the 1360's attempted to undermine the strength of the nobility by employing bourgeois ministerials the rule of the nobles was undisputed.

The history of Jerusalem and Cyprus is one; fourteenth century Cyprus is but a continuation of the state founded by the men of the first crusade. The second period of Jerusalemite history is the first stage of Cypriot; the second and third periods of Cyprus are but continuations and might well be reckoned the third and fourth phases in the history of Jerusalem. Catherine Cornaro, last independent ruler of Cyprus, designated herself queen of Jerusalem, Cyprus, and Armenia, placing the Jerusalemite title first.

While Cyprus is a continuation of Jerusalem much is altered. The Italian cities are more important; the growing merchant class, already apparent in the West, powerfully influenced Cyprus, which was essentially a maritime community and whose wealth was dependent upon trade. Further there is a subtle difference in the geographical situation which must be taken into consideration. No longer were the Frankish lords constantly menaced by Saracen neighbors who desired the extermination of their little state. No longer did king and vassal have to hold together for defense.

One cannot but wonder, in passing from Beirut to Famagusta today, if the refugees who fled across that narrow strait in 1291 felt the same atmospheric change which is so apparent to the visitor now. St Nicholas of Famagusta and Santa Sophia of Nicosia are no less Gothic than are the cathedrals of Tortosa and Beirut; St Hilarion perched high on its mountain, overlooking Kyrenia and beyond across the sea towards Anatolia, is not essentially different from the continental castles of Baniâs, Kalaat-es-Schekif (crusading Belfort), or even mighty Krak-des-Chevaliers. The same palm trees are growing and the same camels and omnipresent donkeys are in evidence, but we sense a subtle difference. Cyprus is of the East yet not oriental. Greek predominates over Arabic. While there is much in common, they are different,—and the same differences were probably noticeable six hundred years ago. Both countries have changed; the centuries of Turkish rule probably have brought them closer together, yet the variations are there and were probably there then. While the history of Cyprus is the sequel to that of Jerusalem, it is one in which the characters have changed considerably and in which new surroundings have had their effect on the plot and on the *mise en scène*.

BOOK I

THE CONSTITUTIONAL DEVELOPMENT OF THE LATIN KINGDOM OF JERUSALEM

CHAPTER 1

THE FIRST KINGDOM, 1099-1174

IN 1231 when the barons of Jerusalem met to protest the actions of Richard Filanger, the marshal of Frederick II, Balian of Sidon, speaking for the barons, said that when the country was conquered it was not by any chief lord but by the whole people, and that the lordship of the realm was founded in election.[1] While this bit of historical evidence was used by Balian to justify his opposition to Frederick's marshal and had no practical application to the actual case in hand, it is true that throughout the twelfth century there was a marked tendency to consider the kingship as elective by the chief nobles of the land. Even when, towards the end of the century, hereditary succession to the throne was frequent, the heir was always elected and the coronation took place only after the nobles had chosen the candidate as their king.

The crusading forces which had founded the kingdom had to elect one of their number as king, for there had been no natural leader among them to whom all would naturally defer. Since the death of Adhelmar of Le Puy, the papal legate who led the crusaders in the first years of the crusade, rivalry and contention divided the various leaders, nor was anyone accepted as first among them. Before Jerusalem was taken, several of the more powerful princes dropped out, Bohemond remaining in Antioch, and Baldwin in Edessa. Robert of Normandy, Robert of Flanders, Hugh of Vermandois were all anxious to return to the West as soon as they could accomplish their vows. Stephen of Blois had deserted the army during the siege of Antioch. When the army reached Jerusalem, Raymond of St Gilles, Tancred, and Godfrey de Bouillon were the only leaders left who could be considered as candidates for the throne of the newly conquered realm. Raymond was unpopular; the bitter hatred between Bohemond and the count of St Gilles had done much to retard the progress of the crusade, and Tancred and the Normans who had come south with the army would never tolerate the election

[1] *Eracles (R. H. C. Occ.*, ii), p. 389.

3

to the kingship of their arch-enemy. Further, Raymond seemed inclined to return to the West, Tancred would never be acceptable to the Provençals, and Godfrey de Bouillon remained the one logical candidate on whose election all parties could unite. Thus a compromise candidate was chosen, a man of the second rank, who had distinguished himself but little during the crusade: thus was created a legendary hero and popular saint.[1]

But Godfrey was not the first king of Jerusalem, for he refused to accept the title and crown, contenting himself with the title of Baron and Defender of the Holy Sepulchre. The probable reason for this was that Godfrey recognized the Pope's claim to Jerusalem as a state of the Church, and not as has been often said because he would not wear a crown of gold where his Savior had worn a crown of thorns.[2]

That Godfrey considered the Church the overlord of Jerusalem is shown by his action at Easter 1100 when he performed homage to the patriarch. At the same time he made a grant to the Church whereby he promised to give the patriarch the city of Jerusalem with the custody of the Tower of David, reserving however, the usufruct

[1] The election took place July 22, 1099, the eighth day after the fall of the city. H. Hagenmayer, '*Chronologie de la Première Croisade*', *R. O. L.*, vi–viii (1898–1901), no. 409; and references cited therein.   William of Tyre, IX, i–ii, 364–367, shows the legend in process of formation.   He tells how the servants of all the leaders were questioned and that those of Godfrey could report no vices and only an excess of piety on the part of their master.   After less than three-quarters of a century Godfrey's election had become the recognition of the best and noblest in the crusading host.   This tradition is well maintained by Col. C. R. Conder, *The Latin Kingdom of Jerusalem*, (London: Palestine Exploration Fund, 1897), pp. 67–69, where a different set of causes for Godfrey's election are given.   F. Chalandon, *Histoire de la Première Croisade*, (Paris: Picard, 1925), p. 291, claims that Godfrey's election demonstrated the essential weakness of the whole system and presaged the monarchy under the control of the barons.

[2] Godfrey's subordination to the Papacy is expounded by Charles Moeller in *Mélanges Godefroid Kurth*, (Liège, 1908), pp. 73–83.   An interesting theory, though hardly one to be seriously considered, is that suggested in the Russian article of G. Laskin, noted in the *R. O. L.*, vii (1899), p. 630, that Godfrey refused to assume the crown because Heraclius had not worn his crown when he brought the Holy Cross back to Jerusalem after his Persian campaign, and because the patriarch of Jerusalem on that occasion celebrated the Holy Offices without wearing his mitre out of reverence for the holy occasion.   The legend of the 'crown of thorns' motif had taken root early and Ludolph von Suchem in 1350 wrote that Godfrey and Baldwin had made a rule that no king of Jerusalem should ever wear a golden crown but should wear instead a crown of thorns, 'which rule' says the pious traveler, 'their successors observe even to this day' (sic!).   (Ludolph von Suchem, *Descriptio Terrae Sanctae*, (translation in *P. P. T. S.*, xxvii,) par. 38, p. 104.)

of the city for life or until such time as he was able to conquer another city for himself.[1]

Godfrey's rule, though short, evinced considerable ability, and it may be safely said that in the first year of its existence the foundations of the state were laid and the general features of its government were determined. Besides continuing the war with the Saracens and winning the great battle of Ascalon, Godfrey distributed fiefs and organized in a rough way the system of courts for the nobles and bourgeoisie.[2] Later Jerusalemite tradition attributed to Godfrey the original code of laws, the *Lettres du Sépulcre*, which was said to have been compiled under the duke's direction by ascertaining the customs and usages of the various peoples who made up the new state.[3]

When Godfrey died on July 18, 1100, the succession caused difficulties. Godfrey's own preference had been for his brother Baldwin, count of Edessa, and the election of Baldwin was carried in a hurried conclave of Godfrey's personal friends and officials, who seized Jerusalem for Baldwin.[4] But the Patriarch Daimbert, who was busy

---

[1] *Chronologie*, no. 455; R. Röhricht, *Regesta*, doc. 29; William Tyre, IX, xvi, 388; H. Hagenmeyer, *Die Kreuzzugsbriefe*, (Innsbruck, 1901), pp. 168–74, 371–403.

[2] Ibelin, ii, 23; Albert Aix, VII, xxxvii, 532, tells how the people produced before Baldwin the benefices which Godfrey had granted them.

[3] Ibelin, iv, 25–26; Novare, xlvii, 521–23.

[4] *Chronologie*, nos. 482, 486, 489; William Tyre, X, i–iii, 401–03; Albert Aix, VII, xxvii, 524; Raoul de Caen, *Gesta Tancredi*, (*R. H. C. Occ.*, iii) cxlii, 705; Fulcher, II, i, 352–53. Concerning the election of Baldwin, Albert says that the barons consulted Godfrey as to a successor and swore to him that they would elect none save his brother or some relative: '*nulli regnum Iherusalem se reddituros nisi fratribus suis aut uni de sanguine eius*'. Raoul says that they asked Godfrey to suggest a successor. Fulcher says that Baldwin was expected by the Jerusalemites to succeed his brother and that he rejoiced in his inheritance: '*Balduino, quod omnis populus Hierosolymitanus eum in regni principem substituendum heredem exspectarent ... gaudens de hereditate ...*'. William says that Baldwin was elected to succeed by hereditary right: ' *Tandem vero, sive supremo domini ducis judicio, sive de communi principum, qui pauci erant, consilio, citatus est dominus Balduinus, Edessanus comes, domini praedicti ducis ex utroque parente frater, ut in regnum accederet jure sibi debitum haereditario, et fratri succederet in eadem cura*'. Ernoul, p. 5, says that the realm escheated to Baldwin. From these statements it is apparent that, whether or not Godfrey proposed Baldwin, his adherents considered Baldwin as Godfrey's heir and that Godfrey's party acclaimed Baldwin on their own initiative. Also, while hereditary succession cannot be argued from such evidence, it does show that by the time William and Ernoul wrote hereditary succession had so far gained acceptance that Baldwin was thought to have inherited the throne.

The leaders in the group which elected Baldwin were Garnier de Gray, Geldemar Carpinel, Wicker l'Alleman, Geoffrey the chamberlain of the duke, Mathew his seneschal, Arnulf of Chocques, and Bishop Robert of Rama.

besieging Haïfa in alliance with Tancred and the Venetians,[1] claimed the reversal of Jerusalem under the terms of Godfrey's grant, and, fearing that Baldwin would not surrender the city to him, requested Bohemond to prevent Baldwin's reaching Jerusalem.[2] These plans miscarried, however, as Bohemond was captured by the Saracens and the letter destined for him fell into the hands of Raymond of St Gilles, who turned it over to Baldwin.[3] Baldwin, who had met Maurice, the papal legate, at Laodicea and secured his support, proceeded south to his new possessions, arriving in Jerusalem the ninth of November, where on the thirteenth he received the oaths and homages of his vassals.[4] Daimbert was conspicuously absent at this ceremony; it was not until the Christmas following that peace was made between the king and patriarch and Baldwin was solemnly crowned as king of Jerusalem by Daimbert in the Church of the Nativity at Bethlehem.[5] Tancred, who had tried to capture Jerusalem while Baldwin was coming down from Edessa, was given the regency of Antioch during Bohemond's captivity, and withdrew to the north.[6]

Though Baldwin took an oath of homage to the patriarch at the time of his coronation, the difficulties between them were by no means ended; the first twelve years of the reign were marked by difficulties with the patriarchs, which ended only with the accession of Arnulf of Chocques to the patriarchal throne.[7]

The reign of Baldwin I was primarily one of conquest. Beugnot

---

[1] *Chronologie*, nos. 484, 487, 488, 496.   The siege was ended with the capture of the city August 20.

[2] *Chronologie*, no. 491; Albert Aix, VII, xxvii, 524; William Tyre, X, iii–iv, 403–06; G. Dodu, pp. 349–52.

[3] *Chronologie*, nos. 493, 495, 499, 501.

[4] *Chronologie*, nos. 503, 506, 514, 515; Fulcher, II, i–iii, 352–70; Albert Aix, VII, xxxvii, 532.

[5] *Chronologie*, no. 524; Fulcher, II, vi, 384–85.   Daimbert retreated to Mount Sion and refused to enter the city.

[6] *Chronologie*, nos. 509, 511, 540, 542.   Baldwin and Tancred were old enemies having come into conflict over Tarsus in 1098. (*Gesta Francorum*, ed. Bréhier, Paris: Champion, 1924, p. 58.)

[7] On the difficulties of the kings with the patriarchs, see chapter 10 below.   E. Hampel, *Untersuchungen über das lateinische Patriarchat von Jerusalem von Eroberung der heiligen Stadt bis zum Tode des Patriarchen Arnulf (1099–1118)*, (Breslau, 1899), relates the details of the struggle of patriarch and king during the first eighteen years of the kingdom.

claims that Baldwin was an active legislator and that he is responsible for laws dealing with military service, confiscation of fiefs, and the celebrated *Assise du coup apparent*.[1] Concerning the first two, as Beugnot cites no specific assise, I cannot say, but I am convinced that the *coup apparent* was the work not of Baldwin I but of Baldwin IV, under whose reign it will be discussed. Nor have I been able to find evidences of any considerable legislative activity under Baldwin I, though in all probability it was he who carried on Godfrey's codification of the laws.

One event of the reign of Baldwin I is, however, of the highest importance in the constitutional development of the kingdom; it shows how the kings sought to make the throne hereditary and how the barons strove to keep it elective. In 1113 Baldwin, whose first wife had died on the crusade, and whose second wife, an Armenian princess, had been repudiated, married Adelaide, widow of Roger of Sicily, who brought with her a rich dower which the kingdom badly needed. In the marriage contract it was agreed that should any children be born of the union, the throne of Jerusalem should pass to the eldest at the death of Baldwin, but that should Baldwin and Adelaide have no issue, the throne should pass on the death of Baldwin to Roger of Sicily, Adelaide's son by her first husband.[2] But it was not at all to the liking of the barons, or of Arnulf the patriarch, that the throne should go to the Sicilian prince, and when in March 1117 Baldwin was sick, and no children had yet been born to Adelaide, Arnulf summoned a council of the clergy and barons which solemnly proclaimed the annullment of the marriage on grounds of consanguinity. Adelaide at once returned to Sicily where she died the following year.[3]

Baldwin died even before his unfortunate wife, succumbing to a fever as he was returning home from a campaign in Egypt in April

---

[1] Beugnot, *Assises*, i, Introduction, p. 22.

[2] William Tyre, XI, xxi, 488–89: 'si rex ex praedicta comitissa prolem susciperet, ei post regis obitum sine contradictione et molestia regnum concederetur . . . si absque herede ex eadem comitissa suscepto defungeretur, comes Rogerius filius eius, haeres existeret; et in regno, sine contradictione et molestia rex futurus, succederet'. Röhricht, pp. 103–04.

[3] William Tyre, XI, xxix, 505. Röhricht, p. 118. It is interesting to speculate what might have been the results both to Jerusalem and the West had Roger become the king of Jerusalem, and combined the crowns of Jerusalem and Sicily.

1118. According to Albert of Aix, the chief barons went to the dying king and asked him whom he desired as a successor, to which he replied his brother Eustache of Boulogne, or his nephew Baldwin de Burg, whom he had left in Edessa when he took the throne of Jerusalem. Though Baldwin's wish may have influenced the votes, the accession of Baldwin de Burg came about purely through election. Nor was the election undisputed, but Joscelin de Courtney, who led the party favoring the count of Edessa, carried the day and Baldwin was elected by the council of the clergy and nobles. The supporters of Eustache had already sent messengers to their candidate summoning him to the East, but Baldwin's partisans urged the necessity of electing a ruler who could take possession at once and Eustache was met in Apulia with the news of Baldwin's election.[1]

Baldwin II is considered one of the strong kings of Jerusalem. Like that of his predecessor, his reign of thirteen years is marked by a constant series of wars against Aleppo, Damascus, and Egypt.[2] Constitutionally his rule is important for the regency during his imprisonment, the council of Neapolis of 1120, the struggle with the Patriarch Stephen, and the election of his successor. Besides these

---

[1] Albert Aix, XII, xxvii–xxx, 707–10: *'diversi diversa dicerent, tandem omnibus acceptum fuit ut Balduinus de Burg in throno regni Iherusalem locaretur'*.

Fulcher, III, i, 616, says merely that Baldwin was *'communiter electus'*.

William Tyre, XII, iii, 513–16, tells the whole story as one in which the claims of the legitimate candidate were overruled by necessity. The adherents of Eustache urged his election: *'nec interrumpendam haereditariae successionis antiquissimam legem'*; Baldwin's election was an usurpation: *'Videtur tamen minus regularem habuisse introitum; legitimumque regni haeredem certum est a debita successione fradulenter exclusisse illos qui eum promoverunt;. . . quia quod factum erat, contra ius et fas, et contra hereditariae successionis legem antiquissimam, nullo modo stare posset.'*

Eustache had accepted the offers of the envoys who came to fetch him to Jerusalem, but when he reached Apulia and heard of the election of Baldwin, he turned back refusing to start a civil conflict, though his escort assured him the election was illegal.

Joscelin was rewarded for his championing of Baldwin, as he had hoped to be, by the grant of the county of Edessa, which he held in fief of the king.

[2] C. R. Conder, *The Latin Kingdom of Jerusalem*, pp. 75–77 et seq., gives a picture of the peaceful life in Palestine which while true in fact gives, I feel, the wrong impression. He says that Jerusalem was more at peace than were the western states at the same period, and dismisses the wars of the Jerusalemites with the explanation that, as they were fought on the frontiers, they did not greatly effect the internal conditions of the country. While the interior of the kingdom was not overrun by invasion and war, the continual struggle on the frontiers could not but materially have effected the internal affairs of the state, also the siege and capture of Tyre can be put on the frontier of the kingdom only by a very liberal interpretation of the term.

major events, several assises have been preserved from the reign of Baldwin II.

The great council of Neapolis, which is the first important event of the reign of Baldwin II, was called by the Patriarch Warmund and the king to reform the abuses in the Church and the morals of the kingdom generally. It was attended by the clergy and chief nobles of the realm, being as much a meeting of the *Haute Cour* as an ecclesiastical council. Among the twenty-five articles which were enacted at this council were measures regarding the payment of the tithes to the Church, regulations concerning slavery, marriage, and other personal relations. This council and its decrees are important for our purposes, not for what we learn about the moral degradation of the Jerusalemites, but because ecclesiastical matters were discussed and rules adopted in a council composed largely of the lay nobility of the kingdom, and that some of its provisions were issued by the king with the consent of his barons.[1]

In the same year the king abolished the dues which had previously been collected on all oil and vegetables entering the David Gate into Jerusalem. This decree was issued in the form of a charter and was witnessed by clergy, nobles, and bourgeoisie.[2]

In April 1123 Baldwin, while campaigning near Antioch, endeavoring to rescue Joscelin of Edessa who had been taken captive, was himself captured by Balak of Aleppo. The barons of Jerusalem elected Eustache Grenier, lord of Caesarea and Sidon and constable of the kingdom, to be bailli during the king's captivity. But Grenier died the following June, and William de Buris, prince of Galilee and lord of Tiberias, who succeeded Grenier in the constableship, was elected to take his place.[3] The regency of de Buris is important as showing the degree of control exercised over the king by the

---

[1] The full text of the decree of the council is to be found in J. D. Mansi, *Sacrorum Conciliorum Nova et Amplissima Collectio* (2nd ed., Paris, 1900), xxi, 261–66. See also William Tyre, XII, xiii, 531; *Regesta*, doc. 89; Röhricht, p. 146. The *Livre au Roi*, xvi, 616–17, contains laws and assises of Baldwin II.

[2] Rozière, doc. 45; *Regesta*, doc. 91; *Assises*, ii, 485–86. Later, between 1128 and 1130, Baldwin remitted the charges on pilgrims entering the port of Acre if their goods were less than 40 besants in value. (Rozière, doc. 46; *Assises*, ii, 486–87; *Regesta*, doc. 125.)

[3] William Tyre, XII, xvii, 537–38; Fulcher, III, xvi, xx–xxii, 658–61, 669–75. The *Documents Relatifs à la Successibilité au Trône* (*Assises*, ii), p. 398, credits Grenier with the Venetian treaty and the siege of Tyre and ransoming the king, events which occurred under de Buris, his successor.

barons. Baldwin had asked the Venetians to assist him in the capture of Tyre, and a fleet under Dominico Michieli came to the East in
1123. In the absence of the king, a treaty was made between the
Patriarch Warmund and William de Buris and the Venetians.
After enumerating the concessions to be granted the Venetians in
return for their aid, the treaty promises that the king will accept
and ratify it upon his release, nor will any other person be accepted
as king until he has confirmed its terms.[1] Thus we see how the
barons controlled the king. Baldwin upon his liberation, after his
ransom had been raised by de Buris, ratified and confirmed the
treaty.[2] The reign of Baldwin II was troubled in the years 1128–30
with the pretensions of the Patriarch Stephen who attempted to
revive the patriarchal suzerainty and control over the kingdom but
Stephen's ambitions were stopped by his death, and his successor
William was entirely amenable to the royal policies.[3]

About this same time the question of the succession came to the
fore. Baldwin had only daughters, and it was necessary to choose
a successor to the throne. The king desired to combine dynastic
with elective claims and to marry his eldest daughter, Melissande, to
the man whom the barons elected as their king. Summoning a
council of his barons, he raised the question and discussed possible
candidates for the hand of Melissande and the throne of the kingdom.
The choice fell on Foulque, count of Anjou, then about forty years
of age, who had been recommended by Louis VI of France and
Pope Honorius II.[4] Foulque arrived at Acre in the spring of 1129

[1] Tafel-Thomas, i, 84–89; William Tyre, XII, xxv, 550–53; *Regesta*, doc. 102. 'Universali-
ter igitur supradictas conventiones ipsum regem, Deo auxiliante, si aliquando egressurus de
captivitate est, nos Gormundus, Hierusalem patriarcha, confirmare per Evangelium faciemus.
Si vero alter ad Hierosolymitanum regnum, in regem promovendus advenerit, aut superius
ordinatas promissiones antequam promoveatur, sicut ante dictum est, ipsum confirmare
faciemus; alioquin ipsum nullo modo ad regnum provehi assentiemus.

[2] May 2, 1125. Tafel-Thomas, i, 90–95; *Regesta*, doc. 105. Baldwin was ransomed and
released in August 1124. (William Tyre, XIII, xv, 576.)

[3] William Tyre, XIII, xxv, 594–95; Röhricht, p. 185; Dodu, pp. 356–57; Mas Latrie, '*Patriarchs de Jérusalem*', R. O. L., i, p. 18. See below p. 205.

[4] William Tyre, XIII, xxiv, 593; XIV, ii, 608; Ernoul, p. 10; *Gesta Ambaziensium Dominorum*, p. 115, and *Gesta Consulum Andegavorum*, pp. 69–70, in L. Halphen and R. Poupardin,
Chroniques des Comtes d'Anjou (Paris: *Collection de Textes*; Picard, 1913). Letter of Honorius II to Baldwin recommending Foulque: Rozière, doc. 15; *Regesta*, doc. 122; Röhricht, p.
185.

and was married to Melissande, the cities of Tyre and Acre being given him in fief.[1]

Two years later, August 21, 1131, Baldwin died. On his death-bed, he summoned Foulque, Melissande, and the chief barons and prelates of the kingdom, and in the presence of the court and with their consent, bestowed upon Foulque and his wife the governance of the realm. On the 14th of September following Foulque and Melissande were crowned in the Church of the Holy Sepulchre.[2]

The reign of Foulque and Melissande seems to have been a joint rule and the charters issued by Foulque usually were issued with the consent of Melissande, his wife. The name of Baldwin, their son, was also incorporated in their acts on occasion. The six acts issued by Foulque as king of Jerusalem which have been preserved, all bear the consent of Melissande.[3] While this in itself would not in any way prove that it was a joint rule,—for the consent of the wife was often included in charters,—when considered in connection with the fact that Melissande retained the governance of the realm after the death of Foulque, it does indicate that the rule was joint and that the king and queen both ruled.

William of Tyre and Ernoul both say very definitely that Baldwin consulted with the barons. William de Buris and Guy de Brisbarre were sent to the West and de Buris carried on the negotiations with Foulque. Apparently Baldwin applied to Louis VI and the Pope for recommendations and then took the matter up with his council again. The *Gesta Ambaziensium Dominorum* says that Louis recommended Foulque to Baldwin.

J. Chartrou, *L'Anjou de 1109 à 1151* (Paris: Presses Universitaires, 1928), pp. 225–239, appendix on Foulque as king of Jerusalem, follows the *Gesta* and says he was recommended by Louis.

[1] William Tyre, XIII, xxiv, 593–94; Chartrou, *L'Anjou*, p. 227, says: *'le roi lui donnait la Ptolemaïde, Tyr, Sur, et Acre'* (sic!). Foulque was thus doubly endowed.

[2] William Tyre, XIII, xxviii, 601–02, XIV, ii, 608; Röhricht, pp. 190, 194. W. Miller, *Essays on the Latin Orient* (Cambridge, 1921), p. 518, says the monarchy was elective until 1131 after which it became hereditary.

[3] Foulque's first charters are issued as regent for Antioch and do not have Melissande's consent. (Rozière, docs. 85, 86; *Regesta*, docs. 149, 157; Chartrou, *op. cit.*,—'Catalogue des Actes de Foulque',—nos. 101, 102, p. 282.) Six acts of 1136, 1138, and 1142, all have the consent of Melissande. (*Regesta*, docs. 163, 164, 174, 179, 181, 210; Chartrou, nos. 103–108.)

The record of a grant made by Foulque to the canons of St Laud of Angers of an ivory reliquary given him by the sultan of Egypt, refers to a personal gift and not to a public act. (*Regesta*, doc. 139a; *B. E. C.*, lix (1898), p. 540.) The consent of Baldwin, their son, is included in the acts of 1138 and 1142. (*Regesta*, docs. 179, 181, 210.) Foulque appears alone on an act of 1132 but only as witnessing. (*Regesta*, doc. 142.)

Baldwin II had done much to strengthen the position of the monarchy; Foulque's rule further increased the royal power and with him the kingdom is often considered to have approached its zenith. The tremendous activity of King Foulque, his interference in the affairs of the counties of Antioch, Tripoli, and Edessa, his leadership in the foreign war which continued throughout his reign, his successful opposition to Zenghi, and his quickness in stamping out revolt at home all contributed to make his reign one which in many ways may be considered the strongest of any Jerusalemite monarch. The reign of Amaury appears to be the more glorious, but Amaury overstepped himself in his dreams of conquest, and the brilliancy of his reign was based on the solid foundations laid by his father.

When Foulque ascended the throne, he became also bailli of Antioch. Bohemond II, who had married Alice, the second daughter of Baldwin II, was killed in a battle with the troops of Imed-ed-Din-Zenghi of Mosul in January 1131, and the Antiochenes at once summoned Baldwin to assume the bailliage for his infant grand-daughter Constance.[1] Although the princess-mother, Alice, opposed her father's bailliage, Baldwin overcame her and took over the affairs of the principality. When Baldwin died the following August, Foulque was offered the bailliage by the Antiochene barons. Alice, taking advantage of the opportunity afforded by Baldwin's death, had seized the bailliage, forming an alliance with Pons, count of Tripoli, and Joscelin of Edessa to prevent Foulque from acquiring control of Antioch. But Foulque defeated the allies and drove Alice from Antioch, whence she retired to Laodicea which had been given her by Baldwin, while Foulque established himself at Antioch as bailli,[2] retaining the regency of Antioch until Princess Constance

---

[1] William Tyre, XIII, xxvii, 598–601. I accept the date of 1131 as given by William, and accepted by Rey, 'Histoire des Princes d'Antioche', *R. O. L.*, iv (1896), p. 356, in preference to February 1130, given by Röhricht, *Königreichs*, p. 188, from Arabic sources.

If one accepts William's date the time seems much better accounted for. By Röhricht's dating there is a gap from the beginning of 1130 to July 1131, while if 1131 is taken as the beginning of the bailliage the time is well accounted for, and it was in 1130 that Bohemond assisted Baldwin against Damascus.

[2] William Tyre, XIV, iv–v, 611–14; Rey, *op. cit.*, p. 357; Röhricht, p. 196. Alice even sought the help of Zenghi.

was married to Raymond of Poitiers in 1136.[1] The whole episode did much to strengthen the prestige of the king in the counties where little regard was generally felt for the royal power. Nor did Foulque's influence end with Raymond's accession, for Raymond kept in close relations with the king; the two princes mutually assisting each other in their wars with the Saracens, especially Zenghi.[2]

In 1132 the peace of the kingdom was disturbed by the revolt of one of the most powerful barons of the realm, Hugh II de Puiset, count of Jaffa. Hugh, a cousin of Queen Melissande, and of the highest Franco-Syrian aristocracy, entered into conspiracy against the king with Romanus de Le Puy, lord of Outre-Jordan. Hugh is reported by William of Tyre to have been the favorite and probably the lover of Queen Melissande. Walter of Caesarea, Hugh's step-son, brought charges of treason against the count of Jaffa in the High Court, but Hugh, conscious of his guilt according to William, did not appear to answer the charges. The court declared him guilty and forfeit, and Hugh fortified himself in Jaffa, calling on the emir of Ascalon for aid. The Egyptians, only too glad to have the opportunity, sent an army which attacked Arsur. However, Foulque beat back the Saracens and besieged Hugh, whose vassals, after failing in their efforts to reconcile him with the king, deserted their lord and went over to the king. The patriarch arranged a peace whereby Hugh was exiled for three years, during which time Foulque held Jaffa. As Hugh left the kingdom and never returned, his fiefs escheated to the crown.[3]

---

[1] William Tyre, XIV, xx, 635; Rey, pp. 358–59; Röhricht, p. 202. Two of Foulque's charters as bailli of Antioch have been preserved. (*Regesta*, docs. 149, 157.) Renaud Mansoer, the constable of Antioch, was left in charge of the government by Foulque in 1132.

[2] Foulque suggested Raymond for the principality of Antioch. Reciprocal aid was given in the campaigns of Montferrand and Baniâs.

[3] The story is told in William Tyre, XIV, xv–xvii, 627–30; Röhricht, pp. 199–201. Hugh was the grandson of Alice de Monthléry, the sister of Melissande de Monthléry who was mother of Baldwin II. Hugh's father, Hugh I, had received the county of Jaffa from Baldwin II, and Hugh had succeeded at his death. Hugh II married Emma, the niece of Arnulf the patriarch, who was lady of Jericho in her own right. She was the widow of Eustache Grenier, and mother by him of Walter of Caesarea and Gerard of Sidon.

Romanus de Le Puy and his son Ralph, both being convicted of treason, were declared forfeit and their fief of Outre-Jordan was given by the king to Paganus, the king's butler. Hugh de Puiset went to the court of Roger II of Sicily where he was given the county of Gargano.

The greater part of Foulque's reign was spent in a series of wars against the Saracens. The increasing strength of Zenghi alarmed the Syrian states, both Christian and Moslem, and in 1139 an alliance was concluded between Jerusalem and Damascus against the atābeg which resulted in the Christian reoccupation of Baniâs, which had been taken from them by Zenghi.[1] The last two years of Foulque's reign were passed in comparative quiet. It was a great era for fortress building; the castles of Ibelin, Blanchegarde, Bersabée, and Krak (Pierre du Desert) were all constructed during Foulque's reign. Some of these were royal castles, others private or given to the Orders. But all were sources of strength to the kingdom.

Another way in which Foulque strengthened his position in the kingdom was by the extension of the domain and by the distribution of fiefs. New conquests and the escheats which came to the crown gave him lands in which he could place vassals devoted to himself. While no such charters of enfeoffment have been preserved, the chroniclers tell of the establishment of Paganus, the butler, in Outre-Jordan, that of Balian 'le vieux' in Ibelin, Renier Bruce in Baniâs, and the escheat of Jaffa to the crown. Joscelin of Caïmont first appears under Foulque, and the first of the great house of Babin gives his assent to a charter of John Patricius, one of his vassals, Foulque and Melissande consenting to the same grant.[2]

Foulque died November 10, 1143, leaving his wife and two sons, Baldwin, aged thirteen, and Amaury, aged seven.[3] Melissande

---

(*Familles*, pp. 338–41, 401–02. See also L. de Mas Latrie, 'Les Comtes de Jaffa et d'Ascalon', *Archivio Veneto*, xviii (1879), 370–417; and 'Les Seigneurs du Crac et de Montréal appelès d'abord Seigneurs de la Terre-au-delà-du-Jordain', *Archivio Veneto*, xxv (1883), 475–94).

Hugh apparently did not leave Jaffa at once as an act of 1133 grants a casale to the Hospital, and acknowledges the receipt of a gift from the Knights of 100 besants and a mule. (*Regesta*, doc. 147; D. L. *Cartulaire*, doc. 97). Rey, (*Familles*, p. 341) infers from this act that Hugh had already lost most of his lands though he had not yet left the country.

[1] William Tyre, XV, viii–ix, 669–71. In a previous campaign in 1137 Foulque had held his own against Zenghi at Montferrand.

[2] Act of 1140: Rozière, doc. 120; *Regesta*, doc. 200. C. Hopf, in a review of Rey's edition of the *Familles*, in the *Revue Critique*, ii (1870), 236, gives a list of the lords of Caïmont, beginning with Joscelin under Foulque.

[3] The exact date of Foulque's death is uncertain. Chartrou, pp. 234–36, presents evidence to show that it was early in 1144. Röhricht, pp. 228–29, says November 10, 1143. Dodu,

at once took up the governance and arranged for the joint coronation of her eldest son and herself. William of Tyre says that the
rule was hers by right and that she was remarkably well fitted for
the position of ruling queen.[1] The coronation took place Christmas
1143. Baldwin and Melissande were both crowned, and the double
rule which Melissande before had shared with her husband she now
shared with her son. There is no mention of any election; the
queen continued in her governance, a new king was associated with
her. The work of Baldwin II was bearing results—a dynasty was in
process of formation, and hereditary monarchy seemed for the
moment to have replaced elective. Several reasons may explain
this: the king's death was sudden and the queen lost no time in establishing herself on the throne; more important was the fact that
Foulque had been a strong and popular king and there was no opposition. His vassals and retainers were willing to accept his son
and there was no one to oppose him. The monarchy was still elective; the barons probably met as the High Court and placed Baldwin
and Melissande on the throne. If we assume, as I think the evidence justifies our doing, that Melissande was queen in her own
right, the matter is still simpler, for the barons would then only have
recognized that the queen took a new colleague to rule with her.
The charters issued during the time that Melissande and Baldwin
both occupied the throne prove, I think, that it was a joint rule and

---

De Fulconis Iherusolymitani Regno (Paris, 1894), pp. 59–60, says 1144. T. A. Archer, 'On the
Accession Dates of the Early Kings of Jerusalem', *E. H. R.*, iv (1889), 89–105, gives either
1143 or 1144. The editors of William of Tyre say November 13, 1144. William Tyre, XV,
xxvii, 701, says 1142, November 13, in the eleventh year of his reign. In XVI, iii, 707, he says
November 10 (4th Ides Nov.), and this date is followed by most of the other chroniclers,
though the year is given generally as 1143. His death was not known in Rome or in Anjou in
January 1144, but was known by September 1144 as evidenced by documents. An act of
1149 issued by Melissande terms it the fifth year of Baldwin III (*Regesta*, doc. 256). Chartrou cites an act of Geoffrey Plantagenet which refers to Foulque as '*nuper defuncti*!'. This
act is dated 1143—the year 1143 ending 26 March, 1144. Mlle Chartrou argues that the
death occurred early in 1144, but none of her arguments hold strongly against November 1143
and William's evidence as to November can not be so lightly dismissed. I have accepted the
date November 10, 1143 as being the most reasonable.

[1] William Tyre, XV, xxvii, 702: '*Reseditque regni potestas penes dominam Milisendem,
Deo amabilem reginam, cui jure haereditario competebat*'. *Ibid.*, XVI, ii, 706; XVII, xiii, 779–
81: '*regni tanquam jure hereditario sibi debiti curam et administrationem sortita est, filiorum
legitimam agens tutelam*'. (p. 779.)

not a regency on the part of Melissande for her son. The reign of Baldwin falls into two periods, before and after 1152; at first the queen and king ruled jointly, with Manasses de Hierges, the constable, as chief advisor. In the second, after Baldwin had rebelled against his mother and Manasses, the king ruled alone with the advice of a large number of barons. A study of the charters of the period from 1144 to 1152 adds materially to our understanding of the relations between mother and son. Twelve charters have been preserved: four were issued by Baldwin and Melissande together,[1] two by Melissande with the consent of Baldwin,[2] four by Melissande alone,[3] and two by Baldwin alone.[4] Manasses appears on five of these charters,[5] his last appearance being on an act of Melissande's in 1151. The charters issued by Melissande alone are of a later date than those issued with Baldwin; the last charter issued by them together is in 1150 and the four by her alone fall between 1150 and 1152. After the breach in the spring of 1152, the charters of Melissande become fewer, and we have only four charters between her dethronement and her death in 1161. Of these the first, of 1155, was issued at the request of Baldwin to confirm a grant he had made,[6] and the other three were issued with his consent in the years 1159-1160.[7]

Of Baldwin's twenty charters issued in the years after 1152, five are granted with the consent of Melissande, Amaury's consent being included on three of them.[8] One, of 1159, is granted at Melissande's

---

[1] In 1144 (*Archives*, ii, B, 124-25; *Regesta*, doc. 227); 1146 (Delaborde, doc. 26; *Regesta*, doc. 240); and 1147 (D. L. *Cartulaire*, docs. 173, 175; *Regesta*, docs. 244, 245).

[2] In 1149 (D. L. *Cartulaire*, doc. 180; *Regesta*, doc. 256), 1150 (D. L. *Cartulaire*, doc. 191; *Regesta*, doc. 262).

[3] In 1150 she confirmed a charter which Baldwin had granted. (*Archives*, ii, B, 129; *Regesta*, doc. 259.)   In 1151 she confirmed a grant previously confirmed by Foulque and herself, and granted a mill to St Lazare. (Rozière, doc. 49; *Archives*, ii, B, 130-31; *Regesta*, docs. 268, 269.)   In 1152 she made a grant to the Holy Sepulchre. (Rozière, doc. 48; *Regesta*, doc. 278.)

[4] In 1144 (Rozière, doc. 34; *Regesta*, doc. 226), and 1150 (*Archives*, ii, B, 128; *Regesta*, doc. 258).   Melissande later confirmed this. (*Regesta*, doc. 259.)

[5] *Regesta*, docs. 240, 245, 259, 262, 268.

[6] *Regesta*, doc. 313; Rozière, doc. 50.

[7] *Regesta*, docs. 338, 339a, 359.

[8] *Regesta*, docs. 293, 306, 321, 322, 325.   Amaury is mentioned on 306, 321 and 325.

request,[1] and the other fourteen do not mention the queen.[2] It will be noted that after 1152 Melissande issued no charters in her own name without mentioning the king, and that Baldwin included her in his but irregularly.

The reign of Melissande and Baldwin was a period of storm and disaster. Zenghi's constant inroads on the northern counties were at last successful, and Edessa fell in 1144, shortly after Foulque's strong arm had been removed. The forces of the second crusade, which came to restore the kingdom, only increased the existing difficulties and stirred up new rivalries, besides plunging the kingdom into a war with Damascus and helping indirectly to throw that state into the hands of Nureddin. Renaud de Châtillon in Antioch was already showing some of that adventurous foolhardiness which was to cost the kingdom so dear at a later date, and was embroiling himself with the Byzantine Empire. The prosperity and security of Foulque's reign was ended, and a period of depression seems to have set in for the Jerusalemites. The barons grumbled and looked for someone on whom to place the blame, finding a victim in Manasses de Hierges, the constable. Manasses was the son of Hodierne, sister of Baldwin II, and was first cousin to Queen Melissande. He came to the East about 1140 and was given the position of constable by Baldwin III and Melissande. On the death of Balian d'Ibelin, he married his widow, Helvis of Rama, thus allying himself indirectly with the house of Ibelin.[3] Manasses seems to have been a man of some ability, but his arrogance and pride in his position as chief adviser of the queen antagonized the other barons and the king, and he eventually became so cordially hated that in 1152, on the advice of some of the barons, the king revolted,

[1] *Regesta*, doc. 336.

[2] *Regesta*, docs. 276, 281, 291, 299, 307, 309, 315a, 341, 344, 352, 353, 354, 355, 366. Nos. 344 in 1160 and 366 in 1161 carry the consent of Theodora, Baldwin's wife, and Amaury. In 1161, Theodora issued a charter in her own name without mentioning Baldwin. (*Regesta*, doc. 367.) An act of allegiance in 1155 is to Baldwin and the patriarch with no mention of Melissande. (*Regesta*, doc. 302.)

[3] *Familles*, pp. 544–45, 619. According to the *Lignages d'Outremer* Manasses' daughters married into the houses of Gibelet, Grangerin, de Brie, and Mimars. (*Lignages* (*Assises*, ii) xxxviii, 470–71.)

had himself crowned again,—this time without his mother,—and
assumed the governance alone. Walter de St Omer, prince of Galilee, and John de Soissons were sent by the king to Melissande with
offers to divide the kingdom, whereby Baldwin should take Acre,
Tyre, and the north while Melissande ruled over Jerusalem, Neapolis, and the south. Melissande accepted the terms offered and retired to Neapolis. Baldwin then deposed Manasses from the constableship which he then conferred upon Humphrey, the lord of
Toron. This angered the queen and difficulties began; the king
encroached on his mother's lands and soon there was open war between them. Isolating Manasses in his castle of Mirabel which
was heavily beleagured, the king attacked Neapolis. When the
queen fled to Jerusalem, he pursued her and besieged her in the citadel. Meanwhile many of her vassals had gone over to the king
until there remained with her only her son Amaury, lord of Jaffa;
Philip of Neapolis; and Rohard, viscount of Jerusalem. Fulcher,
the patriarch, and the clergy intervened in an endeavor to stop the
civil war, but their efforts were unavailing and the king stormed the
citadel which was taken after a bloody fight. Melissande gave up
Jerusalem and all part in the government, retiring once more to her
fief of Neapolis.[1] She reappeared only in 1157, when she assisted
Baldwin de l'Ile and the baillies who were governing the kingdom
while King Baldwin was busy with the war against Nureddin.[2]

The wars against Nureddin and the Egyptians were the most
important events in the second part of the reign of Baldwin III.
In 1153, after a siege of seven months, the Christian army captured
Ascalon, which had long been a dangerous center for Egyptian attacks
on the kingdom, and the city was organized as a fief and given to
Amaury, count of Jaffa, the brother of the king.[3] While the southern frontier was thus secured, the eastern was further imperiled,
for in the same year, and while the Christian forces were besieging
Ascalon, Nureddin of Aleppo conquered Damascus and spread his

---

[1] William Tyre, XVII, xiv, 781–83; Röhricht, pp. 268–70. Manasses was exiled and his
fiefs forfeited. Mirabel went to the Ibelin lords of Rama. Melissande died in 1161. (William Tyre, XVIII, xxxii, 877.)

[2] William Tyre, XVIII, xix, 851. In 1153 Melissande advised Baldwin as to the disposal
of properties in Ascalon. (*Ibid.*, XVII, xxx, 813.)

[3] William Tyre, XVII, xxi-xxx, 794–813; Röhricht, pp. 273–79.

menacing power southward along the eastern frontier, so that his possessions bordered on Jerusalem as well as on the northern counties. The years 1156 to 1160 were marked by wars against Nureddin around Damascus, Baniâs, and Sheizar. Jerusalem was strengthened by an alliance with Byzantium, which was made in 1158 when Baldwin married Theodora, a niece of Emperor Manuel Comnenus.[1]

Baldwin died February 10, 1162 in Beirut, universally lamented by his subjects. His death at the age of thirty-three was considered a severe blow to the kingdom,[2] and the throne devolved by election on his brother Amaury, count of Jaffa and Ascalon. Though Amaury was clearly the nearest heir to the throne, there was considerable question as to his succession and the barons disagreed about electing him king. Amaury was married to Agnes de Courtney, sister of Joscelin III of Edessa and widow of Renaud of Mares. She had been betrothed to Hugh d'Ibelin of Rama, but the match was broken off and she was married to Amaury. As Amaury was distantly related to her, and as he was considered to have stolen her from Hugh, the clergy and barons refused to allow him to become king as long as he kept his wife. But Amaury was a *politique*, and Jerusalem was worth a wife, wherefore he obligingly divorced the lady, who promptly married Hugh d'Ibelin.[3]

The reign of Amaury marks the zenith of the kingdom of Jerusalem. But, as in many other cases, the apparent peak was reached only after the decline had really set in. That Amaury was one of the most gifted monarchs the kingdom ever had is attested by the legis-

[1] William Tyre, XVIII, xxii, 857; F. Chalandon, *Jean et Manuel Comnène*, (Paris, 1912), pp. 439–41. For the wars with Nureddin see W. B. Stevenson, *The Crusaders in the East* (Cambridge: University Press, 1907), pp. 171–84.

[2] William Tyre, XVIII, xxiv, 879; Röhricht, pp. 307–08. Baldwin had fallen sick in Tripoli, where he was cared for by Barak, Count Raymond's Arab physician. When the treatment failed to restore him to health at once the poor Moslem was accused of poisoning the king!

[3] Ernoul, pp. 16–17; William Tyre, XIX, i, 883–84, iv, 888–90; *Familles*, pp. 19–22, 300, 363. The standard biography of Amaury is that of G. Schlumberger, *Campagnes du Roi Amaury Ier de Jérusalem* (Paris, 1906). The more scholarly study by Röhricht, 'Amalrich 1, König von Jerusalem', *Mitteilungen des Instituts für Oesterreichische Geschichtsforschung*, xii (1891), is reproduced in chapters 17 and 18, pp. 308–360, of his *Geschichte des Königreichs Jerusalem*.

William Tyre refers to Amaury's succession: '*in regni solium hereditario sibi jure debitum*'. (p. 884.)

lation which has come down to us from his time.[1] That he was one of the strongest is proved by the character of the same laws. But the 'dream of empire' carried him away and he sacrificed the strength of his state in a vain endeavor to enlarge it by extensive foreign conquests. The helpless condition of Egypt was a deceptive lure, and Amaury succumbed to the temptation. His campaigns in Egypt, though in themselves not unprofitable, precipitated the catastrophe which later overwhelmed Jerusalem by so weakening Egypt that she fell into the hands of the lieutenant of the atābeg and gave Saladin a base from which to extend his empire and to encircle the Christian states.

But it is not as a warrior that Amaury merits our attention here. However ephemeral his conquests and ill-advised his wars, the legislative work which he carried through stands as a monument to his ability and to the strength of the monarchy which produced it. The later kings of Jerusalem and Cyprus swore at their coronation: '*les assises dou royaume et dou rei Amauri et dou rei Baudoyn son fiz, et les ancienes costumes et assises dou roiaume de Jerusalem garderai.*'[2] According to Beugnot, this oath refers to the fact that Amaury issued the *Assises* of the *Haute Cour* and Baldwin those of the *Cour des Bourgeois*.[3] But it is not necessary to go to such lengths to explain this phrase in the coronation oath. Amaury's legislation, and I believe Baldwin's also, is to be found in less extensive works than

[1] William Tyre, XIX, ii, 884, says of him; '*in jure consuetudinario quo regebatur regnum, subtilis plurimum et nulli secundus*'.

Chartrou, *L'Anjou*, pp. 234–35, characterizes both Baldwin III and Amaury as incapable of continuing or even conserving the work of Foulque. C. R. Conder, *Latin Kingdom of Jerusalem*, p. 122, pictures him as indeed a miserable thing: 'neither loved nor respected in his kingdom . . . the frank and generous manners of the former kings were not inherited by this unfortunate monarch, whose avarice betokened the Armenian, and whose gloomy reserve was not accompanied by austerity of life'. On p. 118 he says: 'the successors of Baldwin III were weak and obstinate', and he begins his chapter on 'The Loss of the Kingdom', with the accession of Amaury.

Compare Schlumberger's statement (p. 348) anent the death of Amaury: '*Ce jeune héros mourait à la fleur de l'âge*, . . . *Ce fut une catastrophe déplorable*', and he speaks of the: '*douleur et consternation universelles*' caused by his death.

There is undoubtedly a middle ground, and the *Assise sur la ligece* alone should bring Amaury better treatment than he has received at the hands of Col. Conder.

[2] Ibelin, vii, 30.

[3] Beugnot, *Assises*, ii, Introduction, p. 39,

complete codes. Chapters **XLIII** to **XLIX** of the *Assises de la Cour des Bourgeois* are laws governing maritime cases: they begin with the statement: '*Ici orrés en quel part establi le roi Amauri que deust estre la raison des mariniers et des vaiceaus et des naves.*'[1] Article **CCLXXXVIII** of the same code is an assise of Amaury's altering the law of adultery and permitting the husband to kill the wife and lover if he finds them *in flagrante delicto.*[2] His *Assise of Belfis* regulating the service that can be demanded from a knight is known through the statement of John d'Ibelin of Beirut as reported by Philip de Novare.[3] In the administration of justice Amaury is credited with the founding of the two sets of courts for maritime and commercial cases, the courts of the *Chaine* and the *Fonde.*[4] But the greatest contribution of Amaury to the legislation of Outremer is without doubt his famous *Assise sur la ligece*, which was issued in the first year of his reign. The assise is given in full in Ibelin CXL:[5]

Que les homes des homes dou chief seignor dou reiaume feiscent ligece au chief seignor dou reiaume, par l'assise, des fiés qu'ils tenoient de ces homes, et que toz ciaus qui avoient fait homage au chief seignor, fust par l'assise ou autrement, fucent tenus les uns as autres, et aussi les homes de ces homes de chascune court par sei; et que se le rei voleit aveir la feauté des gens qui estoient manant ès cités, et ès chastiaus, et ès bors, que ces homes tenoient de lui, que il li juracent toz feauté, et que il li fucent tenus par cette feauté de ce que les homes de ces homes li sont tenus par la ligece faite par l'assise au chief seignor. Et fut devisé et acordé lors coment il feroient la ligece par l'assise au chief seignor, et de quei ils sereient tenus à lui par la ditte ligece, et de quei le seignor sereit tenus à ciaus qui la ditte ligece li feroient, et de quei les homes sereient tenus les uns as autres et toz ensemble.

[1] *Assises*, ii, 42–47.

[2] *Assises*, ii, 218.

[3] *Gestes*, par. 202. And see Beugnot, *Assises*, i, Introduction, p. 31, and text p. 455, note c; Schlumberger, *Amaury*, p. 191; and below p. 158.

[4] D. Hayek, *Le Droit Franc en Syrie* (Paris: Editions Spes, 1925), pp. 134, 141. Beugnot, *Assises*, ii, Introduction, p. 24, attributes the *Chaine* to Amaury but the *Fonde* to Foulque. Hayek attributes them both to Amaury, with, I believe, considerable reason.

[5] *Assises*, i, 214–15. Philippe de Novare, l, 526, says: 'Ce est l'assise por que les homes des barons et des riches homes, et des autres homes dou seignor qui ont homes, font liegece au chief seignor des fiés que il tienent de ces homes; et tousjors dit l'on au faire, que il li fait ligese selon l'assise. Et teil la mosist qui ne la seit mie bien'.

See also Jacques d'Ibelin (*Assises*, i), x, 457.

The occasion for the issuance of this assise was a conflict which arose in 1162 between the king and Gerard of Sidon and Beaufort. Gerard had disseised one of his vassals of his tenement without the consent of the king or the court. Amaury championed the cause of the vassal and forced Gerard to reinstate him in his lands. The case was brought up in a full meeting of the High Court.—'*par la cort dou dit rei et dou dit Girart et de toz les barons et les haus homes dou reiaume et de toz ciaus qui avoient homes qui tenoient fiés d'iaus el dit roiaume*';[1]—which would seem to suggest a meeting at which all the suzerains of the realm were present.

That the king was able to carry through an assembly composed of feudal suzerains a measure which practically deprived them of their control over their vassals shows the strength of the monarchy in the first year of Amaury. For while the tenants-in-chief of the crown were already the liege vassals of the king, until this time the arrière vassals had been connected to the crown only through the mediate lords. The effects of Amaury's assise were far-reaching. It made all the holders of fiefs liegemen of the king and consequently peers of each other. This is confirmed by Ibelin in a later chapter where he says that all liegemen of the king are peers of each other.[2] It brought all fief holders under the jurisdiction of the king's High Court and removed them in part from that of their suzerain's court baron.[3] Any vassal who was disseised by his lord could appeal to the king's court, and the king was bound to protect him and not allow him to be disseised except by the decision of the court. If the mediate lord refused to plead his case in the king's court, the king reinstated the arrière vassal in his lands as the case would be considered as having gone to him through default.

Liege homage was reserved to the king; all other homage should reserve the liege homage to the king.[4] Any homage taken to a lord of Jerusalem was not legally liege homage, even though no specific reservation had been made, as liege homage in Jerusalem could be

---

[1] Ibelin, cxl, 214.

[2] Ibelin, cxcix, 319–20; Novare, li, 527; Geoffrey le Tort (*Assises*, i), xv, 448.

[3] *La Clef des Assises de la Haute Cour* (*Assises*, i), ccxiv, 595; Ibelin, cxcvii–cc, 317–22; Novare, li, 526; Jacques d'Ibelin, x–xi, 457–58.

[4] Geoffrey le Tort (ms. B.), ii, 445; Ibelin, cxcv, 313–14.

taken only to the king.[1] If a vassal holding fief from any of the greater lords did not offer his liege homage to the king within a year and a day after receiving the fief, the king could disseise him of his fief which reverted to the mediate lord, while the vassal himself was exiled for the life of the king,[2] or, if he was not disseised, he at least lost all the advantages of the assises and was wholly subject to his lord without redress.[3]

The assise protected the arrière vassal against his mediate lord by allowing him redress in the king's court. But it also protected the king against the greater barons as the arrière vassals could be used as a lever against them. If the lord were summoned to appear in the king's court and did not go, it was the duty of his vassals to urge him to go and warn him that if he did not answer the king's summons within forty days they would affealt themselves from him and place themselves directly under the king. The king was bound to compensate the arrière vassals for any losses they sustained if they affealted themselves in this manner. If he failed to do so the vassals were in a most embarrassing position, for their only chance then was to return to their lord and serve him against the king who had broken faith with them. The *Assises* do not say what would be the lot of the unfortunate vassal whose lord refused to receive him back in such a case.

If the quarrel between the king and the lord came to open war, the vassals should demand that the lord take his case to the High Court within forty days, and in case of refusal should affealt themselves and serve the king against him, as in the case of refusal to answer the king's summons. But if the lord agreed to take the case to the court the vassals were obliged to support him and to fight for him if justice was not done him in the court.[4]

---

[1] Ibelin, cxcv, 313–14. Liege homage can only be taken once and as it is due to the king cannot be given another: 'nul qui est home d'autrui ne peut après faire homage à autre, ce il ne sauve son premier seignor, ou se il ne le fait par son congié, que, il ne mente sa fei vers celui de qui il est avant home ... nul home ne peut faire plus d'une ligece; et que toz les homes des homes dou chief seignor dou reiaume li deivent faire ligece par l'assise; et puisque l'on li deit la ligece, l'on ne la peut à autre faire sanz mesprendre vers lui'.

[2] Geoffrey le Tort (ms. A.), xi, 438.

[3] Jacques d'Ibelin, vi, 456.

[4] Ibelin, cxcvii–cc, 317–22; Novare, li, 526. The vassals of Hugh of Jaffa had affealted themselves and gone over to the king in 1132, when Hugh revolted against Foulque. (William

The *Assise sur la ligece* is unique in feudal annals. At a single stroke it endeavored to accomplish the results obtained in England by the Salisbury Oath and the judicial reforms of Henry II. It is the Norman reservation of fealty, but as G. B. Adams phrases it: 'carrying it a long distance further, to a point never involved or contemplated in the Norman practice.'[1] For it *legalized revolt* and thereby created a weapon which was usable against the king as well as against the mediate lords. In Jerusalem it might have been of value to the monarchy in curbing the power of the great barons and raising against them the alliance of the king and the lesser nobility. Administered by a strong king it would have been a powerful weapon in the hands of the monarchy. Unfortunately after the death of Amaury there was no king of Jerusalem strong enough to avail himself of it, and the increased power which should have been given the monarchy went to the *Haute Cour*, which was dominated by the very lords against whom the assise was aimed. In Cyprus it was for the kings an unmitigated evil, for there were almost no arrière vassals, and the right of revolt given by the assise was used by the tenants-in-chief against the kings. For the king was only chief suzerain of the realm and the same weapons which would work against the lord of the fief were equally available against him.[2] In both realms the assise of Amaury guaranteed the supremacy of the *Haute Cour*.

At the time of its passage, however, the assise shows the strength of the king who could carry such a measure through an assembly composed of the very suzerains whose power it was intended to curb. Probably at no time in the history of the Latin states was

---

Tyre, XIV, xvi, 630.) The assise of Amaury did not establish a new practice but made obligatory one which had previously been optional with the vassals. It also promised the vassals greater security in turning to the king from a revolting suzerain.

The *Assises de Romanie*, art. 28, provide that the vassals shall serve their lord against his lord unless he shall have been proven wrong in the court. See also arts. 49, 88, 209, 212, 216.

[1] G. B. Adams, *Origin of the English Constitution*, (2nd ed., New Haven: Yale Univ. Press, 1920), p. 105. Adams further characterizes it as 'squarely opposed to feudal principles'.

[2] Beugnot, *Assises*, i, Introduction, p. 46, calls it '*une grave erreur*', and condemns it wholly as merely weakening the strength of the larger nobility without adding in any way to that of the king. Grandclaude, p. 151, terms it '*la grande charte de l'Orient Latin*', and explains that while in Syria it was a tool of the king against the barons, in Cyprus it protected the barons against the king.

the king as strong and influential as during Amaury's reign from
1162 to 1174. The king was personally popular and his policies met
with general approval. His ambitions in regard to Egypt, while
opposed by the Templars, were endorsed and encouraged by the
Hospitallers and by the majority of the Franco-Syrian nobility.[1]
His Byzantine alliance, cemented by his marriage with a Byzantine
princess, seemed to give strength and prestige to his kingdom.[2]
But the most striking proof of the influence of the king came at the
time of his death in the peaceful succession of his son Baldwin to
the throne, for Baldwin was a child and a leper. Yet when the
lords, ecclesiastical and lay, assembled to elect a king to rule over
them they elected Baldwin, in spite of his youth and fatal malady.[3]
The hereditary right of the dynasty would seem to have been established.

The death of Amaury marks the close of an era in the history of
Jerusalem. It was an era of conquest and accomplishment, of
strong kings and warlike barons. It was a period in which an elective monarchy was able to assert itself, by the ability of the men
who occupied the throne, over a baronage which considered itself
in every respect the equals of the king.

[1] The Templars throughout opposed Amaury's Egyptian schemes and refused to coöperate with him in the war. The Hospitallers, under the leadership of the Grand Master Gilbert
d'Assaily, encouraged him and even urged him into the last campaign against his better judgment. (William Tyre, XX, v, 948–49.) William's lamentations over the Egyptian fiasco
were *a posteriori* and must not be taken as representative of the state of opinion at the time.
The campaign was discussed and carried in the High Court.

[2] Amaury married Marie, a relative of Manuel's, and an alliance was concluded between
Manuel and Amaury against Egypt. (William Tyre, XX, i, 942.) Amaury, who had been
crowned on his accession to the throne, was crowned again after his marriage.

For a more detailed examination of Amaury's relations with the Byzantine Empire see
my article 'To What Extent was the Byzantine Empire the Suzerain of the Latin Crusading
States', *Byzantion*, vii (1932).

[3] William Tyre, XXI, ii, 1006. Baldwin was the son of Amaury by Agnes de Courtney.
When the marriage had been annulled, Baldwin and his sister Sibylle had been declared legitimate. He was educated by William of Tyre, the historian, who first discovered his affliction
when he was nine years old.

Concerning his accession to the throne William says: '*convenientibus in unum universis
regni principibus, tam ecclesiasticis quam secularibus, consonante omnium desiderio, . . . inunctus
est et coronatus*'.

CHAPTER 2

WAR AND RECONSTRUCTION,
THE TRANSITION YEARS 1174-1210

THE second period in the history of the kingdom of Jerusalem,
that of the loss of Jerusalem, the third crusade, and the reconstruction, runs approximately from the accession of Baldwin IV to
that of John de Brienne, 1174–1210. These dates are admittedly
arbitrary; although the accession of John was not a date of any
importance, it can be considered as the end of that period of reconstruction which followed after the third crusade. By 1210 the first
of the great books of the *Assises*, the *Livre au Roi*, had been written,
and the *assises et bon usages* had become fixed and only awaited the
definitive formulation which the next generation was to bring. The
reign of John de Brienne is itself a prelude to that of Frederick II,
and with Frederick II a new era of Jerusalemite history begins.
Before we can consider thirteenth century Jerusalem, the country
whose institutions can so well be studied in the *Assises* and in the
Mémoires of Philip de Novare, we must first review the years of
semi-anarchy and trouble which sunder it from the state of Amaury
I and which contributed not inconsiderably to shape the later state.

When Baldwin IV ascended the throne of Jerusalem in 1174 he
was but thirteen years old and was already afflicted with leprosy.
Four days after his father's death, on July 15, he was crowned by the
Patriarch Amaury before the assembled barons and clergy. It was
the anniversary of the capture of Jerusalem, seventy-five years after
Godfrey had planted the banner of the Cross on the Holy City.
Before thirteen more years had passed, Saladin was to destroy the
kingdom at Hattin and the city itself would be collecting its forces
to withstand a siege. Though the boy was crowned in his own right
and no regent was appointed, the government of the realm fell
largely into the hands of Miles de Plancy, lord of Montreal and
seneschal of the late King Amaury, who had been one of Amaury's
most intimate friends. There is no reason to believe that Miles'
position was in any way official, or that his power had any more firm

26

foundation than the influence which he was able to exert over the youthful king.[1] But the rule of Miles was unpopular, his arrogance and domineering manner alienated the native born nobility, and in the autumn Raymond III, count of Tripoli, appeared before the *Haute Cour* and demanded the regency for the boy king. Raymond was the son of Hodierne, daughter of Baldwin II, and was second cousin of the king, his closest relative on the royal side of his family.[2] After a session which lasted two days the *Haute Cour* awarded the regency to Raymond, giving him control of the kingdom and custody of the king.[3] About the same time Miles de Plancy was murdered in the street in Acre.[4]

---

[1] William Tyre, XXI, ii–iii, 1006–1007. Beugnot, *Assises*, i, 610, note *a*, claims that de Plancy was regent for Baldwin, but there is no statement to this effect in any of the chroniclers or indication thereof in documents. Rey, *Familles*, p. 638, denies him any official position. He was a Champagnoise who had received Montreal, with the hand of Stephanie de Milly, from Amaury.

[2] William Tyre, XXI, iii, 1007.

Raymond's relationship to Baldwin may be seen from the accompanying table. Joscelin de Courtney was a closer relative, but on the mother's side of the house and not in the royal line.

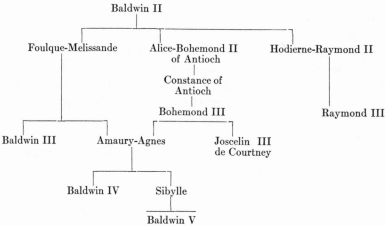

In 1174 Raymond III married Eschive de St Omer, heiress of the fief of Galilee and Tiberias, and as prince of Tiberias was the foremost of the vassals in the principality of Jerusalem. Bohemond III of Antioch was more distant by a generation in descent than Raymond, though he was descended from an older sister.

[3] William Tyre, XXI, v, 1010–1011.

[4] William Tyre, XXI, iv, 1008.

The time was one which required a strong man. Saladin, profiting from the deaths of Nureddin and Amaury with the resultant succession of children both in Syria and Jerusalem and the civil war which had broken out among the heirs of Nureddin, was preparing to establish himself in the empire of the atābeg and then carry out his dream of the holy war against the unbelievers and Trinitarians of Jerusalem. By the end of 1174 he had taken Damascus, Homs, and Hama; Jerusalem was already beginning to feel the menace of the encirclement.[1] The count of Tripoli, commander in chief of the armies of Jerusalem, took the offensive against Saladin at the end of 1174, but arranged a treaty of peace in 1175. But in spite of Raymond's treaty, the king in person led an expedition against Damascus which failed miserably. In 1176 the king and count made a joint expedition against the Saracens.[2] The presence of Raymond in the field most of the time that he was acting as regent explains why he figures on none of the charters issued by Baldwin during the period of the regency.[3]

The regency of Count Raymond ended in 1176 when the king achieved his majority at fifteen, but the increasing illness of the boy monarch and the impending foreign war necessitated the appointment of another bailli.

It had been decided to take the offensive against Saladin and to strike at the heart of his power by a campaign against Egypt. New reinforcements of crusaders from the West under the leadership of Count Philip of Flanders seemed to bring the help which would be needed to guarantee the success of the campaign. But the king was in no physical condition to attempt the long and hard campaign, and it was necessary to have someone act as bailli and take charge of the war. The post was offered to the count of Flanders who refused it, whereupon the bailliage and command of the army were conferred

---

[1] William Tyre, XXI, vi, 1012–13; Röhricht, pp. 366–67; Stevenson, *Crusaders in the East,* pp. 208–212.

[2] William Tyre, XXI, viii–xi, 1017–1025.

[3] Eight charters of Baldwin IV have been preserved from the years 1174–76. In the first, December 13, 1174, Raymond appears among the witnesses. (D. L. *Cartulaire,* doc. 468; *Regesta,* doc. 518.) On none of the other seven does he appear. (*Regesta,* docs. 525, 530c, 537, 538, 539b, 539c, 539d; D. L. *Cartulaire,* docs. 480, 489, 496, 497, 498; Delaborde, doc. 38; *R. O. L.,* iii, 61, no. 117.)

upon Renaud de Châtillon, ci-devant prince of Antioch, now,—by virtue of his marriage with Stephanie de Milly,—lord of Montreal and Krak, who had but recently been released from a long imprisonment in the dungeons of Aleppo.[1] But the projected invasion of Egypt never materialized and Philip returned to Flanders without having accomplished anything, save for a futile campaign against Harenc in company with Bohemond III.

Baldwin resumed the control of affairs after the collapse of the Egyptian scheme and for the next few years ran the government himself. It was a period of almost continuous war against Saladin, the Christians winning a notable victory at Mons Gisard in the south in 1178 and later losing consistently in the east around Baniâs. In 1180 truces were signed with Saladin by both Jerusalem and Tripoli.[2]

Meanwhile Baldwin had become suspicious of Raymond of Tripoli, with the result that decidedly cool relations existed between them. When Raymond wished to come south in 1182, the king refused to permit it, fearing lest he was coming to wrest his throne from him, and it was with this fear in mind that Baldwin had married his sister Sibylle to Guy de Lusignan in 1180. Finally in 1182 a truce was made between the king and the count.[3]

These years when Baldwin ruled alone were probably the constructive years of his reign. In 1178 and 1182 special taxes were levied to conduct the war which brought new methods into the system of tax assessing.[4] And it is to this period that the legislative activity of the reign should be attributed.

[1] William Tyre, XXI, xiv, 1027–29; Röhricht, pp. 370–71; G. Schlumberger, *Renaud de Châtillon* (2nd ed., Paris: Plon, 1923), pp. 179–80.

Philip de Milly of Neapolis had exchanged his fief for that of Montreal and Outre-Jordan in 1161, and had retired in 1169 into the Order of the Templars. His daughter Stephanie carried the fief to her successive husbands, Humphrey de Toron, Miles de Plancy, and Renaud de Châtillon.

[2] William Tyre, XXI, xx, 1037– XXII, iii, 1065; Röhricht, pp. 374–90.

No attempt is made in this book to discuss even generally the foreign wars and the rise of Saladin. These events can be found best chronicled in Röhricht or in Stevenson's *Crusaders in the East*. Foreign affairs are mentioned here only as they affect internal and constitutional matters.

[3] William Tyre, XXII, i, 1062–63; ix, 1077–79.

[4] William Tyre, XXI, xxv, 1048; XXII, xxii, 1109–1112. And see below, chapter on finances, p. 180.

In affirming that Baldwin IV was a legislator one immediately treads on shaky ground. The principal evidence is found in the oath noted above in connection with Amaury to preserve the assises of Amaury and his son Baldwin. But what laws came from Baldwin? Surely not, as Beugnot thinks, the code of the *Assises de la Cour des Bourgeois* for that, as Granclaude has proven, I think, conclusively, dates from the time when Frederick II occupied the Holy City and not from the first kingdom at all.[1] But there is one law attached to the name of King Baldwin which in my opinion can be credited to Baldwin IV. It is the *Assise du coup apparent* which Beugnot attributes to Baldwin I. This law is given in full by Philip de Novare, LXXV:[2] '*Au coumencement, quant les premiers assises furent faites, fu ordené et après use*', . . . (and he gives the old form of the law) . . . '*De toutes ces chozes desus escrites, ai je entendu qu'elles furent aussi assises et devisées et lonc tens usées . . . Mais après avint, au tens dou rei Baudoin, que il li sembla et as preudoumes . . . et . . . le rei Baudoin fist l'assise*'. Now certainly Novare would not say of a law which was repealed by Baldwin I that it had been in use for a long time. This I think proves that the new assise came from one of the later Baldwins, either Baldwin III or Baldwin IV. As between the two I prefer to attribute it to Baldwin IV because of the clause in the oath, though Baldwin III is credited with being a scholar of the law also. And if Baldwin IV did issue assises I think that the period around 1180, when he was ruling alone, is the most probable period of his reign for such activity to fall.

But Baldwin was not destined to rule long. The leprosy, which had long wasted away his body, affected his eyes in 1183, causing blindness. A bailli was needed and the choice fell on Guy de Lusignan, count of Jaffa and Ascalon, the king's brother-in-law and probable successor to the throne. An arrangement was made whereby the king reserved for himself the royal title and the city of Jerusalem with 10,000 besants revenue, giving Guy the management of the rest of the realm. Guy swore not to aspire to the throne while his brother-in-law yet lived, and not to alienate any of the king's

[1] Beugnot, *Assises*, ii, Introduction p. 39; Grandclaude, *Étude sur les . . . Assises*, pp. 66–70.

[2] Novare, lxxv, 546–47.

cities or castles, whereupon the liegemen all swore homage to him as bailli.[1] But trouble soon broke out between the king and Guy, for when Baldwin desired to exchange Jerusalem, which he had kept, for Tyre, which he had assigned Guy, he met with a firm refusal from the count of Jaffa. The anger of the king was justly aroused against his proud and presumptious protegé, and he was not alone in his disapproval of the bailli. The opposition to Guy centered around Raymond of Tripoli and the Ibelins. Baldwin d'Ibelin of Rama had been the unsuccessful candidate for the hand of Sibylle when she was married to Guy, and he and his family resented the slight which had been put upon them.[2] The failure of the Christian arms further weakened Guy's position, nor did the fact that he was supported by Renaud de Châtillon, whose recklessness had brought down upon Krak the army of Saladin, tend to make him more popular.[3]

By 1183 the difficulties between king and bailli had reached a climax, and in a meeting of the *Haute Cour*, at which Raymond, Baldwin and Balian d'Ibelin, and Renaud of Sidon were conspicuously active, it was determined to secure the succession and to crown the five year old Baldwin V king.[4] Baldwin V was Sibylle's son by her first husband William de Montferrat, and the selection of him as successor to the throne cut Guy out of his hopes of succession, which as husband of Sibylle he had legitimately entertained. The coronation of the son instead of the mother ran counter to the accepted laws of inheritance when the fief passed through the mother, and this act was a very deliberate assertion on the part of the *Haute Cour* of its right to elect the monarch. Yet I feel that it was deliberately done counter to the general tendency of political thought, for Guy's eventual succession seems to have been taken

---

[1] William Tyre, XXII, xxv, 1116–17; Röhricht, p. 404. In March 1183 Baldwin issued a charter '*consensu Guidonis . . . et Sibyllae uxoris eius*'. (*Regesta*, doc. 625.)

[2] William Tyre, XXII, xxix, 1127–28.

[3] Renaud constantly pillaged caravans on their way from Damascus to Mecca and return. He had, in 1182, earned the undying hatred of Saladin by his attempt to capture Mecca and Medina.

As Jerusalem was at truce with Saladin, Baldwin tried to stop Renaud in his pillaging, but the lord of Krak refused to heed his suzerain. See Schlumberger, *Renaud de Châtillon*, chapters 7 and 8.

[4] William Tyre, XXII, xxix, 1127–28; Ernoul, pp. 115–16; *Eracles*, p. 6; *Gestes*, par. 38.

for granted by Baldwin IV when he appointed Guy bailli, and the very pains taken to crown young Baldwin during his uncle's lifetime shows that the barons realized that they were running counter to custom. Perhaps the laws of inheritance were not yet fixed—it is quite possible that the male in the second generation would be preferable to the female in the first, or rather that the nephew was preferable to the sister for the inheritance was traced by relationship from the person last seised of the fief. I do not admit that it was merely the normal functioning of the accepted right of the barons to elect their king. Though the throne was still in theory elective, the dynasty had been well enough established so that hereditary right was a very strong factor in determining the succession; it should be noted that William of Tyre, who wrote his history at this very time, constantly refers to succession by hereditary right, even pushing it as far back as Baldwin I. Undoubtedly at the moment the barons did not think over-much about constitutional forms or the respective claims of hereditary and elective theories. They were anxious to be rid of a most unpopular bailli and saw in the coronation of the little prince an easy means of depriving Guy of the bailliage.

After the coronation of Baldwin V the relations between Baldwin IV and Guy became steadily worse. Baldwin tried to have Sibylle's marriage to Guy annulled and to seize Jaffa and Ascalon, and, finally, to insure against Guy's trying to rule for his stepson, ordered that the bailliage of the realm be given to Raymond of Tripoli and the custody of the child to his maternal uncle, Joscelin de Courtney, the seneschal of the kingdom. Raymond was given the city of Beirut to defray his expenses as bailli, and the castles of the king were made over to the Orders to garrison and guard. It was further stipulated, at Raymond's request, that in case of the demise of Baldwin V before he came of age, the regency should continue until his successor had been chosen by an electoral college composed of the Pope, the German emperor, and the kings of France and England.[1] This is a most interesting provision and, I think, proves

[1] William Tyre, XXIII, i, 1133–34; *Eracles*, pp. 1–10; Ernoul, pp. 115–17; Röhricht, pp. 409–10.

Guy and Sibylle had both been present at the coronation of Baldwin V. Guy had been excused from taking the oath of homage to his step-son.

The regent was not allowed to have custody of the heir according to the later *Assises* Ibelin, clxx, 261).

that the barons recognized the hereditary principle in matters of succession. Had they been still working on the theory of an elective monarchy, no such electoral college would have been necessary as they could simply have elected a successor themselves. The delegation of the choice of a successor to the committee of western sovereigns shows that the *Haute Cour* anticipated a disputed succession and did not consider itself competent to decide the matter, which would not have been their attitude had they still maintained their rights of election.

The ordering of the bailliage to Raymond was the last act of Baldwin IV. Consumed by leprosy, the unfortunate king finally 'answered God's summons' on March 16, 1185, dying however with the satisfaction of knowing that his kingdom was in the keeping of the man who was recognized, by his foes if not by his friends, as the ablest warrior of the crusading states.[1]

The most important act of Raymond during the few months that Baldwin V lived was a four year truce which he made with Saladin in 1185. He appears on charters of Baldwin V of May, June, and November, 1185, as giving consent with the title '*comes Tripolitani et totius regni procurator*'.[2]

When little Baldwin died in September 1186, the expected trouble began.[3] Joscelin delivered the body to the Templars for burial, and hastened at once to seize Acre and Beirut for Sibylle. Guy and Sibylle occupied Jerusalem, while Raymond summoned the barons to him at Tiberias. Raymond demanded that, according to the

---

[1] Beha-ed-Din, *Life of Salah-ed-Din P. P. T. S.*, xiii: (London, 1898), p. 112, chap. 35, calls Raymond 'the most intelligent man of that race and famous for his keenness of perception'. Raymond has met with various fortunes at the hands of modern historians, many of whom blame him for his flight at Hattin. He has been accused of desiring to turn Moslem but fearing to do so. William of Tyre was a partisan of Raymond's, and his account is most complimentary to the great count of Tripoli; but a less favorable view of him will be found in Ambroise, *L'Estoire de la Guerre Sainte* (ed. G. Paris: *Docs. Inédits.*, Paris, 1897).

[2] Eracles, p. 13. Documents in: Delaborde, doc. 43; Strehlke, docs. 18, 19; *Regesta*, docs. 643, 644, 657. Pope Urban III addressed a letter to Raymond as bailli. (*Liber Jurium, i*, doc. 345; *Regesta*, doc. 438.)

Raymond made three grants in Tripoli during this time in which he used his title of bailli of Jerusalem, though the grants were made as count of Tripoli. (*Regesta*, docs. 645, 651a, 651b.)

[3] Ernoul, p. 129, note 5; *Eracles*, p. 25, note 5; Röhricht, p. 416. The last mention of Baldwin on a charter is one of April 1186 which is dated: '*Balduino V rege, Eraclio patriarcha*'. (*Regesta*, doc. 651; D. L. *Archives*, doc. 63.)

agreement made before the death of Baldwin IV, he should be allowed to retain the bailliage of the kingdom until the electoral college of Pope, emperor, and kings of France and England should designate a successor. He formally assembled the *Haute Cour* at Neapolis; the great majority of the barons, especially the Ibelins and their adherents and allied families, attended. Meanwhile, Guy and Sibylle had been joined in Jerusalem by Renaud de Châtillon; Gerard de Ridefort, Grand Master of the Templars; Roger des Moulins, Grand Master of the Hospitallers; and the Patriarch Heraclius; while Joscelin sent assurances of support from Acre encouraging Sibylle to proceed at once with her coronation.[1] Sibylle sent to the barons at Neapolis demanding that they recognize her as queen, but they refused until the decision of the chosen electors should be received. When this refusal was brought back to Jerusalem, Heraclius, Sibylle, de Châtillon, and de Ridefort barred the gates of the city and prepared to crown the queen. When des Moulins refused to coöperate in this illegal action they proceeded without him.[2] Two crowns were prepared, and the patriarch placed one on the head of Sibylle and the other on the altar of the Holy Sepulchre, where the coronation services were held. As it was necessary that there should be a king as well as queen, the patriarch told Sibylle that the other crown was for her to place on the brow of the man whom she should choose to rule with her. Her action was dictated in advance and she solemnly placed the crown on the head of her husband Guy;—the worst fears of the barons and Baldwin IV were fulfilled.[3] Renaud meanwhile addressed the people, pointing out that Sibylle was the legitimate

---

[1] Ernoul, pp. 129-35; *Eracles*, pp. 25-29; *Gestes*, par. 43. It must be remembered that the accounts of this civil war come to us from the pen of avowed adherents of Raymond and the Ibelins. Ernoul was the squire of Baldwin d'Ibelin.

Heraclius, like Raymond, has had various interpretations placed upon his character. While undoubtedly he left certain moral qualities to be desired he was not the archvillain portrayed by William of Tyre who was his unsuccessful rival for the patriarchate.

[2] The keys to the chest in which the royal crowns were kept were entrusted to the patriarch and the Masters of the Temple and Hospital. Des Moulins refused to give his key to the patriarch, but threw it out of the window,— and of course it was at once picked up and brought back, and the chest was unlocked without further protest.

[3] Ernoul, p. 134; *Eracles*, p. 29.

When Geoffrey de Lusignan, Guy's brother, heard of the coronation he is said to have remarked: 'If he is now king, he will ere long be God'. ('Dont deuist il bien iestre, pardroit. Dieus'.) (Ernoul, p. 60.)

heiress to the throne, as being daughter of Amaury, sister of Baldwin IV, and in every way '*li plus apareissanz et li plus dreis heirs dou roiaume*'.[1]

Raymond and the Ibelins were of no mind to accept the *fait accompli* and quietly acquiesce. When the news of the coronatioñ reached Neapolis, the barons in council determined to crown Isabelle, the younger half-sister of Sibylle, and her husband Humphrey de Toron. Both Isabelle and Humphrey were young, and it was felt that they would be mere tools in the hands of the experienced count of Tripoli.[2]

The question of the succession in 1186 was a personal one far more than a legal or constitutional one. Sibylle was the elder daughter of Amaury, and the sister of Baldwin IV. Though Amaury had been forced by the patriarch to divorce their mother, Agnes de Courtney, the children were recognized as legitimate and there was never a question as to their right as legitimate heirs. Baldwin IV had been crowned without question, and Sibylle's son Baldwin V as well. But Sibylle's husband was more than the barons would tolerate. It was not that they did not recognize Sibylle's legitimate claims to the throne, but that they would not have Guy as king over them. Had William de Montferrat not died almost immediately after his marriage, or had Sibylle married Baldwin of Rama instead of the Poitevin adventurer, there would probably have been little or no opposition to her succession. But the fact remained that Sibylle had married Guy and now elected to have him as her king. In consequence, as the barons would not have Guy, they had to find someone to replace Sibylle too,—Isabelle stood ready to hand.

Isabelle Plantagenet was the daughter of Amaury by his second wife Marie of Byzantium. After Amaury's death, Marie had married Balian d'Ibelin, bringing Neapolis with her as dower. As Balian was one of his brother's most staunch supporters, the former queen was on the side of the barons and her influence with Isabelle was strong. Isabelle's husband, Humphrey IV de Toron, was the son of Humphrey III the younger of Toron, grandson of the old constable Humphrey II. His mother was that Stephenie de Milly who had

---

[1] *Eracles*, p. 28.
[2] Ernoul, pp. 134–36; *Eracles*, p. 30; Röhricht, p. 419.

married, after the death of Humphrey the younger, Miles de Plancy and later still Renaud de Châtillon. The marriage of the young couple had been celebrated in the castle of Krak while Saladin was besieging it in 1182, and Humphrey, already joint lord of Montreal and Krak, had inherited the fief of Toron at the death of his grandfather in 1179.[1] But though his step-father was one of Guy's most ardent supporters, Raymond and the Ibelins thought they could count on the young, rather scholarly, unwarlike and somewhat weak-willed Humphrey to act as they directed.

There was not, so far as I can find, any claim as a *porphyrogenita* made for Isabelle. Though in Byzantium, whence her mother had come, the claim of the child born to the purple was often urged against elder heirs born before the accession of the parent to the throne, the laws of Jerusalem provided for the inheritance of the children by a first marriage in preference to those by a second. But the barons went back to a more fundamental rule—the right of the *Haute Cour* to elect the ruler. Yet even here they did not try to do more than to designate which member of the ruling house they preferred. They did not attempt to bring in an outsider. Even Raymond of Tripoli, closely connected with the Bouillon-Plantagenet dynasty as he was, did not set up his own candidacy for the throne, though he was the strongest baron in the realm, the recognized leader of the barons against Guy, and was already legally in possession of the government in his capacity of bailli.

The selection seemed good and the chances for success were strong. Though Guy and Sibylle held most of the important cities of the realm, the total of the fiefs held by the baronial faction was impressive: Tripoli, Galilee and Tiberias, Ibelin, Rama, Neapolis, and Toron (as well as Humphrey's claim to Krak and Montreal which could be advanced against those of Renaud). But Raymond and the Ibelins had made their plans without testing their tools.

---

[1] Ernoul, p. 103, tells a delightful story about Saladin at this time:—that the princess sent him a piece of the wedding cake as he lay besieging the castle, and that Saladin inquired in which tower the bride and groom lay, ordering that, in the attack on the castle, that tower should be unharmed. Schlumberger tells the anecdote with all his accustomed vividness and charm of style in *Renaud de Châtillon*, pp. 226–28.

The genealogy of Humphrey de Toron is from the *Familles*, pp. 470–71, and the notes of Mas Latrie in the Bibliothèque Nationale, Ms. *Nouv. Acq. Français*, 6795.

No sooner did Humphrey hear of the scheme to place him on the throne than he fled by night from Neapolis and went to Jerusalem, where he threw himself on the mercy of Guy and Sibylle, performing homage and promising complete adherence to them against his own partisans.[1] This sudden and unexpected flight of their candidate wholly upset the plans of the barons, and they applied to Raymond to release them from their oaths to him. Sadly and reluctantly the count agreed and the barons, with the exception of the haughty Baldwin of Rama, hastened to Jerusalem to do homage to the king and queen. And even the proud Ibelin was forced eventually to become the man of his hated rival, for Guy refused to accept the homage of his son for his fiefs. Though he said the required words, Ibelin refused to kneel, and, as soon as he had made his homage, invested his son with his fiefs and, demanding Guy's permission to leave the country, went to Antioch where he was given fiefs by Bohemond III, which were, according to Ernoul, '*iii tans de tiere qu'il n'avoit laissiés, et castiaus et cités*'.[2]

The years 1187 to 1190 were far too full politically to allow of much institutional development. The steady advance of Saladin, the valiant but futile resistance, the tragedy of Hattin, and the march of the Saracen armies across the mountains and plains of Palestine with the attendant capitulation of the cities, the imprisonment and ransom of the king and many of the chief barons, the crumbling

---

[1] Ernoul, p. 136; *Eracles*, p. 31.

[2] Ernoul, pp. 137–39; *Eracles*, pp. 31–34.

Baldwin appears on a charter of Bohemond III given at Antioch in 1186. His name appears first under the heading '*de militibus*', before those of the seneschal, constable, and chamberlain of Antioch. (D. L. *Cartulaire*, doc. 783; *Regesta*, doc. 649.) Delaville Le Roulx and Röhricht both date this charter as February 1186, basing the date on the confirmation by Urban III at Rome in June. But the confirmation *may* have been June 1187. (D. L. *Cartulaire*, doc. 809.) The charter of Bohemond is a confirmation of a grant made by Bertrand of Margat in February 1186, and Röhricht presumes that the suzerain's confirmation was made at the time of the original grant. The name of Baldwin d'Ibelin would seem to alter this date, however, as he was in Jerusalem in the early months of that year and did not go permanently to Antioch until after Guy's coronation in September. On the other hand he may easily have been in Antioch on a trip in February 1186, before he went there to stay. He appears on a charter of Raymond of Gibelet, given at Antioch under the same date.

Raymond of Tripoli does not appear to have performed homage to Guy, for Ernoul says that when he had released the barons from their oaths he retired to Tiberias, while the rest went to Jerusalem to do homage to the king.

away of the state which the rulers from Godfrey to Foulque had built,—such are but the outstanding events of these crowded years. Much can be drawn from the history of Jerusalem in the last months before the fall,—for the moralist a sermon, for the philosopher a smile at the futile gesturings of the puppets who strove so blindly to avert the overwhelming destiny which pressed down upon them. Russia on the eve of the Mongol conquest is not more pathetic than the little Latin kingdom, cowering in the shadow of great Saladin's advance, yet unable to put a stop to the petty rivalries and constant internal bickerings which divided the councils and prevented all coöperation among the lords whose every effort should have been directed towards holding in check the Moslem power. Amid the havoc of falling cities and broken oaths, heroic martyrdoms and cowardly cringings, the man of the hour appeared in the person of Conrad de Montferrat, who arriving at Tyre just as the city was about to surrender, strengthened its resistance, and succeeded in holding the city as an isolated stronghold against the Moslem torrent. His arrival in July 1187, shortly after the debàcle at Hattin, came at a time when the resistance of the Franks was at its lowest ebb. Sidon and Beirut had just fallen; Jerusalem was frantically organizing defense under Balian d'Ibelin; Guy was in prison; and Count Raymond, after his flight from Hattin, had retired to Tripoli where he was shortly thereafter to die of sickness. Conrad seemed the only man who was capable of keeping his head in the general turmoil and for two years he held Tyre against the Saracen, repulsing attack and enduring siege, not even wavering when his father, a prisoner in Saladin's camp, was exposed and tortured before the walls of Tyre in an effort to break the resistance of the son. In 1188 Guy and many other prisoners were released by Saladin after they had taken oaths not to take arms again against him. However, promptly absolved from such an unchristian oath by a patriotic patriarch, they at once began to collect forces in an effort to regain some of their lost possessions. When Guy appeared in 1189 before Tyre demanding the surrender to him as king of this last city of his former kingdom, Conrad refused to abdicate the position he had won, refusing even to allow the king entrance within the city. Conrad had reason to feel himself a better man than the rash and unfortunate Guy. The king moved south to Acre and in the early summer of 1189 began the siege round which were to center most of the events of the third crusade. In the fall of 1190 during this siege Queen Sibylle died and with her death events become once more important to this study.[1] For the throne had belonged to the queen; Guy was merely king by virtue of her selection and by his position as her husband. At Sibylle's death the throne, according to the laws of Outremer, passed at once to the next heir,—the princess Isabelle. This was Conrad's opportunity. Isabelle's husband, the weak Humphrey de Toron, was obviously unfit to be king. Conrad approached the patriarch and the bishop of Beauvais on the subject of divorcing Isabelle from Humphrey, thus leaving the lady free to marry him. He received encouragement in this design from Balian d'Ibelin, Renaud of Sidon, and others of the barons who had opposed Guy; and Balian's wife, Marie of Byzantium, who was Isabelle's mother, brought pressure to bear on the girl to consent to the divorce. The grounds advanced were that as the marriage had taken place when Isabelle was only eight years old she was then too young to be married. Though the archbishop of Canterbury opposed the divorce and excommunicated Conrad (who seems to have neglected to divorce either of his two former wives), the bishop of Beauvais pronounced Isabelle's marriage to Humphrey annulled and at once thereafter married her to Conrad. The princess, though reluctant, obeyed the demands of her birth and position.[2]

[1] The date of Sibylle's death, which is given by Ambroise as August 1190 (*L'Estoire de la Guerre Sainte*, lines 3897–3902, col. 104), and by Mas Latrie as 15 July, 1190 (Ernoul, p. 267), can be fixed only approximately from charters. She is mentioned in a charter of Guy given at Acre in September 1190 (Strehlke, doc. 25; *Regesta*, doc. 696); also in another charter of 1190 dated by Méry, *Histoire . . . de Marseille*, i, 194–95, as October 25, 1190, and by Bréquigny, *Diplomata, chartae, epistolae* (Paris, 1791), iv, 125, as April 24. Röhricht, *Regesta*, doc. 697, follows Méry as to the date but omits Sibylle from the charter. In his *Geschichte* he dates her death as October 1190 (p. 538), disregarding this charter as of too uncertain date; and in the *Regesta*, *Additamentum*, doc. 703a, p. 47, notes her death as *ca.* 15 Oct. 1190. A letter of October 21, 1190 given in the *Epistolae Cantuarensis* (ed. Stubbs: Rolls Series: *Chronicles and Memorials of the Reign of Richard I*, vol. ii; London, 1865), doc. cccxlvi, pp. 328–29, says that she is dead.

The story of Conrad and of the wars 1187–90 are to be found in Ernoul, pp. 140–258; *Eracles*, pp. 40–150; Beha-ed-Din, *passim*; *Itinerarium Regis Ricardi* (ed Stubbs: Rolls Series: *Chronicles and Memorials of the Reign of Richard I*, vol. i; London, 1864), Bk. I, 5–137, and also Stubbs' excellent preface; Röhricht, pp. 422–537.

[2] Ernoul, pp. 267–68; *Eracles*, pp. 151–54; *Gestes*, par. 50; Ambroise, *L'Estoire de la Guerre*

Guy de Lusignan did not, however, recognize the throne to have escheated to his sister-in-law and continued to consider and call himself king.[1] Conrad never assumed any royal title, nor could Isabelle until she was crowned. She was known as *domina*, while Conrad used his title of marquis and lord of Tyre on his charters; only on a charter of May 7, 1191, did he call himself '*rex Hierosolymitanus electus*'.[2]

The arrival of the armies of France and England under Philip Augustus and Richard added more complications, as Philip at once championed the cause of Conrad while Richard favored Guy. Finally, on July 28, 1191 it was agreed in a meeting held under the presidency of Philip and Richard that the crown of Jerusalem should remain with Guy until his death, when it should go to Conrad, and that until that time Conrad should be given the cities of Tyre, Sidon, and Beirut.[3] Philip's departure for France almost immediately after this left Richard in command of the crusading forces. Trouble soon broke out between Conrad and Richard, and the marquis refused to assist the king in his expedition against Ascalon. After fighting up and down Palestine for some eight months and finally making an advantageous peace with Saladin,—whereby the Christians were to keep Jaffa, Ascalon, and the northern towns which they had recaptured, and were permitted to visit Jerusalem and the Holy Places,—Richard prepared to return home. In an assembly of the host held at Ascalon in April 1192 the question of

---

Sainte, lines 4108–50, cols. 110–111, p. 378; *Itinerarium Regis Ricardi*, I, lxiii, 119–123; Röhricht, pp. 538–39.

Isabelle secured for Humphrey his hereditary lands of Toron and Chateauneuf. The most complete account of the whole story is found in the *Eracles*, but it is far inferior in interest to that of Ambroise who, writing as a zealous partisan of Richard and Guy, condemns Conrad unmercifully and tells how '*li faus marchis . . . voleit le riaume aveir*', and so by his gold and his strong position married the wife of Raimfrai de Thoron '*contre Deu e contre raison . . . car li marchis aveit esposes deus beles dames, joefnes toses*'—and for this sin he was excommunicated and after suffered.

[1] Guy issued five charters between the death of Sibylle and the end of 1192 in which he styled himself king of Jerusalem. (*Regesta* docs. 698, 701, 702, 703a, 705a.)

[2] Conrad issued his charters '*cum*' or '*consensu Isabellae uxoris*' (*Regesta*, docs. 703, 704, 705). It is in the last of these three that he used the Jerusalemite title.

[3] Ambroise, ll. 5041–5066, col. 137; Röhricht, p. 568. It was further stipulated that should both claimants die while Richard was still in the East, Richard should have the power to name the next king.

the kingship was again brought up. The agreement of July 1191 and the departure of Philip had left Richard with practical control of the kingdom. He commanded the armies and dictated policies. But Conrad and the French knights, who had been left behind by Philip under the command of the duke of Burgundy, had not accepted Richard's leadership and had withdrawn, leaving Richard to carry on the war alone. Consequently the army which was with Richard at Ascalon was made up primarily of Richard's adherents and the Syrian nobility of Guy's party. None the less, when Richard announced his intention of leaving for England, the realization of the necessity for union and the knowledge of Conrad's stubborn resistance, combined with an appreciation of his ability and a marked lack of respect for Guy's, caused the barons humbly to request the king that before he left he would order a single king for the country and that Conrad be given the rule. The choice of the barons was not personally pleasing to Richard, but he acquiesced in the election of the host and dispatched his nephew Henry, count of Champagne, to Tyre to notify Conrad of his election as sole king of Jerusalem. Conrad's ambition was at last realized; but not for long, for on April 28, the day after the arrival of Henry with the glad news, Conrad was murdered in the streets of Tyre by some members of the sect of the Assassins.[1]

Guy meanwhile had begun negotiations for the purchase of the island kingdom of Cyprus, which Richard had conquered incontinently on his way to Acre, and in May 1192 he removed to the island leaving the field uncontested in Jerusalem.[2]

[1] Ambroise, ll. 8601–8664, 8715–8909, cols. 230–238; *Itinerarium*, V, xxiii–xxvi, 334–41; *Eracles*, p. 193; Röhricht, p. 614.

Richard was accused of hiring the Assassins to murder Conrad, but the charge was never founded on more than rumor.

An excellent modern account of the whole third crusade and the politics which attended it is to be found in A. Cartellieri, *Philipp II August*, vol. ii, *Der Kreuzzug 1187–91* (Leipsic and Paris, 1906).

[2] Richard had conquered Cyprus and then sold it to the Templars, who, unable to enforce their rule in the island, wished to return it to Richard. Guy bought the Knights' equity in the kingdom and arranged with Richard to pay the rest. He settled Cyprus in May 1192, and as the Templars had been having trouble since the beginning of the year it is probable that he had already planned and probably executed the purchase before Conrad's murder. (*Eracles*, pp. 189–92; L. de Mas Latrie, *Histoire de Chypre*, i, 32–38.) G. Jeffrey, *Cyprus under an English King* (Nicosia: Govt Press, 1926) is a readable and very picturesque account of the

The murder of Conrad and the departure of Guy left the whole question open again but it was soon settled by Richard's arranging for his nephew, Henry of Champagne, who was also a nephew of Philip Augustus and consequently acceptable to both English and French factions, to marry Isabelle and be chosen king of Jerusalem. The marriage took place almost immediately after Conrad's death. Ambroise gives a charming story of how the barons who were encamped outside Tyre elected Henry, and Richard was informed only after the event; but the account in Ernoul, which says that Richard came from Acre to Tyre and brought Henry with him suggesting him for the vacant throne, seems the more reliable.[1] Henry was destined never to have the title of king of Jerusalem, and although he ruled for five years, from 1192 to September 1197, he was never crowned; his charters carry only the title of count of Troyes, with the exception of one in March 1196, in which he designated himself '*Henricus Trecensis comes palatinus et regni Hierosolymitani dominus*'.[2]

Henry's career was abruptly ended in September 1197 by a fatal fall from a tower window, and Isabelle found herself once more a widow; she was twenty-four by now and had already had three husbands! The *Haute Cour* met to consider the question of procuring another husband for the princess. After Ralph of Tiberias had been suggested and rejected on the grounds that he could bring no outside resources to the aid of the kingdom, the selection of the court fell on Amaury de Lusignan, elder brother of Guy, who was constable of Jerusalem and now king of Cyprus, having inherited his brother's kingdom when Guy died in 1194.[3]

---

conquest of Cyprus, drawn from the *Itinerarium* (which the author unfortunately cites throughout as Vinsauf) and with much local color supplied by Jeffrey's intimate knowledge of Cypriot archeology.

[1] Ernoul, pp. 290–91; *Eracles*, pp. 194–95; Ambroise, ll. 8909–9102, cols. 238–43; *Itinerarium*, V, xxviii, 342–43, xxxiv–vi, 346–350. Röhricht, pp. 616–18, follows the account of Ambroise and the *Itinerarium*.

[2] *Regesta*, docs. 707, 709, 710, 713, 716, 716a, 717, 720, 721, 722, 722a, 724, 727, 735. Mas Latrie, *Histoire de Chypre*, i, 121, suggests that Henry was never crowned as he always hoped eventually to return to France.

[3] Ernoul, pp. 309–10; *Eracles*, pp. 220–23.

Amaury had inherited Cyprus from Guy in 1194 and in 1197 had been crowned king by the imperial chancellor. Amaury was constable of Jerusalem 1181–1194 and again in 1197,

The election of Amaury was a clear case of the *Haute Cour's* exercising its power to elect a monarch. The election of Conrad was the same, and so, if we can accept the story given by Ambroise, was that of Henry, though I am inclined to think that Richard had a hand in that affair. Yet Isabelle continued as princess, and all the elective monarchs were married to the legitimist queen. The situation points to a compromise between the two principles of election and hereditary succession. Heredity had progressed far enough so that the barons, in choosing a king, chose a husband for the queen.

It was not until after her fourth marriage that Isabelle was finally crowned queen and her husband king. Consequently Amaury II numbered himself next after Guy in the list of kings of Jerusalem, assuming the title '*Aymericus per Dei gratiam Jerusalem Latinorum rex nonus et rex Cypri*'.[1]

The reign of Amaury and Isabelle, unlike that of Henry of Champagne and Isabelle, is one of some constitutional interest. The country was recuperating from the devastation of the long war against Saladin, and the energies of the rulers and the feudality were devoted to restoring the prosperity of the cities and fiefs which remained in Christian hands. Desultory war against Saladin's heirs (the great Kurd had died in 1193, leaving his empire divided among several heirs, no one of whom could reunit it) around Jaffa, Beirut, and along the coast characterized the reigns of both Henry and Amaury, but with Amaury there is a revival of constitutional inter-

---

when he appears on a charter as king of Cyprus and constable of Jerusalem (Mas Latrie, iii, 606–07; *Regesta*, doc. 737). The *Eracles*, pp. 202–03, variant reading, (Mas Latrie, ii, 9–10, gives a varied story of the same) tells an interesting and not unimportant anecdote concerning Henry and Amaury. In 1194 Henry seized Amaury and threw him in prison for having advised Guy to capture Tyre and for assisting the Pisans, against whom Henry was operating. Amaury said that as he was the constable and Henry's liegeman the prince had no right to treat him so. Henry said he would hold him until Guy surrendered Cyprus to him, but the barons objected and secured Amaury's release from prison. He surrendered the constableship to the prince and departed for Cyprus, where, shortly thereafter, he became king. According to the other version Henry demanded the surrender of Jaffa, which Amaury had as fief from Guy and Sibylle. The whole is confused and merely shows that the prince and the constable had a quarrel in which Amaury was unjustly imprisoned but was released upon the demands of the barons and tried in the *Haute Cour*. Ernoul omits any mention of the story.

[1] Ernoul, p. 310; *Eracles*, p. 223; Röhricht, p. 674. The act from which this signature is taken is one of 1198 given in Mas Latrie, ii, 24–25; *Regesta*, doc. 747.

est. Amaury endeavored to have the codes of laws which had prevailed in the earlier kingdom drafted and had commissioned Ralph
of Tiberias, considered the foremost jurist of the time, to compile
them; but Ralph refused to work with the commission which the
king desired to appoint.[1] Whether or not the *Livre au Roi* was the
work of this committee it is impossible to say. The *Livre* was
issued sometime during the reign of Amaury and may very possibly
have been the result of the work of the commission which Amaury
appointed, but Ralph of Tiberias was not the chairman thereof as
the king desired.

Ralph and Amaury had other troubles besides this. Ralph, it
may be recalled, was the candidate for Isabelle's hand who was
passed over when Amaury was elected, for which he bore the king a
grudge. In 1198, as Amaury was riding from Acre to Tyre, he was set
upon by hired murderers and only with difficulty escaped death. A
force from Tyre, which he raised after his escape, captured and
killed the murderers after wringing from them the fact that they
were hired by Ralph of Tiberias. Amaury at once seized Ralph and,
declaring his fiefs forfeit, banished him from the kingdom. But
Ralph, a clever jurist, saw how he could turn the tables on the king.
Demanding trial by his peers in the *Haute Cour*, he charged the
king with illegal action in disseising and banishing him without trial.
The court sustained Ralph in his charge against the king, and Ralph
then announced that as Amaury was ill disposed towards him he
would no longer remain in the kingdom.[2] It was probably at this
time that Ralph surrendered to the king the fief which he held in

---

[1] Novare calls him '*le sovrain de soutilance de fait de court*' (xciv, 570). Novare, xlvii, 522–
23, and Ibelin, cclxxiii, 430, tell of Ralph's refusal to serve on the committee to redact the laws,
because he did not wish that everyone should know as much about them as he did. Ralph was
seneschal of Jerusalem 1194–1220. After his break with Amaury he went to Antioch where
Bohemond gave him fiefs, but he quarreled with him and, returning the fiefs, went to Constantinople. He was back in Jerusalem at the time of the coronation of John de Brienne in 1210,
and was with John at the siege of Damietta in 1218, where he taught the laws to the young
Philip de Novare. (Novare, xlix, 525.) At some time in his career, presumably after his
return in 1210, he married Agnes, daughter of Renaud of Sidon. His daughter Eschive
married Eudes de !Montbéliard, and a second daughter Heloise married Peter d'Avalon.
(*Familles*, pp. 456–57; Bibliothèque Nationale, Ms. *Nouv. Acq. Français*, 6795.)

[2] Ibelin, cciv, 327–28; *Eracles*, pp. 228–30. Ernoul, pp. 310–11, merely mentions the attack on the king, which was supposed to have been made at the instigation of Ralph.

Tripoli, demanding release from the homage which he had performed for the fief.[1]

The appearance of the *Livre au Roi* was constitutionally the most important event of the reign of Amaury. The chronicles do not mention it, but internal evidence shows that it must date from this period.[2] Amaury's reign was also the first in which Jerusalem and Cyprus were ruled by a single monarch.

Amaury died in 1205, leaving Isabelle in possession of the throne; she survived her husband only for a short time.[3] Her son by Amaury had died shortly before his father, and after Isabelle's own decease the throne devolved on the little princess, Marie. She was Isabelle's daughter by Conrad and was known as '*La Marquise*'. John d'Ibelin, lord of Beirut and Isabelle's half brother, was appointed regent for Marie by the *Haute Cour*.[4] In Cyprus Amaury was succeeded by Hugh, his son by Eschive d'Ibelin, under the regency of Walter de Montbéliard, husband of Hugh's sister Borgogne.

The regency of John d'Ibelin lasted four years, during which time the bailli and the *Haute Cour* carried on a campaign against Melek-el-Adel and negotiated the marriage of the princess. An embassy was sent to France to the court of King Philip to ask a king for the country and a husband for the princess. Philip recommended John de Brienne and in 1208 it was agreed that John should marry Marie.

---

[1] Novare, lxxiii, 543–44.

[2] The date has been established by Grandclaude, pp. 46–50.

[3] Amaury died April 1, 1205. Ernoul, p. 407, note 2; *Eracles*, p. 305; *Gestes*, par. 62; Röhricht, p. 696, note 2. *Familles*, p. 32, and the editors of the *Eracles* say that Isabelle lived until 1208, but this is obviously wrong as proven by the documents. No charters of Isabelle's issued after the death of Amaury exist, and an act of John d'Ibelin's in May 1206 is issued as bailli of the realm with the consent of '*dominae regni Mariae*'. (*Regesta*, doc. 812; Strehlke, doc. 41). This would prove that Isabelle died before this time. That she was dead before December 1207 is also evidenced by the treaty between John d'Ibelin, as bailli, and Hugh of Cyprus, which was approved by the archbishop of Tyre at that time, and in which there is no mention of her. (*Regesta*, doc. 823.)

[4] John was the son of Marie of Byzantium and Balian d'Ibelin, and thus half-brother to Isabelle. He was made constable of Jerusalem by Henry of Champagne but traded the title for the fief of Beirut. The *Eracles*, p. 305, says that the barons met before Isabelle, and elected John bailli immediately afrer the death of Amaury. This is the '*Vieux sire de Beyruth*', who was so celebrated for his knowledge of law and for his resistance to Frederick II in Cyprus and Jerusalem. See below.

The next year was spent in arrangements on John's part, and it was not until September 1210 that he landed in Acre, where he was married to the princess. They were crowned on October 3 in the cathedral of Tyre. At the time of the marriage John was approximately sixty years old, his bride seventeen.[1]

The most interesting feature of this period, which closes with the accession of John de Brienne to the throne, is the series of female successions and the election of men who would combine the office of husband of the queen with that of king of the realm. The question at once arises as to how far the man thus elected was king in his own right and how far he was merely prince consort of the reigning queen. The answer appears in the provision of the *Livre au Roi* which was written under Isabelle and Amaury. It says that the acts of a king who has married the reigning queen and holds his position through her must, after his death, be reënacted by the queen with the approval of the *Haute Cour* to remain valid.[2] While it is possible that this provision was put in to prevent Amaury or any other king in a similar position from trying to act independently of his wife, it might equally appear to be a check on the king imposed by the court, which requires that he submit his acts to it as well as to the queen.[3]

[1] Ernoul, pp. 408–09; *Eracles*, pp. 306–11; *Gestes*, par. 67; Röhricht, pp. 699–701; P. Lafiteau, *Histoire de Jean de Brienne* (Paris, 1727), pp. 105–110.

Ernoul says that the barons themselves elected John on the nomination of a knight in the *Haute Cour*; Lafiteau prefers this version. The *Eracles* says that he was recommended by Philip Augustus, who wished to get him out of France as he was jealous of him for the favors of Blanche of Champagne. The *Gestes* would indicate nomination by Philip. Though Philip may very possibly have nominated him, the cause given by the *Eracles* is hardly to be taken in good faith. I accept Röhricht's estimate of the ages of the couple, though John's seems to be a bit too advanced.

[2] *Livre au Roi*, iv, 609: 'S' il avient que li rois soit mors et est remese la royne de par cuy li reaumes meut, et puis avient que la dame prist autre mary aucun haut home, si com li afiert, par le conceill de ces homes liges, bien sachés que la raison juge et coumande enci à juger que nule don que celuy roi done, ne doit estre tenus après sa mort, se la royne sa moillyer ne l'otroie par la garentie de ces homes liges meysmes; car se elle l'otreie, si com est dit desus, si que l'otroiance d'ele parole au prevelige, si doit estre ferme et estable par tot; mais se elle ne l'otrée, si com est dit desus, et encores soit ce que li rois ses maris en ait fait prevelige a celui ou à cele à cui il a fait seluy don et ceelé dou ceau reau, si ne deit valer celuy don par dreit ne par l'assize.'.

This is exactly the same rule as that which was applied to baillies, whose acts were valid only during their lifetime unless confirmed by the heir in the court. (*Livre au Roi*, vi, 610.)

[3] Beugnot, *Assises*, i, 609 note, points out that the case occurred only once in the history of the kingdom.

Dodu thinks he has clinched the matter and proved that the kings could not act without the consent of their wives by affirming that the name of the queen appears on all charters which have been preserved from any of the kings who held office through their wives.[1] But this is not pertinent, as it was the general custom to include the consent of the wife, and often of the children as well, in any charter, and this was done by private individuals as well as kings. Thus we find Raymond II of Tripoli issuing charters with the consent of his wife Hodierne;[2] Bohemond III of Antioch with the consent of his wife Sibylle;[3] Raymond Rupin with his wife Heloise;[4] and Robert of Frandolio with his wife Agnes.[5] Further Amaury issued charters without the consent of Isabelle, though he normally included it as he had that of his first wife, Eschive d'Ibelin.[6]

A more conclusive proof of the fact that the kings ruled only through their wives is to be found in the fact that the heir of the queen invariably inherited. Thus Isabelle was the heir of Sibylle, Marie the heir of Isabelle, and later Marie's daughter Isabelle inherited from her mother. Guy endeavored to keep his throne after the death of his wife, and was confronted by the opposition of a

---

[1] Dodu, pp. 122–23.

[2] *Regesta*, doc. 233; D. L. *Cartulaire*, ii, doc. 8, p. 902. His son's consent was also included.

[3] *Regesta*, doc. 680; Röhricht, *Amalrich I*, p. 488.

The consent of his son was also mentioned. Bohemond had issued a charter with the consent of his former wife Orgollose. (*Regesta*, doc. 478; Müller, pp. 15–16.)

[4] *Regesta*, docs. 845, 877, 886; V. Langlois, *Trésor des Chartes d'Arménie* (Venice, 1863), docs. 12, 13, 16. The consent of Leo of Armenia was also usually carried in Rupin's charters.

[5] *Regesta*, doc. 284; *Archives*, ii, B, 131.

The consent of four sons and two daughters is also carried. An interesting charter for studying confirmations and consents of all interested parties is a confirmation given by Baldwin of Rama in 1176 of a sale of a casale to Constance of St Gilles by John Arrabitus for 800 besants. Arrabitus held the casale from Balian d'Ibelin, who held it from his brother Baldwin of Rama, who held it from the king. The charter, granted by Baldwin at the request of Arrabitus and his two brothers, carries the consent of Balian d'Ibelin, his daughters and their husbands, and is issued from the king's court. (*Regesta*, doc. 539; D. L. *Cartulaire*, doc. 495.)

[6] Charters issued by Amaury without the consent of Isabelle are: *Regesta*, docs. 761a, 774, 780. Those issued with her consent are: *Regesta*, docs. 740b, 743, 744, 746, 747, 747a, 747b, 747c, 776. *Regesta*, doc. 723 is issued with the consent of Eschive. A charter of 1197 issued as king of Cyprus and constable of Jerusalem, without mention of his wife, falls between the death of Eschive and his marriage to Isabelle. (*Regesta*, doc. 737.)

great part of the nobility; John de Brienne later tried to hold the throne but lost it to the husband of his daughter; and Frederick II himself, king of Jerusalem through his marriage to Isabelle de Brienne, was only recognized as regent for Isabelle's child Conrad. Had the throne been Amaury's instead of Isabelle's, could not Hugh de Lusignan have claimed it on his father's death? This I think is a far stronger argument than that advanced by Dodu on the basis of the charters.

The princes who were elected by the *Haute Cour* had of course a much stronger position than those who were merely prince consorts of the queen. It will be seen in the next chapter that Ralph of Soissons and Henry of Antioch had no power whatever, and did not enjoy the privileges of Foulque, John de Brienne, or Amaury de Lusignan. Yet all these kings of Jerusalem had more in common with Philip II of Spain or Prince Albert than with William of Orange, if it is permissible to seek analogies in the husbands of the English queens.

CHAPTER 3
THE SECOND KINGDOM, 1210-1291

B Y THE thirteenth century the throne of Jerusalem may be said to have become definitely hereditary. The *Haute Cour* still took part in the selection of the king, but it was no longer the electoral group. The court generally confined itself to approving the heir, and, in cases of collateral and disputed succession, to selecting among claimants the closest heir and the person to whom, according to the laws of inheritance, the throne should escheat. As the throne became hereditary so did the regency. Unlike the wholly elective baillies of the early twelfth century, the baillies and regents of the thirteenth century presented to the court their claims to the bailliage and it was granted them by the court upon the presentation of proof that they were the legal heirs to the bailliage. This applies of course only to baillies for minor heirs, and has nothing to do with the many baillies in the thirteenth century who represented the ruler *in absentia*.

The thirteenth century is the century of the *Assises de Jérusalem*, and before examining the historical development of the 'second monarchy' it is advisable to consider what the laws say concerning the succession to the throne and bailliage. The texts of the later and more complete law books assume rather than define the laws of succession, and it is in the *Livre au Roi*, the earliest of the Outremer codes, which dates from the reign of Amaury and Isabelle at the turn of the century, that we must seek the most explicit laws defining succession to the throne and to the bailliage.

Even the *Livre au Roi* assumes an hereditary monarchy. With the case of the heirs of Isabelle in mind, the *Livre* considers the succession as between heirs of a reigning queen. If the queen, through whom the realm escheats, dies leaving heirs by more than one husband the heirs of the first marriage shall inherit the throne. Male heirs have precedence over female, but females by an earlier marriage have precedence over males by a later. Thus a daughter by a first marriage has precedence over a son by a second, though the

49

son by a second would have precedence over an older sister born of the same marriage. The regency is to go to the nearest relative, male or female, on the side through which the throne escheated. If the queen's heirs are of a second marriage, heirs by a first lacking, and the father is living at the time of the death of the queen, the regency for the minor heir shall go to the father until the heir shall have reached his or her majority.[1]

Philip de Novare says nothing concerning the succession to the throne in his treatise on the laws, but his pronouncements on the case of Alice of Cyprus vs. Conrad, as recorded in his *Mémoires*, show that he accepted the laws for the succession to the fief as governing the throne, and adds the provision that the heir must come in person to claim the throne, and that if he fails to come the throne passes to the next heir.[2]

John d'Ibelin, likewise, does not mention succession to the throne, except in his chapter on the coronation where he says the patriarch shall ask the people to accept the king whom he is crowning as the legitimate heir; but he descants fully on the subject of the laws of succession to fiefs, and the same laws are applicable to the throne which was in every respect a fief.[3] James d'Ibelin merely says that the king shall proclaim himself and state his claims as heir to the throne.[4]

---

[1] *Livre au Roi (Assises, i), v, vi, 609–10; Documents Relatifs à la Successibilité au Trône et à la Régence (Assises, ii), p. 398.*

As Grandclaude, pp. 49–50, 119–20, suggests, this law was very probably devised to protect Marie *'la Marquise'*, Isabelle's daughter by Conrad, against any claims that might be advanced by Amaury, Isabelle's son by Amaury II.

It was in conformity with this theory, though previous to the writing of the law, that Raymond of Tripoli had claimed the regency for Baldwin IV; it was under this law that John d'Ibelin, Isabelle's half-brother, had been given the regency for Marie.

The *Assises de Romanie*, art. 217, provide that if the mother through whom the fief escheats dies before being invested of the fief, her husband shall not have the bailliage for her heirs, who have thus become the heirs of her parents, but the bailliage shall go to the next of kin in her family.

[2] *Gestes des Chiprois*, pars. 225–26; *Eracles*, p. 420. 'Il est coustume au royaume de Jerusalem que le plus dreit heir et le plus aparant emporte l'eritage par raison, tant que plus dreit heir de ly veigne ...' (*Gestes*).

While Conrad was the heir, in his absence, Alice was next heir and so inherited.

[3] Ibelin, vii, 30. The laws for the succession of fiefs are to be found in: Ibelin, cxliv–clvii, 217–37, clxxv–clxxvi, 275–77; Novare, lxvi, 536–37, lxxi–lxxiv, 542–46, lxxxii, 554; Geoffrey Tort, i–v, 435–36; Jacques d'Ibelin, xxxi–xxxv, lxix, 461, 468.

[4] Jacques d'Ibelin, i, 453–54.

The decision of the *Haute Cour* in the dispute between Hugh of Antioch-Lusignan and Hugh de Brienne in 1264 added the rule that among collateral heirs the throne should pass to the oldest living male relative in the nearest degree of relationship to the person *last in seisin* of the kingship.[1]

The very absence of any simple statement in regard to the hereditability of the throne shows how well established heredity was by the time the jurisconsults wrote their books. The fief had become hereditary and the throne followed the law of the fief. The laws of Jerusalem, like all the early codes of law, concern themselves not with general principles known to all, but with details which need special exposition and clarification. It is with minor heirs, regencies, and collateral heirs that the *Assises* are concerned.

The king reached his majority in all probability at the age of fifteen. The only definite statement in any of the laws is that of the *Livre au Roi* which says that the king shall be crowned when he has reached the age of twelve and that a regency shall be appointed until he shall be of an age to govern the kingdom.[2] Coronation of course did not imply majority; Baldwin IV, Baldwin V, and Henry I of Cyprus were all crowned when they were minors.[3] Fifteen was the age of majority for the fief and we may assume that it was also that for the majority of the king.[4]

---

[1] *Doc. Rel. Succ. Tr.*, pp. 401–415. And see below.

[2] *Livre au Roi*, vi, 610. This occurs in a passage relative to the regency of the father for an heir through the mother: '*Si tost come il sera en l'aage de douse ans, si det estre courounés ou en Jerusalem ou dedens Sur; et si juge la raison que li peres deit aver le baillage dou reaume et de ses anfans, jusque li plus ainsnés soit d'aage de justiser et de gouverner son reaume.*'. In the Morea the heir could claim investiture at fourteen and investiture must be granted, but he did not enter into enjoyment of the lands or revenues before he was fifteen. (*Assises de Romanie*, art. 85.)

[3] Baldwin IV at thirteen years with Raymond of Tripoli as regent; Baldwin V at five years with Raymond as regent; Henry I at eight years with Alice, his mother, as regent. The *Eracles*, p. 398, says that Henry came of age in 1232 at the age of fifteen, seven years after his coronation. It was then that the bailliage of Frederick II for Henry ended according to the claims, and law, of the Cypriots.

[4] Novare, xxi, 495; Ibelin, lxxi, 114, clxix, 259; *Clef des Assises*, ccxxi, 595. The *Assises d'Antioche*, v, 16, make the majority fifteen years and knighthood. The lord could advance the age of the majority, but once agreed upon it could not be altered. Dodu, p. 124, and Mas Latrie, i, 171, 324, agree that fifteen was the age for majority. Beugnot, *Assises*, i, 259, admits fifteen the age for a private fief, but p. 610 note *c*, says: '*Cependant tout indique que la loi fixait à quatorze ans la majorité des rois de Jérusalem*', a statement for which I can find no proof or corroborative evidence.

Until the heir should have come of age the regent exercised the royal powers. As we have seen the bailliage was given to the closest heir on that side of the family through which the throne escheated. If there was no apparent relative who could claim the bailliage, the *Haute Cour* elected a bailli; or if there were too many relatives the court decided which was to have the charge.[1] The custody of the heir was not given to the bailli, but to the closest relative on that side of the family through which the throne did not escheat, though there were several times when this rule was violated. The principle behind this was that the bailli was always an heir of the minor ruler and while it was proper that he should have charge of the administration of the realm, it was not safe for him to be given custody of the child whose demise might make him heir of the realm.[2] But in cases

---

[1] In the early period the baillies, like the kings themselves, had been elective by the *Haute Cour*, and Eustache Grenier had been elected as bailli for Baldwin II during his captivity. (William Tyre, XII, xvii, 538.) The baillies who served during the illness of Baldwin IV were in part elective and in part appointed by the king himself, but these are not cases of bailliage for a minor, but rather fall into the group of baillies for an absent lord.

In Cyprus the bailliage was complicated by the claim of the suzerain to act as bailli for the minor heir, as evidenced by the struggle with Frederick II discussed in this chapter. The bailliages exercised in Antioch by Baldwin II, Foulque, and Baldwin III might be considered as bailliages by the suzerain were it not that they were essentially bailliages by election of the *Haute Cour* of Antioch. This is clearly evidenced by the action of the nobles in the struggle between Baldwin II and Foulque, on the one hand, and Alice of Antioch, on the other, when, though Alice was the mother of the heir, the barons supported the suzerain whom they had asked to assume the bailliage. (This matter is discussed in the chapter on the relations of the kings with the great counties.)

The regency of Raymond of Tripoli for Baldwin IV is a case of the nearest relative on the side through which the realm escheated receiving the bailliage from the court. The case of Hugh of Antioch-Lusignan, discussed below, is an even better case of the heir presenting his claims before the court.

[2] Ibelin, clxx, 261: 'Et se il avient que l'eir seit merme d'aage, et aucun ou aucune, qui li apartient de là dont le fié muet, vient avant requerre le baillage si come il deit, il le deit avoir dou fié; mais l'enfant ne deit mie estre en sa garde, se le fié li peut escheir; car en cest endreit a une assise qui dit, que baill ne deit mie garder mermiau . . . L'enfant deit estre en la garde dou plus preuchein de ces parens ou amis, à qui le fié ne peut escheyr; et deit avoir son vivre covenablement de son fié'.

Thus when Raymond of Tripoli was given the bailliage for Baldwin V, the custody of the child was given to Joscelin de Courtney, his maternal uncle. (Ernoul, pp. 116–17.) A violation of this rule occurred in the case of the bailliage of Walter de Montbéliard for Hugh I of Cyprus, and the evil results were apparent when Hugh claimed to have been shamefully treated by his brother-in-law from whom he demanded a strict accounting. (*Eracles*, p. 305, 315–16; Mas Latrie, i, 171–73.) Alice of Cyprus seems to have been given full custody of her

where the father was bailli for the child who inherited from its mother, the father was given custody of the child as well as the bailliage of the kingdom.

While the bailli held office he exercised all the powers pertaining to the king. But his acts were valid only during his tenure of office, and had to be confirmed and reënacted by the heir upon reaching his majority if they were to remain in force.[1] This applied to grants of land, appointments to office, and assignments of revenue as well as to governmental actions.[2] Forfeitures ordered under the bailli were also valid only during his tenure of office. This was inevitable as forfeiture was the penalty for refusal to perform homage, and the liegemen were not required to do homage to anyone except the ruler himself. Refusal of homage to the bailli entailed forfeiture of the fief while the bailli was ruling, but when the heir took over the government, if the vassal offered homage it had to be received and his fiefs restored.[3]

Further, the bailli was held to a strict accounting for all his acts and for the revenues of the realm during his period of rule, and the

---

son Henry, as well as the baillliage of the realm, but she was bailli as the mother and not as any possible heir to the throne. In the Morea the the next heir after the minor heir was given both bailliage and custody, but he was strictly responsible for the maintenance of the child. (*Assises de Romanie*, art. 39.)

[1] *Livre au Roi*, vi, 610. The same law applied to the husbands of reigning queens. (*Livre, au Roi*, iv, 609.)

[2] In 1210 the truce with the Saracens made by John d'Ibelin, as regent for Marie, lapsed, since it was not renewed by Marie and John de Brienne. (Ernoul, p. 409.) When Alice of Cyprus succeeded Frederick II as bailli of Jerusalem, she revoked all his grants and appointments and made new appointments to the offices of the realm. (*Assises*, ii, 400.) This is interesting as showing one bailli revoking the acts of a preceding bailli.

The bailli could pledge the heir to accept his acts if he had any means of guaranteeing acceptance, as was the case with the treaty with Venice made by Warmund, the patriarch, and William de Buris, the bailli for Baldwin II, who guaranteed the king's acceptance of the treaty. This was secured by the power of the patriarch and the elective power of the *Haute Cour*, which was superior to the royal power. (William Tyre, XII, xxv, 550–53; *Regesta*, docs. 102, 105.)

In 1170 Amaury, acting as bailli of Tripoli, promised the validity of an act to the Hospitallers, but what he guaranteed was that he would help the Hospital to keep the lands should the count of Tripoli not agree thereto. It was merely a matter of force and not any right. (D. L. *Cartulaire*, doc. 411; *Regesta*, doc. 477.)

[3] *Doc. Rel. Succ. Tr.*, p. 398. Ibelin explains carefully that homage was a contract binding equally upon both parties and that, as a minor cannot be held to a contract, it was not wholly legal to do homage to a minor. As homage was due only to the liege lord and not to his representative or bailli, the liegeman could refuse to do homage until the heir came of age. But as the bailli had been deprived of the service of the feif he could claim the forfeiture thereof dur-

heir could demand an accounting before the *Haute Cour*. The bailli was held not to have in any way diminished the value of the realm and was amenable to the court had he done so.[1]

The fortresses of the kingdom were not entrusted to the bailli but were kept under the control of the court, being assigned to some baron or often to one of the Orders to guard until the king should come of age.[2]

Finally, the bailli was limited by those three things concerning which a man is answerable only to his lord, namely his life, his honor, and his fief.[3] Yet this was not as great a limitation as it might seem to be, as the bailli could bring the case into the *Haute Cour* and after the court had heard it there was no appeal or reversal of its decision. As the king himself was not able to act on any of these three matters without the approval of the court, the bailli was as powerful as the king in this respect, in fact if not in theory.

---

ing the term of his regency and until the vassal would offer to do homage to the lord and resume his feudal obligations.

This same rule applied in the case of an heiress who married without the consent of the bailli. He could distrain her fief during his regency, but she could make her peace with the lord when he came of age, and the forfeiture imposed by the bailli was invalidated.

The *Assises de Romanie*, art. 39, provide that the vassals need perform homage to the bailli only if he is the next heir, and they shall always reserve the rights of the minor heir.

[1] This was common to all feudal law. For the classic exposition see Magna Carta, articles 4 and 5, and the commentary in McKechnie, *Magna Carta*, (2nd ed.; Glasgow: Maclehose, 1914), pp. 205–212.

The most celebrated case in the East is that of Hugh I of Cyprus and Walter de Montbéliard. Hugh accused Walter of cruelty to his person and peculation with the royal revenues, and summoned him into the court; but Walter fled to the continent without waiting trial. Hugh demanded that Walter pay him 200,000 besants, which, he said, were in the treasury when Walter became bailli, and in addition pay him 40,000 besants to compensate for the bodily suffering he had endured at the regent's hands. (*Eracles*, pp. 315–16.)

The accounting demanded by Frederick II from John d'Ibelin will be considered below.

[2] *Doc. Rel. Succ. Tr.*, p. 401: '*Les homes liges deivent garder les fortereces dou reiaume, quant les heirs sont mermes d'aage, ou quant il sont hors dou pays et il ne sont entrés en leur reiaume si come il deivent*'.

Thus during the minority of Baldwin V under the regency of Raymond of Tripoli, the fortresses were guarded by the Templars and Hospitallers. And, as will be shown, when Tyre was taken from Filanger in 1243, Philip de Montfort kept it though Alice of Cyprus and her husband were recognized as baillies of the realm. (*Gestes*, par. 232; *Eracles*, p. 423; and see below.)

[3] *Doc. Rel. Succ. Tr.*, p. 398: '*et sera valable ce que se fera devant lui*, (the regent) *sauve de trois choses de quei on ne deit respondre senon devant son seignor qui est à eaus tenus de fei et eaus à lui, ce est à assaveir, de son cors et de son fié et de son honor.*'

Having examined the statements of the *Assises* in regard to the kingship in the thirteenth century, the history of the kingdom of Jerusalem can now be resumed where it was left at the end of the previous chapter,—with the accession of John de Brienne, husband of Marie '*la Marquise*'. For two years John and Marie ruled jointly, until in 1212 Marie died in giving birth to a daughter Isabelle. While John used the title of 'tenth king of Jerusalem' throughout his reign and seems to have considered himself king in his own right, it is safe to say that he ruled after the death of Marie as regent for their daughter.[1]

John's reign is not one of any constitutional importance. The chief event of the fourteen years in which he occupied the throne of Jerusalem was the fifth crusade, in which the Jerusalemite, Antiochene, and Cypriot forces served together with crusaders from the West under the leadership of King Andrew II of Hungary, Archduke Leopold II of Austria, and the earls of Chester and Salisbury. The crusaders were at first successful in capturing Damietta at the mouth of the Nile. Although King John was theoretically the commander-in-chief, divided councils and failure to coöperate, combined with the stubbornness of the papal legate Pelagius, cardinal of Albano, soon caused the crusade to fail utterly, and all the advantages won in 1219–20 were lost in 1221.[2] Disgusted, John

---

[1] Ernoul, p. 411; *Eracles*, p. 320; Röhricht, p. 702, and note 5.

Eracles says: '*Li rois Johan demora en la seignorie por la baillage de sa fille, apres la mort de sa feme la roine Marie*'. John's charters prove very little.

A charter of July 1211 and one of April 1212, mention Marie as co-factor or consenting. (Rozière, doc. 145; D. L. *Cartulaire*, doc. 1383; *Regesta*, docs. 853, 858a.) But one of January 1212 does not mention the queen, though the consent of the patriarch is mentioned. (Méry, i, 226–27; *Regesta*, doc. 855.)

After the death of Marie, John issued his charters in his own name without any mention of Isabelle until one in March 1221 when her consent is given. (Strehkle, doc. 55; *Regesta*, doc. 940; some charters of John not mentioning Isabelle are *Regesta*, docs. 892, 898, 899, 927, 930, 934, 953.) The fact that John did not mention Isabelle and that he later tried to secure the throne for himself until his death shows that he at least wanted to rule in his own name; the ready acceptance of Frederick by the barons shows equally well that they never considered that he did. The statement of the *Eracles* reflects an opinion some years after the fact when later developments had already influenced the perspective.

[2] The fifth crusade was a dismal affair. The Hungarian and Austrian crusaders campaigned a while in Syria and had mostly gone before the campaign against Egypt was begun. John was elected chief of the combined armies and took command, but was opposed by Pelagius from the moment of his arrival. They did take Damietta and the Egyptians

returned to his kingdom, and in 1223 set out for the West in search of a husband for his daughter, leaving Eudes de Montbéliard bailli in Jerusalem in his absence.[1] The match which John contemplated for his daughter was certainly a brilliant one. Frederick II, emperor of the Holy Roman Empire and king of Sicily, was the most brilliant figure in Europe, and his sun was in the ascendant in 1223. The protegé of Honorius III, with victories at his back and the troubles with the Lombard cities and his rebellious son still in the future, Frederick seemed to John and to the Pope ideally suited to assume the leadership of the crusading movement which was dear to both of them; his alliance with Isabelle of Jerusalem seemed an excellent way to stimulate his interest in Jerusalem and to bring help to the crusading states. Consequently the advances made by John were heartily endorsed and seconded by Honorius and the marriage was arranged. But John made a fatal error in trusting the marriage negotiations to Herman von Salza, Grand Master of the Teutonic Knights; for von Salza was more interested in Frederick than in John and he did not carry out John's instructions that the marriage was to be so arranged that John could retain the throne of Jerusalem for life, Frederick and Isabelle to succeed only after he was dead. Trusting to von Salza to arrange the matter as he had ordered, John left Italy and went to

---

offered very favorable terms of peace which John and the most of the barons wished to accept, but Pelagius hoped for more and refused the Egyptian offers, pushed an expedition up the Nile, and brought the whole crusade to a disastrous end. The materials for the study of the fifth crusade have been collected or analyzed by R. Röhricht, *Quinti Belli Sacri Scriptores Minores* (Paris, 1879), *Testimonia Minora de Quinto Bello Sacro* (Paris, 1882); the same scholar began a study of the crusade in his *Studien zur Geschichte des Fünften Kreuzzuges* (Innsbruck, 1891). *Eracles*, Ernoul, and the chronicle of Oliver von Paderborn (Stuttgart, 1894) give the best narrative accounts from the western point of view. Röhricht's *Königreichs*, pp. 717–756, give the latest results of the author's researches in what was his field of special interest.

[1] John had married Stephanie, the daughter of Leo of Armenia, in 1213 shortly after the death of Marie. When Leo died in 1220 John left the army in Egypt and went home, preparing to raise the claims of his wife to the Armenian throne. But before he could advance them, Stephanie and their son died, thus completely upsetting John's schemes. (*Eracles*, pp. 320, 349.) He returned to the army at Damietta, went on the Nile campaign, and returned to Jerusalem wholly discouraged. Herman von Salza went to the West immediately after the failure in Egypt to report the causes of the failure of the crusade. He may have opened negotiations with Frederick then; at any rate Frederick sent galleys to Jerusalem to bring John and his retinue to Italy. (*Eracles*, p. 355.)

France, where he was present at the funeral of his old lord and friend, Philip Augustus, and where he assisted at the coronation of Louis VIII in Paris on August 6, 1223. From France he went to Santiago de Compostella on a pilgrimage,—and stayed in Spain to marry Berengaria of Castile. He returned to Italy the following year, only after the marriage negotiations between Frederick and Isabelle were completed. While John remained in Italy, the bishop of Patti, who was promoted to the archiepiscopal see of Capua later that same year, went to Syria where he acted as the proxy for the emperor in the marriage ceremony, which was performed at Acre, and in the coronation, which took place at Tyre immediately following. Isabelle, now queen of Jerusalem, received the homages of the liegemen of the kingdom. Then sailing for Brindisi, the little queen came to Frederick who married her in person, crowning her empress of the Holy Roman Empire and queen of Sicily (9 November, 1225). It was only after the marriage that John de Brienne discovered that his plans had miscarried and that von Salza had not secured for him the throne of Jerusalem for the remainder of his life. Frederick at once demanded from John the seisin of the kingdom, and from the Syrian barons, who had escorted the queen from Tyre, the homages due him as king. John was taken aback, but could only accept the *fait accompli* and surrender the throne to his son-in-law. Frederick sent the bishop of Melfi to secure the homages of the Jerusalemite barons to him as king, and confirmed Eudes de Montbéliard in the bailliage until he should come in person to Syria. John had no recourse but to stir up trouble for Frederick with the Pope.[1]

The Pope had for some years been urging the emperor to fulfill the vow of the crusade which Frederick had taken in 1215, but the em-

---

[1] The story of the marriage and Frederick's duping of John is told at length in: *Eracles,* pp. 355–60; *Gestes,* pars. 86–88; Ernoul, pp. 449–55. Modern accounts are in: J. Lafiteau, *Histoire de Jean de Brienne* (Paris, 1727), pp. 330–53 *et passim;* W. Jacobs, *Patriarch Gerold von Jerusalem* (Aix-la-Chapelle, 1905); E. Winkelmann, *Kaiser Friedrich II* (Leipsic, 1889–97), pp. 199, 219–29; Röhricht, pp. 757–64.

Isabelle appears on a charter of January 1226 as: '*Romanorum imperatrix, Ierusalem et Siciliae regina*'. (Strehlke, doc. 59; *Regesta,* doc. 975.)

Lafiteau says that Frederick would have assassinated John but that he escaped. Frederick's infidelity and the cruel manner in which he treated his wife only intensified John's resentment and hatred.

peror had been able to secure postponements. Honorius was inclined to blame Frederick for the failure of the fifth crusade, for the armies had waited for him to arrive and had become weakened through the prolonged delay and inactivity; when Frederick married Isabelle and became himself king of Jerusalem, the Pope hoped to see the long postponed vow at last fulfilled. As Frederick could not depart for the East at once, it was agreed that he would start on the crusade not less than two years later. Frederick seems to have intended sincerely to fulfill his promises in 1227. Honorius had been right in estimating that Frederick king of Jerusalem would be more interested in a war in the East than was Frederick the crusader. Accordingly, in 1227, the emperor prepared an army and despatched Thomas d'Aquina, count of Acerra, to Syria with the advance guard, appointing Acerra bailli of Jerusalem to replace Eudes de Montbéliard. When, in the midst of his preparations, Frederick was suddenly taken sick and was unable to set sail, he applied to Pope Gregory IX, who had succeeded Honorius, for another postponement. As it happened, the interruption was probably as annoying to Frederick as to the Pope for Frederick had negotiated a treaty with Melek-el-Kamel, sultan of Egypt, whereby, in return for assistance to be given Egypt against their enemies of Damascus, the emperor was to receive the city of Jerusalem from the Egyptian sultan. Gregory IX, who knew nothing of this treaty, thought Frederick's request for a postponement merely another attempt to avoid going on the crusade. Without waiting for any explanation Gregory launched a bull of excommunication against Frederick. Nothing daunted, the emperor, when he had recovered from his illness, continued his preparations and on June 28, 1228, set sail for Syria with a large army. The excommunicate emperor was undertaking the crusade in the teeth of papal opposition![1]

---

[1] *Eracles*, pp. 363–66; Ernoul, pp. 457–60; Röhricht, pp. 764–69; Röhricht, 'Die Kreuzfahrt des Kaisers Friedrich II', *Beiträge zur Geschichte der Kreuzzüge* (Berlin, 1874–78), i, 1–112; W. Jacobs, *Patriarch Gerold.*

The treaty with Egypt is given in Michaud, *Bibiothèque des Croisades* (Paris, 1829), iv, 429–30; *Regesta*, doc. 992.

Honorius III had been Frederick's tutor and was inclined to be lenient with him, though before his death even Honorius broke with the emperor. The new Pope, Gregory, was an uncompromising defender of the rights of the Church and had little sympathy for Frederick.

But it was not as king of Jerusalem that Frederick sailed, for on April 25, 1228, Isabelle gave birth to a son, the future Conrad IV, and herself died from the ordeal of childbirth the fourth of May following. Thus Conrad was legally king of Jerusalem and Frederick was only regent for his son. When the news of Isabelle's death was received in Acre, the liegemen met and in the *Haute Cour* elected John d'Ibelin of Beirut and Balian of Sidon baillies for Conrad pending the arrival of Frederick. Ibelin declined the honor and Eudes de Montbéliard was returned to the bailliage once more with Balian as his colleague.[1]

In July 1228, Frederick reached Cyprus, where he landed at Limassol and established himself in the palace of Philip d'Ibelin, which was vacant since Philip's death the year previous. There he was met by Thomas of Acerra, Richard Filanger, his marshal of the Empire whom he had sent on ahead of him, Balian of Sidon, John d'Ibelin, and the Cypriot barons. Frederick then demanded and received the homage of the eleven-year-old king, Henry of Cyprus, over whom he claimed suzerainty on the grounds of his father, Henry VI, having accorded the royal crown to Amaury in return for vassalage.[2]

Although he was still a child, Henry had already been crowned in 1225 by his uncles Philip and John d'Ibelin, who feared lest Fred-

---

The Lombard League had just been reorganized and had taken the field against Frederick when he started on his crusade, and it was but natural that Gregory thought the postponement merely another attempt of Frederick's to avoid going. Frederick had actually sailed but had to return. The part of the army which went on in 1227, under the command of Henry of Lembourg, spent its time fortifying Sidon and Caesarea.

[1] *Assises*, ii, 399.

A charter of 1226 shows Isabelle consenting to Frederick's grants. (Strehlke, doc., 59; *Regesta*, doc. 975.) But after her death Frederick continued to use his title of king of Jerusalem, and it is not until 1243 that Conrad appears on his charters as giving consent. (*Regesta*, docs. 978, 994, 995, 997, 1003–14, 1016, 1034, 1064, 1089, 1112.) In November 1243 is the first charter of Conrad in his own name; it is a confirmation of the custody of Ascalon to the Hospital which Frederick had already granted. (*Regesta*, doc. 1112a; D. L. *Cartulaire*, doc. 2308.)

[2] *Eracles*, p. 367: 'il requist a avoir par le droit de l'empire le baillage dou roi qui estoit inerme et de sa terre, et les homages dou roi et de ses homes; et en ce n'ot nul contredit, ains li fu fait tout ensi come il l'avoit requis. Quant il ot receus les homages, il retint le roi en son ostel'.

The granting of the royal crown of Cyprus by Henry VI is told in: *Eracles*, pp. 209–212; Mas Latrie, i, 127–28.

erick should claim the bailliage over the boy. Philip had held the regency until his death in 1227, when John received it. Thus when Frederick landed and claimed the bailliage, John was in possession of the office, and had antagonized the emperor by crowning Henry without asking his permission.[1] When the emperor demanded the custody of Henry, Ibelin could only agree, as Frederick was Henry's suzerain, but Ibelin did not recognize Frederick as bailli.

From 1228 to 1243, the so-called 'Lombard War' dominated the history of the Latin states: Frederick and his agents and partisans on the one hand and the Ibelin factions on the other fought out the control of the kingdom. The Ibelins, like the Guelphs in Germany, maintained the constitutional rights of the feudal baronage against the imperialists, and, more successful than their western counterparts, established in Jerusalem and Cyprus that rule of law so well illustrated by the *Assises* which were written by the most famous member of their family. The history of this war is told in detail in the *Mémoires* of Philip de Novare, the jurist, who was an ardent adherent of the Ibelin house and who himself played no unimportant part in the struggle. These *Mémoires*—their author called them *L'Estoire et le Droit Conte de la Guerre qui fu entre L'Empereor Federic et Messire Johan de Ybelin, Seignor de Baruth,*—have been preserved in the compilation known as the *Gestes des Chiprois*, and form our chief source for the whole period.

The trouble started in July 1228 when Frederick, after taking

---

[1] When Hugh I of Cyprus died in 1218 the bailliage for the infant Henry was given to Alice, the mother, who was given custody of the child and all the revenue of the kingdom, while Philip d'Ibelin was given control of the state. The *Gestes* say that Ibelin was appointed by the *Haute Cour*, the *Eracles* that Alice appointed him. At any rate Ibelin held the powers of the bailliage and the lieges did homage to him and promised to obey him until Henry should come of age. Alice later married Bohemond of Antioch and tried to get the administration of the kingdom transferred to him but the court refused as they had sworn to obey Ibelin. Alice later appointed Amaury Barlais, a powerful Cypriot noble, as bailli, and Ibelin seems to have surrendered to her will, but the barons rejected Barlais and restored Ibelin. Barlais fled to Tripoli where he organized an anti-Ibelin faction. Philip kept the regency until his death, when the barons elected his brother John to carry on the rule. But throughout Alice had had the revenues of the kingdom, the Ibelins having only the political powers. (*Gestes*, pars. 96, 98, 110-115, 123; *Eracles*, pp. 360-62; Mas Latrie, i, 197, 215, 231-32.)

When the Ibelins had crowned Henry, Frederick had protested but had from that distance been unable to do anything. When he came to Cyprus, however, he had not forgotten the slight put upon him by the Ibelins and planned to humble them.

possession of the young king, demanded of John of Beirut that he render an accounting of his bailliage since the death of Hugh, and that he surrender his city of Beirut to the emperor as a fortress of Conrad's kingdom which should be in the hands of the regent. This demand took place at a banquet which the emperor gave at Limassol, in the old palace of Philip d'Ibelin, in the presence of the assembled Outremer baronage. John of Beirut at first thought the emperor was amusing himself with some practical joke, but he soon found that Frederick was in earnest. The emperor was undoubtedly instigated to attack the Ibelins by the influence of Gauvain de Chenchi, who had been driven from Cyprus by the Ibelins and who had fled to Frederick in Italy where he *savoit mout d'oizeaus, et si fu mout honoré a cele court.*[1] To the demands of the emperor, Ibelin replied that he held Beirut as a fief from the king,—since it had been granted him by Amaury and Isabelle,—and this he would prove willingly in the *Haute Cour* of Jerusalem; that as for the bailliage of Cyprus, neither Philip nor he had ever enjoyed any of the revenues of the kingdom which had been given to Alice of Champagne, and this he would prove before the *Haute Cour* of Cyprus. The closing line of his speech, as reported in the *Gestes*, gives the spirit of his party in their whole struggle: *Et sire, vous soiés certains que pour doute de mort ou de prizon je ne feray plus, se jugement de boune court et de loyale ne la me faisoit faire.*[2] With this the emperor had to be satisfied for the moment; it was agreed that John should give two of his sons as hostages that he would appear, and that twenty barons should pledge their persons and goods as further security. Frederick received the hostages and imprisoned them in chains.[3] From this incident the trouble began anew.

The espisode does not seem necessary, for both sides were determined to carry the matter further, and, as soon as troops had been recalled from Syria to Cyprus, the emperor moved from Limassol to Nicosia, whither John of Beirut had previously fled. John retreated to the strong fortress of St Hilarion, called then *Dieu*

---

[1] *Gestes*, par. 117. We have followed the *Gestes* throughout in our narrative of the Lombard war

[2] *Gestes*, par. 127.

[3] *Gestes*, par. 128; *Eracles*, pp. 367–68.

d'Amour, in the mountains near Kyrenia, and prepared to resist. But Frederick was much disturbed by news which he had from the West to the effect that the armies of the Pope and John de Brienne were ravaging his possession in Italy, and he was anxious to get on to Syria and accomplish his crusade that he might sooner return to the West. Consequently, after a siege of a fortnight, he consented to a truce whereby Ibelin surrendered St Hilarion to a garrison of King Henry, and took an oath of fealty to Frederick as suzerain of the king of Cyprus, though he still refused to accept him as bailli. It was agreed that Ibelin was not to be further punished for his resistance to the emperor, and both parties promised to accept the decision of the *Haute Cour* as final in the quarrel between Frederick and the lord of Beirut. This truce having been arranged, Frederick went to Acre in September, accompanied by Ibelin and the greater part of the baronage. Imperialist garrisons were left to guard the chief fortresses of the island. Towards the end of the year Frederick sent back Stephen of Botron as his bailli for Cyprus.

At Acre the barons of Jerusalem at once recognized Frederick as regent for Conrad; and Balian of Sidon and Eudes de Montbéliard surrendered to him the bailliage of the kingdom. But the ban of excommunication which had been launched by the Pope raised the opposition of the clergy and the Orders against the emperor; both the Templars and Hospitallers refused to recognize him or answer his appeal. The Teutonic Knights, more German than religious under the mastership of Herman von Salza, disregarded the papal ban and allied themselves with the emperor.

In spite of the opposition of the clergy, Frederick went about his business of the crusade, proclaiming the war of Christ, a device whereby the Orders could join him as it did not involve any recognition of his authority, and took his army to Jaffa.

But there was little fighting to be done, for neither the emperor nor the sultan, al-Kamel, had any great desire for war; Frederick's chief desire was to get back to Italy and al-Kamel was anxious to consolidate the conquests which he had just made from Damascus. Consequently a treaty was arranged which renewed in general the terms of the old friendship, and Frederick was given official control over Jerusalem, Bethlehem, Nazareth, Jaffa, Toron,

Caesarea, and Montfort, though the Moslems were privileged to worship in the mosques and in the places sacred to their belief.[1] From Jaffa Frederick went to Jerusalem, where he assumed the crown of Jerusalem, crowning himself since there were no clergy present, as Patriarch Gerold had placed the city of Jerusalem under the interdict. Leaving a small garrison in the city under the command of Eudes de Montbéliard, Frederick returned to Acre and thence set sail for Italy on May 1, 1229.[2]

Before he left, Frederick appointed baillies to represent him in both Jerusalem and Cyprus. The bailliage of Jerusalem was conferred upon Balian of Sidon and Eudes de Montbéliard in the presence of the *Haute Cour* at Acre, while about the same time the emperor sold the bailliage of Cyprus for three years to five barons,— Amaury Barlais, Amaury de Bethsan, Gauvain de Chenchi, William de Rivet, and Hugh de Gibelet, all enemies of the Ibelins,—receiving in return 10,000 marks. In taking the bailliage Barlais and his associates swore to the emperor to drive the Ibelins out of Cyprus forever.[3]

The emperor had not long been gone from Syria when Alice of Cyprus appeared before the *Haute Cour* demanding the throne of Jerusalem as the most legal heir of King Amaury, in view of the fact that Conrad had never come to the East to claim his inheritance. But the *Haute Cour* was not yet ready to throw off the Hohenstaufens, and the barons informed her that they were the lieges of Frederick, who held the country as regent for Conrad, himself as yet a minor. However they sent an embassy to Conrad to ask that he

---

[1] *Gestes*, pars. 128–39; *Eracles*, pp. 368–74; Ernoul, p. 460 ff.; *Assises*, ii, 399; Mas Latrie. i, 242–51; Röhricht, *Königreichs*, pp. 774–90; *Beiträge* as above. The text of the treaty with Melek-el-Kamel is given in: Mas Latrie, iii, 626–29; *Regesta*, doc. 997.

[2] Letter of Herman von Salza: *Regesta*, doc. 1000; *M. G. H. Epistolae XIII Saec.*, i, doc. 383, p. 299; Huillard Bréholles, iii, 99–102.

Letter of Patriarch Gerold: *Regesta*, doc. 1001; *M. G. H. Epis. XIII Saec.*, i, doc. 384, pp. 299–304; Huillard Bréholles, iii, 102–110. See also: *Eracles*, p. 374; Ernoul, pp. 465–66.

[3] *Gestes*, pars. 138–39; *Eracles*, p. 375; *Assises*, ii, 399. Balian of Sidon and Garnier l'Alleman were the baillies originally appointed but Garnier resigned and de Montbéliard took his place. The argument given in the *Assises* would indicate that de Montbéliard was appointed in the *Haute Cour*. Frederick left garrisons of Lombards, Germans, and Flemings in Cyprus to help control the island.

come to Acre within a year that his lieges might do homage to him personally.[1]

Meanwhile, in Cyprus, the five baillies, endeavoring to drive out the Ibelins, began a war with the adherents of that house in which they ravaged the Ibelin fiefs. John of Beirut returning from Syria with an army, forced the baillies to retire with their royal prisoner to the strong citadel of Kyrenia and the series of castles which defended the northern part of the island, St Hilarion, Buffavento, and Kantara. Ibelin was successful in forcing the surrender of all but St Hilarion in a short campaign; the siege of Hilarion, however, took ten months and did not end until June 1230, when the garrison surrendered and King Henry was delivered over to the Ibelins. A peace was made whereby the baillies, Amaury Barlais, Amaury de Bethsan, and Hugh de Gibelet surrendered and swore never to make war on the Ibelins again, in return for which they were allowed to keep their fiefs. De Chenchi and de Rivet had been killed and so were beyond the power of the Ibelins; but their families were allowed to keep their estates.[2] The Ibelin victories in Cyprus by no means ended the struggle with the emperor, but, in combination with the situation in the West, they did secure a year's cessation of hostilities.

Frederick had returned to Italy to find the papal armies, led by John de Brienne, ravaging his southern kingdom, and his control throughout the peninsula seriously menaced. He had thrown all his energies into a campaign which had driven the Apostolic armies back into the Papal States, and had forced from the Pope the treaty of San Germano (1230). Then, having made his peace with Rome, he

---

[1] *Eracles*, p. 380: 'requist le roiaume de Jerusalem si come le plus dreit heir qui fust aparant dou roi Haimeri son ayol'. Mas Latrie, i, 262–63, says that Alice claimed the bailliage of the realm, but the statement of the *Eracles* shows that it was the kingdom itself that she claimed. If Conrad's rights were passed over she had claims to the kingdom, but she certainly had no claims to the bailliage for Conrad. After Conrad came of age Alice was given the lordship, which was more bailliage than seisin of the throne, but then it was the power of the *Haute Cour* to select the bailli when the king was absent and had appointed no regular bailli that was operative.

[2] It was during the period when they were trying to drive out the Ibelins, that the baillies earned the undying hatred of Philip de Novare, whom they first tried to buy over to their side and later tried to murder. Novare's intense loyalty to the Ibelins and his legal knowledge were dangerous to the Barlais party at the time, and his literary ability has succeeded in blackening their reputation for posterity.

turned his attention towards remodeling the constitution of his southern kingdom. Jerusalem, like Germany, was neglected the while the emperor consolidated his absolutism in his favorite state. As soon, however, as he had secured himself effectively in the *Regno*, Frederick revived his eastern schemes and dispatched an army under Richard Filanger to the East in the summer of 1231. When Ibelin heard of the dispatch of the fleet, he hurried to Cyprus and prepared the defense of the island; so that when the imperialists arrived at Cape Gavata they were unable to land and were forced to proceed to the mainland of Syria.

Ambassadors from the emperor then came to Henry of Cyprus demanding the total expulsion of the Ibelins from Cyprus, both John of Beirut and all his relatives. To this Henry replied that he would not, and could not, comply with this demand, especially as Ibelin was his own close relative, and to enforce the emperor's demand would necessitate his own exile. Unable to attack Ibelin in Cyprus, Filanger occupied Tyre and began to besiege Beirut. Ibelin at once demanded assistance from Henry, which was granted, and the Cypriots prepared to relieve Beirut. Barlais, de Bethsan, and de Gibelet deserted to the imperialists, claiming that they were bound by their oath to Frederick rather than by that given to Henry or John d'Ibelin, as Henry was still a minor and Frederick was still the legitimate bailli.

Filanger, after securing Tyre and investing Beirut, went to Acre, where he summoned the *Haute Cour* and presented letters of Frederick appointing him bailli in Jerusalem and legate in Outremer. The appointment was accepted by the barons, and Filanger entered upon that disastrous administration which was destined to alienate almost the entire Jerusalemite population. The barons, led by Balian of Sidon, assembled the *Haute Cour* and protested against the seizure of Beirut, for, they argued, the kings of Jerusalem had always sworn to observe the assises and usages of the kingdom and Frederick had so sworn; and one of the fundamental laws of Jerusalem was that no liegeman could be dispossessed of his fief except by the judgment of his peers in the *Haute Cour*. Though Ibelin had offered to prove his case in the court, Filanger had disseised him of his fief of Beirut without any semblance of trial. As loyal lieges of the realm, the barons were prepared to assist in punishing Ibelin if the court should decide him worthy of forfeiture, but until the court should have so decided, they could not permit the bailli summarily to confiscate the fief, wherefore they demanded that Beirut be returned to Ibelin. Filanger held a conference with some of his colleagues at Beirut and finally replied that he was the bailli of the emperor and that the latter had ordered him to seize Beirut and, as the order seemed thoroughly reasonable to him, he would continue to carry it out against Ibelin. This answer, denying as it did the supremacy of the assises and the law, and clearly stating Filanger's intention to act in a despotic manner without the assent of the *Haute Cour* and in open violation of the laws, threw the moderate party into the Ibelin camp; Balian of Sidon, Eudes de Montbéliard, Garnier l'Alleman, and others who had formerly supported Frederick joined the Ibelin faction against Filanger. Further support was added to the Ibelin cause when the citizens of Acre, both knights and bourgeoisie, who were associated in the *Frarie de St André*, a religious fraternity, organized themselves into a commune and declared themselves ready to support John of Beirut.[1]

The kingdom was now divided into two hostile camps. Supporting the imperial claims were the western troops,—the Lombards—whom Frederick had sent under the brothers Filanger,—the Teutonic Knights, Barlais and his partisans, and the Pisans. They held Tyre and Sidon and had invested Beirut. With the Ibelins sided the majority of the baronage of Jerusalem and Cyprus,—forty-three

---

[1] The whole story is derived from the: *Gestes*, pars. 139–60; *Eracles*, pp. 376–92. Philip de Novare wrote a poem after the manner of the *Reynaud the Fox* epic in which he satirized Frederick and the baillies and told the story of the war in allegorical verse. This poem is quoted at length throughout the *Gestes*. A very convenient chronology of the war is found in Ch. Kohler's edition of the *Mémoires de Philippe de Novare* (Paris; Champion, 1913; *Classiques Français du Moyen Age*), pp. 134–38, but it must be remembered that the paragraph numbers in Kohler differ from those in the other two editions of the *Gestes*.

Good secondary accounts of the war are to be found in Mas Latrie, i, ch. xi, 254–300; Röhricht, ch. xxiv, pp. 798–828; H. Müller, *Der Langobarden Krieg auf Cypern* (Halle, 1890). A brief narrative account in English is in the review in the *Edinborough Review*, clxxxii (1895), 440–467, under the title 'Medieval Cyprus'. F. von Löher, *Kaiser Friedrich II Kampf um Cypern* (Munich, 1878), was written before the discovery of the *Gestes*.

For a more detailed account of the formation of the commune at Acre see my 'Communal Movement in Syria', in *Haskins Anniversary Essays* (Boston: Houghton Mifflin, 1929), pp. 124–28.

important lords in all,—the commune of Acre, the king of Cyprus, and the Genoese; their centers were Cyprus, Acre, and Beirut. Between the two parties were the clergy,—headed by the patriarch and Peter, archbishop of Caesarea,—the Templars, Hospitallers, Venetians, Bohemond of Antioch, and a few lords. Pope Gregory IX urged mediation and wrote the rebels asking that they submit to Frederick; the neutral group vainly endeavored to keep peace but were unable to prevent the outbreak of hostilities.[1]

The first battle of the war took place at Casal Imbert, between Tyre and Acre, on May 3, 1232; and the Cypriots who were commanded by Anseau de Brie were disastrously defeated. The main part of their army fled to Acre taking with them King Henry; John d'Ibelin, who had not been present at the battle, arrived, accompanied by Eudes de Montbéliard and Balian of Sidon, only in time to collect the scattered remnants of his army.

Encouraged by the victory, the Lombards turned their attention to Cyprus, where Barlais had already begun a partial conquest of the island. Additional troops were dispatched to the assistance of Barlais; and Kyrenia, Famagusta, Nicosia, and Kantara were captured by the imperialists. The only important fortresses remaining in the hands of the Ibelins were soon St Hilarion and Buffavento. But the imperialists' victories were short lived, and Ibelin and Henry soon had an army in Cyprus which, with the help of the Genoese, recaptured Famagusta, Kantara, and Nicosia. The imperialists retreated to the neighborhood of St Hilarion where, on June 15, five weeks after the battle of Casal Imbert, the two armies met again. This battle at Agridi reversed the position after Casal Imbert and the imperialists were forced to take refuge in Kyrenia, where they concentrated their forces.

The position of the imperialists was one of considerable danger and Filanger endeavored to get assistance from Armenia, Tripoli,

---

[1] *Gestes*, pars. 160–67; *Eracles*, p. 394.

The letters of Gregory IX are given in: Huillard Bréholles, iv, 376–78; D. L. *Cartulaire*, docs. 2025, 2026. The treaty between Henry of Cyprus and Genoa is in: Mas Latrie, ii, 51–56; *Regesta*, doc. 1037; *Liber Jurium*, i, doc. 693.

Eudes de Montbéliard and Balian of Sidon were not with the Ibelins until after the battle of Casal Imbert. They tried to remain loyal to Frederick but could not tolerate Filanger's despotism after Casal Imbert.

and finally from the West, going in person to Italy accompanied by Barlais and de Bethsan. Henry of Cyprus, who had reached his majority in May, convened his *Haute Cour* and formally confiscated the lands of the Barlais group, declaring them forfeited for treason, and bestowing them on loyal barons.[1]

Meanwhile the siege of Kyrenia dragged on; the Cypriots could not cut off the communications of the besieged with the sea, which prolonged the resistance. It was not until the late spring of 1233 that the defenders of the city, discouraged by the successes which the Ibelins had been gaining on the mainland and despairing of any help from the West, finally capitulated.[2]

In Acre the Ibelins had profited by an attempt of the emperor to conciliate the Jerusalemite baronage. Realizing the unpopularity of Filanger, Frederick had sent to the East the bishop of Sidon with letters replacing Filanger in the bailliage by Philip de Maugastel. But when the letters had been presented to the *Haute Cour*, the barons refused to accept the new appointment, claiming that Balian of Sidon and Eudes de Montbéliard were still the legitimate baillies, as they had been appointed by the emperor in the meeting of the

---

[1] The Barlais were lords of Arabian and Zekanin in the kingdom of Jerusalem, which fiefs were apparently left in their possession as Amaury's son John sold these fiefs to the Teutons, and his younger son Amaury tried to get them back. (Strehlke, docs. 81, 106, 107; Bib. Nat., Ms. *Nouv. Acq. Fr.* 6794.)   Nothing is known of Barlais after his forfeiture.

Amaury de Bethsan was chamberlain of Cyprus and a member of the house of Bethsan in Jerusalem.

Hugh de Gibelet was a relative of the Ibelins, being related to Melissande of Arsur, John's wife, according to *Gestes*, par. 111.   The other four were all related to each other but Hugh was an outsider.   I cannot fit him into the Gibelet family, though Hugh is a family name with them.   Perhaps he was related to Arnesius de Gibelet who appears with the Ibelins on so many charters of Henry I.

At any rate, while they were forfeited in Cyprus, these barons were not forfeit of their fiefs in Jerusalem.   As we have seen, de Chenchi and de Rivet being dead before the submission, their families were left in possession of their fiefs.

[2] *Gestes*, pars. 167–204; *Eracles*, pp. 394–402, give narratives of the war.

During the siege of Kyrenia occurred a pathetic incident.   Henry I had been officially married to Alice de Montferrat, daughter of the despot of Salonica, the marriage being arranged by Emperor Frederick.   Henry had never seen his wife, who was brought to Cyprus by imperialist agents and who was held in Kyrenia.   She died during the course of the siege and a truce was declared to enable Henry to get the body and give it a proper funeral.   She was buried as queen of Cyprus in the cathedral of Santa Sophia of Nicosia, though her husband had never seen her until the day of the funeral. (*Gestes*, par. 194; *Eracles*, pp. 402–03.)

court, and an action performed in the court could not be undone by letter. A violent discussion arose which ended when John of Caesarea, the spokesman for the barons who opposed de Maugastel, sounded the tocsin and called in the mob of Acre which broke up the meeting with considerable personal violence.[1]

The fall of Kyrenia ended the attempt of Frederick to assert his control in Cyprus; though he refused to recognize Henry as having attained his majority before the age of twenty-five years, Frederick did not attempt any longer to enforce his bailliage. But the emperor was still officially bailli of Jerusalem for Conrad, and was still possessed of Tyre. In fact, however, the real power on the mainland, as in Cyprus, was John d'Ibelin, who, as mayor of the commune of Acre, was the dominant figure in the government of the country.[2] Ibelin was determined to rid the East of the Hohenstaufens and planned an attack on Tyre, Frederick's last stronghold. But action on these lines was deferred by the intervention of Pope Gregory IX who, having become reconciled with Frederick some time since, endeavored to restore peace in the East. Letters were sent to the clergy, the masters of the Orders, and to Ibelin himself demanding that the rebellion against the emperor end, and that amends be made to Frederick for the wrongs done him.[3] The letters proving unfruitful, the archbishop of Ravenna was sent as legate to Syria, but he was able to recommend only the continuance of Filanger's administration. The barons sent envoys to the Pope to present their pleas against the emperor, and a general peace was drawn up on the basis of a plan previously outlined by Gregory in a letter to Frederick in February 1236.[4] The main idea of the Apostolic See was to arrange a peace which would strengthen the imperial control and at the same

---

[1] *Gestes*, par. 205; *Assises*, ii, 399–400; Röhricht, pp. 826–27; Huillard Bréholles, xii, 347. De Maugastel was a Syrian baron and Frederick hoped to conciliate the nobles by appointing him.

[2] Ibelin had been elected mayor of Acre in April 1232. (*Gestes*, par. 181.) In 1247 Pope Innocent IV formally absolved Henry of Cyprus of his oath of allegiance to Frederick and took him under the protection of the Papacy. (Mas Latrie, ii, 63–64.) This ended any theoretical control of the Empire over Cyprus, and put the seal on the work done by the Ibelins when they drove the imperialists out of the island.

[3] Letters of the Pope given in: Mas Latrie, iii, 640; D. L. *Cartulaire*, doc. 2118.

[4] Letter of Gregory IX to Frederick II, February 21, 1236 in: *M. G. H. Epis. XIII Saec.*, i., doc. 674, pp. 571–73; *Regesta*, doc. 1070.

time prove acceptable to the barons who were fighting for the preservation of their legal and constitutional liberties. As Conrad and Frederick, according to·Gregory, are the legitimate rulers of Jerusalem, they and their baillies should be obeyed '*in ordinatione castrorum et officialium, perceptione reddituum et iurium aliorum, que in ipso regno ad regem de antiqua et obtenta consuetudine spectare noscuntur, salvis assisiis necnon antiquis et approbatis consuetudinibus regni predicti*'. The citizens of Acre should dissolve their commune and depose the officials set up thereby. Filanger should be restored and assisted by de Montbéliard until the following September when the bailliage should be conferred upon Bohemond of Antioch. The bailli should be appointed by the emperor, the barons having at no time any right to elect one. Security should be promised all the revolting barons save the Ibelins and these should be tried in the *Haute Cour* '*per iudicium regni iustitiam . . .   terre consuetudinibus et assisiis observatis*'.

Such a peace was obviously wholly objectionable to the Ibelins and their allies, and both the commune of Acre and the *Haute Cour* of Nicosia denounced it. It was at this critical period that John d'Ibelin, '*le vieux sire de Baruth*', died. He had been the heart, soul, and brains of the baronial party, and much of the success which they had gained had been due to his bravery, sound judgment, and qualities of leadership. He fought to maintain the privileges of his class but was ever the lover of the law and the enemy of tyranny. Fortunately many of his best qualities were inherited by his son Balian, who succeeded him in the leadership of the party, ably seconded by his cousin Philip de Montfort.

While the Lombard war was dragging to a close, Palestine was visited by two bands of crusaders under Thibaut of Champagne, king of Navarre, and Richard, earl of Cornwall. But beyond the reconquest of Ascalon these expeditions accomplished nothing and their effects were but slight. It was during the stay of the French crusaders in Acre that Alice of Cyprus married Ralph of Soissons.

Alice had suddenly become a most important pawn in the game of politics in Jerusalem, for on April 25, 1243, Conrad would attain his majority and Frederick's bailliage for his son would be terminated. The majority of Conrad had been agreed upon by the Ibelin party as the date for the beginning of offensive hostilities against Filanger in Tyre, for once Frederick's bailliage was ended they would no longer be in any way bound to respect his agent. Filanger had taken the occasion of the departure of the English crusaders to launch an attack on Acre, but it had been repulsed by Philip de Montfort with the aid of the Venetians and Genoese, and the imperialists had been driven back to Tyre. An immediate attack on Tyre to follow up their victory had been strongly advocated by some of the baronial leaders, but it was finally agreed to wait until after April 25 as thus they would legally preserve their loyalty to their legal ruler and his representative.[1]

As soon as Conrad became of age, he sent messengers to the East with letters appointing agents to rule for him. The barons assembled in the *Haute Cour*, June 5, together with representatives of the Genoese, Venetians, Templars, and the city of Acre, to decide upon the recognition of the messengers. Ralph of Soissons came before the court and presented the claims of his wife Alice, as heir of King Amaury, and Philip de Novare urged the barons to accept Alice, legally justifying the proposed action. For while Conrad was the true heir, until he should come to claim his inheritance in person, the next heir could legally claim the bailliage. Wherefore Novare suggested that the *Haute Cour* recognize Alice as bailli, reserving always the rights of Conrad should he come in person to the East. This advice seemed sound to the barons of the court and the oath was administered to Alice and Ralph, who swore to obey the assises and customs of the kingdom and to protect the Church and the poor in their rights and privileges. Following this they were consecrated and the lieges performed homage to them.[2]

---

[1] *Gestes*, pars. 212–225; *Eracles*, pp. 413–20; Letter of Marsiglio Georgio, the Venetian bailli, October 1243, in: Tafel-Thomas, ii, 354–57; *Regesta*, doc. 1114.

The exact chronology cannot be clearly established as the narratives are confused and the documents only afford a partial check. Röhricht, pp. 855–57, and Mas Latrie, i, 323–24, are the best modern accounts.

[2] There are four accounts of this meeting, three of which are by eye witnesses and participants: that of Marsiglio Georgio, Venetian bailli, who wrote a report of the meeting to the Seignory of Venice the following October (Tafel-Thomas, ii, doc. 299, pp. 351–89); that of Philip de Novare found in his *Mémoires* (*Gestes*, pars. 225–26); that of John d'Ibelin of Arsur found in the *Documents Relatifs à la Successibilité au Trône et à la Régence* (*Assises*, ii, 399–400); and the account in *Eracles*, p. 420, which is shorter and much less reliable, and was very

Though Alice might have had some claims to the bailliage as half-sister of Marie, '*la Marquise*,' her claim as presented was through Isabelle Plantagenet and Amaury I. She was the daughter of Isabelle by Henry of Champagne, and so, after Marie and her heirs, heir to the the throne of Jerusalem. She had previously claimed the throne itself and had been rejected by the barons who were faithful to the line of Marie, but they were now quite willing to recognize her as heir after Conrad and to give her the bailliage of the realm reserving Conrad's rights. Conrad's coming of age ended the regency of Frederick, and Conrad's failure to appear in person opened the throne to the next heir according to Alice. The court apparently did not accept this statement of the case and Conrad continued to be titular king; but the powers of the kingship were given over to Alice and her heirs, who assumed with the title of *seignors* of Jerusalem the seisin of the kingdom. The seisin made them more than baillies,

---

apparently done some time after the event. There are minor discrepancies in the various accounts:—Novare's inclusion of the Pisans, staunch supporters of Frederick who could hardly have been expected to be there; Marsiglio's and Ibelin's contradictions as to whether the archbishop of Tyre or the archbishop of Nicosia presided; and a few other minor details; but the main events are the same in all. The *Eracles* account gets it rather mixed up and places the whole occurrance in 1240 before Conrad came of age.

Ibelin gives the best statement of Alice's claims: 'car l'assise et l'usage dou reiaume de Jerusalem est tel, et aussi celui de Chypre; et puisque le droit heir est en son aage, que pere et mere pert le baillage, et por ce l'aveit perdu l'empereor Federic . . . et . . . la royne Aalis . . . come le plus dreit heir aparant requerant en la court; et diseit que puis que son nevou le rei Conrat esteit d'aage et il ne veneit en persone entrer en son reiaume, que le plus preuchein heir i deveit entrer; et que elle esteit le plus preuch in heir de là où le reiaume moveit, et que ce esteit elle prest de prover tot ensi come la court esgardereit ou conoistreit que prover le deust: et por ce lor prioit elle et requereit que letres ne messages que le rei Conrat aveit mandé ou mandast ne deussent acuillir; que se sereit contre l'assise et l'usage doudit reiaume, douquel il ne pooient en nulle maniere aler à l'encontre.' (*Assises*, ii, 400.)

Novare shows what the court did: 'que il meïssent la reÿne Alis en saizine dou reyaume de Jerusalem, come le plus dreit heir aparant, et ly feïssent homage et service, par ensi que, tantost come le roy Conrat venroit au royaume de Jerusalem, que il fussent quite a la reÿne Alis, et a luy feïssent ce qu'il deüssent'. (*Gestes*, par. 226.)

The *Annales de Terre Sainte*, pp. 440–41, say Alice was recognized *as queen* in 1242. This can, I think, be considered merely an error on the part of this later chronicle.

The rule concerning the heir having to come in person to claim the fief was operative also in the Morea, where William de Villehardouin used it unjustly against Marguerite de Passavant in 1261. She was absent as an hostage for William when she inherited the fief of Acova, and though William was responsible for her absence, he confiscated her fief because she did not appear in person to claim it. (Longnon, *La Chronique de Morée* (*Soc. Hist. Fr*: Paris, 1911), pp. 197–99; *Assises de Romanie*, art. 36.)

but they were less than kings as they did not have royal title or coronation.

This ambiguous position of Alice was most convenient for the barons. They asserted Alice's powers against Thomas of Acerra whom Conrad had sent as his bailli to Syria, and at the same time refused to grant Ralph and Alice possession of cities on the grounds that during a regency they should be controlled by the lieges as they were subject only to the *Haute Cour*.[1]

The matter of their legal position being settled, the barons proceeded with the business of clearing the imperialists out of the country, and with the aid of the Venetians invested Tyre, where Lothaire Filanger, Richard's brother, was strongly maintaining an imperial base. The siege of the city lasted twenty-one days and that of the castle dragged on after the city had been taken. When it finally surrendered it was not because it was about to fall but because the Ibelins had been fortunate enough to capture Richard Filanger as he was returning to the East, after having been to Italy to see his master, and the surrender of the city was made the price of Filanger's ransom. The fall of Tyre ended the imperial resistance and the 'Lombard war' was over. Ralph of Soissons demanded that Tyre be given to him as bailli, but was met with the refusal of the barons; and Tyre was kept by Philip de Montfort, who announced his willingness to surrender it as soon as he was sure that Conrad would not come to claim his throne, but who meanwhile consolidated his own power in the city. Balian d'Ibelin occupied Acre in similar manner, and Ralph in disgust returned to France. The *Haute Cour* solemnly nullified all the acts of Frederick as bailli and deposed Raymond de Gibelet, his seneschal. By the summer of 1243 the last of the imperialists had been expelled and the constitutional party had completed their triumph.[2]

---

[1] *Gestes*, par. 232; *Eracles*, p. 423.

And when Marsiglio Georgio complained of actions against Venetians, the barons answered that if the spoliation was done by the bailli of the ruler it could be undone, but if by the king it could not be undone as Conrad was king, and Alice was not the legitimate ruler. (Tafel-Thomas, ii, 357.)

[2] *Assises*, ii, 400–01; *Gestes*, pars. 227–31; *Eracles*, pp. 422, 426–27; Marsiglio Georgio in Tafel-Thomas, ii, 355–57; *M. G. H., Epis. XIII Saec.*, ii, doc. 564, p. 399.

Richard Filanger went back to Sicily; Lothaire to Antioch where Bohemond gave him fiefs;

The rule of Alice of Cyprus in alliance with the Ibelins lasted until 1246 when she died and the lordship of Jerusalem passed to her son, Henry of Cyprus. Henry appointed Balian d'Ibelin of Beirut his bailli in Jerusalem, at the same time granting Tyre as an hereditary fief to de Montfort. Henry used the title *'rei de Chypre et seignor del reaume de Jerusalem'* in his charters. Balian held the office of bailli for only a year, and at his death in 1247 the bailliage was conferred on his brother, John of Arsur, who held it intermittently until 1258.[1]

Meanwhile the city of Jerusalem, Ascalon, and many smaller towns had fallen into the hands of the infidels once more, and Melek Saleh Najm-al-din Ayyub's Khwaresmian Turks had defeated the Christians at Gaza in 1244. St Louis had taken the Cross and after his ill-fated expedition to Egypt had spent some years in attempting to bolster up the tottering Latin kingdom (1248–54). In 1253 Henry of Cyprus died leaving his throne to his infant son, Hugh II, under the regency of his queen, Plaisance of Antioch, sister of Bohemond VI. A projected marriage between the widowed queen and Balian d'Ibelin, son of John of Arsur, which would have further increased the Ibelin control in Jerusalem, was abandoned due to the opposition of the prince of Antioch.

In 1257 Bohemond brought Plaisance and Hugh to Acre and de-

Thomas of Acerra went to Tripoli whence in 1248 the Pope was writing to have him expelled. (D. L. *Cartulaire*, doc. 2470.) At the same time the Pope ordered the Hospitallers to break off all relations with Frederick. (D. L. *Cartulaire*, doc. 2471.)

Within a year after the departure of the imperialists from Tyre, the Turks had taken Jerusalem. Frederick's rule was ended and his work gone to naught.

[1] *Gestes*, pars. 257–59 (The *Mémoires* of Philip de Novare ended with paragraph 229 of the *Gestes*, the rest is a continuation by a later hand, probably Gerard de Montreuil); *Eracles*, pp. 436–444; Mas Latrie, i, 337–38.

A charter of Henry showing the use of the title is found in: Mas Latrie, ii, 66–67; *Regesta*, doc. 1200.

John of Arsur was bailli 1247–48. When St Louis came to the East John surrendered the bailliage to one John Fuinan; but Fuinan was unable to cope with the quarrel of the Genoese and Pisans in Acre, and John of Arsur had to take back the bailliage. Some time before 1254 he again resigned the office, for his nephew John d'Ibelin of Jaffa was bailli at the time of the death of Conrad and the accession of Conradin. John of Jaffa gave up the bailliage in 1256 and John of Arsur was recalled once more. He retained the position until his death in 1258. During his last term of the bailliage John of Arsur and Geoffrey de Sargines, the seneschal and commander of the soldiery which Louis IX had left in Syria, made a treaty with Egypt.

manded that Hugh be recognized as heir to the kingdom and that the bailliage be given Plaisance for her son. John of Arsur surrendered the bailliage; and the desired oath, saving always the rights of Conradin,[1] was taken to Hugh by the barons of the *Haute Cour*, the Templars, Teutonic Knights, Venetians, and Pisans. The Genoese, Catalans, and Hospitallers, who were at feud with the Venetians, Pisans, and Templars, refused the oath. Plaisance reappointed John of Arsur to the bailliage and left him to settle the war and suppress the Genoese. When John died the year following, Geoffrey de Sargines, seneschal of the kingdom and commander of the French troops which St Louis had left behind him in Palestine, succeeded to the bailliage.[2]

In 1261 Plaisance died, and the succession to the bailliage of both Jerusalem and Cyprus was at issue. The bailliage of Jerusalem was claimed by Isabelle de Lusignan, the younger sister of Henry of Cyprus, who had married Henry of Antioch, the younger son of Bohemond IV. It was not however until 1263 that Isabelle and Henry, her husband, came to Acre where they were accepted by the *Haute Cour* as baillies, though the barons refused to swear allegiance to them as they had not brought with them the legitimate heir. Leaving Henry at Acre, Isabelle returned to Cyprus.[3] Isabelle did not, however, make any effort to secure the bailliage of Cyprus but allowed her son, Hugh of Antioch-Lusignan, who later became Hugh III, to claim the bailliage in the *Haute Cour* of Nicosia. Hugh de Brienne, the son of Marie, who was Isabelle's elder sister, also allowed the claim of his cousin to the bailliage of Cyprus to pass unchallenged.[4]

---

[1] Conradin became the Hohenstaufen claimant on the death of his father Conrad in 1254.

[2] *Eracles*, pp. 441–444; *Rothelin Eracles*, p. 634; *Gestes*, par. 268; *Assises*, ii, 401.

De Sargines appears as seneschal on a charter of October 1258 on which John of Arsur is constable and bailli. (*Regesta*, doc. 1269; Strehlke, doc. 127.) He is bailli in April 1263 (*Regesta*, doc. 1325), but by July 1264 he is seneschal and Henry of Antioch is bailli. (*Regesta*, doc. 1332a.)

[3] *Eracles*, pp. 446–47; *Gestes*, pars. 313–20.

[4] Hugh de Brienne had been brought up by his aunt Isabelle, and it has been suggested that he did not wish to oppose the aunt who had befriended him; wherefore it was not until after her death that he entered his claims against his cousin. (Mas Latrie, i, 385–88.) See genealogical table in appendix, and *Familles*. Also the elaborate genealogical article by Mas Latrie, 'Généalogie des Rois de Chypre', *Archivio Veneto* (1881).

But when Isabelle died in 1264 and Hugh of Antioch claimed the bailliage of Jerusalem, Hugh de Brienne entered a counter claim and the case was brought before the *Haute Cour*.[1]

The two claimants were of the same degree of relationship to the minor king, both being sons of his aunts. Hugh de Brienne's case lay in the fact that his mother was the elder sister of Henry, the father of Hugh II, while Hugh of Antioch-Lusignan's mother was the younger sister. To this, Antioch-Lusignan countered that he was himself older than Brienne. He further insisted that the relationship should be traced, not from their common ancestor, Alice of Cyprus, but from the person last seised of the bailliage, which was his own mother Isabelle. He pointed out that Marie, Brienne's mother, was dead at the time of the decease of Henry of Cyprus, and the dead cannot inherit. Thus the claims of her line were invalid. The bailliage had passed from Plaisance, who had assumed it on the death of her husband Henry, to Isabelle, her sister-in-law, and not to Brienne, her nephew. And, Antioch-Lusignan claimed that, since his mother Isabelle had been in full seisin of the bailliage at the time of her death, he, as her heir, was now entitled to it. Both claimants produced precedents from cases of private law and it is interesting to note that Brienne endeavored to cite an opinion of Philip de Novare as authoritative. A lengthy debate ensued which lasted for several days. The account of the speeches has been preserved by John d'Ibelin of Jaffa, the jurisconsult. The decision of the *Haute Cour* was in the outcome given to Hugh of Antioch-Lusignan on the grounds that he was the eldest living male relative in the first degree of relationship to the minor, and was most closely related to the person last seised of the office.

The importance of this case is at once apparent and it was used as a precedent in later cases,—notably, the succession of Hugh IV in 1324. It established the rule that inheritance was to be determined from the person last in seisin of the fief or office and not from a more remote ancestor, and further that the elder male relative, though de-

---

[1] The details of this great debate are taken from the account in the *Documents Relatifs à la Successibilité au Trône* (*Assises*, ii), pp. 401–15. Mas Latrie, i, 399–407, gives an abridged but full account with many quotations.

scended from a younger sister, had precedence over a younger male descended from an elder sister.[1] Hugh of Antioch-Lusignan was thus possessed of the bailliages of both Jerusalem and Cyprus when Hugh II died in December 1267. His succession to the throne of Cyprus and to the seignory of Jerusalem was not seriously disputed, as he had proven his relationship to Hugh II when he received the bailliage of Jerusalem. Hugh de Brienne did make a vain attempt to oppose him but failed, and Hugh of Antioch-Lusignan was crowned king of Cyprus on Christmas day 1267 by William, patriarch of Jerusalem, who was visiting in Cyprus.[2]

The last step in the aggrandizement of Hugh III was when after the execution of Conradin in 1268 he became king of Jerusalem. There was at this time a serious controversy over the succession, as rival claims were introduced by Marie of Antioch, the granddaughter of Isabelle Plantagenet through Melissande, who was daughter of Isabelle and Amaury II and wife of Bohemond IV.[3]

Both claimants were descended from Isabelle Plantagenet. Hugh was the grandson of Alice of Cyprus, Isabelle's daughter by Henry of Champagne, her third husband. Marie was the daughter

---

[1] *Assises*, ii, 419–22, for the argument in 1324. Article 130 of the *Assises de Romanie* establishes these same rules of succession, influenced perhaps by this case in Jerusalem.

[2] *Eracles*, p. 456; *Gestes*, par. 355; *Assises*, ii, 415. The editors of the *Eracles* give the date of Hugh's death as November 11, which Röhricht, *Königreichs*, p. 938, corrects to December 5.

[3] *The Doc. Rel. Succ. Tr.* (*Assises*, ii), pp. 415–19, discusses this debate as occurring when Hugh II died and does not mention Conradin as dead. From this account Mas Latrie, i, 424–25, and ii, 73, note 2, concludes that the debate occurred before Conradin's execution on October 29, 1268. But the statement in the *Gestes*, par. 369, is conclusive: 'Il avint que le roy Hugue de Chipre . . . quant il vy que Conradin fu mort, le quel fu, luy et le dit roy Hugue, enfans de couzin et de couzine jermaine, car Corrat quy fu fis de l'empereor Federic, et fu pere de Conradin, et la mere dou roy de Chipre Hugue de Lezegniau (et le roy Conrat) furent jermains de ii seurs, de la ou le royaume de Jerusalem meut, et por ce le dit roy Hugue se fist courouner dou royaume de Jerusalem'. Amadi, Florio Bustron, and the *Lignages d'Outremer* (*Assises*, ii), p. 444, agree that it was after Conradin's death, but Mas Latrie discards their evidence as later. It must be remembered that Mas Latrie did not have the *Gestes*, which were discovered only after the publication of his book. Röhricht, p. 947, accepts it as after Conradin's death.

Placing the death of Conradin on October 29 as the date before which the debate could not have occurred, we can place the date of April 11, 1269, as the latest date on which it could have occurred as Geoffrey de Sargines died on that day, and Geoffrey was the first man to take homage to Hugh after the court had given its decision. (*Assises*, ii, 419; *Eracles*, p. 457.)

of Melissande, Isabelle's daughter by her fourth husband. Thus while Hugh was descended from the child of an earlier marriage which was an important point in his favor, Marie was one generation closer to their common ancestor. Marie tried to keep the argument one of degree of relationship to Isabelle of Jerusalem, since it was through relationship with her that the relationship with Conradin would be established. Hugh, on the other hand, shifted it to relationship to Hugh II, who had enjoyed the seignory of Jerusalem as heir of Alice of Cyprus, who had been recognized by the *Haute Cour* as the closest heir after the descendants of Marie *'la Marquise.'* There was no escaping this point, and Marie of Antioch admitted that Alice of Cyprus had been legally recognized as the closest heir after the Hohenstaufen branch of the family. But she contended that when Alice of Cyprus died the seignory should have gone to her mother Melissande instead of to Henry I of Cyprus. Hugh countered by stressing the inheritance from the person last seised of the seignory and claimed that Henry, the son, was the heir of Alice rather than Melissande, the sister. Marie claimed inheritance from Isabelle, and insisted that Melissande the daughter had better rights than Henry the grandson. Precedent favored Hugh, for the rule that inheritance should be based on relationship to the person last seised of the seignory had been laid down in the previous case against Brienne. The investiture of Alice of Cyprus gave her the seignory and made her children, rather than the descendants of a collateral line of Isabelle's descendants, the legitimate heirs. Further circumstances favored Hugh. He was already exercising the powers of the king, having been previously granted the seignory, and his claims had been accepted by the *Haute Cour* before Marie raised any question. That Hugh was also king of Cyprus and was allied by marriage with the powerful families of Ibelin and Montfort, while Marie was a spinster, also counted in his favor. The *Haute Cour* decided the

---

The mention of Geoffrey in a charter of April 19 seems to imply that he was dead by that time. (D. L. *Cartulaire*, doc. 3334.) Thus the debate must have occurred in the early months of 1269, allowing time for the news of the death of Conradin to reach the East.

The question debated between Hugh and Marie was not the bailliage of Jerusalem, which Hugh already had, but the throne itself, and it was that to which Marie later sold her claims to Charles of Anjou.

case in favor of Hugh and did homage to him. Marie refused to accept the decision of the *Haute Cour* and, on the day of Hugh's coronation, again protested, announcing her intention of carrying the case to the Papal Curia. Leaving the kingdom, she went to Europe, where she placed herself under the protection of Charles of Anjou, the king of Sicily.[1]

The question of Marie's claims came up before the Council of Lyons in 1273, but no definite decision was given. Representatives of the kingdom of Jerusalem who were present claimed that the case had been finally settled in their own *Haute Cour* and that no appeal could be made after the verdict was once given nor had any court in the world appellate jurisdiction over the *Haute Cour* of Jerusalem. But while no decision in favor of Marie was ever officially given by the Curia, the Pope favored her claims and it was through the agency of Gregory X that Marie sold her rights over Jerusalem to Charles of Anjou.[2]

In 1277, shortly after Hugh III had withdrawn from Acre due to his inability to enforce his rule over the Templars and the *Frarie*, there arrived in the East Roger de St Severin, count of Marsico, bailli of King Charles, who presented letters from Charles and the Pope demanding that Acre be surrendered to him and that homage be done to Charles. Balian d'Ibelin, whom Hugh had left as his bailli in Acre, surrendered the citadel readily enough, but the barons at

[1] Hugh was crowned September 24, 1269 (*Eracles*, p. 457; *Annales Terre Sainte*, p. 454; Röhricht, p. 948), and his first charter as king dates from November 1269. (*Regesta*, doc. 1368; D. L. *Cartulaire*, doc. 3371.)

The claims of Marie were supported by the Templars while Hugh was supported by the Hospital. It was the continued opposition of the Templars which forced Hugh to abandon Acre in 1276.

The sources for this debate and Marie's appeal are: *Assises*, ii, 415–19; *Gestes*, pars. 369, 375; *Eracles*, pp. 464, 475–76; and the documents cited below.

[2] Marie sold her title to Jerusalem for 1000 gold pieces and an annuity of 4000 livres of Tours. The charter of Charles of Anjou confirming the purchase, issued March 18, 1277, shows the date of the final transfer of the claims. It was confirmed by Charles II in 1289. (*Regesta*, docs. 1411, 1486.)

The Council of Lyons gave no decision on the matter. Mansi, *Sacrorum Counciliorum*, XXIV, cols. 37–135 (cols. 62–67, notes on proceedings), does not mention Jerusalem. Röhricht, pp. 975–76; Mas Latrie, i, 445–59; and R. Sternfeld, *Ludwigs des Heiligen Kreuzzug nach Tunis und die Politik Karls I von Sizilien* (Berlin, 1896), p. 303 ff.; are modern accounts.

first refused to perform homage. When Hugh, to whom they appealed, refused to act in any way, they yielded and made homage to Charles, accepting St Severin as the bailli of the rightful king. Two years later, in 1279, Hugh made a vain attempt to capture Acre but his Cypriot troops deserted; St Severin and the Templars were left in control of the capital.[1] Meanwhile the Latin states had been crumbling away before the attacks of the Mameluke sultans of Egypt. From 1263 to 1277, Bibars-el-Bondocari had ravaged the Christian counties and had captured Arsur, Jaffa, Antioch, and many other cities and fiefs. His successor, El-Melek-el-Mansur Kelaoun, continued his conquests. The Mongol invasion promised relief to the harassed Christians, who still clung to the hope that had led the Popes and St Louis to send John of Piano Carpini and Fra William of Rubriquis to the courts of the Great Khan under the misapprehension that in the Mongol they would find a liberator from the Saracen. Following the lead of the Armenian kings, the Syrian lords made treaties with the Mongol Mangu-Timour,—St Severin alone allying with the Egyptians. But the first wave of Mongol advance had been broken, and Kelaoun stopped the invaders sharply at Homs in October 1281, after a terrific battle which cost both sides the flower of their armies. The Mongols were turned back and Kelaoun was free to go on with his conquests of Christian lands.

The baillies of Charles of Anjou might have been able to stave off the final conquest by the Egyptian, for they were in alliance with him, but the Sicilian Vespers upset Charles' imperialistic plans. The Sicilian monarch had to retrench and could less well afford to spare the troops necessary to maintain his control in Syria. St Severin was recalled to the West, and Eudes Pelechin was left in command in Syria. Pelechin continued the Egyptian policy and secured another treaty in June 1283.[2] In the same year, Hugh III made another attempt to seize Acre but was repulsed. The following

[1] *Eracles*, pp. 474–79; *Gestes*, pars. 396–401; *Annales Terre Sainte*, pp. 456–57.

[2] The treaty with Egypt is summarized in: D. L. *Cartulaire*, doc. 3832; *Regesta*, doc. 1450. The narrative of the last years of the Latin kingdom is given in the *Gestes*, pars. 419–516. The *Eracles* dwindles and stops altogether at 1277. Most of our information comes from the Arabic sources, especially Makrizi's history of Egypt (trans. Blochet in *R. O. L.*, viii–xi (1900–1908)) and from European chronicles. The *Annales Terre Sainte* carry through to 1291 but are at best only fragmentary annals. The fall of Acre is the subject of a special account, the

year Hugh III died and was succeeded by his son John, who ruled from April 1284 to May 1285, being in turn succeeded by his brother, Henry II. Further Angevin reverses in the West, and the consequent weakening of the garrison at Acre, enabled Henry to gain control of Acre in 1286. Pelechin was driven out and Henry established his uncle, Philip d'Ibelin, as bailli in Acre, while he returned to Nicosia, after having received the crown of Jerusalem at Tyre.[1]

The expulsion of the Angevins untied the hands of the Egyptians; Kelaoun once more invaded the principalities. Laodicea fell and Tripoli; only his sudden death in October 1290 prevented Kelaoun from completing his conquests. As it was, the glory of blotting out the Latin kingdom and expelling the unbelieving Trinitarians from Syria fell to Kelaoun's son, Melek-el-Aschraf, who in 1291 captured Acre, Haïfa, Tyre, Sidon, and Beirut. The Christian refugees fled to Cyprus where under different conditions, on an island not constantly exposed to Moslem attacks, they continued their lives under the same laws, institutions, and dynasty under which they had lived in Syria. But it was a different life, and though the history of Cyprus is a continuation of that of Jerusalem, it is a new chapter with many variations.

In tracing the foregoing sketch of the constitutional development of the kingdom of Jerusalem the thread of continuity was the successions to the throne and the bailliages. The most important consitutional events center about the laws of inheritance, but there were other developments in the thirteenth century which must be noticed before concluding this chapter. In the field of jurisprudence the thirteenth century stands out in Outremer history; it was

---

Excidium Urbis Acconis, published in Martène, *Amplissima Collectio*, v. 757–784; and the *Oesterreichische Reimchronik* (*M.G.H. Deutschen Chroniken*, v, 2, 2), has a full account thereof.

Röhricht, 'Die Eroberung Akkas durch die Muslimen', *Forschungen zur Deutsche Geschichte*, xx (1879), 96–126; 'Der Untergang des Königreichs Jerusalem', *Mittheilungen des Instituts für Oesterreichische Geschichtsforschung*, xv (1894), 1–58 (reprinted with slight modification in the *Königreichs Jerusalem*, pp. 996–1032), and 'Études sur les derniers temps du royaume de Jérusalem', *Archives*, i, 617–52, ii, 365–409; all give detailed narrative accounts by the great German scholar of the history of Jerusalem. Mas Latrie, i, 475–99, discusses the fall of the kingdom; and C. L. Kingsford, 'Sir Otho de Grandison', *Transactions of the Royal Historical Society*, 3rd series, iii (London, 1909), gives a graphic account of the fall of Acre.

[1] Gestes, pars. 437–39.

then that the great books of Philip de Novare, John d'Ibelin, the *Assises de la Cour des Bourgeois*, and the treatises of James d'Ibelin, Geoffrey le Tort, and the *Clef des Assises de la Haute Cour* were written.

The fourteenth century could order only that the book of John d'Ibelin should be made the official code of the kingdom of Cyprus, and add the few scattered laws which are found in the *Bans et Ordonnances des Rois de Chypre*. In the fifteenth century the book of Ibelin was translated into Italian for the Venetian rulers of Cyprus. The thirteenth century may then be considered as the time when the science of jurisprudence was at its height and when the customs and usages of the kingdom became fixed.

In the realm of administration, an important innovation was undertaken in 1250 when the barons of the *Haute Cour* ordered that records of all the transactions which took place within the court should be kept.[1] Those for the *Cour des Bourgeois* seem to have been begun at once but the records of the *Haute Cour* only began to be kept at all regularly during the reign of Henry II and were possibly never kept in Jerusalem at all.[2]

As regards the relationship between the king and the *Haute Cour*, after the Ibelin party defeated the imperialists and Alice of Cyprus and her heirs received the governance of the realm, the *Haute Cour* stood supreme and unquestioned. The government was in the hands of the feudal oligarchy, dominated by the house of Ibelin, and even the Lusignans had to play a minor rôle on occasion.

In 1272 the Cypriot barons opposed Hugh III's attempt to order them overseas for military service, and the opposition was led by James d'Ibelin. The matter was, however, compromised and the

---

[1] *Abrégé Assises Cour Bourgeois* (*Assises*, ii), xiii–xvii, 246–49, gives an account of the meeting of the *Haute Cour* in which this was ordered. It was one of the meetings held at Acre while St Louis was there.

[2] *Abrégé*, xviii, 249–50. Henry made a special ordinance that the *Haute Cour* should keep records. The earlier provisions do not specify whether they refer to both courts or only the *Bourgeois*, but one may infer that while designed for both they were put into effect only in the lower. At any rate Henry provided that clerks be appointed to keep the records of the High Court, showing that they had not been kept until that time. An assise of Hugh IV (*Bans et Ordonnances*, xxviii, 371–72) completes the organization of the registers and enumerates the material which should be contained in them. But it refers of course only to Cyprus.

barons consented to follow the king, but with a definite time limit of four months.[1]

But the constitutional development of Jerusalem in the thirteenth century can best be seen in the study of the episodes of the war between the Ibelins and Frederick which have already been considered. We can see there the working of the laws governing bailliages, the insistence of the barons on the submission to the law and to the trial by peers in the *Haute Cour*, the right of revolt when the assises have been violated and fair trial has not been accorded a liegeman, and throughout the loyalty of lord to man and vassal to lord, which was the essential base on which the feudal system rested.

The period after the close of the 'Lombard war' was one of continuous troubles for Jerusalem; the foreign wars occupied the attention of the rulers and barons. The princes could not maintain peace between quarrelsome factions within the kingdom, and the menace from without continually increased; all this finally precipitated a state of semi-anarchy which stifled all constitutional growth. That the kingdom fell is partly the fault of the Lusignans, who spent the energy of the realm in futile war with the Angevins, and who retired to Cyprus leaving the country without a leader. But more blame attaches to the Templars, Hospitallers, Genoese, Venetians, Pisans, and those lords of Outremer who constantly quarreled among themselves. When they should have been consolidating their resources for common action against a common enemy, they attacked one another and kept up a state of continuous civil war within the weak and tottering kingdom. Jerusalem had fallen to Saladin in 1187 because of this internecine strife. The century which elapsed brought no cessation and merely made the way easy for Sultan Melek-el-Aschraf to realize the ambitions of his great predecessor.

[1] *Document Relatif au Service Militaire* (*Assises*, ii), pp. 427–34; *Eracles*, pp. 462–64; and see below under limitations on service in the chapter on the military establishment.

BOOK II

THE ADMINISTRATIVE MACHINERY OF THE LATIN KINGDOM

CHAPTER 4

THE HAUTE COUR

'IN THE Assises of Jerusalem we have indeed the most perfect picture of the ideal feudal state, and they are themselves the most complete monument of feudal law. . . . For the administration of justice there was the High Court at Jerusalem, which was originally intended to have jurisdiction over the great lords, but gradually became in effect the king's Council of State dealing with all political affairs'. Thus C. L. Kingsford describes the *Haute Cour* of Jerusalem, and expresses a theory which,—G. B. Adams notwithstanding,—is accepted as substantially correct.[1] Nowhere is the purely feudal character of the Outremer state more apparent than in the High Court which united in a single body of barons all the functions and powers of the state. If feudalism implies a weak monarch and a strong aristocracy, then the ideal feudal state existed in Jerusalem. 'In no country of Europe', says Dodu, 'was society established in a manner more in conformity with the principles of feudalism'.[2]

The cardinal governing body of the kingdom was the *Haute Cour*; had modern theories and terminology been known in the thirteenth century it would have been referred to as the 'sovereign body' in the state. It included within its sphere of activity the modern departments of executive, legislative, and judiciary. Its word was law, or rather its interpretation of the existing body of custom made law, and the king who endeavored to act without the advice of, or contrary to the decisions of, his High Court found himself confronted with a legalized rebellion on the part of his subjects. Neither of the great imperialist phrases '*Quod principi placuit legis habet vigorem*' nor '*Rex legibus solutus est*' were valid in the Latin crusading states.

With powers, when fully developed, as extensive and all-inclusive as those of the English *Curia Regis* under William the Conqueror or

---

[1] *Cambridge Medieval History* (New York: Macmillan, 1926), V, 303–04. G. B. Adams, *Origin of the English Constitution* (2nd ed., New Haven: Yale University Press, 1920), pp. 186–94, maintains a rather unique theory concerning the ideal feudal state which he finds in many ways best revealed in Norman England.

[2] Dodu, p. 160.

Henry I, the High Court of Jerusalem aimed at the subordination of the monarch and the keeping of the king *primus inter pares*, a mere president of the council of his vassals and his peers. As regards its political competence says Dimitri Hayek: 'elle était le conseil directeur du gouvernement, une sort de directoire militaire; à ce titre, elle accaparait la souveraineté réelle et partageait le pouvoir législatif avec les sages hommes, tout en gardant, par ailleurs, sa suprême prépondérance.'[1]

The powers of the *Haute Cour* passed through several stages of development. In the first years of the kingdom the *Haute Cour* exercised considerable power and influence. The king's hands were tied by the struggle with the ecclesiastical power and by his subordination to the Church, so that the baronage retained much of the power which had been theirs when they elected Godfrey king and established the monarchy. Kingship was elective and the barons of the High Court kept an effective check on the monarchs they had created.

But as the kingship increased in strength under the rule of Foulque, Baldwin III, and Amaury, the court lost some of its strength and gradually became subject to the royal will. The reign of Amaury and the legislative action which that monarch carried through show what the relative strength of the king and court was in this period. This is likewise illustrated by the peaceful succession of father by son, and of brother by brother. While Baldwin III, Amaury, and Baldwin IV were all elected to the throne the election in these cases was little more than a formality, and the royal influence predominated over the free election of the baronage. But perhaps the most illuminating act of this period is the celebrated *Assise* of Amaury of 1162 which changed the composition of the *Haute Cour* and brought the arrière vassals into direct relation with the king. It is incredible that the barons of the *Haute Cour* desired this, as its immediate result was that the court was weakened while the king grew stronger.

But the troubles of the reign of Baldwin IV, the lingering illness of the leper king, and the need for a strong leader against the Saracen

[1] D. Hayek, *Le Droit Franc en Syrie pendant les Croisades* (Paris: Editions Spes, 1925), p. 59.

inroads gave the baronage a chance to recuperate their waning strength and to become again the real governing body of the realm. The election of Baldwin V against the claims of his mother, the regency of Raymond of Tripoli, and the turning to Isabelle after the death of Baldwin V all manifest increased activity on the part of the barons. The anarchy which followed Hattin further enhanced the powers of the court, never to be lost thereafter. Throughout the thirteenth century the king was always subject to the control of his council.

One of its very sources of strength lay in the fact that the *Haute Cour* in Jerusalem never developed that differentiation of function and personnel which characterized the history of the western curias in the late twelfth and thirteenth centuries. It always remained the old feudal council of the vassals, though its membership was greatly extended by the inclusion of the arrière vassals after 1162. There is little difference between the *Haute Cour* and the council of the early Capetians. In Jerusalem there never developed any differentiated bodies such as the Exchequer, King's Bench, Common Pleas, Council, or Parliament of England; no *Chambre des Comptes, Parlement,* or *Consiel du Roi* as in France; no *Dîwâns* as in Sicily. Jerusalem knew no justiciars like those of southern Italy; no itinerate justices like those of the Anglo-Norman kingdom; not even baillies like those of Philip Augustus in France. The student of the *Haute Cour* of Jerusalem will find himself thoroughly at home in the councils of the early Capetians or the first four Norman rulers of England, but he will become lost at once in the courts of Philip the Fair (he will even have difficulties in those of Philip Augustus) or of Henry III or Frederick II.[1]

In England the first step in the breakdown of the old curia was the differentiation of function, so that the members of the curia met in

---

[1] For the early stages of the development of the English curia see: J. F. Baldwin, *The King's Council in England during the Middle Ages* (Oxford: Clarendon Press, 1913), chaps. 1–3; C. H. McIlwain, *The High Court of Parliament* (New Haven: Yale University Press, 1910), introductory chapters; G. B. Adams, *Councils and Courts in Anglo-Norman England* (New Haven: Yale University Press, 1926). The best account of the councils under the early Capetians is in A. Luchaire, *Histoire des Institutions Monarchiques de la France sous les Premiers Capétiens* (2nd ed.: Paris, 1891), i, 243–77. See also P. Viollet, *Histoire des Institutions Politiques et Administratives de la France* (Paris, 1890–1903), ii. For Norman institutions see C.

specific sessions for specific purposes. The barons of the curia assembled to receive the accounts of the sheriffs, a special meeting for financial session, and it was only slowly that the barons *in* the Exchequer became the barons *of* the Exchequer.[1] The same is true of the courts of King's Bench and Common Pleas; only gradually can the cleavage of these departments from the parent stem be recognized. The same barons who sat in the Exchequer also sat on the bench for common or royal pleas; they were justices of the curia sitting sometimes for financial, sometimes for other pleas. The function developed before the special body which cared for it. But in Jerusalem the whole council always sat on all matters; there was no differentiation either of function or of personnel.

The High Court, which sat normally at Jerusalem in the first period of the kingdom and at Acre in the second (though it could meet anywhere that was agreed upon and for military purposes met at any convenient spot, such as at Saphoria in 1187), was composed of all the vassals of the king. Membership was dependent upon the tenure of a fief, which could be either in land or money, and the king could not appoint members to the body.[2] Ecclesiastics were members by virtue of their holdings, and the western communes which held possessions in the realm were represented in the *Haute Cour*. Leaders of bands of crusaders were generally invited to attend the meetings of the court; and Dominico Michieli the Venetian, Philip of Flanders, Louis VII of France, Prince Edward of England, and others are to be found at meetings. While St Louis was in the East he attended many meetings and presided over some, and the same may be said for Frederick II and Richard of England. The bourgeoisie,

---

H. Haskins, *Norman Institutions* (Cambridge, Mass: Harvard University Press, 1918), and his 'England and Sicily in the Twelfth Century', *E. H. R.* xxvi (1911). F. Chalandon, *Histoire de la Domination Normande en Italie et en Sicile, 1009–1194* (Paris, 1907), ii; and E. Jameson, 'The Norman Administration of Apulia and Capua', *Papers of the British School of Rome* (London: McMillan, 1913), vi, give information on Norman Sicily, though the best study by far is that of Haskins cited above.

[1] R. L. Poole, *The Exchequer in the Twelfth Century* (Oxford: Clarendon Press, 1912). For an intensive study of the differentiation of the English administrative offices see T. F. Tout, *Chapters in the Administrative History of Medieval England* (Manchester: Manchester University Press, 1920), i, introductory chapters.

[2] In the principality of Achaia only liegemen were members of the prince's court. (*Assises de Romaine*, art. 72.)

who met on occasion with the court and who appear on charters, were, I believe, similarly invited to attend the meetings but were never members of the court.[1]

The materials for the study of the *Haute Cour* are insufficient to determine whether or not there ever developed, as there did in the West, a greater and smaller council. If by the 'smaller council' one understands a definite group of barons who attended the king and advised him, Jerusalem did not develop one. Before 1162 the membership was not overly large as there were not many liegemen of the king; and while after the inclusion of the arrière vassals the number greatly increased, the entire membership of the court very seldom attended the meetings and there did not develop any set group which transacted business. In some of the more important sessions of the court, especially in those where the barons were assembled at the military array and plans of campaign were discussed, the number in attendance must have been great; but for ordinary purposes the number varied from half a dozen to twenty as shown by the charters given *coram rege*. Ibelin says that two or more liegemen with the president,—the king or his representative,—were sufficient to make a court; and Usamah tells how Foulque appointed six or seven knights to 'arise and judge this case for him' when he appealed to the king to secure damages for injury done his property during time of truce.[2]

But the group which surrounded the king was not a fixed one. The names of those who attested charters do not indicate any definite group who composed the small personal council of the king. The grand officers were not invariably present, though usually there was one or more of them. Humphrey de Toron the constable, Philip

---

[1] On the composition of the *Haute Cour* see: Beugnot, *Assises*, i, Introduction, 16; Dodu, pp. 160–71; Hayek, *op. cit.*, pp. 58–68; H. Prutz, *Kulturgeschichte*, pp. 213–32. For the bourgeoisie in the court see Dodu, pp. 273–75.

Frederick II was king of Jerusalem and so was by right a member and president of the court while he was in the kingdom.

[2] Ibelin, clxiii, 252; '*quant le seignor ou home qu'il ait establi en son leuc, et deus ou plus des homes dou seignor sont ensemble, ce est cort*'. The *Clef des Assises*, lx, 584, says: '*le seignor et trois de ces houmes*'. See Hayek, *op. cit.*, pp. 65–67; Usamah (ed. Hitti), pp. 93–94. In the Morea minor affairs could be adjudicated by a small number of lieges, but those bringing suit could demand a larger number if the case was important. (*Assises de Romanie*, arts. 4, 13.)

of Neapolis, William the marshal, and Frederick archbishop of Tyre witness most of the acts of Amaury I but are not universally found thereon.[1] Under Henry I of Cyprus the Ibelin family practically monopolized the council, but the membership of any meeting may well be said to have depended upon those who happened to be present at the moment.

One of the fundamental duties inherent in the position of fiefholder was attendance at the court when summoned, and he was also held obliged to go out, upon his lord's command, to judge disputes and make inquests.[2] Yet this was no system of justices comparable to the justices-in-eyre of England for it was not a prerogative of the king and was not in any way connected with the king's justice. In every respect the court baron was like the *Haute Cour* and the count could dispatch his vassal to make inquest as well as could the king. These inquests were used in connection with cases of *novel disseisin* which were 'esclarsi par l'enquesicion', and these cases did not come into the king's court at all, being heard in the regular court baron of the suzerain, unless, as was more often the case, they were adjudicated out of court by the lord. While Jerusalem had *novel disseisin* and *morte d'ancestor*, and while these pleas were decided by use of the inquest, the itinerate justices who administered these assises in England did not develop in the East.[3]

Nor did the court in Jerusalem ever become fixed, but until the end of the kingdom moved about with the king, though the king's presence was not necessary and he could appoint a representative to preside over the court in his absence. Further, and this is one of the most important features of the Jerusalemite system, the king was equally amenable to the jurisdiction of the court along with any of his vassals.[4] All members of the court were peers, and trial by peers being the fundamental formula of Outremer law, the king as well as any of the barons was subject to the decisions of the court.

[1] *Regesta*, docs. 397, 400, 412 (none are found on 413), 449, 450, 452, 453, 465, 466, 467.

[2] Ibelin, ccxvii, 347.

[3] Ibelin, ccxlviii, 396; *Clef des Assises*, lxxvi, lxxix, lxxxi, 585; deal with *novel disseisin* and *morte d'ancestor*.

[4] Ibelin, ii, 23: 'et establi que lui et ses homes et leur fiés et toz chevaliers fucent menés par la *Haute Court*', referring to Godfrey's establishment of the court. Geoffrey le Tort, xv, 448, says that all are peers: 'qui que il soient, hauz au bas, povres au riches'.

Having thus far seen what the *Haute Cour* was not and did not become let us turn our attention to what it was and to a consideration of its functions and powers. In general we must observe the court of the middle thirteenth century for it was to that period that the *Assises* refer, but we have also much evidence as to the actions of the court in the twelfth century.

As the advisory and executive council of the king the *Haute Cour* decided all matters of policy. By it the earlier kings were elected, to it the later kings presented their claims, and the approval of the court was necessary before any prince could assume the kingship. Godfrey had been elected by a council of the leaders; Baldwin was elected by the chief lords of the kingdom; when Baldwin died the court elected Baldwin II over the claims of Eustache of Boulogne. It was the court which approved the selection of Foulque of Anjou as successor to Baldwin II and which confirmed him in the kingship after the death of his father-in-law.

The activity of the *Haute Cour* in electing monarchs and regents during the period up to the fall of Jerusalem and through the stormy years covered by the third crusade has been discussed in a previous chapter and need not be repeated here. In 1198 the court elected Amaury de Lusignan, then king of Cyprus and constable of Jerusalem, king of Jerusalem and husband of the reigning queen; and ten years later negotiated the marriage between their princess Marie 'la Marquise' and John de Brienne.[1]

In the thirteenth century, while the monarchy had become definitely hereditary, the court decided the claims of aspirants to the throne and the decision of the court was necessary before the heir could receive the homages of the barons. Thus Hugh of Antioch-Lusignan and Hugh de Brienne disputed the succession in 1264 for the bailliage of Jerusalem, and Hugh III four years later won the throne from Marie of Antioch in the High Court of Acre. Thus the court in 1243 appointed Alice of Cyprus bailli of Jerusalem, in the expectation that Conrad would forfeit his inheritance through failure

---

[1] Ernoul, pp. 309–10, 407–09; *Eracles*, pp. 306–08; *Gestes*, par. 67. The court had arranged the marriage of Baldwin III to Theodora of Byzantium in 1157. (William Tyre, XVIII, xvi, 846.)

to appear before the court to claim it within the appointed year and a day.[1]

In the election of baillies the court exercised full powers; even after the bailliage, like the kingship itself, had become hereditary, it chose the bailli from the various relatives and candidates. Nor was this confined to the *Haute Cour* of Jerusalem; the courts of Antioch and Tripoli exercised the same powers within their counties; and from 1101 when the barons of Antioch called in Tancred to rule over them in the absence of Bohemond, to 1288, when those of Tripoli rejected the bishop of Tortosa, appointed bailli by the Princess Sibylle, the courts of these counties elected their baillies and approved their princes.[2]

The court advised the king in all matters of policy even intervening in ecclesiastical matters. The council of Neapolis of January 1120, which met to reform the customs of the clergy and is included by Mansi among the councils of the Church, was also a meeting of the *Haute Cour*; Eustache Grenier, William de Buris, Barisan the constable of Jaffa, Baldwin of Rama, and other secular lords were present, besides King Baldwin himself.[3]

War and peace, treaties of alliance, and tax levies were discussed and voted in the court. In 1139 Foulque held a council to decide upon the alliance with Damascus; in 1148 the council determined on war with the same state; in 1177 the alliance offered by Manuel Comnenus was debated in the court.[4] Of course there is nothing un-

[1] It must be observed that the court appointed Alice bailli when Conrad came of age and that the barons took homage to her reserving the rights of Conrad should he come within the year and a day to claim his throne. The consecration of Alice however made her ruler of the kingdom though legally Conrad could not have been considered to have lost his claims before April 26, 1244, and it was not until the death of Conradin that Hugh III could assume the title of king. Ibelin, clxxii, 267, gives the law that the heir must appear within a year and a day. The incidents of Alice's election are found in *Gestes*, par. 226, and above p. 71, note 2.

[2] See in general: E. G. Rey, 'Résumé Chronologique de l'Histoire des Princes d'Antioche', *R. O. L.*, iv (1896), 321–407. For the election of Tancred see: *Chronologie*, No. 538; Fulcher. II, vii, 390–93. For the rejection of the bailli in 1288: *Gestes*, par. 467; Röhricht, p. 994 ff.

[3] *Regesta*, doc. 89; J. D. Mansi, *Sacrorum Conciliorum Nova et Amplissima Collectio* (2nd ed.: Paris, 1900), xxi, 262–66; William Tyre, XII, xiii, 531.

[4] William Tyre, XV, vii, 668–69; XVII, i, 759; XXI, xvi, 1031. An extreme case is that of Baldwin I consulting his vassals in Edessa before be accepted the throne of Jerusalem. (Albert Aix, VII, xxxi, 527.)

usual in the kings' submitting such matters to their councils, which was a common practice throughout the West; where Jerusalem differed from the Anglo-Norman or French monarchies is that while in the West the kings listened to the advice of their councils, in the East they were bound by their decisions. The Jerusalemite council was more like the council devised by the Provisions of Oxford than that which respectfully advised Henry II, save that it had no definite composition as did the revolutionary English body.

The king could initiate plans and suggestions but the final word came always from the barons in the court. *'Res nova novo indiget consilio, nec est in domino principe solum hoc effectui mancipare. Oportet enim, ut cum suorum . . . fidelium consilio, super hoc plenius deliberet'*,[1] was the reply of the Antiochene barons to the Basileus Manuel when they repudiated the treaty whereby Raymond had ceded Antioch to the Byzantines, for the ruler may not alienate any portion of his realm without the consent and approval of his vassals.[2] How far the king was subject to his council is well shown by the provision of the treaty of 1123, drawn up between the barons and the Venetians, in which it was provided that if the king did not accept the treaty he would not be allowed to return to his throne and that no successor would be accepted who did not agree to the provisions of the treaty.[3]

Esgart de la court was necessary for much routine business and no fief could change hands or be sold without the approval of the court. Fiefs for sale were exposed in the court, and the court acted as a registry bureau for sales, gifts, and mortgages of feudal property. After the reign of Henry II of Cyprus (1268–1324) the court maintained a special secretary who recorded such matters, but this is a

---

[1] William Tyre, XV, iii, 660.

[2] William Tyre, XV, xx, 690–91: 'sed neque eamdem absque conniventia civium et procerum, transferendi dominium in aliam personam habuisse, vel principum regionis transigendi ullam aliquo jure, alterutri illorum concessam. Quod si in hoc vel uterque, vel alter, obstinate perseverare praesumerent, futurum esse, ut urbe et universis finibus illorum ejectos, extorres faciant ejus, quam cum detrimento fidelium suorum contra jus venalem proposuerant, hereditatis'. The Antiochenes also argued that Raymond was only prince through his wife and so exceeded his powers.

[3] William Tyre, XII, xxv, 550–53; Tafel-Thomas, i, 79–90; *Regesta*, doc. 102.

fourteenth century practice and applies to the court of Cyprus rather than that of Jerusalem.[1]

An action once taken in the court was irrevocable unless altered or rescinded by the court itself, and the monarch could not with impunity disregard the court's decision. *'Nulle choze faite par court n'en doit estre desfaite, se elle ne se desfait par la condision de la court meismes'* says the *Clef des Assises de la Haute Cour.*[2] Usamah noticed this and commented on the fact that the king accepted the decision of the barons and to what extent—'the knight is something great in their esteem'.[3]

And there are many instances where the barons forced their ruler to accept their decisions when they were contrary to his own desires. Baldwin I was forced by his barons to abandon his Sinai campaign;[4] Tancred was compelled by his vassals to obey Baldwin's summons to succor Edessa when he would gladly have refused assistance;[5] in 1182 the court forced Baldwin IV to make peace with Raymond of Tripoli, with whom he had broken due to the intrigues of the queen mother.[6] One celebrated occasion where the king reversed the decision of the court resulted in disaster, when Guy de Lusignan, after having been advised by the court to remain in camp to await Saladin in July 1187, disregarded the counsel of his vassals and ordered the march to Hattin.

Two very illuminating cases are found in the matter of selection of baillies. When Alice of Cyprus received the bailliage of Cyprus for her child Henry in 1218, the court appointed her uncle, Philip d'Ibelin, bailli to administer the realm while leaving Alice the enjoyment of the revenues. An oath was taken by the barons to Philip to obey

---

[1] *Abrégé Cour Bourgeois*, xviii, 249–50. See *Regesta*, doc. 1027; D. L. *Cartulaire*, doc. 1996 for sale of fief exposed for sale in the court of Acre.

The lower courts were also registry courts and the *Haute Cour* followed their practice in establishing a secretariat.

The *Assises de Romanie* contain several provisions showing the necessity of transfers being registered in the court.

[2] *Clef des Assises*, clxxvii, 592; *Assises Cour Bourg.*, xxvi, 33.

[3] Usamah (ed. Hitti), p. 94.

[4] Albert Aix, XII, xxii, 703; XII, xxvi, 706. Baldwin was in the midst of besieging a city when his men refused to serve longer.

[5] Albert Aix, XI, xxi, 672–73.

[6] William Tyre, XXII, ix, 1077–79.

him as bailli until Henry should have come of age. Alice later married Bohemond V of Antioch and demanded that the bailliage be transferred to him, but was met by the refusal of the barons on the grounds that having taken the oath to Philip as bailli until Henry came of age they could not now transfer their oaths to another, though they admitted that Philip was only bailli for Alice.[1] When Philip died before Henry's majority the bailliage went to his brother John, lord of Beirut. The other case is that of Philip de Maugastel. When Frederick II had been in Syria he had appointed as his baillies Balian of Sidon and Eudes de Montbéliard, the appointment being made in the full session of the *Haute Cour*. In 1229 he endeavored to alter his appointment and sent letters ordering that Philip de Maugastel should be recognized as bailli. But when the letters were read in the court the barons refused to permit the change and John of Caesarea, speaking on behalf of the barons, said: '*ce que l'empereor mandeit esteit à l'encontre de ces assises et de ces usages, por ce qu'il voleit desfaire par letres ce qu'il aveit fait devant court: et que ceste chose ne poeient il faire ne soufrir*'.[2]

In addition to its political and advisory functions, the *Haute Cour* was the legislative body, in so far as one can be said to have existed. The kingdom of Jerusalem, in common with other feudal states, recognized no legislative power but did admit of the interpretation of existing custom both by the courts and by special assises. The basis of the law of Jerusalem was that code prepared by the wise men appointed by Duke Godfrey at the time of the conquest. Omitting here all discussion of the relation of this code to the later *Assises* of Jerusalem, which are, whatever their origin, purely thirteenth century law, it is sufficient to note that the laws of Jerusalem were based on the feudal customs of eleventh century Europe as brought to the East by the men of the first crusade. To this original code the later kings made additions, and these additions were known under the inclusive name of *Assises*. But while these assises were issued by the kings and bear their names, they were essentially

---

[1] *Gestes*, par. 98. *Eracles*, pp. 360–62, makes the story even more pointed by saying that Alice herself had appointed Philip instead of his having been elected by the court, but the *Gestes* are here better authority and should be followed in preference.

[2] *Assises*, ii, 399.

the work of the High Court, and rested for their enforcement upon the sanction given them by that body. *'En cest païs est l'usage autant vaillable come l'assise'*, says Philip de Novare.[1] The term assise was a flexible one in the twelfth and thirteenth centuries and included a variety of forms of legislation and administrative edict. They were practically any kind of legal precept which differed from unwritten custom.

The *Assizes of Clarendon* and *Northampton* in England are a series of disconnected rules adopted on variant subjects by the curia at a single session. The *Assize of Arms* is a single administrative ordinance. Jerusalem made no more differentiation than did England. *'Les assises'*, says Ibelin, *'ne pevent estre en pluisors choses provées, que par le lonc usage, ou por ce que l'on l'a veu faire et user come assise'*.[2] This admits almost any recognized custom as the equivalent of an assise and of equal value with more definitely established laws. Where there is no assise, Ibelin declares, custom should be followed; and where the court recognizes and records this custom it shall be considered as being an assise. In 1250 the barons of the realm assembled to draw up a code of laws and it was agreed that the records of the court were better indications of the law than any written rules.[3] For while the general principle of the law might be incorporated in a code, the most authoritative guide to practice was the record of the decisions of actual cases as tried in the *Haute Cour*. Feudal law was always largely case law; Bracton's *Note Book* is hardly less valuable than his treatise on the laws; and in Jerusalem the decisions of the High Court were the real laws of the land. True law is enforced law,—the barons of Jerusalem were Austinian before Austin.

Custom was the basis of all law. *'Sous le régime de la féodalité primitive il n'existait qu'une seule loi'*, says Beugnot, *'la loi féodale; loi conventionnelle, absolue, immuable'*.[4] The custom of the people

---

[1] Novare, lvi, 530. For the foundation of the courts and the codification of the laws by Godfrey see: Ibelin, i–iii, 22–25; Novare, xlvii, 521–23; and the discussions in Beugnot's Introduction to the *Assises*, vols. i and ii; Hayek, *op. cit.*; Dodu, and especially Grandclaude *Étude Critique*.

[2] Ibelin, cxi, 182–83. But *'esgart . . . n'est assise ne ne doit estre tenue pour assise'*. (*Clef des Assises*, cxxiii, 588.)

[3] *Abrégé Cour. Bourg.*, xiv–xvi, 246–48.

[4] Introduction to *Assises*, i, 41.

made the first code which was prepared under Godfrey and Baldwin I. To it were added assises which were themselves merely interpretations of custom, at least in the minds of those who made them. Assise and usage went hand in hand, and the formula used throughout the legal treatises of Jerusalem is '*par l'assise ou par l'usage*' which is derived from the phrases of the *Livre au Roi:* '*Et ce est dreit et raison par l'assise*', or, '*par l'us et par l'assise*'.

That the assises were often new laws mattered not, and in no way affected the theory which lay behind them. Law was interpreted by the courts; the same men who made up the court set down their interpretations in a written document so that there would be no further disagreement or question on the matter. Legislation and adjudication were all one. In the assises of the kings of Jerusalem which have come down to us in one form or another, several kinds of rules are illustrated. The assise of Amaury *sur la ligece* was a revolutionary law which bound the arrière vassals directly to their liege lord.[1] The assise of the same monarch concerning the service that might be demanded of a knight during a siege, known from the place of its issuance as the *Assise of Belfis*, was probably not more than an administrative order of the day during the campaign.[2] The *Assise of Neapolis* of 1120 was a set of rules governing the payments to be made to the patriarch, and was drawn up by a church council to which members of the lay nobility, as the High Court, were added.[3]

Other celebrated assises are those of King Baldwin: *du coup apparent* and *de la bailliage des rues.*[4] Henry II created the secretaryship of the High Court by assise. The *Assise de la bailliage des rues* is of particular interest for it shows clearly how necessary the consent of the High Court was in establishing any sort of law or ordinance.

[1] See the discussion of this assise in Chapter 1 above.

[2] The assise is given in the *Gestes*, par. 202. See G. Schlumberger, *Campagnes du Roi Amaury Ier de Jérusalem* (Paris: Plon, 1906), pp. 192–93, for a discussion and presentation of this view.

[3] Mansi, *Concilia*, xxi, 262–66; William Tyre, XII, xiii, 531–32; *Regesta*, doc. 89. F. Chalandon, *Histoire de la Première Croisade* (Paris, 1925), p. 311, refers to this assise as '*pour le royaume de Jérusalem, le plus ancien document de droit écrit qui nous soit parvenu*'.

[4] Novare, lxxv, 546–48; Ibelin, cxiii, 185; Geoffrey le Tort, xxii, 441,—for the *coup apparent*; for the *bailliage des rues—Assises Cour. Bourg.*, ccciii, 225.

Beugnot, *Assises*, i, Introduction, 22, attributes both of these assises to Baldwin I but without giving conclusive evidence for his attribution of them to this monarch.

This assise, which was a simple police measure dealing with the streets of the towns, was never considered legal as the court had not passed upon it. The *Assises de la Cour des Bourgeois* says of it: *'Bien sachés que la raison ne prent mie à droit nus de VII sos et demy d'escouver les rues, por ce que li rois Bauduins y mist ces establissemens sans le conseill de ces homes et de ses borgeis de la cité.*[1]

The age of Amaury I was a great period for legislation and the memory of the work of Amaury was preserved in the later oath sworn by the kings: *'et les assises dou royaume et dou rei Amauri et dou rei Baudoyn son fiz, et les ancienes costumes et assises dou roiaume de Jerusalem garderai'.*[2]

The law of Jerusalem was local law. While it was based generally on the law of France, or rather, on the laws of various fiefs which owed allegiance to the French king, it was yet not exactly French law. In the feudal ages each fief had its own law and the 'law of the land' was the law of the fief. The principality of Antioch, while it followed generally the laws of Jerusalem, still had its own law and custom distinct from that of the principality of Jerusalem. Cilician Armenia, situated between the Byzantine Empire and the Latin

---

[1] *Assises Cour Bourg.*, ccciii, 225. Notice also that the word here used is *establissemens*, which was used interchangeably with *assise*. As the decree directly effected the bourgeoisie they should also have been consulted in this matter. But I feel that Beugnot goes too far in claiming, as he does in his note to this assise, that the bourgeoisie had a share in legislation and and the illegality was due to their not being consulted. The lack of validity of the assise is due to the failure to submit it to the *Haute Cour*. Jerusalem recognized the same theory as the West that persons directly affected by any act should be consulted in the ordaining thereof, but the definite acceptance of the measure was in the hands of the barons of the court.

Grandclaude, *op. cit.*, pp. 10–25, studies the types of law and the participation of the various classes in the making thereof.

[2] Ibelin, vii, 30. Later tradition attributed to Amaury II the legislative work of Amaury I. Novare, xlvii, 521–23, tells how Amaury II employed Ralph of Tiberias to rewrite the old laws, but that the codification did not take place due to the quarrel between the king and Ralph. Amaury II wished the old laws, which were lost with the fall of Jerusalem, to be rewritten and preserved and none would have been better suited to this task than the veteran jurisconsult who became the master of Novare. See Grandclaude, p. 101–02; and Beugnot, Introduction to the *Assises*, ii, 10–11.

William of Tyre, XIX, ii, 884, gives a picture of Amaury I: *'in jure consuetudinario, quo regebatur regnum, subtilis plurimum, et nulli secondus'*. Baldwin III was also devoted to the study of law and William says of him (XVI, ii, 706): *'Juris etiam consuetudinarii, quo regnum regebatur Orientale, plenam habens experientiam; ita ut in rebus dubiis, etiam seniores regni principes eius consulterent experientiam, et consulti pectoris eruditionem mirarentur'*.

states, had its own law, which while based essentially on the Byzantine Syro-Roman law showed influence of the practices of the Frankish states.[1] When Hugh de Brienne appealed to the French law he was met with the answer: '*ne requiers je riens par l'usage de France, mais par l'usage de ce royaume le requiers je; ne en ce royaume n'est il pas l'usage tel comvous dites qu'il en est en France, ains est tout le contraire*'.[2] And when Frederick II claimed the regency by the law of the Empire he was informed that the courts of Acre and Nicosia were the final authorities respectively in Jerusalem or Cyprus.[3]

Not French, not Imperial (Lombard), not Roman (for in the whole treatise of Ibelin there is but one reference to the Justinian code: '*el code de l'empereor Justinien qui est un des meillors livres de leis des empereors que il firent ancienement*'),[4] the laws of Jerusalem were the product of the country, the men who inhabited it, and the conditions under which they lived. The law was based on custom as they·remembered it, and was modified to meet the needs of their situations as seemed best to the leaders assembled in the *Haute Cour*.[5]

The *Haute Cour*, as the chief law court of the kingdom, administered, interpreted, and enforced this law. Its jurisdiction covered

[1] *Assises d'Antioche*, Armenian text with French translation (Venice: *Société Mekhithariste*, 1876).

The Armenian code is to be found in the edition of J. Karst, *Sempadscher Kodex oder Mittelarmenisches Rechtsbuch* (2 vols: Strassburg: Trübner, 1905). The basis of the Armenian code was in the Byzantine law and the old Syro-Roman code, but, in law as in institutions, Armenia copied somewhat from her southern neighbors.

[2] *Assises*, ii, 406.

[3] *Gestes*, par. 127. Albert Aix quotes Baldwin I that '*gentilium decreta et nostra non conveniant*'. (Albert, XI, xxii, 673.)

[4] Ibelin, cxcii, 309.

[5] In closing this discussion of the law it must be pointed out that the above statements refer only to the law as administered by the High Court,—the law of the nobility, essentially the law of the fief. Beugnot, in the Introduction to volume 1 of the *Assises* says: '*En Occident le droit commun avait pénétré dans le droit féodal et modifié, conformément à ses règles particulière·, les usages de la féodalité, tandis qu'en Orient le fief continuait d'être la source unique de toutes les relations sociales des nobles entre eux*'. (p. 63.)

The *Assises de la Cour des Bourgeois* include, however, much that is derived from the Roman law. The chapters of the *Assises* which are written in Latin and are taken from the Roman law are believed by Beugnot, with sufficient grounds, to have been the work of a later interpolator; but the Old French text contains many principles derived from the Roman law.

a noble in every phase of his life except the three aspects of religion, marriage, and testament, which were reserved for the church courts, and the relations which he had with his inferiors, which were attended to by the *Cour des Bourgeois*.[1] Certain cases did not need to be brought into the court, but these were all minor affairs and included only '*que le seignor a et tient*', defense against a more distant heir in cases of inheritance, and recovery of a fief '*par l'assise usée de la novele desaisine*'.[2]

The cases which the High Court was competent to hear included murder, rape, assault (*coup apparent*), wardship, debt, recovery of slaves, sales and purchases of fiefs and horses, default of service or homage, inheritance of fief, disseisin (except *novel*), and all the cases of a purely feudal nature. Treason was always tried in the High Court.[3] The court records of the sessions of the High Court of Cyprus have not been preserved and the court of Jerusalem never kept any, for records were only begun under Henry II and Jerusalem practically never was in his possession. But the chroniclers have preserved accounts of some of the more celebrated cases and much light can be thrown on the work of the court from a review of some of these. Probably the most illuminating instance is the case of Frederick II vs. John d'Ibelin of Beirut, in which the emperor illegally disseised Ibelin without trial in court, and in which the king of Cyprus and the barons of both realms supported Ibelin, alleging that it was one of the fundamental laws of the kingdom that no free man could be disseised of his fief except by judgment of his peers.[4] The action of the barons in this case was wholly in accord with the law. If a liegeman wrongs the king, the king may punish the man

---

This is easily explained by the fact that the Franks took over, from the law in use in the country, rules applicable to the lower classes; and these rules were based on the Roman law as found in the old Syro-Roman law book which had been used throughout Syria since the Roman times and which had become the custom law of the Syrians. The Franks took over what to them was the custom of the people,—and that custom was Roman law. (See Beugnot, Introduction to *Assises*, ii, 36 ff.)

[1] *Clef des Assises*, ix, 579. Hayek, pp. 72–74, gives an excellent discussion of the competence of the High Court.

[2] Ibelin, ccxlviii, 396.

[3] Ibelin, lxxx, 128–29. See Appendix on Law of Treason.

[4] See above chapter 3.

but only through the court. '*Ne peut il* (le roi) *mie metre jà main sur son home lige sans esgart de ces pers*', says the old *Livre au Roi*.[1] The king should summon the court and the man should be tried; if guilty his peers surrender him to the king's mercy. But if the king seizes him without the verdict of the court, he is considered to have committed the first wrong and the vassal has redress against him. This redress takes the form of refusal of service or, if the case be severe, revolt on the part of the other vassals of the king. John d'Ibelin of Jaffa, with his uncle's and his own experience in mind, sets down the law that if the lord seizes his vassal and imprisons him '*sanz connaissance de sa court*' the fellow vassals shall demand his release. If the lord refuses they shall release him by force, though if the lord intervenes in person violence may not be used against him. In this case they shall refuse all service until their peer has been released and given fair trial in the court. The same holds good if a man's fief is seized, in which case the barons shall continue their opposition until the fief is restored.[2]

Refusal of service and revolt were also legal if the lord refused to hear the plea of a liegeman in his court, or refused to abide by and render justice according to the decision of the court; also if the lord did not pay the vassal what was owing to him and the court decided in favor of the vassal.[3]

Among the cases reported by the chroniclers in which the vassals opposed the king when he acted without the consent of the court is that of the imprisonment of Amaury de Lusignan by Henry of Champagne, when the barons demanded and secured his release.[4] When Amaury II disseised Ralph of Tiberias without the trial by his peers, the lord of Beirut and the other vassals refused all service and forced the restoration of Ralph.[5] In these cases the barons used the agency of the court to protect their peers and themselves against the attacks of the monarch. Trial by peers was ingrained in the ideals and practices of the Outremer baronage. Through the

[1] *Livre au Roi*, xxv, 623–24.

[2] Ibelin, cci–ccii, 323–24; Jacques d'Ibelin, viii, 457; Geoffrey le Tort, xxx, 442.

[3] Ibelin, cciii, 325; Geoffrey le Tort, xxx, 442.

[4] *Eracles*, p. 208; the prince submitted and the revolt was not resorted to.

[5] Ibelin, cciv, 327–28, cites the case of Ralph of Tiberias to prove the law.

weapon of the High Court they protected themselves in what they considered to be their rights, and in the court they banded together to oppose any infringement of their rights. Thus it was that in the High Court of Nicosia the barons, lead by James d'Ibelin, refused the military service in Syria which Hugh III demanded from them,— which debate was heard by Edward Longshanks who was then crusading in the East.[1]

To summarize then, the High Court, including and representing the feudal baronage, controlled the policy of the king and the direction of the affairs of state; it interpreted the old laws and, albeit unconsciously, made new ones; and finally it defended its members against any attack upon, or diminution of, their rights. In so doing it preserved in its purest form the feudal system of the eleventh century; and at the same time so weakened the state by preventing the development of a strong monarchy that the state could not survive the constant pressure which was exerted upon it by the stronger Moslem states to the south and east.

All that has been said of the *Haute Cour* of the kingdom applies equally to the courts baron of the great vassals. Ibelin lists twenty-two seignories which had courts baron in the 1180–90's, just before the fall of Jerusalem.[2] These were, so far as can be determined, in personnel and function replicas of the *Haute Cour* and had similar competence over local matters.

The non-noble members of society had their own courts, a discussion of which will be found in the following chapter.

[1] *Assises*, ii, 427–34; *Eracles*, pp. 462–64.
[2] Ibelin, cclxx, 419–21.

CHAPTER 5
THE LESSER COURTS

THE *Haute Cour* was the judicial organ of the feudal nobility. But while they were the governing class, the nobility were by no means the greater part of the population of the kingdom, and below the High Court spread a network of courts for non-nobles. *'Le duc Godefroi establi deus cours seculiers, l'une la Haute Court, de quoi il fu gouverneor et justisier; et l'autré la Court de la Borgesie'.*[1] The *Haute Cour* and the *Cour des Bourgeois* are often referred to as the High and Low courts, but this is confusing, and it should be constantly borne in mind that this distinction is proper only in the sense that they ministered to the needs of the upper and lower classes of society, and should never be taken to mean that the High Court had any appellate position over the Low. Both courts were sovereign within their own spheres and there was no appeal from the one to the other, *'En nostre court'*, says Philip de Novare, *'n'a point d'apeau'.*[2]

The dominating principle of Outremer jurisprudence was that of judgment by one's peers, and the two courts High and Low were created to adapt this principle to the two main classes of society. For

---

[1] Ibelin, ii, 23. The material contained in this chapter is very largely a review of more exhaustive treatises on the courts of the Latin kingdom. The most important work on this subject is that of D. Hayek, *Le Droit Franc en Syrie* (Paris: Spes, 1925). The introductions to Beugnot's edition of the *Assises de Jérusalem* are comprehensive but in part sadly out of date. Dodu has a fair chapter on the courts and Grandclaude contains some considerable material. Prutz, *Kulturgeschichte*, book III, chapter iii, pp. 213-32, discusses the laws and court system; and there are several other scattered and detailed studies and monographs on special points. The sources are all derived from the *Assises de Jérusalem*. As so much has already been done on this subject we have given it a more cursory treatment than less studied fields.

[2] Novare, lxvi, 537. There never developed in Jerusalem intermediate courts or appellate courts such as those of the justiciars in Calabria or the eyre courts in England. The lord's *Cour des Bourgeois* did not become the king's by the presence of the royal viscount, as the county court in England became the royal court by the presence of the king's justiciar. The royal vicecomital courts were located in the domain fiefs, and the lower courts on fiefs held by vassals belonged to the justice of the fief and were in no way under the royal control. The court system of Jerusalem resembled most closely that of France before Philip Augustus. In the principality of Achaia appeal could be made from the lord's court to the prince's, and from the prince's to the emperor's. (*Assises de Romanie*, art. 143.) Not so in Jerusalem.

the classes inferior to these,—for the native Syrians,—special native courts were created under their own native judges. Slaves had no legal position and were considered as chattels and judged in the court of their owner,—usually the High Court.

The High Court has already been discussed in our preceding chapter and we have seen that its jurisdiction included all nobles and all matters pertaining to noble tenure, and that it was the regular court for all cases civil or criminal which concerned knights.

The *Cour des Bourgeois* had the same competence for the free non-noble Frankish citizenry. It included within its jurisdiction all cases which were essentially concerned with the Frankish bourgeoisie. In criminal matters it included murder, treason, theft, rape, and assault, as well as the less serious petty offenses. It was the highest criminal court for the non-noble population, and in its jurisdiction over crimes involving life and limb, it took over the higher jurisdiction from the lesser courts of the *Fonde, Chaine,* and the native courts. Trial by battle was a legal form of proof in the *Cour des Bourgeois* as well as in the High Court.[1] Cases between noble and bourgeois were heard in the lower court, in accordance with the general rule that mixed cases were to be heard in the court of the inferior party.

The presiding officer in the *Cour des Bourgeois* was the viscount chosen by the lord who controlled the court from among his liegemen; he was merely the president of the court and had no part in its judgments, though he carried them out once they had been made. As head of the constabulary, he arrested malefactors and commanded the night watch. His chief lieutenant was the master sergeant, known by the Arabic title of *mathesep*, originally an inspector of markets, weights and measures, and later the assistant to the viscount. The viscount and *mathesep* each commanded a corps of sergeants who acted as police as well as performing various duties around the court.[2]

---

[1] *Assises Cour Bourg.,* xxiii, 32, list the pleas which may be heard in the court. *Ibid.,* ccxliv–cccii, 183–226, give the penal code. The special courts of *Fonde* and *Chaine* had, as will be seen, very limited jurisdiction, and referred their major cases to the vicecomital court.

[2] For the viscount see p. 135, Hayek, pp. 92–93, contends that the viscount need not be a noble, in spite of the definite statement to that effect in the *Abrégé;* but he is unable to cite any cases where the viscount was non-noble. It was only under Henry II of Cyprus that the state began to prosecute criminals.

The most important members of the *Cour des Bourgeois* were the jurors. They were twelve in number and were appointed by the lord of the court from among his freeborn Catholic Latin bourgeoisie. They had a threefold duty: as judges they decided on the verdict of the court and assigned the proof to be made (i.e., battle, oath, ordeal, etc.); as counsel they were required to give advice and to assist the litigants. Each litigant was allowed to demand counsel at the opening of the trial and one of the jurors was assigned to him to act as his counsel. When they acted as counsel, they could not of course participate in the verdict. Lastly the jurors were witnesses to any charters, grants, deeds of sale, and the like which were made in the court.[1]

The *Cour des Bourgeois*, like the *Haute Cour*, was a court of record as well as of law, and for this purpose there were attached to it from the earliest times scribes (*écrivains*) who kept the records of the court. At first these records were merely calendars of grants and charters witnessed in the court, but after 1250 they were expanded into real registers of the transactions of the court.[2]

The *Cour des Bourgeois* met every Monday, Wednesday, and Friday, except on saints days, at a fixed time and place, unlike the High Court which met at call and very irregularly.[3]

In Cyprus there was but one High Court and one *Cour des Bourgeois*, but in the principality of Jerusalem, courts of both kinds were granted to the barons who held '*court et coins et justice*'. Ibelin lists twenty-two lords who held courts baron, besides the king, and thirty-three *cours des bourgeois*, besides the four belonging to the king at Jerusalem, Neapolis, Acre, and Daron.[4]

The lords' courts were exact replicas of the king's courts, except that the lord presided over his high court and appointed the viscount

---

[1] *Abrégé Cour Bourg.*, ii, 236–37; Hayek, pp. 93–105.

[2] *Abrégé*, xiii–xviii, 246–50, tells of the creation of the registers. While none of these records have been preserved, charters with the signatures of the jurors are extant. D. L. *Cartulaire*, doc. 1996, certifies the sale in the *Haute Cour* of a fief to the Hospital and carries the names of the witnesses. Mas Latrie, iii, 677 note 2, gives a charter from the vicecomital court of Acre, on which the twelve jurors witness a sale to the Teutonic Knights.

[3] *Abrégé Cour Bourg.*, vii, 239.

[4] Ibelin, cclxx, 419–21. The *Livre au Roi*, xxxix, 634, lists only twelve barons as having what was termed in the West 'high justice', but implies that there might be others. Ibelin's list gives the situation as of the reign of Baldwin IV–V around 1180–90. For Cyprus see *Bans et Ordonnances*, xxviii, 371.

for his lower. If the king came to the meeting of the baron's court it became for that session the High Court of the realm, though this was not true of the lower courts. Jerusalem never developed the fictitous parage of the royal justiciar who was in law the peer of every subject of the king.

The native Syrian population were governed in the earlier years of the kingdom by their own courts and under their own laws.[1] These courts, composed of native jurors under the presidency of a native *reis*, who corresponded to the viscount, had competence over minor cases which on the criminal side did not involve life or limb, and on the civil side did not exceed the value of one mark silver. They were of small importance as they were soon absorbed by the courts of the *Fonde* in the cities and remained only in the rural villages and casales.

The *Cour de la Fonde* was a court especially created to deal with commercial cases in the market towns and from this function derived its name. Through the circumstance that the great bulk of its cases were those of the natives, it soon extended its sphere of activity and included the native courts in the towns where it was situated. It was composed of a bailli and six jurors, two Frank and four native, appointed by the lord of the town. Its competence included commercial suits, civil suits of merchants, and minor cases between natives. The law followed was that of the *Cour des Bourgeois* and major cases were sent up to that tribunal. It was also a court of record and bureau of registry for sales, other than land, and other commercial transactions, and also an office for the collection of the sales and purchase taxes.[2] That each religion was to take oath on its

---

[1] Ibelin, iv, 26, says clearly that they were under their own laws and their own judges: '*que il fucent menés par l'usage des Suriens . . . selonc lor usages*'. Beugnot, *Assises*, ii, Introduction, p. 24, accepts this at its face value and grants the free use of native law. Dodu believes that while native custom law was used at first it was later abandoned. Hayek, pp. 128–29, and Rey, *Colonies Franques*, p. 78, claim that they were governed throughout by the law of the *Cour des Bourgeois*. As the bourgeois law was derived largely from native law, this may very possibly have been the case. Hayek's thesis is weakened by his admitted prejudice, for he writes '*comme libanais et comme chrétien*' (p. 7), and concludes his work with the pious wish that Syria may once again come completely under French law. (p. 157).

[2] *Assises Cour Bourg.*, ccxli, 171–73 (ccxlii–liii, 173–81, lists the tariffs on various goods). Hayek, p. 132, claims that the *Fonde* developed from the native courts by adding the Frankish jurors and replacing the native *reis* by the bailli.

own holy book in the court of the *Fonde* was perhaps a relic of the earlier custom of trying each people under their own laws.

A special court for naval and maritime cases was organized in the larger port towns. Known as the *Cour de la Chaine* from the chain which closed the entrances to harbors in the Middle Ages, this court had special jurisdiction over cases arising from shipping, shipwreck, and maritime business. It was also a registry office and customs house where the anchorage tax and the customs duties were paid. It consisted of a bailli and jurors who were drawn from the sailors and merchants, thus adhering to the rule of trial by peers. It had no criminal jurisdiction and its civil was limited to suits under the value of a mark silver. More important cases were sent to the *Cour des Bourgeois*, but the *Chaine* held preliminary hearings on major maritime cases before they were sent to the bourgeois court.[1]

In none of these inferior courts was trial by battle permitted and all of them sent their more serious cases to the *Cour des Bourgeois*. The state had, in the time of the kingdom of Jerusalem, not yet taken upon itself the rôle of prosecutor, and unless a plea was introduced by the victim, or an accredited relative or associate, no action was taken by the court. The court would summon the defendant in both criminal and civil cases but would not arrest a criminal against whom no plea was lodged.[2]

In addition to the courts of the kingdom considered above were the courts of the Church and the foreign consulates, which acted in special and restricted spheres, totally apart from the regular courts. Of the church courts little need be said here; like the ecclesiastical courts throughout the Christian world, they operated under the rules of the canon law. Their competence included all clerics, and under this head came the members of the various religious Orders—the Templars, the Hospitallers *et al.*—as well as the regular and secular

---

[1] *Assises Cour Bourg.*, xliii–xlix, 42–47. Though the exact date of the founding of this court is not known, I agree with Beugnot, Rey, and Hayek, in attributing it to the reign of Amaury I whose activity in maritime legislation is attested by the code of maritime law which bears his name. The oldest charter mentioning it is from 1188 when Conrad granted the Pisans the revenues from the *Chaine* of Acre. (Müller, p. 33; *Regesta*, doc. 674.)

[2] Ibelin, lxxxii, 130–31, lists those who may bring a plea on behalf of the victim of a murder. Under Henry II the viscounts were authorized to arrest criminals and public prosecution began, but this was after the loss of Jerusalem and was effective only in Cyprus.

clergy and the friars. They had jurisdiction over church property and over all those cases between laymen which were associated with the sacraments of the Church. The *Assises* set aside as belonging to the church courts all matters relating to the Catholic faith, marriage, and testament.[1] The Church extended its rights to the furthest limits, and claimed the right to judge all relations between man and wife on the basis of its acknowledged authority over the sacrament of marriage. It also handled all cases of bastardy and legitimation. As the church courts could not impose a sentence which would result in the loss of life or limb, they were forced to work at times with the secular courts. In cases of disputes between clerics and laity, the viscount and jurors of the *Cour des Bourgeois* would go to the church court and assist in the verdict.[2]

The last group of courts to be considered in the discussion of the judicial system in the crusading states is that of the consular courts of the Italian and Provençal cities. These courts were established by special grants to the colonies of Italians resident in the Levantine towns, or to the communes of Venice, Pisa, and Genoa themselves. Similar courts were established in the Byzantine Empire under the Comneni. The earliest grant of extraterritorial jurisdiction in the kingdom of Jerusalem is found in that treaty drawn up between the doge of Venice and the barons of Jerusalem in 1123.[3] This privilege was extended to Antioch by the grant of Renaud and Constance in 1153.[4] The Genoese got their first court, in 1187, by a treaty with the barons of Jerusalem, and, in 1189, Bohemond III granted them

---

[1] *Clef des Assises*, ix, 579. And see below under Church relations. William Tyre, XX, xxx, 998–99, records the refusal of the Templars to answer in the king's court for the murder of the emmissaries of the Assassins and their insistence that they were subject only to the canon law and their own courts.

The *Assises de Romanie*, art. 149, provided that questions of validity of testament should be heard in the church court, but if it concerned the false testimony of a witness it should be heard in the lay court. The enforcement of the provisions of a testament from an unwilling executor would have to be done in the church court.

[2] *Abrégé Cour Bourg.*, lxxii, 292; Hayek, pp. 150–55.

[3] Tafel-Thomas, i, 84–89; William Tyre, XII, xxv, 550–53; *Regesta*, doc. 102; and see below chapter on Italian communes.

[4] Tafel-Thomas, i, 133–35; *Regesta*, doc. 282. Raymond had in 1140 promised the Venetians speedy justice in his own courts (Tafel-Thomas, i, 102–03; *Regesta*, doc. 197).

courts in Antioch and Laodicea.[1] Pisa received its first court in 1156 by the grant of Baldwin III.[2]

These courts had ordinary jurisdiction over all cases arising between members of their own communes; in cases of disputes arising between members of different communes or between an Italian and a Frank, the case was heard in the court of the defendant. But capital crimes were at all times reserved for the royal courts or the court of the lord of the town.

In addition to this extraterritorial jurisdiction over all members of their own communes the Italian corporation had control over the districts in the cities which had been granted them, with the right to hear cases of all people living in their quarter. Later the lords recalled this right in part and excepted liegemen or holders of bourgeois tenements from the jurisdiction of the foreign court.[3]

So much for a sketch of the court system of the kingdom of Jerusalem. With the exception of the consular and church courts, all the courts applied the law of the kingdom as it is found in the works of the jurisconsults and the *Assises*. This law, as has been said, was, for the lower courts, a combination of principles from the Roman and feudal laws and was current custom. In matters of procedure the courts of Outremer followed the usual practice of calling upon some form of the *Iudicium Dei*, especially the judicial combat which was required for major crimes, or of accepting the oaths of the litigants. In 1140 Usamah witnessed a combat and also a trial by ordeal of water in the bourgeois court of Neapolis.[4] Charters were

---

[1] *Liber Jurium*, i, doc. 363; *Regesta*, doc. 659; Röhricht, 'Amalrich I', *Mitteilungen des Instituts für Oesterreichische Geschichtsforschung*, xii (1891), p. 488; *Regesta*, doc. 680.

[2] In Tyre; Müller, pp. 6–7; *Regesta*, doc. 322. Courts were granted in Acre in 1168 and in Tripoli in 1187: Müller, pp. 14, 25–26; *Regesta*, docs. 449, 662. See Appendix for lists of grants to commercial communes.

[3] Tafel-Thomas, ii, 351–89, 389–98; *Regesta*, docs. 1114, 1116. Tafel-Thomas, iii, 150–195; *Regesta*, doc. 1413; Heyd, i, 322; Hayek, pp. 144–49.

[4] Usamah (ed. Hitti), pp. 167–69. Ibelin, lxxxi, 129, gives the cases which must be decided by battle in the *Haute Cour*. The ordeal was used in the *Cour des Bourgeois* but not in the *Haute Cour*. But even where it was used it could not be forced on the litigants. (*Assises Cour Bourg.*, ccxlvii, 202.) No attempt is made in this study to discuss the court procedure; the treatises of Ibelin and Novare are manuels of procedure and deal with every phase of it, and it has already been studied in special works.

invalid as proofs unless supported by the witnesses. *'Nule chartre ne vaut riens sans guarens'* says the *Assises de la Cour des Bourgeois.*[1]

The *counsel*, which was a necessary part of trials in the High Court and ordinarily used in the bourgeois, was a peculiarity of the Outremer law. The litigant would demand counsel at the opening of the case and the lord would appoint some member of the court to act in that capacity. The liegeman who refused to act as counsel when appointed forfeited his court-right and his fief. It was the duty of the counsel to advise and assist the litigant through the mazes of the legal formulae, and to assist him or say for him the exact words in which charges had to be brought or refuted. The procedure was extremely ritualistic and, as in the West, failure to use the exact words of the oath caused loss of the case. To prevent this the eastern courts allowed what was termed *retenail*. The counsel requested at the beginning of the hearing that the case be heard subject to *retenail*, and Novare warns anyone against attempting to carry the case through without this precaution.[2] *Retenail* gave the right to say again the formula if a mistake was made the first time. Once the verdict of the court had been given there was no appeal to a higher court, nor beyond *retenail* could there be a new trial. In the *Haute Cour* the dissatisfied litigant could always attempt to prove the court guilty of false judgment, *'la court fausser'*, but this was a rather strenuous method and was seldom resorted to, for it entailed challenging each member of the court to single combat and defeating them all within a single day. Ibelin says that the court should assemble at one end of the field and ride forth one by one to the battle. Further, the court does not mean the group of men who gave the verdict but the entire membership of the court, for in questioning the truth of the verdict the accuser throws doubt upon the honor of the court and every member thereof. If the challenger failed to conquer the entire court

---

[1] *Assises Cour Bourg.*, cxlvi, 100.

[2] Novare, lxvi, 537. Ibelin, xv–xxi, 40–46, tells under what circumstances a man shall plead and also those occasions when he may not, as against his lord or his vassal. (Though if the court ordered he had to plead against his vassal.)

in a single day he was to be hanged at sundown.[1] And even this was allowed only in the *Haute Cour*, in the *Cour des Bourgeois* the verdict once given was irrevocable.

[1] Ibelin, cx, 179–182; lxxxvii, 560–62. But if the challenger accuses a single member of the court and not the whole court he need fight that member only, for he has not thrown discredit upon the court. Or he may accuse several members individually, and so long as he says that the individual was false, and does not mention the court, he will have only to fight the individuals directly mentioned and personally insulted. At sundown all those who had been defeated were hanged.

In the *Cour des Bourgeois* there was no such battle allowed. Since battle between nobles and non-nobles was forbidden the bourgeoisie could not have defended themselves had a noble chosen to defy them. Novare says that in the *Cour des Bourgeois* anyone who declared the court false should have his head cut off incontinent: '*et le gringor merci que le seignor en puist aver, selon ceste assise, si est de faire coper la lengue*', which would indicate that the beheading of obstreperous nobles was not always possible, and that a milder course was easier to follow. Further, if the accuser recanted his charge of dishonesty and admitted the honor and integrity of the court, he could save his head or his tongue, but would lose the case in which he was at law, and also lose his court-right for a year and a day.

CHAPTER 6

THE GRAND OFFICERS AND THE CHANCERY

IN REFERRING to the personnel of the *Haute Cour*, mention has been made of the grand officers of the realm; some consideration of them in comparison with their western counterparts necessarily belongs in a study of the monarchical institutions of Jerusalem. The grand officers, especially the chancellor, are a fair indication of the character of the monarchy; the more centralized states had more elaborate bureaucracies while in the more loosely knit countries the older system of household officials sufficed to carry on the central administration.

Jerusalem most closely resembles the France of the early Capetians from the point of view of grand officers. There can be little doubt but that the grand officers of Outremer were derived from those of France under Philip I. The seneschal, constable, marshal, chamberlain, and chancellor are found at both courts; there is no mention in Jerusalem of the justiciar, so important in the Norman states, and the logothete, who assumed such great prominence in Sicily, is in Jerusalem merely a subordinate clerk. It is in the use of such lesser officials as the turcopler, admiral, dragomen, and viscounts of the ports that the most noticeable differences between eastern and western practices are to be found, and it is of these that we know the least.[1]

---

[1] For the study of grand officers in general see: A. Luchaire, *Histoire des Institutions Monarchiques de la France* (2nd ed.: Paris, 1891), i, 163–206; and a shorter account in Luchaire's *Manuel des Institutions Françaises* (Paris, 1892), pp. 518–556; C. H. Haskins, *Norman Institutions* (Cambridge, Mass.: Harvard, 1918); L. Halphen, *Le Comté d'Anjou au XIe Siècle* (Paris: Picard, 1906), pp. 98–112; J. Chartrou, *L'Anjou de 1109 à 1151* (Paris: Presses Uniersitaires, 1928), pp. 107–162; J. H. Round, *The King's Serjeants and Officers of State* (London, 1911); T. F. Tout, *Chapters in the Administrative History of Medieval England* (Manchester: Manchester University Press, 1920); L. W. Vernon-Harcourt, *His Grace the Steward and Trial of Peers* (London: Longmans, 1907); J. L. A. Huillard-Bréholles, *Historia Diplomatica Friderici Secundi* (Paris, 1852–61), xii, Introduction; F. Chalandon, *Histoire de la Domination Normande en Italie et en Sicile* (Paris, 1907), vol. ii; L. Cadier, *Essai sur l'Administration du Royaume de Sicile sous Charles I et Charles II d'Anjou* (*Écoles Françaises d'Athènes et de Rome*: Paris, 1891), pp. 168–277.

Furthermore, the eastern officers did not undergo the same changes in character that their western counterparts suffered. True, in Cyprus the grand officers developed somewhat and new officials found their way into the heirarchy, but in Jerusalem and throughout the twelfth and thirteenth centuries the grand officers continued to be very much what they had been at the time of the founding of the kingdom. The chancellor, for example, always remained the royal secretary and never developed that judicial and writ-issuing power which enhanced the position of this functionary in the West.

Before we consider the individual dignitaries a few fundamental differences between East and West should be indicated. In the East the offices were seldom hereditary and there are few cases of the position passing from father to son. The Ibelins did, it is true, hold nearly all the grand offices of Cyprus and Jerusalem, but the offices were not hereditary and, while each generation of Ibelins held posts, the son seldom occupied the position which his father had held. The grand offices were held for the duration of the reign and a regent could, and often did, appoint his own set of officers.[1] Another difference is that in the East the grand offices did not become titular as they did in the West; the general tendency in the West was for the offices to pass into the hands of some great baronial family and thereafter become purely titular, a minor official performing all the duties of the office save those of a purely ceremonial nature. The counts of Champagne became hereditary seneschals of France, the Bohun earls of Hereford hereditary constables of England, and the Bigods and Howards held the English marshalship; as the offices passed into these families they tended to become more purely titular and honorary. In Jerusalem this was not the case and the grand offices remained always a species of royal patronage.

Further, the grand offices of Jerusalem were normally filled from among the lords of the *principality* of Jerusalem and never from the counts of the great semi-independent states. No prince of Antioch or count of Edessa or Tripoli ever held any grand office in the kingdom.

[1] Thus Alice of Cyprus revoked the appointments made by Frederick II and appointed her own officers. (*Assises*, ii, 400.) Earlier, Henry of Champagne demanded that Amaury de Lusignan give up the constableship of Jerusalem to which he had been appointed by Baldwin IV. (*Eracles*, pp. 202–03, variant reading; and in Mas Latrie, iii, 595–96.)

Joscelin III de Courtney was seneschal, but it was under Baldwin IV and only after the loss of the county of Edessa when his lands were confined to Jerusalem.

The great counties, the patriarchate, and the Orders all had their own sets of officers, and even some of the larger seignories in the principality of Jerusalem, such as Jaffa and Galilee, had theirs. Lists of the more important officers can be found in the appendix of this work.

The seneschal was, in theory at least, in the East as in France, the first of the grand officers. In France the seneschal certainly occupied the most important post; its holders became so powerful that Philip Augustus thought fit to suppress the office completely. In England, under the title of Lord High Steward, the seneschal rose from a more menial rank to considerable power under the Angevins, and in the fourteenth century presided over the Peers' Court. One of the first officers to develop in Anjou, the seneschal had considerable power in that county, whence the prestige of the office spread to England and Normandy. In Norman Sicily, under Frederick II, the seneschal was unimportant; and under Charles of Anjou he was merely the official in charge of the accounts of the hôtel of the prince.[1]

In Jerusalem the powers of the seneschalship were akin to those of the French dapiferate before its great increase of power.[2] The seneschal was the master of ceremonies and carried the sceptre on the coronation day; at the feast after the coronation he served the king, and performed the same services at the four great festivals of the year when the king appeared in all his regalia. The seneschal had charge of all the baillies and clerks of the royal treasury, except those of the household, who were under the chamberlain, and they were responsible to him. He was essentially a financial administrator and presided over the *Secrète*, ordering all payments made therefrom,

---

[1] Vernon-Harcourt, *op. cit.*; Round, *King's Serjeants*, pp. 68–76; W. Walker, *Royal Power in France under Philip Augustus* (Leipsic, 1888); J. W. Thompson, *Development of the French Monarchy under Louis VI le Gros* (Chicago, 1895); P. Durrieu, *Les Archives Angevines de Naples* (*Écoles Françaises d'Athénes et de Rome*: Paris, 1886–87), i, 39; Huillard-Bréholles, *op. cit.*, xii, 137.

While in France the seneschal developed his powers in the twelfth century, in England it was only in the thirteenth and fourteenth centuries that he became of major importance.

[2] Ibelin, cclvi, 407–09; vii, 29–31; Dodu, pp. 156–57.

farming out the rents, receiving the returns of the tax farmers and of the baillies, and controlling the employment and dismissal of treasury baillies and clerks.

The seneschal had general supervision of all fortresses and castles and could transfer the garrisons from one castle to another, though he had no power over the governors of the castles and the king's orders were always superior to those of the seneschal.

In the court the seneschal could hear pleas, save those which concerned the life, fief, or honor of the pleader, at times when the king or his regular representative was not present; if the case had been begun before the king and left unfinished, no matter what the subject, the seneschal was empowered to sit on it. He could convene the High Court and preside over it.[1] Thus in matters judicial the seneschal was the *alter ego* of the king, and he occupied the same rôle in military affairs, attending the king in battle or, in the absence of the king or his official representative, taking his place in the battle array and commanding the king's company. And when the battle had been won, the seneschal received the king's share of the spoils and guarded it.[2]

As the king's personal representative the seneschal was easily the first of the grand officers in dignity of rank, but in actual power the dapiferate was surpassed by the constableship. However, some of the seneschals of Jerusalem were men of outstanding ability; Hugh de St Omer, Miles de Plancy, Joscelin de Courtney, Ralph of Tiberias, Geoffrey de Sargines, John de Grailly, and Philip d'Ibelin were all important seneschals in the twelfth and thirteenth centuries.

Contrary to the western practice, where the constable was merely a military officer (and only developed into prominence after the suppression of the dapiferate in France), the constable of Jerusalem was the chief officer of the kingdom.[3] In a state which was per-

---

[1] *Assises*, i, 3; this was at least true by the fourteenth century in Cyprus, for Philip d'Ibelin, seneschal of Jerusalem, convened the court in the absence of the seneschal of Cyprus.

[2] Ibelin, cclvi, 407–09.

[3] In Sicily and in England the constable was always a military officer as in early eleventh century France. An interesting parallel to the importance of the constable in Jerusalem is to be found in the office of the *staller* in the court of the Norwegian kings. This officer, who seems to be most closely related to the constable of any of the officers, was the chief official

manently at war, as was the kingdom of Jerusalem, the constable as head of the army easily surpassed the seneschal in influence. In the coronation ceremony, the constable carried the royal banner before the king in the procession to and from the church, and held the king's horse when he mounted and dismounted. For this service he received the king's horse.[1]

In military matters, the constable had charge of the disposition of troops in battle unless the king or his bailli explicitly ordered the array; if the king or bailli was not present in person in the battle the constable had supreme command and had all the powers of the king, save that he might not strike a liegeman but only kill his horse under him. When the king was present the constable commanded a picked troop, having the choice of men after the king's own company had been made up. The *Livre au Roi* specifies that the constable's should be a double troop and that it should hold the first position in the battle after the turcoples.

On campaigns the constable was the military judge and could settle all cases, whether of knights or of bourgeoisie. The *sodeers* (mercenaries) were his particular charge and he settled all cases of claims for pay, whether the claimant was a knight, sergeant, or squire. The *sodeer* demanded his pay from the constable who then collected it from the lord by whom it was owed. If the debtor had no money the constable could seize and sell his goods to obtain the amount owed. In case the lord denied the debt, the matter was taken before the court and the burden of proof was on the lord, who had to prove that he did not owe the debt claimed.[2] The constable represented the *sodeers* in cases before the court and saw that justice was done them. This gave him a judicial position, and the constable had the power, when the king or bailli was not present, to

---

in the Norweigan service in the eleventh century. (L. M. Larson, 'The Household of the Nor-wegian Kings', *A. H. R.*, xiii (1908), 474–78.)

In Armenia the title of constable was adapted to the old *sbaçalar (stratelates)* who com-manded the army and had the first position in court ceremonies. (E. Dulaurier, 'Étude sur l'Organization Politique, Religieuse et Administrative du Royaume de la Petite Arménie', *Journal Asiatique* (1861), 63–64).

[1] Ibelin, cclvii, 409–11, vii, 29–31; *Livre au Roi*, xiv, 615–16; Dodu, pp. 157, 177–78; give the duties, powers and rights of the constables in Jerusalem.

[2] Ibelin, cxxxiv, 209–10.

demand from each member of the court his opinion, and to preside over the court.[1] The list of constables of Jerusalem contains many of the great names of the Outremer baronage: Eustache Grenier, William de Buris, Humphrey de Toron, Amaury de Lusignan, John d'Ibelin of Beirut, Walter and Eudes de Montbéliard, John and Balian d'Ibelin of Arsur, and others. In the fourteenth century the title was held by several members of the reigning house of Lusignan of Cyprus.

The marshal was everywhere the lieutenant of the constable, and substituted for him when the constable could not appear in person. Always connected in some way with horses, the marshal in France never became considered a grand officer until the sixteenth century. In the Empire and England though the marshal never got entirely away from his connection with oats, hay, and horses' supplies, the office underwent considerable development, and the marshals of the Empire were among the most important officials, being used for important duties, as illustrated by Richard Filanger, Frederick II's imperial marshal who became his legate in the East.[2] In Jerusalem the marshal remained always a military officer and held his office in sergeantry from the constable, owing him liege homage after the king and the lords from whom he held fiefs.[3] At the coronation the marshal accompanied the constable, receiving the royal banner from his hand when the constable assisted the king to mount his

[1] Ibelin, cclvii, 410: 'Et quant cort est ensemble por jugement ou por recort faire ou por conseill ou por avoiement, sanz le rei ou sanz celui qui est en son leuc, il (le conestable) peut et deit demander l'avis de chascun, ou faire le demander au mareschal, ce il viaut; et peut destraindre chascun de dire ou de soi aquiter si come il est usage; et peut comander à retraire l'esgart ou la conoissance ou le recort ou l'aveement que la court a fait, auquel que il vodra de ciaus de la court.'

The *Livre au Roi*, xiv, 615, says: 'Bien sachés que li counestables est tenus d'oyr et d'entendre les clains et les tors que l'un chevaler fait à l'autre, se li rois nel veut oyr et n'est en la terre. Et par devant le counestable deivent estre jugiés et chastiés les mausfais as chevalers, par dreit.'

[2] Round, *King's Sergeants*, pp. 82–98; Huillard-Bréholles, *op. cit.*, xii, 137 ff.; J. Declareuil, *Histoire Générale du Droit Français* (Paris: Sirey, 1925), pp. 461–62.

[3] Ibelin, cclvii, 411: 'Et si (le conestable) *deit aveir l'omage dou mareschau, sauf les rei et les autres persones à qui il est tenus de fei, ce est assaveir de ce dont l'office de la mareschausié est tenus à celui de la conestablie'*.

Ibelin, cclviii, 412–14, and *Livre au Roi*, ix–xv, 612–16, deal with the office of marshal. The rules seem to refer to a single marshal and not to several.

horse. At the feast the marshal held the banner behind the king, and after the celebration was ended and the constable had escorted the king home (receiving therefore the king's horse), the marshal escorted the constable to his house, receiving in turn the horse of the constable.

It was the marshal who was directly in charge of the *sodeers* and who received their oaths. He heard disputes between them save such as were concerned with pay or involved death penalties. The marshal's court was common to almost all countries where the office existed, though the court tended to merge with that of the constable and it was through the control over this court that the French marshals got much of their power at a later period. For each *sodeer*, the marshal in Jerusalem received four besants, except for those of the king's household over whom he had no jurisdiction and for whom he collected nothing. He took down the names of persons guilty of default of service and reported them to the constable, who could either punish them himself or order the marshal to do so. Through the marshal both king and constable issued their orders to the army and he acted as official spokesman.[1]

In battle the marshal carried the royal banner and commanded the troop just preceding the king's own. After the battle, at the order of the constable, he took charge of the distribution of the spoils and made over to the seneschal the king's share thereof. The marshal took charge of all horses captured and employed them in replacing those which had been killed or mutilated in the battle. This replacement of horses was known as *restor* and was one of the most important duties of the marshal. Before the battle the marshal inspected the arms and equipment of the knights and sergeants and ordered the *sodeers* to make necessary repairs on their armor. He then examined all the horses, evaluated, and listed them, thus accepting them for *restor*. If a horse was killed or maimed the owner applied to the marshal who ordered a new horse of equal value to be substituted, or ordered the payment to its owner of its value. That

---

[1] In England the marshal witnessed the expenditures of royal officials and kept tallies of the payments made out of the treasury. He controlled the prison of the Exchequer and King's Bench courts in the later period. (Round, *op. cit.*)

any one who disobeyed the command of the marshal lost his right of *restor* was a factor which greatly contributed to the marshal's power.

Among the marshals of Jerusalem only Eudes de St Amand, Joscelin de Courtney, Hugh Martin, and John de Gibelet were men of any great consequence. While in most countries there were several marshals serving concurrently, in Jerusalem there seems to have been but one marshal at a time, though in Antioch we do find two marshals holding office simultaneously.

The chamberlain was connected in a more personal manner with the king than were any of the other grand officers. In France in the eleventh century he had been an officer of major importance but he quickly sank to a subordinate place and his duties became largely ceremonial and personal. In Jerusalem we find him in charge of the personal finances and household accounts of the king.

On the day of coronation the chamberlain dressed the king for the ceremony and, bearing the royal sword, marched at the head of the procession. At the church he took the crown, sceptre, and other regalia from the other officers and passed them on to the king. At the dinner he served the king's wine,—and received therefore the king's golden cup. When the lieges made homage to the king it was the chamberlain who presided and who dictated the form of the oath which they were to take. As each vassal was bound to give a present to the chamberlain on this occasion, the office was a lucrative one.[1] The office carried with it in Jerusalem a fief of five casales near Acre, and in 1179 John de Bellême, then chamberlain, sold the fief to Joscelin de Courtney for 7500 besants. There is no evidence whether or not any land was subsequently attached to the office.[2]

[1] Ibelin, cclix, 414.

Ibn Djubair (*R. H. C. Or.*, iii), p. 455, reported that the treasurer-chamberlain had charge of all imposts and that all revenues were returned to him. But he refers to Count Raymond of Tripoli as chamberlain under Baldwin IV, which practically destroys any value in his statement. This is a fairly representative statement and shows the inaccuracies of the Arab writers as regards anything concerning the internal history of Jerusalem. They were unfamiliar with the Frankish institutions and confused them hopelessly, so that while the Arabs are invaluable as sources for the external history of the crusading states they are practically worthless for the internal and administrative.

[2] Strehlke, doc. 10, pp. 10–11; *Regesta*, doc. 579. See L. de Mas Latrie, 'Le Fief de la Chamberlaine et les Chambellans de Jérusalem', *B. E. C.*, xliii (1882), 647–52.

Among the chamberlains of Jerusalem but few celebrated names occur, Amaury de Lusignan held the title between 1175 and 1178 before he became constable, and Rohard and Renaud de Caïphas were marshals in the first quarter of the thirteenth century. The name Chamberlain became affixed to descendants of Renaud as a surname, though the office passed out of the hands of the family almost at once.

Concerning the office of butler almost nothing is known in Jerusalem. The *Assises* do not mention it but the signatures of several butlers prove the existence of the office in the kingdom. The duties were probably purely ceremonial as in the West and it never developed to any importance. Eudes de St Amand held the office after having been marshal.[1]

The chancellor, the last of the grand officers, developed but slightly in Jerusalem from the models found in the West in the late eleventh century. At first glance the Jerusalemite chancery seems to be remarkably backward and undeveloped, but, when one considers the chanceries of France, Anjou, the Holy Roman Empire, and even Normandy at the end of the eleventh century, it becomes apparent that the Outremer chancellor had progressed somewhat over the crude practices of the West at the time of the inception of the office in the East. The Jerusalemite chancery may be criticized for not developing further, for, with a foundation almost contemporary in time and under very similar circumstances, the Norman-Sicilian chancery worked out an elaborate organization; but the trend in the crusading states was always rather Capetian than Norman; and the chancery, reflecting the decentralized monarchy, remained merely an office for the issuance of royal charters.

The Jerusalemite chancery none the less compares very well with the chanceries of France, Anjou, or even Normandy, before the the reforms of Henry II in the latter states and of Philip II in France. While the number of documents which have come down to us from Jerusalem is wholly inadequate for a complete and intensive study of the Outremer chancery, the documents we have show many advanced characteristics.

---

[1] See Appendix to this work and Ducange, *Les Familles d'Outremer*, pp. 615–37, for lists of grand officers. Ducange gives some biographical data when possible.

As in the West the chancellor in Jerusalem was always an ecclesiastic, but the connection between the chancery and the royal chapel seems never to have existed as a feature of the Jerusalemite system. In the Empire it became the custom, as the chancellor's duties increased, to have a titular archchancellor and several clerks,—chancellors, protonotaries, and scribes who did the work of the office.[1] In the East, while the chancellorship was connected with some of the most important ecclesiastics of the kingdom, most of the charters which have been preserved were issued by the chancellor himself, though enough examples of the employment of a subchancellor or notary remain to prove that all charters did not necessarily come from the hand of the titular chancellor.[2]

[1] In the Empire the archbishop of Mayence was archchancellor of Germany, and the archbishop of Cologne archchancellor of Italy. Among the important ecclesiastics who held the office of chancellor of Jerusalem may be noted: Ralph, bishop of Bethlehem, chancellor 1146–1174; William, archbishop of Tyre, chancellor 1174–1183; Peter d'Angoulême, bishop of Tripoli, chancellor 1185–1191; Joscius, archbishop of Tyre, chancellor 1192–1200; Simon, archbishop of Tyre, chancellor 1226–27.

The imperial protonotary developed considerable power and possessed his own seal. In Sicily the protonotary also developed and was in charge of a bureau which recorded all privileges and administrative acts. The logothete in Sicily prepared the documents and the chancellor merely affixed the seal, but the logothete was one of the most important officials of the realm and it was he who received ambassadors and acted as the king's spokesman. (Cadier, *Administration de Sicile*, pp. 194–213; Durrieu, *Archives Angevines*, i, 41; Huillard-Bréholles, xii, 131–34.)

[2] A charter of Baldwin II in 1120 was drawn up by Brando '*clericus et cancellarii (regis) consanguineus*', and Paganus, the chancellor, signed among the witnesses. (H. F. Delaborde, *Chartes de Terre Sainte*, doc. 8; *Regesta*, doc. 90.) This Paganus was chancellor 1115–1128 and appears on charters throughout that period. (*Regesta*, docs. 76b, 79, 89, 90, 90a, 91, 102, 109.) While he attended the council of Neapolis, his position in the church is not known. In attesting this charter he signs after the last of the priors and before Eustache Grenier and William de Buris.

Ralph, bishop of Bethlehem and chancellor, had a vicechancellor named Stephen as shown by a charter of Nov. 29, 1160, where he signs:—'*Datum per manum Stefani, Radulfi, Bethlemitae episcopi regisque cancellarii, in hoc officio vicefungentis*'. (D. L. *Cartulaire*, i, doc. 296; *Regesta*, doc. 355.)

William of Tyre had charters drawn up for him by assistants named Peter (D. L. *Cartulaire* i, doc. 480; *Regesta*, doc. 525), and Lambert (D. L. *Cartulaire*, i, doc. 496; *Regesta*, doc. 537): '*Datum per manum Lamberti capellani*'.

A charter of Guy de Lusignan of 1186 was drawn up by Joscius '*sacerdotis regis*' (Strehlke, doc. 20; *Regesta*, doc. 650); another in 1191 by Gerard, '*capellani regis*' (*Liber Jurium*, i, doc. 392; *Regesta*, doc. 702).

Baldwin, '*capellani domini regis in hoc vicefungentis*', prepared a charter of Amaury II in 1198. (Mas Latrie, ii, 24–25; *Regesta*, doc. 747.)

Jerusalem developed no system of writs,—but she developed no royal justice; she had no chancery courts,—but she had no common law and no appelate jurisdiction; she evolved no chancery registers, —but she evolved no strong monarchy and administrative bureaucracy. If the Jerusalemite chancery failed to come abreast of that of the Anglo-Norman kingdom, Norman Sicily, or France, it was because Jerusalem had no Henry I or Henry II, no Roger, no Philip Augustus or St Louis. If we compare the charters of Foulque of Anjou in Anjou and in Jerusalem, the Jerusalemite are easily the more advanced.[1] The charters of Baldwin I compare not unfavorably with those of Robert Curthose.[2]

It is only after the great administrative reforms of the twelfth and thirteenth centuries in western Europe that the chanceries develop so considerably there, and Jerusalem never experienced those reforms. True, the papal chancery had forged ahead in the earlier period, but the Papacy was a well organized government with a highly trained and efficient secretariat, which was never the case in any of the crusading states.

John de Brienne had a charter of 1212 drawn up by '*Guidanus regis capellanus*' (Méry, i 226; *Regesta*, doc. 855), and one in 1211 by Baldwin and one in 1217 by John de Vinopera, notaries. (Rozière, doc. 145; *Regesta*, doc. 853; D. L. *Cartulaire*, ii, doc. 1526; *Regesta*, doc. 892.)

Conrad de Montferrat, lord of Tyre, had charters drawn up regularly by Bandinus a scribe. (Müller, pp. 26–28; Méry, i, 192; *Regesta*, docs. 665, 666.)

These charters are cited only to show the use of vicechancellors and notaries in place of the chancellors. But, as will be seen, the great majority of the acts were drawn up by the chancellors themselves.

[1] J. Chartrou, *L'Anjou de 1109 à 1151*, pp. 253–284, gives the register of Foulque's acts. Of the 108 acts registered 98 are from Anjou and 10 from Jerusalem. Of the 98 from Anjou only five have the seal affixed, while three are signed with a cross. Of the ten from Jerusalem five have seals. None of the Angevin acts were drawn up by a chancellor, while five of those from Jeruslem were. While this argument is obviously based on absurdly insufficient materials, the average of the Jerusalemite acts is certainly higher than those of Anjou, except in the matter of quantity.

[2] According to the materials which have come down to us Baldwin I issued thirteen charters and one letter in a reign of eighteen years. (*Regesta*, docs. 34, 41, 43, 45, 51, 52, 57, 59, 68a, 74, 76a, 79, 80, 85.) Robert Curthose issued thirty-nine in fifteen years. (Haskins, *Norman Institutions*, pp. 66–70.) These are only the charters that have been preserved and the Norman archives are recognizedly much better preserved than are those of Outremer. The Norman charters do not show any types of act which are not found in the Jerusalemite; all are simple grants or confirmations of previous grants. The Norman titles were not more fixed than were the Jerusalemite, neither having, in this period, become at all settled.

The chancery of Jerusalem knew but one type of document,— the charter granting something,—and even the treaties with the Italian states are in charter form. The many forms of writs and records which the western chanceries worked out were never achieved in the East. Nor did the chancellors develop any judicial powers as did those of France and particularly England, where the writ-issuing power of the chancellor transformed the secretary of the curia into an equity court. In Armenia the chancellor of the kingdom, the archbishop of Sis, had a court, but it was as archbishop and not as chancellor.[1] The chancellors of Jerusalem who were bishops and archbishops had their ecclesiastical courts, but these had nothing to do with their position as chancellor.

The number of charters and documents which have been preserved from Jerusalem is pitifully small, and the preservation of such as we have is due to their having been kept in the archives of religious houses or communes. From the twelve year reign of Amaury I, probably as strong a king as Jerusalem ever had, when we can presume the royal chancery was as busy as at any other period, only twenty-eight documents have been preserved, though this does not include several letters to western princes. Of these twenty-eight charters, twelve are confirmations of grants and sales previously made;[2] twelve are grants of land or money to religious Orders or houses, the Hospitallers, Teutonic Knights, the Holy Sepulchre, and St Lazare;[3] three are grants of privileges to the Pisans;[4] and the last is a grant to Philip Rufus of two casales, for which Philip surrendered the 1300 besants income from the port taxes of Acre which he had obtained by a previous grant.[5]

Twenty-two of these twenty-eight charters were drawn up by the chancellor or by his vice-chancellor; four are published only in abstracts[6], of the two which we know were not drawn up by the chan-

---

[1] V. Langlois, *Le Trésor des Chartes d'Arménie ou Cartulaire de la Chancellerie Royale des Roupéniens* (Venice, 1863), p. 19. The archbishop's court was second only to the court of the king itself.

[2] *Regesta*, docs. 400, 416, 422a, 450, 453, 457a, 465, 487, 501a, 513a, 514, 517b.

[3] *Ibid.*, docs., 397, 512 (to St Lazare), 488 (to Holy Sepulchre), 496 (Teutonic Knights), 413, 423a, 452, 466, 477, 516, 517a (to Hospital), 451a (Josaphat).

[4] *Ibid.* docs. 412, 449, 467.

[5] *Ibid.* doc. 517

[6] D. L. *Cartulaire*, docs. 355, 388, 451, 454; *Regesta*, docs. 423a, 457a, 501a, 517a.

cellor one was granted by Amaury as regent of Tripoli and so did not emanate from the royal chancery, and the other, an award given in a dispute between the Hospitallers and the Church of Ste Marie Maioris, was drawn up by the patriarch.[1] Most of them mention the seal, '*concedit et sigillo confirmat*' being the usual formula.[2]

Diplomatically, the chancery of Jerusalem worked out well its single form of charter; while there are variations during the early reigns, after Baldwin III the chancery forms and formulae became fairly well fixed.

The method of dating was both by the Christian era and by the Roman indictions. The year began at Christmas after the custom of the imperial and of the eleventh century papal chanceries.[3] The year of the reign was sometimes given on the charters of the princes of Antioch though it is not found on those of the kings of Jerusalem.[4] A charter of the patriarch of 1168 is dated: '*Anno ab Incarnatione Domini MCLXVIII, a captione Jerusalem LXIX*'.[5]

The charters of the kings of Jerusalem began with an invocation of the Trinity. The form was either: '*In nomine Sancte et Individue Trinitatis, Patris, Filii et Spiritus Sancti*', or simply: '*In nomine*

---

[1] *Regesta*, docs. 477, 516: ('*Factum Amalrico patriarcha*'.)

[2] One of the exceptions is the charter cited above, prepared by the patriarch.

[3] Mas Latrie, ii, Introduction, pp. 20–25; Delaborde, Introduction, pp. 8–10. The Cypriot chancery changed about 1465 and adopted the Venetian style which began the year on March 1st. The Hospitallers, after their occupation of Rhodes, used two systems of dating,—the Roman calendar for external use, and for internal use a calendar which began the year on the 15th August, the feast of the Assumption of the Virgin and the anniversary of their conquest of the island. The Armenians also used a varied system of dating, sometimes following the Dionysian Christian era used by the other Outremer states, sometimes the Armenian era which began on July 11, 552 A.D. With this they combined the Greek indiction, which differed from the Roman in that it began the year on September 1st while the Roman indiction began on January 1st. (Langlois, *Chartes d'Arménie*, p. 15 ff.) A charter of Leo III to the Venetians in 1271 reads: '*en l'an de Ermenie set cenz e vint e un, e a l'endition dex Grex, chi se au mois de jenvier . . . en l'an nostre segnor Jesu Christ mille et dues cens e sittante un*'. (Langlois, pp. 150–53.)

The Empire began the year at Christmas and so did the Papacy until the pontificate of Urban II in 1088. After that time the Papacy followed the Florentine, Pisan, and Christmas systems interchangeably. But while the papal year began at Christmas the Roman indiction began January 1st. (A. Giry, *Manuel de Diplomatique* (Paris, 1894), pp. 96–129.)

[4] Bohemond III especially dated by the year of his principate. (*Regesta*, docs. 424, 451, 493, 511, 523, 550, 555.)

[5] Rozière, doc. 160; *Regesta*, doc. 455.

Patris, Filii et Spiritus Sancti", while occasionally the form was: '*In nomine Sancte et Individue Trinitatis*'; but after Baldwin III the longer form was the most common.[1]

The seignorial charters, issued by the barons in their own courts, show the use of all the forms, though they incline to the shorter invocations, occasionally omitting them altogether.[2] The Armenian chancery favored the: '*In nomine Patris, Filii et Spiritus Sancti*'.[3]

The invocation was normally followed by the phrase: '*Notum sit omnibus tam presentibus quam futuris*', though this varied and was by no means universally used.[4]

The kings of Jerusalem numbered themselves from Baldwin I and gave their number from him regardless of their name. Baldwin I designated himself: '*Balduinus ab exsultante clero, principibus et*

---

[1] As the basis of these observations I have gone carefully through all the charters contained in: Delaborde, *Chartes de Terre Sainte*; Delaville Le Roulx, *Archives à Malte*; Strehlke, *Tabulae Ordinis Theutonici*; and the charters given in the appendix of the *Assises de Jérusalem*, volume ii. As Strehlke omits invocations in his edition of many of the texts but little could be gained from those contained in his work.

The form '*In nomine Sancte et Individue Trinitatis*' is found only on a charter of Baldwin I and on one of Raymond of Tripoli (*Assises*, ii, docs. 4 and 24).

The '*In nomine Patris, Filii, et Spiritus Sancti*' is found on charters of Baldwin II (*Assises*, doc. 7), John de Brienne and Marie (*Assises*, doc. 50), and Henry of Champagne (Strehlke, doc. 29). A charter of Baldwin I of 1115 has the form '*In nomine Domini Jesu Christi*' (Delaborde, doc. 5).

All the rest of the thirty-nine royal charters given in these collections have the full invocation '*In nomine Sancte et Individue Trinitatis, Patris, Fillii et Spiritus Sancti*.' (*Assises*, docs. 6, 10, 11, 13, 14, 15, 16, 26, 30, 31, 32, 33, 34, 35, 36, 39, 48, 49; Strehlke, docs. 1, 15, 20; D. L. *Archives*, docs. 9, 21, 50, 51, 54, 55, 57; Delaborde, docs. 6, 8, 18, 26, 29, 33, 34, 36, 38, 43, 46.) From this evidence it is safe, I feel, to state that after Baldwin III the longer form which had been in use earlier became more regular and was employed as the normal form of invocation by the chancery, though there were always exceptions to the rule.

[2] *Assises*, ii, docs. 21–25, 27–29, 37, 38, 40, are baronial charters using the long form; docs. 42–45, 47 *etc.* use shorter forms which are more common.

[3] Charters of Leo II and Heyton carry the form cited (Langlois, docs. 1, 2, 6, 8, 9, 19). The longer form current in Jerusalem appears in docs. 5, 10, and 15. A charter of Raymond Rupin (14) has '*Sancte et Individue Trinitatis*'. A charter of 1236 issued by Heyton and Elizabeth has the invocation: '*Voluntate beneficii Dei patris et gracia domini nostri Jhesu Christi et beneplacito sancti spiritus*' (doc. 18). The treaty of 1252 with Julian of Sidon has '*En nom de notre Segnor Jhesu Crist*' (doc. 20).

[4] This phrase is found more regularly on the earlier than on the later diplomas. The French form, which appears on the documents in the thirteenth century was '*Conne chose seit a toz ceaus qui sont et seront*'.

populo, primus rex Francorum';[1] Baldwin III used the title: '*Baldui-nus per gratiam Dei in Sancta civitate Hirusalem rex quartus*';[2] Baldwin IV was '*Latinorum rex Sextus*'.[3] Amaury II was ninth king of Jerusalem and John de Brienne tenth.[4] This custom was peculiar to Jerusalem and was not carried over to Cyprus, where the kings attached no number to themselves. Hugh III used the form: '*Hugue, par la grâce de Dieu XIIe roy de Jherusalem latin et roi de Cipre*'.[5]

The title used by the kings of Jerusalem varied throughout the earlier reigns. Baldwin I termed himself: '*Dei gratia rex Jheroso-limitanus Dei amore et timore*',[6] '*Dei gratia rex Jherusalem*',[7] '*Dei gracia Latinitatis Jherosolimorum rex*',[8] '*Balduinus, regnum Ierosolimitanum dispositione Dei obtinens*',[9] and simply '*ego Baldui-nus*' without any title at all,[10] as well as the more elaborate title cited in the preceding paragraph.

Baldwin II used the forms: '*Dei gratia rex Jherusalem Latinorum secundus*'[11] and '*Dei gratia latinitatis Jerosolimorum rex secundus*'.[12] Foulque followed the '*rex Jherusalem Latinorum*' of Baldwin II.[13] Baldwin III used the title: '*per Dei gratiam in sancta civitate Jeru-salem Latinorum rex quartus*',[14] though he sometimes shortened it by

[1] Charter of Baldwin I: William Tyre, XI, xii, 472; *Regesta*, doc. 59.

[2] Strehlke, doc. 3; Rozière, doc. 54: 'per gratiam Dei in sancta Iherusalem Latinorum rex quartus'.

[3] D. L. *Archives*, doc. 39.

[4] Strehlke, docs. 34, 38, 55; Delaborde, doc. 46.

[5] Charter of 1270: Mas Latrie, iii, 660. The same form occurs on an act of 1269 given in D. L. *Cartulaire*, doc. 3371.

Amaury used the same form: '*Aymericus per Dei graciam rex Jerusalem nonus et rex Cipri*' (Strehlke, doc. 34). Hugh I called himself merely '*Hugo, Dei gratia rex Cypri*' (Rozière, doc. 176). Henry I used the form '*Henricus, Dei gratia rex Cipri*' (Mas Latrie, iii, 639), and no number was given any of the Cypriot kings.

[6] Charter of 1115: Delaborde, doc. 5.

[7] In 1115: Delaborde, doc. 6.

[8] Charter of 1112; D. L. *Cartulaire*, doc. 28. A charter of 1110 has the phrase '*gratia Dei*'. (*Ibid.*, doc. 20.)

[9] In 1114: Rozière, doc. 29.

[10] In 1100: Rozière, doc. 122. This was in all probability before his coronation; the charter is the one in which he made his peace with the Church. (*Regesta*, doc. 34.)

[11] Delaborde, doc. 18.

[12] *Ibid.*, doc. 8.

[13] D. L. *Cartulaire*, doc. 116.

[14] Strehlke, docs. 1, 2, 3.

omitting the 'civitate.'[1] Melissande used the simple form: 'Dei gratia Jerusolimorum regina'.[2] After Baldwin III the full form of 'per Dei gratiam in sancta civitate Jerusalem Latinorum rex' was accepted as the correct title and was used by Amaury I, Baldwin IV, Baldwin V, and Guy.[3] Amaury II shortened it somewhat and combined his Cypriot title in the form: 'per Dei gratiam Iherusalem Latinorum rex nonus et rex Cipri,' and referred to his wife, Queen Isabelle, as 'illustris' or 'venerabilis' 'regine'.[4] John de Brienne called himself 'Dei gratia Latinorum Ierusalem rex decimus et comes Brenensis', though the Brienne title was later omitted.[5] Isabelle de Brienne issued charters as 'Romanorum imperatrix, Ierusalem et Siciliae regina',[6] thereby following generally her husband's title of 'Dei gratia Romanorum imperator semper augustus, Ierusalem et Sicilie rex'.[7]

When the kings of Cyprus became virtual rulers of Jerusalem they used the title: 'par la grace de Dex rei de Chypre et seignor del reaume de Jerusalem',[8] and after Hugh III finally received the Jerusalemite crown he assumed the title: 'par la grace de Dieu dozime roy

---

[1] Delaborde, docs. 26, 29, 33; D. L. *Cartulaire*, doc. 244. A charter of 1147 has the form 'Dei gratia Jerosolimitanorum et sancte civitatis Latinorum quintus rex' (D. L. *Archives*, doc. 9). As Delaville LeRoulx points out the *quintus* is obviously a scribe's or copyist's error.

[2] Delaborde, doc. 34.

[3] Charters of Amaury I: Strehlke, docs. 5, 6, 7, 8; D. L. *Archives*, doc. 21; Delaborde, doc. 36.

Charters of Baldwin IV: Strehlke, docs. 10, 11, 12, 13, 14, 15, 16, 17; D. L. *Archives*, docs. 39, 50, 51, 54, 55, 57; Delaborde, doc. 38.

Charters of Baldwin V: Strehlke, docs. 18, 19; Delaborde, doc. 43.

Charters of Guy: Strehlke, docs. 21, 22, 23, 25, 27. The form 'rex nobilis Iersolimis' occurs on 20.

[4] Mas Latrie, ii, 24; Strehlke, doc. 34 (omits *Latinorum*), 35, 36, 38.

[5] Strehlke, docs. 49, 50, 53, 55, 57; Delaborde, doc. 46.

[6] Strehlke, doc. 59.

[7] Strehlke, doc. 76.

Conrad in 1243 issued a charter as 'Conradus, Frederici imperatoris filius in Romanorum regem electus, heres regni Ierosolimitani'. (Strehlke, doc. 93.) In 1252 Conrad issued a charter to the Hospitallers under the title of 'Conradus Dei gratia Romanorum in regem electus, semper augustus, Hierusalem et Sicilie rex'. (D. L. *Cartulaire*, doc. 2615.)

Conradin in 1268 called himself 'Jerusalem et Sicilie rex, dux Suevie'. (Müller, pp. 100–01.)

[8] Mas Latrie, ii, 66; Strehlke, doc. 105,—charters of Henry I. As king of Cyprus he used merely the title 'Dei gracia rex Cipri'. (Strehlke, doc. 71.) See Mas Latrie, ii, 51–56. Hugh I and Alice had also used the simple form of the Cypriot title. (Mas Latrie, iii, 608, 611; D. L. *Cartulaire*, docs. 1354, 2033.)

de Jerusalem latin et roy de Chypre'.[1] The title of Jerusalem took precedence over that of any other state save the Empire in the titles of the titular kings of Jerusalem. Charles II of Anjou, king of Sicily, used the title: '*Karolus secundus Dei gratia rex Jherusalem, Sicilie, ducatus Apulie et principatus Capue, Provincie et Forcalquerii comes*'.[2] Similarly, Charlotte de Lusignan and James the Bastard of Cyprus placed the Jerusalemite title before that of Cyprus and Armenia.[3]

Following the name and title of the king on the diploma came the consent clause in which the assent of the wife, heir, mediate lord, or other interested person might be given. The use of this consent clause was always recognized but it was not always included in the charters and the practice in this respect was far from regular.[4]

At the end of the charter was the *factum est* clause. Delaborde discusses this phase of Outremer diplomatics in the introduction to his *Chartes de Terre Sainte*, pages 8 to 10. After Baldwin III the date line was usually broken so that the names of the witnesses came be-

---

[1] Mas Latrie, iii, 660; D. L. *Cartulaire*, docs. 3323, 3371. John was the tenth, Frederick II the eleventh, king in the numbering. As Conrad had never come to Syria he was not included in the numbering and Hugh became the twelfth after an interregnum.

[2] Mas Latrie, ii, 91; D. L. *Cartulaire*, doc. 4207,—charters of 1295 and 1293. Charles I had used the long and elaborate title of '*Karolus Dei gracia illustris rex Jherusalem, Sicilae, ducatus Apuliae et principatus Capuae, Almae Urbis senator, Andegavi, Provinciae, Forcalquerii et Tornodori comes, romani imperii in Tuscia per sanctam romanam ecclesiam vicarius generalis (regnorum eius Jherusalem anno 2, Siciliae vero 13*'.) (E. G. Rey, *Recherches Géographiques et Historiques sur la Domination des Latins en Orient* (Paris, 1877), p. 45.)

[3] '*Charlote, par la grace de Dieu royne de Jerusalem de Chippres et d'Armenie*',—charter of 1462 (Mas Latrie, iii, 118). '*Jacobum, Dei gratia Yerusalem, Cypri et Armenie regem illustrissimum*',—charter of 1467 (Mas Latrie, iii, 176).

The kings of Armenia were more truly oriental in the elaborateness of their titles. They owed their elevation to the kingship to the emperor and the Pope and were for a time careful to acknowledge their indebtedness. Leo II issued a charter in which he explained himself as '*Leo Dei gratia rex Armeniorum, filius Stephani et de potenti genere Rupinorum, postquam, divina clementia promotus sum ad regalem dignitatem et sublimatus regali corona per manus Romani imperii*' (Langlois, *Chartes d'Arménie*, p. 105), and in another charter nine years later (1210) he styled himself: '*Leo, filius domini Stephani bone memorie, Dei et Romani imperii gratia, rex Armenie*' (Langlois, p. 115).

The period of gratitude for their elevation did not, however, outlast the first king and Heyton in 1245 used the title '*Dei gracia rex Armenie*' (*Ibid.*, p. 143). Another form used by Heyton was '*Christi Dei fidelis rex Armenie, filius Constantini stirpis regie*'. (*Ibid.*, p. 141.) Leo III evolved the title '*Lion, en Crist Deu feel, roy de tote Hermenie, fiz dou Deu amant e bien aorant sant roy d'Armenie, Hayton, en Crist reposé*' (*Ibid.*, p. 151–52).

[4] The consent of the wife and heir has been discussed already above, p. 47.

tween the line carrying the year and indiction and that carrying the day and month. The year and indiction followed the phrase *'factum est'*, while the day and month followed the *'datum est'*. When the phrase was not divided but read *'factum et datum est'* the entire date followed.[1] These generalizations do not always hold true, however, and several charters have the *factum* and *datum* clauses both following the signatures of the witnesses, and the whole date often followed the phrase *'actum est'*.[2]

Latin was of course the language of the Outremer chanceries throughout the twelfth century. The first chancery to adopt French as its official language was that of Antioch which used the vernacular as early as 1228.[3] Henry I of Cyprus adopted French as early as 1234, though Latin continued to be used for some purposes and for the next two decades French and Latin were used interchangeably in Cyprus.[4] By 1291 Latin had been discontinued altogether and Italian had begun to be used, as evidenced by the grant of Henry II to the Pisans.[5]

The three Orders followed Antioch and Cyprus in the adoption of the vernacular. Charters of the Hospitallers and the Teutonic Knights were drawn up in French as early as 1239.[6] This did not

[1] A charter of Baldwin IV of 1183 (Strehlke, doc. 17), illustrates the divided date line. It reads: *'Factum est hoc anno ab incarnatione domini MCLXXXIII indictione XV. Huius rei sunt testes Guido . . . et al . . . Datum Accon per manum Guillelmi Tyrensis archiepiscopi regisque cancellarii, XIII Kal. aprilis.* An act of Baldwin II (Rozière, doc. 44) shows the single date line: *'Factum est et datum in palatio regis apud Achon, anno dominice incarnationis MCXXVIII indictione IV, mense martio'.*

[2] Strehlke, docs. 31, 32, 34, 35, 36, 38. Acts of Henry of Champagne and Amaury II carry the two lines separately but both following the witnesses. Strehlke, doc. 49, an act of John de Brienne reads: *'Actum anno incarnate verbe MCCXVII Mense Augusti'.* Docs. 50, 53, 55, etc. also carry the entire date after *actum* and omit the signature of the chancellor.

[3] Charter of Bohemond IV to the Teutonic knights (Strehlke, doc. 61; *Regesta*, doc. 979). Latin was still in use in 1219 as evidenced by a charter of Raymond Rupin of that date (Strehlke, doc. 51). After 1228 French was used continuously in Antioch.

Bohemond also used French in Tripoli, his first Tripolitan charter in the vernacular coming from 1236 (Strehlke, doc. 81).

[4] Charters of 1234 (Mas Latrie, iii, 638), 1236 (Méry, i, 419), 1237 (D. L. *Cartulaire*, doc. 2174), and 1253 (Strehlke, doc. 105), are in French. Charters of 1233 (Mas Latrie, ii, 56), 1234 (*Ibid.*, iii, 639), 1239 (*Ibid.*, iii, 642), and 1248 (*Ibid.*, iii, 648), are in Latin.

[5] Müller, p. 108.

[6] Charter of Hospital in Strehlke, doc. 87, or D. L. *Cartulaire*, doc. 2224. Charter of Teutons in D. L. *Archives*, doc. 73.

mean that Latin was abandoned, for both Orders used Latin as well as French thereafter.[1] The first charter of the Templars to be written in French which has come down to us dates from 1252,[2] though an agreement of 1243 between the Temple and Hospital which is written in French may have come from the Temple chancery as well as from that of the Hospital.[3]

French was introduced into the Jerusalem chancery when the kings of Cyprus, who had used the vernacular at home, became lords of Jerusalem and brought over with them their chancery practice in this respect. The first French charter issued by the Jerusalemite chancery dates from 1252,[4] the same year in which the first French document appeared from the Armenian chancery.[5]

The change from Latin to French often produced amusing combinations within a single document, as in the charter of John de Gibelet which reads: '*In nomine patris, filii et spiritus sancti. Ge Johan de Gibeleth, fiz de Guillaume de Gibeleth, de bone memoire, faz asaveir à toz ceaus qui sunt present et qui sunt avenir . . .*'[6]

The Church was naturally the last stronghold of Latin and the bishops and patriarchs continued to employ Latin in their chancer-

---

[1] Latin charter of Hospital of 1240 given in Strehlke, doc. 89. Latin charter of Teutons of 1244 given in Strehlke, doc. 98. A treaty between the Hospital, Temple, and Teutons in 1258 (Strehlke, doc. 116) written in Latin was prepared in the chancery of the Holy Sepulchre.

[2] D. L. *Archives*, doc. 79; and in Delaville LeRoulx, *Documents concernant les Templiers* (Paris, 1882), doc. 19.

[3] D. L. *Cartulaire*, doc. 2296. Delaville LeRoulx (*Archives*, p. 12) says that after 1235 French was the official language of the chanceries of the Hospitallers and Teutons but we can find no proof of this early a date. The Temple has no act in French earlier than that of 1252 or at the earliest 1243. Latin was still used in 1240 as shown by a charter of Armand de Périgord (*Archives Orient Latin*, ii, B, pp. 155–57, doc. 39) but the continuance of Latin does not of course preclude the use of French as well.

[4] Charter of Henry I from Acre,—Mas Latrie, ii, 66.

[5] Marriage alliance with Julian of Sidon: Langlois, *Chartes d'Arménie*, doc. 20. It is signed by King Heyton in Armenian. The Armenian chancery was always multilingual as Armenian was used for internal documents. After the accession of Leo II in 1187 grants to foreigners were made in Latin or French; French became official under Heyton. (Langlois, p. 12.) In 1271 a treaty of Leo III with the Venetians is in French (*Ibid.*, doc. 25); a treaty with the Genoese in 1288 is in Latin and Armenian (*Ibid.*, doc. 26); and in the fourteenth century Latin, French, Italian, and Armenian were all used. (*Ibid.*, docs. 30, 31, 32, 34.)

[6] D. L. *Archives*, doc. 75. A letter of Ochin of Armenia has the invocation in Latin, the body of the text in Italian and the signature in Armenian. (Langlois, doc. 33.)

ies until the end of the kingdom, though on rare occasions French charters were issued by ecclesiastical chanceries.[1]

The charters were witnessed and sealed, the seal being affixed by the chancellor. As the Outremer practice differed not at all from that of the West in this, and as the sigillography of the Latin Orient has already received extensive consideration at the hands of competent scholars no attempt will be made to touch upon the subject here.[2]

In regard to the witnesses, there seems to have been but little system to the order in which they signed. Save that the clergy signed first on most occasions no rule can be established, and even here if the members of the Orders are considered as clergy the rule breaks down.

Among the grand officers there was no apparent order in signing and it is almost safe to say that the most important individual signed first. If the chancellor were witnessing the charter instead of drawing it up his signature preceded that of the other officers,—but it was as a cleric. A rapid survey of a few charters picked wholly at random will show this point. A charter of Baldwin I in 1115 is witnessed by: the patriarch and four prelates, Eustache Grenier, William de Buris, Baldwin of Rama, three other barons, Ulric viscount of Neapolis, six more barons, Gerard the chamberlain, Pisellus (viscount of Jerusalem), and another baron.[3] On another document of the same year, issued by Roger, bishop of Rama, with the consent of Baldwin I, the signatories are: three members of the chapter of Josaphat, the patriarch, the king, three bishops, Eustache Grenier,

---

[1] Charter of the bishop of Nazareth of 1255 (D. L. *Archives*, doc. 84), and charter of bishop of Bethlehem of 1262 (Strehlke, doc. 123), are in French.

[2] The standard work on the sigillography and numismatics of the Latin states has been done by Gustave Schlumberger, especially his *Numismatique de l'Orient Latin*, and his 'Quelques Sceaux de l'Orient Latin au Moyen Age', *Mémoires de la Société Nationale des Antiquaires de France*, lxiv (1905), 253–73.

The Marquis de Voguë also contributed to the study of the sigillography of the crusading states. ('Monnais et Sceaux des Croisades', *Mélanges de Numismatique*, ii (1878), pp. 168–96, and other articles.) Delaville LeRoulx and Delaborde have discussions of seals in the prefaces to their documents, and E. G. Rey's studies on the social life of the Franks in Syria and on the architectural remains deal in places with the sigillography. A short bibliography is given in L. Bréhier, *L'Église et l'Orient* (5th edition: Paris, 1928). Langlois, *Chartes d'Arménie*, pp. 16–19, has a study of the seals of Armenia.

[3] Delaborde, doc. 6; *Regesta*, doc. 80.

Simon the constable, five barons, Pisellus (viscount of Jerusalem), Paganus the chancellor, and Gerard the chamberlain.[1]

An act of Baldwin II of 1120 is witnessed by: bishops, abbots, priors, Peter Barchionensis, Paganus the chancellor, Brando a cleric, Hugh Caulis the constable, William of Tiberias, Eustache Grenier, Pisellus (viscount), eight barons, Anschetin the viscount, Paganus the butler, John the chamberlain, and six more barons.[2] In an act of Baldwin III of 1146 the order of officers is constable, butler, viscount of Neapolis, marshal.[3] In the charters of Amaury I, Humphrey de Toron the constable regularly signed before Miles the seneschal, while William the marshal followed somewhere after the latter.[4] Under Baldwin IV there is no semblance of order. A charter of 1180 has the signature of Renaud de Châtillon followed by Seneschal Joscelin de Courtney; and on an act of February 1182 Renaud again signs first, followed this time by Renaud of Sidon, with the Constable Amaury signing only fifth. In another charter of the same month, Guy de Lusignan, count of Jaffa and Ascalon, signed before Prince Renaud, who was followed by Joscelin the seneschal and Amaury the constable; and on a charter of the following April Raymond of Tripoli witnesses first, followed by Joscelin and Renaud de Châtillon.[5] A charter of Guy de Lusignan has the order of: count of Jaffa, constable, marshal, viscount of Acre, and chamberlain.[6] While the seneschal preceded the constable on two charters of Amaury II in 1198,[7] on an act of John de Brienne the constable signed first.[8]

This shows a marked difference from the western practice where a definite order of signature among the grand officers was the rule. In France after Louis VII the order was always seneschal, butler,

[1] *Regesta*, doc. 76b; *R. O. L.*, vii (1899), doc. 7, pp. 117–18.

[2] *Regesta*, doc. 91; Rozière, doc. 45.

[3] *Regesta*, doc. 240; Delaborde, doc. 26.

[4] *Regesta*, docs. 449, 451a, 453. But on a charter of 1171 William signed before Miles. (*Regesta*, doc. 487.)

[5] *Regesta*, docs. 593, 614, 613, 615; D. L. *Archives*, doc. 55; Strehlke, doc. 14; D. L. *Cartulaire*, doc 625; Strehlke, doc. 15.

[6] *Regesta*, doc. 698; D. L. *Cartulaire*, doc. 917.

[7] *Regesta*, docs. 743, 744; D. L. *Cartulaire*, doc. 1032; Strehlke, doc. 35.

[8] *Regesta*, doc. 934; Strehlke, doc. 53.

chamberlain, and constable.[1] The failure of Jerusalem to develop any definite order of precedence among the grand officers can largely be explained by the lack of importance of any ceremonial in a court as loosely organized as was that of most of the Latin kings. Further the offices were always connected with the individuals and the stronger men took precedence even though they held lesser offices.

Before closing this chapter on the officers of the kingdom of Jerusalem, one officer remains to be considered, who, while not one of the grand officers of the realm, was yet an important official in the administration,—the viscount.

The viscount is the only local officer of whom we have any considerable knowledge, and of his powers and duties the sources give us all too little information. In general the Outremer viscount corresponded roughly to the French or Angevin *prévôt*, the Norman viscount, or the English sheriff. Yet there are many points of difference and only the most general resemblances are traceable. Unlike the French *prévôt*, the viscount in Jerusalem was drawn from the ranks of the lesser nobility and the office could be held only by a knight and a liegeman of the king.[2] There were in the principality thirty-seven viscounties if we can estimate the number of viscounts by the number of *cours des bourgeois*.[3] Of these the four royal viscounts located at Jerusalem, Acre, Neapolis, and Daron, were the most important; and the viscounty of Jerusalem was one of the major administrative offices of the kingdom, being held by such men as Eudes de St Amand and Peter de Cresque.[4] After the fall of Jerusalem the viscounty of Acre became the most important, when that city was made the capital. Besides the four royal viscounts there were the thirty-three viscounts appointed by the barons who had fiefs which could claim high and low justice.

The viscount was the representative of the lord and was the president of the lord's *cour des bourgeois*. The viscount was under oath to administer justice fairly and by the assise, and if there existed no

---

[1] Luchaire, *Histoire des Institutions*, i, 170 and note 1. After the offices had become titular the seals of the officers were affixed in proper order by clerks.

[2] *Abrégé Cour Bourgeois*, part I, chap. ii, pp. 236–37.

[3] Ibelin, cclxx, 419–20.

[4] E. G. Rey lists the viscounts of Jerusalem and Acre (*Familles*, pp. 643–48).

assise, by reason. He gave advice to all who asked it unless the request was treasonable. He arrested all criminals and carried out the judgments of the court.[1]

In addition to these judicial duties the viscount was the financial agent in his area, and collected all the taxes, rents, dues, fines, escheats, forfeitures, and redevances. The royal viscounts made returns to the *Secrète* quarterly, turning in to the treasury what remained of the monies collected after they had paid all the expenses of their viscounties. Whether or not the viscounts held their offices in farm, as did the English sheriffs and Norman viscounts, it is not possible to say definitely, but I am inclined to think that they did. We know from Ibn Djubair that the customs were farmed out, and, as tax-farming was a well established practice, there is every reason to believe that the viscounts farmed the revenues of the districts under their control.[2]

As the local administrative official the viscount issued the proclamations, bans, and ordinances of the king and enforced their observance. He commanded the sergeants and was responsible for their equipment and arms. Together with the *mathesep*, his mastersergeant, he commanded the night watch, alternating with him in making the rounds. The viscount of Jerusalem was often also the *chatelain* of the Tower of David, the chief fortress of the city. While there are no records concerning the military duties of the viscount, this fact would lead one to suppose that, like the Norman viscount, he had the charge of the garrison of the town. He probably also led the sergeants who were expected to serve from the cities '*quant le grant besoin est en la terre dou reiaume*'.[3]

Concerning the lesser officials in the kingdom of Jerusalem we know nothing. *Turcoplers* were commanders of the irregular troops known by that name and, from the later Cypriot office of Grand Turcopler, it is possible to conjecture that they were merely military

---

[1] The duties of the viscount are given in the *Abrégé Cour Bourgeois*, part I, chaps ii–iii, vii, pp. 236–41; *Assises Cour. Bourg.*, iii–iv, 21; and *Les Bans et Ordonnances des Rois de Chypre* (*Assises*, ii), pp. 371–72. D. Hayek, *Le Droit Franc en Syrie* (Paris, 1925), pp. 88–93, discusses his judicial duties.

[2] Ibn Djubair (*R. H. C. Or.*, iii), p. 449, and see the chapter in this book on the financial administration.

[3] Ibelin, cclxxii, 426.

officers. *Logothetes* seem to have been mere clerks. Special viscounts of the ports were probably the presidents of the courts of *Chaine* and *Fonde*. The *mathesep* was the assistant of the viscount. These and other titles of lesser officials, such as dragomen, appear here and there in the charters and documents; but little can be determined either of the duties or powers of the office or of the men who held them.

If it seems strange that Jerusalem never developed various groups of local officials who should mutually check each other as the *prévôts*, *baillies*, and *enquêteurs* did in France, or the sheriff and coroner did in England, it should be remembered that these officers were all agents of the royal power and that it was when one became too powerful that another was established to keep him in check. In Jerusalem the royal power was never sufficiently strong for its agents to need such checks. The feudal nobility were never reduced in power by the usurpations of the royal officers. The king's agents functioned only in the royal domain lands and the feudal lords controlled their fiefs with a minimum of interference from their suzerain. While the viscounts may have become as independent as did the *prévôts*, and while the crown was powerless to prevent this, their insubordination was trivial as compared with the independent attitude of the great landed feudatories.

CHAPTER 7

THE MILITARY ESTABLISHMENT, KNIGHT SERVICE AND FEUDAL TENURE

IN THE kingdom of Jerusalem the chief concern of the government at all times was to defend itself against Moslem neighbors who were constantly hovering on their borders and awaiting a favorable opportunity to regain some of the lands taken from them by the Christian forces. This constant vigilance materially affected the whole life of the people and caused their feudal relations to differ materially from those of a more peaceful western Europe, although feudal Europe was itself sufficiently turbulent. The extensive feudal service, the dominance of the knightly class, and the scarcity of urban communes came about in part because the kingdom was organized for perpetual warfare.

The historians of the first crusade give fabulous numbers for the armies of the Cross. Certain modern historical critics believe that when a medieval writer saw a large number of men he put down a convenient number of thousands and considered the matter no further. As Delbrück has pointed out the 300,000 to 600,000 warriors of the first crusade should be reduced to some 60,000 people of whom about 10,000 were fighting men.[1]

A large proportion of the fighting forces of the conquering crusaders was killed in the conquest, and many returned home after fulfilling their vows, leaving but a small force to defend the newly-conquered Holy Land. William of Tyre reports the army of the crusaders at the battle of Ascalon, before many had returned to Europe, as 1200 knights and 9000 infantry. In 1101, according to Fulcher of Chartres, Baldwin I had only 300 knights and an equal number of infantry, with which he garrisoned Jerusalem, Jaffa, Rama, and Haïfa.[2] When in September 1111 Baldwin I marched to the relief of Antioch, the total Christian army was estimated at 16,000 troops, of

---

[1] H. Delbrück, *Geschichte der Kriegskunst* (2nd ed., Berlin, 1923), iii, 229–35.

[2] William Tyre, IX, xii, 380; Fulcher, II, vi, 389; *Chronologie*, no. 527.

whom some 4,000 were the soldiers of the king.[1] The greatest force ever mustered by the kings of Jerusalem was that which was destroyed at Hattin by Saladin, and the figures differ with each authority, Röhricht estimating that some 20,000 men were collected on this occasion.[2] John d'Ibelin, writing in the middle of the thirteenth century, estimated the total feudal military establishment of the kingdom, exclusive of Antioch-Tripoli, at the time of Baldwin IV, as 577 knights and 5025 sergeants, exclusive of the mercenaries and troops of the Orders.[3] The *Gestes des Chiprois* lists 568 knights and 4075 sergeants.[4]

This enumeration of course includes only the troops owed by regular feudal service. Since the armies provided by feudal services were wholly inadequate to defend the realm, the Christian princes of Syria added thereto soldiery of various types. First, in addition to the knights and sergeants owed by the landed fief-holding vassals, there were many owed by the holders of money fiefs, for land was scarce in Syria and many fiefs were granted out of the revenues of the cities. Besides these were the various types of native soldiery, the *turcoples*, cavalry and foot, who received regular pay and were under the especial charge of the marshal. Lastly the three great religio-military Orders, the Templars, Hospitallers, and Teutonic Knights were the military mainstay of the kingdom; they supplied knights, sergeants, and in some instances ships.

The East had no communal militia, for there were no communes, except for the short-lived attempts at communal government in Antioch, Acre, and Tripoli, all of which arose out of special emergencies. But contingents were secured from the Italian communes in the coastal cities, and the naval assistance furnished by the Italians made possible the conquest of the coastal towns. Bands of crusaders

---

[1] Albert Aix, XI, xl–xli, 682–83. Joscelin of Turbessel brought 100 knights and 50 foot, Baldwin of Edessa 200 knights and 100 foot; Albert lists the various contingents which made up the army, not however giving the numbers of troops in each.

[2] Röhricht, *Königreichs*, p. 428 and footnote 3. The different sources give all the way from 5000 to 63,000. Röhricht after sifting the evidence accepted 20,000, a figure accepted by several and approximated by others. Rey, *Colonies Franques*, p. 113, accepts 20 or 21 thousand.

[3] Ibelin, cclxxi–ii, 422–27. From evidences of the men named in the lists they date from the reign of Baldwin IV or V just before the loss of the kingdom.

[4] *Gestes*, pars. 520–521.

constantly arriving from the West also supplemented the military forces, though they often caused more trouble than they did good.

Theoretically the king of Jerusalem was the supreme commander of the armies, but actually the command was divided among many chiefs. Beha-ed-Din noted with some apparent disgust that the Franks had gone out to hold council before a battle, 'for it is their custom, when it is a question of war, to take counsel together on horseback'.[1] The histories of Outremer are full of accounts of conferences held before deciding on a plan of campaign; the famous council held before the fatal decision of Guy de Lusignan to march to the relief of Tiberias,—when Count Raymond so strenuously opposed the suicidal attack and advised a waiting policy,—is one of the most celebrated events in the whole history of the crusading states.[2] Almost equally famous is the great council held in 1148 at Acre, when, against the advice of the prince of Antioch,[3] it was decided to attack Damascus, a decision which contributed so largely to the failure of the second crusade.

In 1168 the Templars refused to take part in the expedition which Amaury was organizing against Egypt, and sent no troops because they considered it an unjust and unprovoked attack on an ally;[4] there are numerous other cases in which one or another of the counts or princes refused to serve in what seemed to them an unjust or unprofitable campaign. Probably the worst case of divided control ruining a campaign was during the expedition of 1218 against Egypt, commonly called the fifth crusade. John de Brienne, king of Jerusalem, Hugh, king of Cyprus, Andrew, king of Hungary, Leopold of Austria, and the masters of the Orders were the chief leaders of this campaign. John had been elected leader of all, but the Pope sent his legate with full powers of command; the guidance of the crusade fell into the hands of the incompetent legate, Pelagius Galvano of Albano,

---

[1] Beha-ed-Din, *Life of Salah-ed-Din* (P. P. T. S.: London, 1897), p. 14.

[2] *Eracles*, pp. 48–52; Oman, *History of the Art of War in the Middle Ages*, (2nd. ed., Boston: Houghton Mifflin, 1923), i, 324–333, discusses at length the council and the whole campaign of Hattin, showing 'what might have been'.

[3] William Tyre, XVII, i–ii, 758–60.

[4] William Tyre, XX, v, 949. Ibelin, ccxvii, 346, says a vassal must serve where his lord decrees, but the Templars were allies and not vassals of kings.

with the result that Pelagius' attempts to direct the war sent most of the rulers back in dudgeon to their homes.[1]

Added to the evils of divided command and insubordination was the further difficulty that often the crusaders had no very definite idea as to whom they should fight. The second crusade is but one example. Perhaps the most amusing council of war to decide on the plan of campaign was that held in 1123 when the men of Jerusalem and the Venetians were allied to capture some coastal cities but were extremely uncertain which particular city should be their point of attack. Some favored Ascalon, while others held out for Tyre, as the most profitable to be taken. After much discussion the matter was settled in a manner peculiarly characteristic of the crusaders, though hardly in keeping with the shrewd business methods of the Venetians. The names of the two cities were written on two slips of parchment and laid on the altar of the church. An innocent child was led to the altar and directed to draw one of the slips, which, when done, gave the decision of God to the attack on Tyre. In the case under consideration the decision was not unwise, but the method was certainly not deserving of the good results which came from it.[2]

Service from the fief was the normal type of military service, in the East as in the West. In Jerusalem the vassal, according to John d'Ibelin, owed service on horse and fully armed, wherever the king might summon him within the realm, and he must serve as long as the lord decreed, up to a year. Nor did the king himself have to be present in the army, but the vassal must serve as directed.[3] The *Clef des Assises* stipulates that those who owe personal service must serve from the beginning of one year to the next; and there is nothing in any of the laws to indicate that any time limit attached to the military service which could be demanded from the liege

[1] Ernoul, pp. 413–430, 439–447; D. L. *Cartulaire*, doc. 1671; *Eracles*, pp. 343, 349.

Even King John left the army which he could no longer command and returned home, protesting to Rome against Pelagius' interference.

[2] William Tyre, XII, xxiv, 549–50. In 1094 Alexis Comnenus had used a similar method to decide concerning a campaign against the Polovtzes, also in 1116 against the Turks; Alexis drew the slips himself. (Chalandon, *Essai sur la Règne d'Alexis Ier Comnène*, (Paris, 1900), pp. 152–53.)

[3] Ibelin, ccxvii, 345–48.

vassal.[1] William of Tyre, in referring to the expedition of 1166 against Egypt, says that the knights assembled at Ascalon having with them food necessary for the 'constituted days';[2] this would indicate that some definite time limit was set, though William does not say how many the 'constituted days' were. It may be supposed that, the length of the campaign having been decided upon in the meeting of the *Haute Cour*, which arranged military matters, and the lord having summoned his vassals for the term agreed upon, should the campaign last longer than the time stipulated, the lord was responsible for the expenses of the vassals after the expiration of the term. But there seems to have been no limitation as to the length of time which could be demanded as the vassals' regular service at their own expense, provided it was agreed upon in advance.

In the West the time which the vassal was required to serve was normally forty days. In Normandy the vassal had to serve the forty days at his own expense and thereafter at his lord's. Brussel differentiates between the service due from liege homage, which was unlimited in time, and simple homage, which had a forty day limitation.[3] The limited service was, in his opinion, a later development from a time when all service was unlimited.

Boutaric, on the other hand, thinks that at first service was less than forty days and that this term was later imposed as a minimum upon liege service. Guilhiermoz, supporting Brussel, points out that the limitation to forty days was a characteristic of the thirteenth century, and traces its spread to the fact that forty days service was the amount required in the Albigensian Crusade to gain an indulgence.[4] The Morea had four months service in the field and four more in castle guard.[5] Norman Sicily recognized a forty day unit of service at the expense of the vassal, though service was rendered for other periods of time varying from two weeks to

---

[1] *Clef des Assises*, cclxviii, 598.

[2] William Tyre, XIX, xiv, 904: '*Assumptis sibi ad dies constitutos necessariis alimentis*'.

[3] Brussel, *Usage Générale des Fiefs* (Paris, 1750), pp. 105–06; P. Guilhiermoz, *Essai sur l'Origine de la Noblesse en France au Moyen Age* (Paris, 1902), p. 275.

[4] Boutaric quoted in A. Luchaire, *Manuel des Institutions Françaises* (Paris, 1892), p. 197; Guilhiermoz, *op. cit.*, pp. 277–83.

[5] *Assises de Romanie*, arts. 70–71.   And the last four months he must be ready to go on call.   This division of time applied particularly to lieges.

the entire year.[1] In the Germanies the time was six weeks, at the end of which the vassal could go home for a forty day rest. In Anjou the vassal served, as in Normandy, for forty days at his own expense and thereafter at his lord's.[2] In England, though there was a theoretical recognition of the forty days, service for longer periods was exacted.[3]

The argument of Brussel and Guilhiermoz that the limitation to forty days was an innovation would receive support from the practice in the Latin kingdom where no limitation was placed on the service within the realm. Dodu explains the unlimited service in Jerusalem by the statement that while the service was perpetual, all military service rendered by vassals was at the expense of the lord, and that the feudal vassals received pay for their services and could force their suzerain to pay them before they served him. Dodu draws a sharp distinction between the pay given to regular feudal vassals who held the fiefs and received this pay in addition, and that given the holders of money fiefs.[4] To prove his thesis Dodu cites several passages from the texts of the *Assises*. His first reference is to *Le Livre de Jean d'Ibelin*, CCXXIV, p. 355, which discusses how the man shall appeal in the court in refusing a summons for service when the pay which is due him has not been paid. In this chapter Ibelin says that if the time fixed for the payment has passed and no payment has been made, the man is free from service and may disregard the summons. But in chapter CCXXI, which Dodu ignores, Ibelin had already discussed the manner in

[1] F. Chalandon, *Histoire de la Domination Normande en Italie et en Sicile, 1009–1194* (Paris, 1907), ii, 573–74. But if the vassal could prove that he had not received a proper summons the whole expense was on the lord.

[2] *Les Établissements de Saint Louis* (ed. P. Viollet, Soc. His. Fr.: Paris, 1881–84), iii, 31; Guilhiermoz, *op. cit.*, p. 276. But the Angevin vassal could not be forced to serve more than forty days outside the county.

[3] C. H. Haskins, *Norman Institutions*, (Cambridge, Mass.: Harvard, 1918), p. 20 ff.; F. Pollock and F. W. Maitland, *History of English Law* (2nd ed.; Cambridge, 1899), i, 254.

[4] Dodu, pp. 192–95: 'Comme dans ce pays le service militaire était permanent, la solde fournie par le suzerain au vassal n'avait pas la même signification qu'en Occident. Tout homme qui possédait un fief et qui, à raison de ce fief, était obligé à un service personnel, recevait une solde. Ce fait est attesté par un grand nombre de textes. Mais il n'y avait aucune analogie entre un fief de cette nature et un *fief de soudée* proprement dit. Il importe donc de les distinguer soigneusement l'un de l'autre'. The three following pages are full of citations to prove this thesis; we have endeavored to refute them in our text.

which a man shall refuse to respond to a summons when his lord owes him anything or when he is not receiving the revenues from his fief. The two chapters must refer to different types of fiefs and it is quite possible that Ibelin's earlier chapter refers to land fiefs and the second, quoted by Dodu, refers to money fiefs. The next chapter to which Dodu refers is Ibelin, CCXXXVI, pp. 376–379. In this chapter Ibelin starts:—'*Se un home ou une feme est assenée de son fié en un leuc qui ait tant valu de quei il puisse estre paié, et le seignor l'ait pris ou fait prendre, et que par ce li est sa paie defaillie*—', and the term of the payment passes, the man may distrain his lord for his pay or refuse service. The important word in this sentence is the *assenée* which is a term used in reference to assignment of a fief, money rental, or revenue. Thus this paragraph can refer to a fief of a money rent, and to the land against which the rent is levied, as well as to a fief in land. Further in chapter CXLIV (p. 218) Ibelin says that a man who himself conquers a territory may subinfeudate it and may say:—'*Je tel doins à tei et à tes heirs tel ou tels casaus . . . ou tant de besanz assenés en tel leu*'. This very clearly throws into opposition the grant of certain lands against that of certain monies levied on lands. In the first case the lord grants the lands themselves as a fief to the vassal, in the second he retains possession of the lands but grants a certain sum from the revenues thereof to the vassal. Chapter CCXLII (388–89), is devoted to payment when '*un home ou une feme est assené de son fié . . . sur les rentes d'un casau ou d'autre leuc*'.[1]

The habit of the kings and barons of Jerusalem of granting fiefs against the revenues of certain cities and towns is well established and is proved by many charters, a few of which, selected at random from the middle period of the kingdom, are used here for illustration. In 1136 Foulque granted the Marseillais 400 besants from the taxes of Jaffa;[2] in 1159 Melissande granted the Hospitallers 3 *quintaria* and 300 *libri* of oil from the produce of Neapolis;[3] in 1160 Baldwin

---

[1] Albert Aix, XII, xxx, 709–10, tells how Baldwin II reserved certain cities for his own rule but granted out the revenues thereof to barons as fiefs. And again Albert, VII, xxxvii, 532, says that Baldwin I confirmed the benefices which Godfrey had granted of revenues of cities.

[2] Méry, *Histoire de Marseille*, i, 182; *Regesta*, doc. 163.

[3] D. L. *Cartulaire*, doc. 279; *Regesta*, doc. 339a.

III confirmed a charter whereby Renaud Falconarius granted freedom to take reeds from the river near Acre for which Renaud was to have one fifth of the profits from the honey jars which are made of these reeds.[1] In 1168 Amaury granted to the abbey of Josaphat the sum of 1500 besants from the revenues of Egypt when he should have conquered that country.[2] The same monarch granted the brothers of St Lazare a rental of 72 besants a year to be collected in four installments from the revenues of the David Gate in Jerusalem.[3] In 1174, the year after his former grant, the king confirmed a grant of 40 more besants to be collected quarterly from the revenues of the port of Acre, which had formerly been the payment made to Walter, lord of Blanchegarde, and which the latter now gave the brothers.[4] In 1174 Amaury sold to Philip Rufus the casales of Arabian and Zekanin with their appurtenances for the 1000 besants which Philip had in revenues from Acre and for the service of one knight. In the same charter he granted Philip back 800 besants from the revenues of Acre for the service of two knights.[5]

Baldwin IV granted a great number of money fiefs. In 1178 he granted Peter de Cresque 30 quintaria of wine from the lands of Bethcart and Rama; in 1179 he confirmed the grant of 40 besants which Guy de Scandalion made to the Hospitallers from his revenues in Tyre; and in March 1183 he granted Joscelin de Courtney, his seneschal, 1000 besants from the revenues of Acre.[6] Another grant to Joscelin in November 1183 shows several interesting points. Baldwin concedes to Joscelin the rental (termed *assise*) of 1000 besants from the revenues of Acre which Philip Rufus possessed for life. This Joscelin shall hold and enjoy until Philip shall pay him the 2000 besants which he borrowed from him against this rental as security. But as long as he, Joscelin, shall have the rental, he must render the service of two knights

[1] Paoli, *Codice Diplomatico*, i, doc. 50; *Regesta*, doc. 344.

This implies that Renaud had rights over the river and the reeds therein, else he could not sell them.

[2] *R. O. L.*, vii (1899), doc. 37, p. 146; *Regesta*, doc. 451a.

[3] *Archives*, ii, B, 144; *Regesta*, doc. 487.

[4] *Archives*, ii, B, 145; *Regesta*, doc. 512.

[5] Strehlke, doc. 7; *Regesta*, doc. 517.

[6] Paoli, i, doc. 206, p. 248; *Regesta*, doc. 556; D. L. *Cartulaire*, doc. 555; *Regesta*, doc. 590a; Strehlke, doc. 17; *Regesta*, doc. 625.

which Philip had been accustomed to give for this rental. If Philip should die before he has repaid the money, Joscelin shall collect the 2000 besants from the king and surrender to him the rental of Acre, for the rental was only given to Philip as a life fief. But as long as Philip shall live and Joscelin shall have the rental, he must serve for it with two knights.[1] Here we see not only a money fief, but one granted for life only, and also that such fiefs, like fiefs in land, could be placed as security for a loan. The king is also most concerned in insuring that military service due from the fief be regularly performed.

In 1198 Bohemond of Tripoli granted the Hospitallers 1000 besants a year from the revenues which he held from the port of Acre, and the king (from whom as lord of Acre he held his revenues) confirmed the grant.[2] Thirty years later, in 1229, the Emperor Frederick II granted Conrad of Hohenlohe a rental of 6000 besants from the revenues of the port and the market at Acre for the service of nine knights, and promised him another fief of similar value in Jerusalem for only five knights when the city should be recaptured.[3] These examples are sufficient to prove conclusively that money fiefs against the revenues of some port or town were regularly granted by the kings and princes of Jerusalem as a means of securing armed support.[4]

That these grants in rental were made to men also holding fiefs in land is proved by the case of Joscelin de Courtney. We have already seen that Baldwin granted him a revenue of 1000 besants from Acre, and that he had the use of the 1000 besants from Acre which had

---

[1] Strehlke, doc. 13; *Regesta*, doc. 608.   Novare, lxxviii, 550, says money fiefs when pledged as security for debts must be registered in the *Secrète* and the transaction must take place there before witnesses.

[2] D. L. *Cartulaire*, doc. 1032; *Regesta*, doc. 743.

[3] *Archives*, II, B, 166–67; *Regesta*, doc. 1008.

[4] Ibelin, cxliv, 218–19, provides that if the grantor of a money fief dies before any payment has been made to the grantee, the heirs of the grantor need not continue to grant the fief, as the legal enfeoffment had not been completed, the grantee never having been seised of the fief.

In cases of litigation concerning money fiefs, the means of recovery was through appeal to the records of the royal *Secrète*, where the enfeoffment should have been registered by the contracting parties.   As noted above when the money fief was pledged as security for debt the transaction had to take place in the *Secrète*.   (Novare, xxxiv, 511, lxviii, 550; *Clef des Assises*, ccxviii, 595.)

been granted to Philip Rufus. A charter of 1183 confirms his purchase of fourteen towns from Geoffrey le Tort, and establishes an arrangement whereby Joscelin owes two knight's service, and Geoffrey the rest of the service which was due from the fief.[1] In 1186 he was granted six casales for four knights service, and in addition Toron, Neufchâtel, and Baniâs, the fiefs formerly held by Humphrey de Toron, which he should hold for the same service which Humphrey had given.[2] Joscelin also held: houses in Acre, casales from the fief of the king's chamberlain, 500 besants from Acre and 500 from Tyre, rights of free sale in Acre of sugar and honey from his fief of Lanahiam, and the fief of John Baner (100 besants of Acre and four carrucates of land in Caïmont) which fief he, Joscelin, had subinfeudated to Garnier de Paris for the service of one sergeant and two horses.[3] The total holdings of Count Joscelin formed one of the greatest seignories in the East, and much of his wealth came from the many money fiefs which he held. That many of the vassals who held landed fiefs also held money fiefs is undoubtedly true, but that money was paid the holders of landed fiefs as such, as Dodu insists, I do not believe to be the case.

Ibelin, in his list of the knights due from the various fiefs of the principality of Jerusalem, enumerates the services due from the different land fiefs:—from Jaffa and Ascalon (100 knights), Galilee (100), Sidon (100), Krak and Montreal (60), seignory of Joscelin (24); and then lists the knights due from the various bishoprics and cities:—Jerusalem (61), Neapolis (75), Acre (80), Tyre (28), Daron (2). The list ends with the seignory of Beirut (21). Ibelin clearly differentiates between the knights due from the seignories and those due from the cities.[4]

An examination of the lists of service due from one of the cities shows that it is service due from barons of the realm and not from the bourgeoisie. The city of Acre owes eighty knights; ten of these

[1] Strehlke, doc. 16; *Regesta*, doc. 624.

[2] Strehlke, doc. 21; *Regesta*, doc. 653. Humphrey's lands were in the hands of the enemy. Joscelin was to have them if they were recovered. If Humphrey the younger should get them back through a decision of the *Haute Cour*, Joscelin was to have the lands which Humphrey had traded for them.

[3] Strehlke, docs. 10, 14, 22; *Regesta*, docs. 579, 614, 654.

[4] Ibelin, cclxxi, 422–26.

are owed by the constable (presumably Amaury de Lusignan as the men mentioned in the list fixes the list within the years 1182–91 when Amaury was constable); seven are owed by Balian the chamberlain. This Balian the chamberlain is Balian of Jaffa who was chamberlain under Baldwin V and is mentioned in the charters of Baldwin IV and V.[1] Paganus de Caïphas owed seven knights. He was one of the leading barons of Syria and appears often on the royal charters.[2] Raymond de Scandelion who owed seven knights,[3] Philip Rufus[4] and Walter le Bel[5] who owed one knight each, and William de Molembec[6] who owed two, are all barons who are to be found signing charters throughout this period. These examples prove that the

[1] *Regesta*, docs. 587, 588, 643, 644, where Balian of Jaffa appears as chamberlain. The charter of Baldwin V of June 1, 1185 contains the names of Miles, '*pincerna*'; Balian, '*camerarius*'; Paganus, lord of Haïfa; Walter Duras, marshal; William de Flor, viscount of Acre; William de Molembec; and Peter of Lydda, chancellor. (*Regesta*, doc. 644.)

Most of these men are among those listed by Ibelin.

[2] He was the son-in-law of Joscelin Pisellus from whom he held a fief of 20 knights. He also owed two knights for a revenue of 1200 besants from the port of Acre, which Baldwin III had given him and Amaury confirmed by a charter of 1169. (Strehlke, doc. 5; *Regesta*, doc. 465.)

Paganus was quite prominent as a supporter of Conrad de Montferrat and appeared on several of his charters. (*Regesta*, docs. 674, 703, *etc.*) In 1168 a charter of Walter of Galilee confirms an exchange made by Paganus and Foulque, the constable of Tiberias, whereby Paganus traded to Foulque the lands which he held as a fief from Walter for a revenue of 850 besants which Foulque had from the king and the Templars in payment for his castle of Safita. Paganus agreed to continue to render the one knight's service to Walter which he had previously owed for his lands. (Strehlke, doc. 4; *Regesta*, doc. 447.) See *Familles*, pp. 266–67.

[3] Raymond was a common witness on the charters of Bohemond III and IV and also appeared on acts of Baldwin IV and Henry of Champagne. (*Regesta*, docs. 606, 710, 742, 758, 792, 799, 807, 816, 839.) See *Familles*, p. 428.

[4] Philip Rufus owed two knights for a fief of 800 besants in the revenues of Acre which he held from the king. He was lord of Arabian and Zekanin which he had received in exchange from Amaury I, for a revenue of 1000 besants in Acre which he had held by previous grant, and owed one knight for the fief, as he had for the rental. (Strehlke, doc. 7, *Regesta*, doc. 517.) The date of the charter of exchange with Amaury is 1174, too early for one to believe that the one knight he owed for Acre in Ibelin's list could refer to the rental which he exchanged to Amaury. Further, in listing the knights due from the seignory of Count Joscelin, Ibelin lists two as due from the lands of Philip Rufus,—i.e. Arabian and Zekanin which Joscelin got from Philip as security for a loan in 1181. (Strehlke, doc. 13; *Regesta*, doc. 608.)

Philip was a man of considerable importance and the king referred to him as '*consanguinius meus*'.

[5] Walter was viscount of Acre under Guy in 1191, and appeared on charters of Amaury and Hugh I of Cyprus. (*Regesta*, docs, 698, 723, 729, 844; *Familles*, pp. 646–47.)

[6] He appears on charters from 1173 to 1223 (*Regesta*, pp. 156–75 *passim*).

men who owed the service from the cities were not bourgeois but were barons of the realm. Often they owed their personal service for some other fief, and the service they owed in the cities was in all probability for a money fief levied against a rental in the city. Prutz in his *Kulturgeschichte der Kreuzzüge* comments particularly on the knight service for money fiefs which was so characteristic of the crusading states, and remarks that the relations of vassalage there were dependent on money.[1]

The feudal service of Outremer was far more French than Norman and there never developed in the crusading states any definite knight's fee. We can best trace the growth of a seignory in the East from the documents in Strehlke's *Tabulae Ordinis Theutonici* which show the steps by which the great seignory of Count Joscelin was built up. It is impossible to find in this or in any other of the great fiefs any system of knight's fees, or even any consistent value in cash against which the service of a knight was charged. Several elements entered into this, and the law of supply and demand can be seen in operation. When the supply of knights was low and when the Saracens invaded the country reducing the value of landed fiefs and rendering less secure the receipt of rentals levied against the revenues of the towns, the price of a single knight was comparatively high. On the other hand in times of comparative security, or when a new crusade from the West had brought a large number of knights to the East, the value of the knight's fief was appreciably lower. When Guy de Lusignan settled Cyprus, at a time when refugees from the mainland were clamoring for land in Cyprus, he established a ratio whereby a knight's fief should be one which produced a revenue of 400 besants, and that of a squire or turcopler who had two horses and a full suit of armor should produce 300 besants. And these fiefs *'furent assené en terre'*.[2] But that was in a time of particular stress when land was at a premium; and the normal average

---

[1] Prutz, *Kulturgeschichte*, pp. 166, 182–83: *'Auch Ritter thaten im heiligen Lande Söldnerdienste. Daran nahm man dort um so weniger Anstoss, als die den Franken eigenthümliche Ausbildung des Rentenlehens den ritterlichen Vassalen ohnehin schon dem Söldner genähert hatte'.* (p. 183).

[2] *Eracles*, p. 192; Mas Latrie, ii, 8–9. When he had enfeoffed 300 knights and 200 squires he had hardly enough land left to pay 70 knights in the domain.

value of a knight's holding on the continent was somewhat higher. A charter of 1169 shows a grant of a rental of 1200 besants a year on the revenues of Acre for the service of two knights, and an augment of 600 besants for an additional knight, making a straight fief of 600 besants a knight.[1] In 1174 Philip Rufus traded his revenue of 1000 besants in Acre for which he owed the service of one knight for the fiefs of Arabian and Zekanin for which he owed the same service, but he agreed to give two knights service for another revenue of 800 besants in Acre.[2] This would indicate that the value of a knight's fief in money had dropped considerably and that the king was reclaiming a revenue which was not bringing in adequate service with land which was not at such a high premium, and that Philip, who apparently desired to keep the money as well, was having to pay higher for it in service. In 1181 Joscelin de Courtney bought from Philip Rufus the revenue of 1000 besants at Acre which he held for life and for which he owed two knights service.[3] From this we may infer that between 1174 and 1181 the value of the knight had increased somewhat and that Philip had been given an extra 200 besants a year for his two knights service. When we remember that 1174 was the last year of the reign of Amaury I, a period of Jerusalemite successes and prosperity, and that by 1181 the Saracen menace had already begun seriously to disturb the Christians, the fluctuation is understandable. When Frederick II wanted men in 1229 he gave 6000 besants for ten knights' services—a rate of 600 besants per knight.[4] Thus we see the money fief of a knight varying from 400 besants to 600 and even 1000, depending on the need for men and the relative security of the revenues against which the fiefs were laid. In 1261 we find a knight receiving 500 besants, and another case where he was paid part in cash and part in kind.[5]

---

[1] Strehlke, doc. 5; *Regesta*, doc. 465.

[2] Strehlke, doc. 7; *Regesta*, doc. 517, and see note 42 above.

[3] Strehlke, doc. 13; *Regesta*, doc. 608.

[4] *Archives*, ii, B, 166–67; *Regesta*, doc. 1008.

In 1179 Joscelin purchased a fief carrying two knights' service for 7500 besants, but that was the purchase price of the land and does not help in trying to determine the value in annual revenue. (Strehlke, doc. 10; *Regesta*, doc. 579. This is the fief of the chamberlain which Ibelin lists as serving with two knights.)

[5] The charter by which Balian d'Ibelin sold his fief of Arsur to the Hospital in 1261 (D. L. *Cartulaire*, doc. 2985; *Regesta*, doc. 1302), shows the amounts which the knights and sergeants

Money fiefs were more secure than land fiefs, for the ports against whose revenues the money fiefs were granted were less exposed to Saracen attack than were the inland territories. Yet even they were not too secure and the *Livre au Roi* provides that if the king cannot pay his lieges they may sell their armor and live off the produce of the sale, and are meanwhile free from service under arms. The king should, when he is able, make up to them their expenses and their back pay, but it is especially provided that if the king's own revenues are cut off through pestilence, bad crops, or enemy invasion, he shall not be obliged to make up the back pay to the lieges.[1] The provision in so many of the grants, that if the revenues specifically granted are not forthcoming, the amount promised shall be made up from the revenues of some other port or from the general revenues of the kingdom, shows that even the best of securities were at times uncertain and that it was no unprecedented thing for a vassal to be deprived of his promised revenues.[2]

In the case of fiefs in land the vassal was freed from all service due from the fief if the land fell into the hands of the enemy and his lord did not make every effort to recover it. For failure on the part

---

received at that time for their services: knight service with four horses was worth 500 besants in one case; 200 besants, 50 measures of grain, 70 of barley, 50 of oil and 10 of lentils in another case. One sergeant received 72 besants and 2 livresons for the supply of three horses and the *restor* of two.

[1] *Livre au Roi*, xxvii, 625: 'C'il avient par aucune mauvaise année ou par autre raison que li rois ou la rayne soit si povres de ces rentes qu'il ne paie ses homes liges, la raison juge et comande ce enci à juger, que les homes liges ont tant de poier et d'avantage qu'il pevent bien vendre tout leur harneis pour leur vivre et remindre à pié, et jà ne tenront harnois por servir lor seignor, puis qui lor defaut de lor paie. Et toutes les oures que li rois avera poier de paier ou qui les semondra de servise faire, si juge la raison que li rois est tenus tout premier de paier les jusque à celuy jor, tout auci com il ont adès tenu harnois com tenir doivent. Mais c'il avient que yre de Dieu vint et pestilence qui ardi tous les blés et tos les biens dehors, ou que Sarasins vindrent qui tout prirent ce don li rois les paiet et don il fornisset sa terre, la raison juge que li rois n'est puis tenus de paier ses homes liges, se non de tant com il aura receu et tenues les rentes en son poier et non de plus, par dreit ne par l'assise'. Philip de Novare gives the last part verbatim, lviii, 531.

[2] A good example of this is the charter of Amaury I to the Hospital of Ste Marie of the Germans in 1173 in which he grants them 400 besants from Neapolis, and four casales, and one robbas of grain from every carrucate of land which the king holds in Jerusalem and Neapolis. And if the revenue is not forthcoming from these sources it shall be made up from the revenues of Acre. (Strehlke, doc. 6; *Regesta*, doc. 496.) A cursory glance through the grants to any of the Orders will show how common this provision was.

of the lord to protect his vassal in the possession of his fief was a breach of the feudal contract and automatically absolved the vassal from all allegiance and services. If, on the other hand, the lord made every effort to recover the land and could not, the vassal was freed from all service as long as the land was unrecovered but was still bound to his allegiance to his lord.[1] There was one item of considerable expense which the Outremer warrior had no need to worry about. That was the cost of replacement of horses killed or wounded in battle,—always a heavy item in medieval warefare, and especially so in warfare against the Saracens whose archers wrought particular havoc among the horses. Though the knights themselves were comparatively safe in their armor their steeds were ready targets for the Moslem arrows and the average of casualties among the horses must have been high. In order that the ardor of the warriors should not be dulled by consideration for their horses and worry over the expense of replacing them, the king accepted the responsibility and guaranteed the replacement of all mutilated beasts at a value assessed before the battle. This system, called *restor*, was an important feature of the crusading military system. It has already been shown that it was the duty of the marshal of the kingdom to inspect and assess the value of the horses before the battle, and to replace those killed or reimburse their owners afterwards.[2]

---

[1] *Livre au Roi*, xxviii, 625.

I have assumed in the discussion of these laws that the passage in the *Livre au Roi*, xxvii, referred to money fiefs. Dodu uses this passage to help prove that all vassals were paid, but I think that it can better be interpreted as referring to money fiefs in contrast to the landed fiefs in the next paragraph. As the term is lieges, the payment of mercenaries cannot be meant, and as the men were allowed to sell their armor and live off that until their money was provided, it would indicate that they were not men possessed of land fiefs or else they would live off them and not have to sell their armor. I can find no evidence which would incline me to Dodu's thesis concerning the payment of landed fief-holders.

In the Morea the knight whose land was captured by the enemy, so that he could not perform the services due, could recommend the land to his lord for two years and two days, or until it should be recovered, and was free of service meanwhile (*Assises de Romanie*, art. 55). No service was due from a fief while the holder was in prison, if he had been captured while serving his lord. (*Ibid.*, art. 106.)

[2] The laws governing *restor* are given in the *Livre au Roi*, x–xiii, 613–15. Usamah tells the anecdote concerning Tancred, that on occasion when he reproached his men for lack of valor, they replied that they feared not for themselves but for their horses, whereupon Tancred promised to replace all horses that were hurt, and the men went into battle with lighter hearts. (Usamah, ed. Hitti, p. 96.) I cannot say whether this is supposed to be the beginning of this practice or not.

Possession of a land fief demanded *personal* military service. The laws are very explicit in regard to the rendering of personal service for fiefs. Ibelin says that if a man holds several fiefs he shall do liege homage and personal service to the lord from whom he holds his first fief, and perform simple homage for the others for which he shall serve through a knight.[1] But in Jerusalem by the *Assise* of King Amaury of 1162 all the barons were liegemen of the king and so personal service would always be required for fiefs held from the crown. Philip de Novare goes into this matter and says that if a fief owing personal service to the king escheats to a man who already holds a fief which owes personal service to one of the chief vassals of the king it makes no difference, as the king would be served either way. But if the fief escheating owes service to another vassal, the man owes personal service to two lords, who might go to war with each other.[2] By the time of John d'Ibelin this matter had been decided by having liege homage done to the first lord, but when Novare wrote it was still unsettled apparently. If a man has a fief which requires personal service and cannot fulfill his service for it, and another fief escheats to him, Novare says that the lord may confiscate the second fief for the lifetime of the man, but shall give it up if one of the heirs of the man will do personal service for it.[3]

The *Livre au Roi* also specifies for the personal service in regard to fiefs held from the crown and says that if a fief escheats to a liege-man of the crown he must serve for the new fief with another knight.[4] As liege homage and liege service were required of any fief held from the king, it may be safe to assume that since money fiefs seemed to have the same status as fiefs in land, a money fief from the king would receive personal service rather than a land fief from another lord. It is immaterial for the most part as the vassals of the king's vassals were the vassals of the king according to the *Assise* of Amaury, and the king received personal service from them all. Yet money fiefs could be used in the East as in the West to secure more directly an arrière vassal who held his lands from some great lord.

---

[1] Ibelin, cxlviii, 223–24, ccxi, 336.

[2] Novare, lxx, 540–41. The *Assises de Romanie*, art. 99, provide that in case of war between lords the vassal served the lord to whom he first rendered homage.

[3] Novare, lxviii, 538.

[4] *Livre au Roi*, xxxviii, 633–34. But if the fief escheats to a man who has no fief he shall render personal service for it.

The Church and the military Orders were not held to give personal service. The Hospital, in several of its charters purchasing lands, promises to perform the services due from the fiefs except the personal service. Thus a charter of the 1260's, in which the terms of the sale of the seignory of Arsur are contained, stipulates that the Hospital will perform all the services which Balian d'Ibelin had rendered to Hugh, king of Jerusalem and Cyprus, save the service of the body.[1]

Default of service and refusal to reply to the summons were heinous crimes and punished by immediate forfeiture,[2] though the forfeiture was only for life. Further, if the man came but left before his time of service was completed, he was considered to be in default of service and forfeited his fief.[3] But default of service had to be proven in the court, for unless the man was officially summoned by the royal *bannier* he was not required to serve. In Jerusalem the *bannier* was held to prove by the witness of two other liegemen that he summoned the defaulting baron three times. If then he had not come, he was declared forfeit. If no witnesses would testify that he was thrice summoned, he might appear and swear that he was not summoned and no penalty would be imposed upon him. In Antioch, on the other hand, the defaulting baron might clear himself by swearing that he was not summoned and if he so swore, any number of witnesses to the contrary were unavailing and he went free and unpunished.[4]

Though long and continuous military service was exacted from the barons of Jerusalem, and though the service was at their own expense, there were yet many limitations to what the king could demand. No knight could, according to the *Livre au Roi* and Ibelin,

---

[1] D. L. *Cartulaire*, doc. 3047.   Balian kept out the rentals which he had from Acre and Neapolis and for which he also owed service to the king.   The date is not certain on this charter. A charter of Raymond of Antioch of 1149 permits his vassals to grant to the Hospital any lands they wish so long as the knight service is not thereby diminished.   (D. L. *Cartulaire*, doc. 183; *Regesta*, doc. 253.)

[2] Ibelin, cxci, 305–06, ccxx, 351; *Livre au Roi*, lii, 643–44.

[3] Ibelin, ccxxii, 353.   Thus Hugh III confiscated the fiefs of two knights one of whom refused to follow him to Syria, and the other of whom returned before the campaign was ended. (*Assises*, ii, 429.)

[4] *Livre au Roi*, lii, 643–44; *Assises d'Antioche*, i, 8–10.

be required to serve after he had passed the age of sixty years, though this applied only to personal service and he was held to send knights for those fiefs which he held by virtue of service through others.[1]

Service outside the realm was also strictly limited by the laws and even more in practice. The *Livre au Roi*, the oldest expression of the laws and customs of Outremer, says that the king has no legal right to demand service outside the realm for his own profit or need, '*por nul besoing de luy qu'il en ait*',—but that if he orders his vassals to serve for the profit or need of the realm,—'*por le profit dou reaume ou por le besoing de la terre*'—the liegemen are held to serve at the expense of the king. And if the king offers fair pay and the liegeman refuses to serve, he is held to be in default of service, and his fief is forfeit.[2] Ibelin gives a later version of the law regarding service outside the realm. Outside of the limits of the realm the liegeman owes three services, says the great jurist: first, for the marriage of the lord or one of his children; second, to guard and defend the faith and honor of the lord; and third, for the apparent need of the seignory and the common profit of the land. But all services outside the realm are at the expense of the lord.[3]

The *reaume* refers to the principality itself, and Antioch, Edessa, and Tripoli were all considered outside of the limits within which

[1] Ibelin, ccxxvi *bis*, 358–59. Beugnot gives two texts, one of which says sixty and the other forty years. The forty is obviously an error. Ibelin says that a man should supply arms and horses after he has ceased to perform service in person. In Chapter ccxxviii, 362, Ibelin says that no woman past sixty shall be held for service, nor shall she after that age be forced to marry to supply a knight.

The *Livre au Roi*, xlvii–xlviii, 641, says that a man over sixty, or one who is sick, wounded, or helpless, may have his fief free of service unless he is sick through his own dissipation, in which case he must supply someone to serve for him. Also, as above, fiefs held by the service of a knight shall be served for through knights, and are not quit of their service though the lord may not have to serve for the fief held by personal service. The *Assises d'Antioche*, i, 10, provide that a man past sixty is exempt from service. The *Assises de Romanie*, art. 89, provide that when a man passes sixty his fief shall be served for by his son or by a knight. A leper shall send a knight to perform service for him (art. 67).

[2] *Livre au Roi*, xxix, 626.

[3] Ibelin, ccxvii, 347: '*Et hors dou reiaume sont il tenus d'aler et de faire treis choses por le seignor; l'une est por le mariage de lui ou de aucun de ces enfanz; l'autre por sa fei et s'onor garder et defendre; la tierce por le besoing aparant de sa seignorie ou le comun prouffit de sa terre*'.

The *Assises de Romanie*, art. 65, are specific that the vassal need not serve outside the limits of the principality, but must cross the sea to reach another part of the principality if necessary.

free and unlimited service was due.[1] In our chapter on the relations of the kings with the great counties we shall have occasion to notice the service given in the counties by the barons of Jerusalem.

When the kings of Cyprus became kings of Jerusalem a complicated problem arose in regard to the limits of the realm. Many of the lords held fiefs in both realms and so were held for service in both; but there were some whose holdings were only in one of the two kingdoms and there was some difficulty in determining what service could be demanded in Jerusalem from knights holding only in Cyprus.

The question of service owed by the Cypriot barons was the subject of a dispute held between Hugh III and the barons led by James d'Ibelin in 1272. The king called on Edward of England, who was at that time in the East on crusade, to hear the debate. The knights owed service, according to Hugh, at the desire and need of the king, and thus should serve outside the realm as well as within. For the barons of Jerusalem had served in Edessa, Antioch, Tripoli, Damascus, and Egypt under their kings; and Cyprus was ruled by the same laws as Jerusalem. And the barons of Cyprus had in times past served in Adalia, Rhodes, and Armenia, as well as in Syria. Under Amaury II they had served on the continent, and Cypriot knights had garrisoned Jaffa which Amaury held as count before he became king of Jerusalem. They had followed Henry to Damietta, and to the relief of Beirut during the Lombard war. And they had gone to Damietta when Louis IX attacked it, and had followed Hugh III himself to Syria. And for these reasons, the nature of their oaths and the precedents of their sires, Hugh considered that they owed service on the continent at his discretion. To the demands and arguments of the king, James d'Ibelin replied that their oaths did not bind them to unlimited service at the king's discretion and that they were not bound to serve outside the limits of the realm. Knights did not owe service on the sea by any interpretation of their oaths. The king was trying to turn their good deeds to their disadvantage, for in the past they had, in excess of their duty, served overseas for

[1] Albert Aix, XI, xviii, 671, shows Baldwin I asking his vassals to serve voluntarily in relief of Edessa. While they were under no obligation to serve, the king asked them to come as friends and allies.

their love of God and their lord, but this should not create a precedent which could operate against them. Never was this service rendered through the summons of the king. For when they served at Beirut it was because John, the old lord of Beirut, had come before the *Haute Cour* and asked the king, who was then a minor, to help him, and had asked the barons for their aid; and they had gone to help him willingly, but not through any summons. And when they had served at Damietta they had been summoned by the king, but they had gone to him and said, 'Sire, you have had us summoned and we do not heed your summons nor do we believe that we owe you this service; but we will go for God and for our honor', and the king had replied, 'You have spoken well, and I will stand the expense'. And to the king's claims, he, James d'Ibelin, thus replied that the barons of Cyprus had given more than was necessary but would not be forced into yielding up that which was always a free gift. And there were those yet living who would testify that the house of Ibelin had led them across the seas more often than that of Lusignan, so that if precedent made the rule the Ibelins might demand service rather than the king.[1]

The *Document* which supplies the details of this argument does not state the outcome, but the *Eracles*, which mentions the 'discord between the king of Cyprus and his men for the service which the king demanded of them outside the isle of Cyprus and which they did not believe they owed', under the year 1272, says that in 1273 an accord was reached whereby the barons recognized that they owed the king service outside the isle of Cyprus, in Jerusalem, or wherever he pleased, four months out of the year, and that they must serve in person where the king himself or his son went.[2]

---

[1] *Document Relatif au Service Militaire (Assises,* ii), pp. 427–34. Ibelin's closing paragraph is as perfect an example of the defiant attitude of the great barons towards the king as may be readily found, and ranks with the boast of Earl Bigod to his king, that he would neither die nor serve. Ibelin said: 'Et encores mostrons noz certainement par genz qui sont encores plainz de vie, que les homes dou reiaume de Chypre ont plus servi hors doudit reiaume le lignage de Ybelin, que monseignor le rei ne ces ancestres; et se l'usage de leur servise les aservist, par tel raison leur poreient demander ciaus de Ybelin come monseignor le rei leur demande.' (p. 434.)

[2] *Eracles,* pp. 462–64. When Frederick II had demanded service in Syria, old John d'Ibelin of Beirut had urged his adherents to serve not for love of the emperor but for love of Christ, and so that no one could ever say that the Ibelins were friendly to the Saracens and refused to help reconquer the Holy Land. (*Gestes,* par. 126.)

Another limitation to the service which the lord might exact from his man was that created by the special *Assise* of King Amaury at Belfis on his campaign against Egypt, whereby no man was compelled to follow his lord to the siege of a city or castle where his horse could not carry him. This limitation was not always enforced and John d'Ibelin of Beirut reproached himself with not observing it when Anceau de Brie was killed at the siege of Kyrenia while storming the walls, which under the terms of the assise he could not have been required to do.[1]

The knights who owed service for fiefs—either in land or money—formed the backbone of the army of the Latin kingdom. In addition to the fiefs which brought knight's service were those held chiefly by the Church which brought sergeant service, and which could be called upon like the regular lay fiefs. The sergeants owed by the towns fall into this same group. Ibelin, after listing the knights owed by the various fiefs, gives a chapter on the sergeants which he terms: *'Ces sont les aides que les yglises et les borgeis deivent, quant le grant besoin est en la terre dou reiaume de Jerusalem.'*[2] In this chapter he lists 6025 sergeants owed by the various churches, monasteries, and cities. The bishop of Bethlehem owed 200 sergeants, that of Lydda 200, that of Acre 150; the archbishop of Tyre owed 150, that of Caesarea 50; the city of Caesarea owed 50, Neapolis 300, Tyre 100, Jaffa 100; the patriarch and the chapter of the Holy Sepulchre owed 500 each. The abbeys of Josaphat and Mount Sion owed 150 each, and that of the Mount of Olives 50.

These sergeants owed by the bishops and abbots were owed for fiefs held by them for sergeant service. The cities did not have communal militia but served for their lands and privileges with sergeants whom they hired and supplied. These sergeants generally were not

---

[1] *Gestes*, par. 202: *'Jamais chevalier ne deüst ni feïst servise a afaire de ville, ne de chasteau, ni en leuc que cheval ne peüst porter, se il ne fust assegié, ou sur son cors defendant'*.

Beugnot, *Assises*, i, Introduction, p. 31, interprets this to mean that a knight need not serve at a greater distance than his horse could carry him in a single day. But the assise was passed when a knight was killed storming a wall, and, as Schlumberger points out (*Amaury I*, p. 193), was passed to guarantee that knights need not serve as infantry in sieges. Schlumberger thinks it was merely an order of the day, and not meant as a permanent assise.

The Morea had a law whereby a vassal should not be constrained to serve in any place where the lord did not send a sufficient supporting force. (*Assises de Romanie*, art. 22.)

[2] Ibelin, cclxxii, 426–27. The *Gestes*, par. 521, list 4075 in 1291.

summoned at the first call, and were often held as a sort of reserve for the army. Albert of Aix and Fulcher tell of Baldwin I sending to the patriarch to assemble a body of *'fideles'* and bring them to the army at Rama, and say that the patriarch brought 150 foot soldiers.[1]

In addition to these feudal levies, both knights and sergeants, were the able-bodied citizenry who could be called on in time of urgent need. This was done through the publishing of the king's ban summoning all loyal men to the aid of the country. This *arrière ban*, or as it was known in the Germanies, *landwehr*, included all the men capable of bearing arms, irrespective of whether they held land or not. The early kingdom shows several cases of the calling out of the *arrière ban*. In 1104 the king summoned all the people for the siege of Acre, and William of Tyre in telling of it used the phrase *'convocatis viribus et populo universo'*, so that there can be no doubt but that the non-feudal populace is meant.[2] In 1122 when the Egyptian fleet attacked Jaffa, the patriarch and Eustache Grenier, the constable, with the other chief men, raised a militia, according to William. This is a doubtful instance and may or may not refer to anything more than the regular feudal levy.[3] No possible doubt attaches to the statements of William that in 1126 Baldwin assembled the men of the kingdom from the greatest to the least for the war against Damascus[4], and that in 1153 all the men of the kingdom took part in the siege of Ascalon.[5] Ernoul, in telling of Baldwin IV's armament at Ascalon against Saladin, says that he found he had only 500 knights and so summoned the *arrière ban*, and that in the battle the bourgeoisie came out after the knights had charged, and slaughtered the fleeing foe.[6] Likewise in 1187 King Guy, at the advice of the Master of the Temple, summoned to Saphorie all who were able

---

[1] Albert Aix, IX, xlix, 622; Fulcher, II, xxxi, 489–94; *Chronologie*, no, 753.

[2] William Tyre, X, xxviii, 442.

[3] William Tyre, XII, xxi, 544. In the same doubtful class is the statement of Albert of Aix, XII, xi, 695, that Baldwin I summoned all who were in the vicinity of Jerusalem and all the cities he possessed and thus got 700 knights and 4000 footmen.

[4] William Tyre, XIII, xviii, 582: *'congregatus est de mandato domini regi et principum, universi regni populus, a maximo usque ad minimum, voce praeconia, per urbes singulas'*.

[5] William Tyre, XVII, xxi, 795: *'convocatis igitur universi regni viribus, et populo unanimiter conveniente'*.

[6] Ernoul, pp. 42, 45: *'Ançois que li arrière bans venist à Escalonne . . . si prisent les bourgois de Jherusalem et grant partie de ciaus de le tiere qui de plus loing venoient'*. (p. 42.)

to come and sent out the *arrière ban*.[1] In 1218 when John de Brienne had gone to Egypt with the pick of the fighting men of the kingdom, Walter l'Alleman, who was ruling at Acre in place of the king, called on the townsmen and the Genoese to help defend the city of Caesarea against the attack of Melek-el-Moaddan of Damascus.[2]

The Genoese, Pisan, and Venetian communes were often called upon to assist in the defense of the cities, and as a rule were given extra privileges in return. As the relations of the kings of Jerusalem to the Italian cities are considered in another chapter, it will suffice to notice here that many valuable services were rendered by these foreigners both in the conquest and defense of the kingdom, and that they supplied valuable auxiliaries to the regular troops of the various eastern Latin states; though they could only be called on to defend the cities, they served as allies in many offensive campaigns.

In addition to these troops of western origin were the troops, largely natives, who were hired as mercenaries.[3] It should not be thought that all holders of fiefs in land or money were of Frankish descent, for there were many native landholders; nor were all mercenaries natives, for many who came to Syria from the West accepted service as mercenaries; but the Frankish warrior was usually granted a money fief and not hired outright, and most of the mercenaries were native Syrians, Armenians, or Maronites. The chief branch of the native auxiliaries were the *Turcoples*. Usamah calls them the archers of the Franks,[4] and they seem to have been light armed cavalry recruited from half-breeds and natives.[5] These *turcoples* were directly under the marshal of the kingdom and took their orders from him, having no native leaders of their own.

[1] Ernoul, p. 156.

[2] *Eracles*, p. 334.

[3] William Tyre, XIII, xvii, 581, tells how Baldwin II in 1125 raised an army '*interventu pecuniae*'.

[4] Usamah, (ed. Hitti), p. 79.

[5] William Tyre, XIX, xxv, 925, calls them '*equites levis armaturae quo turcopulos vocant*'. Albert Aix, V, iii, 434, refers to them as '*ex Turco patre et Graeca matre procreati*'.

It is probable that Albert got his description from Raymond of Aguilers, who uses almost identical terms. The *turcoples* seem to have been light armed cavalry, probably archers, and of non-Frank stock. (See Dodu, p. 205.) The Byzantines used similar troops, and in 1101 Alexis gave a troop of *turcoples* to Raymond of Toulouse to help Stephen of Blois and the Lombard crusaders. (Chalandon, *Alexis I*, p. 226.)

Besides the *turcoples*, there were Frankish mercenaries who remained in Syria and served for regular pay. Examples of these are
found in the men left by Walter d'Avenes who in 1218, upon depart-
ing for the West, left forty knights in Syria and paid them for one
year;[1] in the hundred knights left by Louis IX under the command
of Geoffrey de Sargines in 1254;[2] and in the forces under Richard
Filanger which Frederick II sent to Syria.[3] A very good example of
how men were hired as mercenaries who had come to the East as crusaders on one of the later expeditions is found in the memoir of
Amaury de Roche, commander of the Temple in France, in which
he suggests that the Pope be asked to pay for the retention of the
fifty knights led by the count of Nevers, who can be hired for the
sum of sixty livres Tournois for each knight.[4]

In a country as poverty-stricken as the kingdom of Jerusalem
usually was, the question how mercenaries should be paid was
often a serious one. The provisions of the *Assises* and the numerous
anecdotes which have come down in regard to securing the money
for payment of soldiers cannot refer wholly to the payment of holders of money fiefs; for the money fief was levied on, and money was
usually secured from, the revenues of a certain town. The mercenary,
however, who served for a definite sum payable by the king or some
lord often had trouble in collecting his due. The laws are full on this
point. Failure to pay is one of the things which can be appealed in
the *Haute Cour*.[5] Ibelin says that the *sodeer* shall appeal to the
constable if he does not receive his pay, and the constable shall secure it for him.[6]

The contracts were evidently made month by month, on the first,

[1] *Eracles*, p. 326.

[2] *Eracles*, p. 441; *Rothelin Eracles*, p. 629.

[3] *Eracles*, pp. 385–86.

[4] Mas Latrie, ii, 71; *Regesta*, doc. 1347.

This dates from about 1266. In 1222 Philip Augustus, in his will, left 150,000 silver marks
to the king of Jerusalem and to the Templars that they might each support 100 knights for
three years. (D. L. *Cartulaire*, doc. 1755.) That the pay for soldiers in the crusading states
was relatively high is evidenced by Usamah's anecdote of Tancred, who taunted his men that
they received as much as 100 Moslems but could not break a line of Moslem infantry. (Usamah, ed. Hitti, p. 96.)

[5] Ibelin, lxxx, 128.

[6] Ibelin, cxxxiv–v, 209–11.

as Beugnot points out, for Ibelin says that if the lord discharges his *sodeer* after three days he must pay him for the full month's service, but if the *sodeer* demands his discharge the lord need not pay him if he serves three days into the next month.[1] If the *sodeer* has contracted to serve the month he may not leave before the term of his contract is ended unless he shall inherit a fief which demands his personal service, or shall become a monk or priest, or marry, or shall take the Cross and go in God's service whither his lord would not lead him. But if he shall quit his service under any other circumstances he shall forfeit his fief if he holds one, or his harness if he is a common *sodeer*. Cases of knights come before the constable, those of the squires and sergeants before the marshal.[2]

Sodeers were maintained by the king, as well as by the liegemen who employed them to serve as extra knights for their fiefs. The king, who as we have already seen, only received exemption from making good the payments due from money fiefs when the country was ravaged by famine, pestilence, or the Saracens, was often hard pressed to raise the money to pay his mercenaries. King Guy used the money which Henry II of England sent as part of his penance for the murder of Becket to hire knights and footmen.[3] The testament of Philip Augustus provided for the granting of monies to the king and to the Temple to hire troops. William of Tyre tells the story of how Baldwin of Edessa tricked his father-in-law, Gabriel of Meletenia, into supplying the money to pay his men by pawning his beard. Joinville tells of securing money to pay the men by breaking into the coffers of the Templars.[4]

---

[1] Ibelin, cxxxvi, 211.

[2] Ibelin, cxxxvii, 211–12. Ibelin differentiates between those who serve for a fief and those who serve for pay: '*Quant aucun home, chevalier ou autre, demorre à seignor à fei ou à fiance à terme mouti, il ne se peut devant le terme partir dou servise son seignor, se n'est por les choses après dittes*', and give the causes above cited. The penalty for desertion before the end of the term was for the knight confiscation of his armor and equipment, and for the simple soldier having his hands pierced with a hot iron. This was excessively severe for breach of contract and was considered as desertion from the army rather than as simple civil contract violation. The pilgrim could return home without penalty, even though he had contracted to serve for a longer term than he stayed.

[3] *Eracles*, pp. 46–47.

[4] D. L. *Cartulaire*, doc. 1755; William Tyre, XI, xi, 469–72; Joinville (ed. De Wailly: Paris; Firmin Didot, 1874), lxxv, 208–10.

In 1149 when Antioch was threatened by Nureddin, Amaury, the patriarch, contrary to his custom, gave of his own money to hire soldiers. (William Tyre, XVII, x, 775.)

The conversation between Amaury I and Thoros of Armenia illustrates excellently the uncertain means employed by the kings of Jerusalem to pay their mercenaries. Thoros marvelled at the fact that all the lands and castles of the kingdom belonged to religious Orders of one type or another and asked how the king got troops, seeing that only three castles remained to him. Amaury replied that he hired them. Thoros seeing that he had not enough rents to afford a large force asked where he got the money, to which the king replied: '*Jou les emprunte tant com jou puisse mius fere*', whereat Thoros pitied him for his defenseless realm and personal weakness.[1]

The Orders, however, supplied valuable military assistance to the kingdom. Pledged to continuous warfare against the enemies of Christ, they held the frontier fortresses and guarded the pilgrim roads throughout Palestine. The Orders were especially valuable to the kingdom through their defense of border fortresses and castles. While some of these castles were the property of the Orders, others were royal castles entrusted to them for safekeeping.

For special services the kings often granted the Orders special concessions, such as a larger share of the booty or extra lands or revenues. In 1168 Amaury I promised the Hospital extensive revenues to be levied on certain Egyptian cities, and first share in the spoils (after the king should have taken out his half) in return for 500 knights and 500 *turcoples* which the Hospital supplied for the Egyptian campaign.[2] In 1220 John de Brienne granted the Teutonic knights half the plunder to be taken at Damietta.[3] Other charters grant the Orders the right of taking the king's share of the spoils if the king shall not be in person in the host.[4]

The Orders acted independently and had their own navies as well as land forces. The navy of the Hospital was one of the most important war fleets of the later Middle Ages, especially after the Knights moved to Rhodes and Malta, but even in the period of the Latin kingdom they had a considerable fleet, and a letter of Nicholas IV in

---

[1] Ernoul, pp. 27–29.

[2] D. L. *Cartulaire*, doc. 402; *Regesta*, doc. 452.

[3] *Archives*, ii, B, 166; *Regesta*, doc. 930.

[4] A charter of Baldwin IV of 1177 (*Regesta*, doc. 553a) makes a grant to the Order of Avis with the stipulation that the land granted shall revert to the donor if the Order ceases to keep up the war against the Moslems.

1292 shows the Pope appealing to the Master of the Hospital to assist the king of Armenia defend his country.[1]

The kingdom of Jerusalem itself had no navy and was dependent on the fleets supplied by the Italian communes, the Orders, and such occasional ships as were possessed by the various counts and barons. The *Gestes* tell how in 1232 the *poulani* of the ports armed vessels, and the king (Henry) gave them fiefs (presumably money) for this naval service.[2] But the major part of the naval armament of the Latin states in the earlier period of their history was supplied by allied fleets of Italians, and the great concessions which were granted to the Venetians, Genoese, Pisans, Marseillais, and Barcelonese were given largely as payment for naval assistance rendered the Frankish armies. In the later period after the loss of Syria, the fleet became the chief arm of the kingdom of Cyprus, but the continental kingdom of Jerusalem had none.[3]

Over this heterogeneous military force the king of Jerusalem had theoretical control. His was the command of the army, and the allies and the soldiery of the Orders served under him. The several occasions when great forces came from the West are exceptional, and need not be considered here. When the crusaders assembled to attack Egypt in 1218 they elected John de Brienne commander of the entire force. But, as we have seen, the command was too divided and the pretensions of the legate, Pelagius, ruined the expedition. The discord between Richard of England and Philip Augustus which so destroyed the efficiency of the third crusade is known in fact and in fiction. During this crusade the rival rulers of Jerusalem played

---

[1] D. L. *Cartulaire*, doc. 4183.

[2] *Gestes*, par. 181.

[3] The kings borrowed or hired ships on many occasions, generally from the Italians but often from individuals. In 1153 Gerard of Sidon commanded a fleet of fifteen galleys at the siege of Ascalon, the ships probably being supplied by the Marseillais. Raymond of Tripoli built a fleet when he wished to send his sister in honor to Constantinople, and turned it over to pirates to ravage the Greek coasts when the sister was refused. (William Tyre, XVIII, xxxiii, 878.) J. Longnon, *Les Français d'Outremer* (Paris, 1929), p. 130, believes that Jerusalem had a fleet of its own and says there was one in the Red Sea, but (p. 140) says that the navy amounted to little and that, while the king had arsenals at Tyre and Acre, he relied on the fleets of the Italians and the Orders.

For the standard account of the naval assistance given by the Italian cities see W. Heyd, *Histoire du Commerce du Levant au Moyen Age.*

rôles decidedly subordinate to the great European monarchs. The second crusade was another case of divided command and the soldiers of Jerusalem, France, the Empire, and Antioch could not get along together; nor could the Orders agree with any of them, and the result was the fiasco before Damascus. When St Louis came to the East he played a large part in governing the country while he was there, and the sixth crusade was under his command with the king of Cyprus as an attendant ally.

But in normal times the king was supposed to have control. The Orders and each of the great counties were always independent and could make their own treaties, declare war and make peace, without any reference to the king or his policy, but as far as the principality of Jerusalem went the king held control. The command of the army was retained by the king or entrusted to the constable who commanded in his absence.

The king had control over all castles and fortresses and could requisition private castles in time of need.[1] But the king could not, according to the *Livre au Roi*, alienate the castles or fortresses of the kingdom to the enemy, and, no matter how great his need, could not surrender them to the Saracens on his own authority. If the king did this without consulting the *Haute Cour* the barons had the right to revolt against him.[2]

In a way the military position of the king of Jerusalem was characteristic of his entire position. He had theoretical powers but was constantly hindered in exercising them by a baronage, jealously guarding their rights and privileges, whom he had to consult on all points. When he could assert himself over his barons, he was hampered by outside interference; and his unfortunate kingdom, ill enough united at best, was torn by the conflict between opposing factions and divergent ambitions of those who came to reëstablish it.

[1] A charter of Amaury II of 1198 grants the Teutonic Knights the tower over the gate of St Nicholas at Acre with the provision that the Knights must surrender it back to the king on demand. (Strehlke, doc. 35.)

[2] *Livre au Roi*, i, 607; a prohibition which assumes the right of the king to control castles in ordinary circumstances. The seneschal had as part of his duties the control of the castles.

In the Morea the prince could surrender castles to the enemy only with the consent of his council of liegemen. (*Assises de Romanie*, art. 19.) Castles in the Morea were allowed to be built only by the prince, the twelve great barons, and the lords who held high criminal justice. (*Assises de Romanie*, art. 94.)

CHAPTER 8
ADMINISTRATION OF FINANCE

CONCERNING the administration of finances in the kingdom of Jerusalem it is impossible to speak with any certainty owing to the almost total lack of evidence and the very inconclusive character of the scanty materials which have been preserved. Practically all that we know of the financial administrative system is derived from the texts of the *Assises*, as no rolls, writs, or accounts have come down to us. Scattered references here and there help to piece out our general picture but the whole must necessarily be vague and shadowy.

No evidence of an elaborately organized exchequer system has been preserved, and it is fairly safe to assume that the Latin states of Outremer did not develop financial bureaucracies in any way comparable to the exchequers of Norman Sicily or England. While argument from silence is always most unsafe, it is reasonable to assume that had there been an exchequer the *Assises* would have included some mention of its officials, as they so carefully include the financial duties of the officers whom they mention, and as their accounts of the various court officials are so full. It is true that no records of any of the administrative departments of the kingdom of Jerusalem have been preserved; the fall of the capital city before Saladin and the subsequent transference of the government to Acre, followed a century later by the removal to Cyprus, caused all governmental records to be destroyed, including the registers of the *Secrète*, which we know to have existed, and the *Lettres du Sépulcre*, which may or may not have been an eastern Domesday Book.

It is impossible to prove conclusively that there was not an exchequer,—it would be equally impossible to prove that one had existed. The monarchy was, on the whole, very loosely organized and its institutions were of the simplest feudal type; with these a centralized exchequer system would agree but badly. The Franks found certain Graeco-Saracenic financial administrative features in use in their conquered possessions and did not discard them. They continued to use the *Secrète*, with its system of registers, which

166

had been employed in Syria before the crusades, but they did not add much to it or develop it as did the Norman conquerors of Sicily; the latter finding almost the same system in use in the island, developed it into an intricate financial and administrative organization. The easy adaptability of the Norman as compared with the intransigeance of the French has been often remarked; the crusaders kept the older system but were satisfied with it as it was, the Normans developed and expanded its possibilities to the utmost.

What little we know concerning the central treasury of Jerusalem can be briefly set forth. The head of the financial administration was the seneschal. He had charge of the properties and revenues of the crown and received the accounts of the treasury officials. All officials were responsible to him, save the clerks of the king's household, who were under the supervision of the chamberlain, and it was by the seneschal or by his order that all payments were made from the treasury.[1] Any profits accruing to the king as the result of a successful battle were turned over to the care of the seneschal.

The central treasury bureau was the *Secrète*, headed by the *bailli de la Secrète*, and manned by a staff of *écrivains* and *receveurs*.[2] In the *Secrète* were kept registers,—the only registers of which we have definite notice in the kingdom. But the *Secrète* was more than a mere chamber of accounts. There the horses were registered for *restor* by the marshal.[3] To the *Secrète* the viscounts made their quarterly returns. There charters were registered for security, fiefs in land or money were pledged as security for loans, and lords paid their vassals the amounts of their money fiefs before witnesses.[4] This bureau with its accounts and registers must have been taken over by the

[1] Ibelin, cclvi, 407–09. Payments for *restor* required the order of the marshal as well.

[2] For even this bit of information we are forced to go to thirteenth century Cyprus, and the existence of a *bailli de la Secrète* in Jerusalem cannot be definitely proven. In Cyprus the office became quite influential in the fourteenth century, and Rey gives a list of the (fourteenth century) baillies (*Familles*, pp. 667–69), to which should be added the name of Henry de Gibelet, who was *bailli de la Secrète* in 1232. (*Gestes*, par. 177. John d'Ibelin left him as his commander in Cyprus when he went to Syria in that year.)

It was to the *bailli de la Secrète*, in fourteenth century Cyprus, that foreigners presented themselves to establish their nationality and to secure the commercial privileges and exemptions to which they were entitled.

[3] *Livre au Roi*, x–xi, 613–14.

[4] Ibelin cl, 227; Novare, xxxiv, 511; lxxviii, 550.

Franks from the previous administrative system and the very name comes from the Byzantine σεκρῆτον, though the institution was in part Saracenic as well as Byzantine.[1] The viscount, who made his returns quarterly to the *Secrète*, was the regular local agent for the collection of the domain revenues and the general taxes and dues. Like the Norman officer of the same title

[1] The all inclusiveness of the *Secrète* registers does much to explain the absence of chancery registers in Jerusalem, for charters and grants which were registered by the chancery in the West were registered by the *Secrète* in the East.   As none of the *Secrète* registers have been preserved it is impossible to tell whether there was but one set of books or whether there were within the *Secrète* several separate bureaus, each devoted to some specific business.   The whole institution was carried over from the previous administration and we know that the Saracen register and financial system was highly developed.   In Fatimite Egypt there were three *dîwâns*: one which recorded the lands and land tax; one which recorded persons and poll tax; and a third which received the returns of the local agents, listed the feudal holdings, controlled the palace expenditures, and audited accounts.   (See Worms, 'Recherches sur la Constitution de la Propriété Territoriale dans les Pays Mussulmans', *Journal Asiatique*, 3rd series, xiv, 4th series, i, iii, especially xiv, 321–338, 347–48.)

It was from a combination of Byzantine elements with this Saracenic system that the Normans in Sicily developed their *Dîwân at Tahik al ma'mûr* which is found under Roger II as a part of the *curia*, and which in 1161 appears under the Greek title of *Secreton*.   After 1174 this broke down into two bureaus: the *Dîwân* or *Duana de Secrètis*, which controlled the royal finances and the domain; and the *Duana baronum*, which administered feudal finances and matters pertaining to fiefs.   The *Duana de Secrètis* was further divided into two *dîwâns* which administered domain revenues, and markets, sales, etc. respectively.   (See Haskins, 'England and Sicily in the Twelfth Century', *E. H. R.*, xxvi (1911), 652–55; Chalandon, *Domination Normande*, ii, 647–53; R. von Heckel, 'Das Päpstliche und Sicilische Registerwesen', *Archiv für Urkundenforschung*, i (1908), 376–94.)

But while the Normans were influenced in the development of their institutions by the Saracens, they derived their chancery registers and their register systems essentially from the papal and Byzantine models; and the registers of Sicily were the descendents of the old Roman registers through the papal and Byzantine as much if not more than through the Perso-Arabic.   (Haskins, *op. cit.*, pp. 443–447; K. A. Kehr, *Die Urkunden der Normannisch-Sicilischen Könige* (Innsbruck, 1902).   H. I. Bell, 'Aphrodito Papyri', *Greek Papyri of the British Musuem*, iv (London, 1910), discusses in the Introduction how the Arabic registers came through the Persian from the Roman Empire.)

The *Secrète* of Jerusalem included all the types of work done by both the *Duanas* of Sicily, and Jerusalem did not develop a special *Duana Baronum*; but what differentiation there may have been within the single *Secrète* it is impossible to say.   We do not even know whether or not Jerusalem had any regular tax registers or land books.   It may be assumed that it did, for the Arabs had full registers and the Franks took over the system, including a poll tax on all Moslems.   That there was some sort of a *Livre des Fiefs* for Jerusalem in the reign of Baldwin IV is evidenced by the enumeration of services owed by the fiefs and cities in Ibelin's chapter CCLXXI, for he must certainly have copied his list from some older document.

The earlier registers were not, in western Europe, divided as to contents.   In France the

or the French *prévôt*, he collected the revenues, paid out the necessary expenses of his viscounty, and returned the balance to the *Secrète*. He also collected the fines from the justice which he administered as president of the *Cour des Bourgeois*.[1]

On occasion the entire revenues of a city or country would be farmed out for a period of years. In 1198 Amaury II summoned the liegemen to elect two men to whom he could farm the rents and revenues of Acre. Under Frederick II a company was formed by Amaury Barlais, Amaury de Bethsan, Gauvain de Chenchi, William de Rivet, and Hugh de Gibelet to farm the revenues of Cyprus; and they were instructed to make the payments due to the emperor's baillies in Jerusalem. They purchased the farm of Cyprus for three years for a payment of 10,000 marks.[2]

The collection of the customs duties at the ports was farmed out to individuals, as Ibn Djubair explains in his account of the customs office at Acre through which he passed.[3] This corresponds to the system in Sicily and south Italy under Frederick II and Charles of

---

books kept by Philip Augustus included all sorts of material, and even when St Louis had a second copy of the register made, it contained the same materials and did not differentiate. Only as the various departments of state broke off from each other did separate registers develop in France. In England where rolls were used instead of books, the public matters gradually were put on one set of rolls and the private on another,—but that was a development of the thirteenth century. The Sicilian registers had been kept on rolls under the Norman princes, but Frederick II adopted the form of books which were bound by years and which included matters of every description of which the emperor wished to keep a record. It was not until Charles of Anjou that the various materials were sorted and separate books were kept. (Heckel, *op. cit.*, pp. 448–59.)

More might be said concerning the registers and the *Secrète* if it were at all possible to determine when they developed. Were they in existence when Philip Augustus came to the East on the crusade? If so (and as they were inherited from the preceding administration they were probably there from the time of the Frankish conquest), did they have any influence on the system of French registers which were established by Philip in 1194 on his return to France? Probably not, for the French monarchs must have been familiar with registers in the West,—those of the Papacy or Sicily,—but it is an interesting speculation and it would be strange indeed to find the underdeveloped Jerusalemite register system affecting the occidental.

[1] *Abrégé Cour Bourgeois*, vii, 241: 'Encores doit le visconte et par court faire amasser les rentes dou seignor et faire les garder à la court, si come il sera devizé ci après; de laquelle rente se doivent faire les despens de la visconté; de laquel entrée et yssue se doit rendre à conte à la Segrete dou Roi par l'escrivain de la court chascun trois mois'.

[2] Ernoul, p. 311, for bailliage of 1198. For that of 1229 see: *Gestes*, par, 139; *Eracles*, p. 375.

[3] Ibn Djubair (*R. H. C. Or.*, iii) p. 449.

Anjou, where a corporation called the *Magistri procuratores et portulani* held the customs duties in farm, paying the sum contracted to the government and assuming all the risks and profits. In Sicily and Italy the *portulani* appointed the port captains and officers, though two officials were appointed by the king and district vicar to assist and check the company's servants.[1] I presume that these farmers of the port revenues in the kingdom of Jerusalem were the officials to whom reference is made under the title viscounts of the ports.

In the Norman kingdom the difference was made between revenues which were under a *Duana de Secrètis* and the customs duties and revenues. The latter were farmed by the *portulani*. Under Frederick II the *Secrètis'* revenues were collected by the royal chamberlains on the mainland and farmed out in Sicily. Under the Angevins the farm system was extended from Sicily to include both parts of the kingdom. The materials from Jerusalem do not permit of any conclusion as to whether or not any such general distinction existed between revenues payable to the *Secrète* and others, and I am inclined to believe there was not, as the *Secrète* had a wide scope and all funds seem to have passed through it. There is, however, a similarity between the two practices; the viscount, like the Italian chamberlain, collected the dues other than customs, and the special farmers had charge of the port revenues. While the corporation of tax farmers never extended its activities to the domain and other such taxes in the East, the viscount probably farmed them himself. I believe that the Jerusalemite system was a cross between the the French and the Sicilian, that the viscount more closely resembled the *prévôt*, and that the customs farm was like the Sicilian, both countries having followed Byzantino-Saracenic institutions found by the conquerors. This would agree with the general thesis that the Franks brought with them officers and institutions with which they were familiar in the West and adapted them to their new surroundings and conditions, but that for new conditions with which they were not familiar at home they retained the old Byzantino-Saracenic institutions which they found in use.[2]

---

[1] Huillard-Bréholles, *Historia Diplomatica Friderici Secundi*, xii, 416–18; P. Durrieu, *Archives Angevines de Naples*, i, 54–57; L. Cadier, *L'Administration du Royaume de Sicile*, pp. 23–25.

[2] In Jerusalem as in France it was, I believe, the district rather than the officer who was

The revenues of the kings of Jerusalem included all the regular feudal and domainial sources of income and, in addition, the extensive profits from the customs duties at those ports and border towns which were in the hands of the king. These port duties belonged to the king as lord of the maritime cities and not as king, for the lords of Beirut, Tyre, and other cities controlled the revenues from their own cities.

The income from the domain was considerable in the flourishing period of the kingdom, for the domain included the more important ports with their customs duties. When Baldwin II ascended the throne he reserved for the crown the cities of Neapolis, Jaffa, Ascalon, Acre, Sidon, Tiberias, and St Abraham's (Hebron) in addition to the royal city of Jerusalem.[1] Many of these cities had been granted away as fiefs before the fall of Jerusalem, and in the period of the second kingdom only Acre remained to the king; but in the earlier days the crown must have derived much profit from its cities. In addition were the agricultural domain lands possessed by the king, known as *censive* lands, whose serfs paid all the usual dues and services, *corvée, angaria*, the gifts at specified times of the year, and the payments for use of pasture, forest, and stream. The king had also the *terraticum*, a tax on bourgeoisie, as well as on agricultural peasants.[2] It is impossible to determine the exact extent of the lands reserved for the king's domain and not granted out as fiefs, but the kings of Jerusalem seem to have been recognized as theoretical owners of all lands not specifically granted to vassals, and while most of the land was granted out some was reserved for the king. That some land was preserved as domain is proven by the case of Cyprus

---

responsible for the revenues. Grants were levied against the revenues of the town, not against the farm thereof.

For French finances and the administration thereof see A. Borelli de Serres, *Recherches sur Divers Services Publics du XIIIe au XVIIe Siècles* (Paris, 1895), i, 'La Compatabilité Publique au XIIIe Siècle', p. 12 ff..

[1] Albert Aix, XII, xxx, 709–10.

[2] Beugnot, 'Mémoire sur le Régime des Terres dans les Principautés fondées en Syrie par les Francs à la suite des Croisades', *B. E. C.*, xiv (1852–53), 529–45, xv (1854–55), 31–57, 236–62, 409–29, especially pp. 417–27; Dodu, pp. 242–43; Rozière, doc. 144; R. Preston, *Rural Conditions in the Kingdom of Jerusalem* (Philadelphia: University of Pennsylvania, 1903), p. 38 ff., claims that there was no personal domain other than that worked by serfs and that the lord had no lands on which the serfs owed part time service.

where Guy granted out nearly all the lands in fiefs so that he had but twenty knights in domain; and Amaury, finding that he had not enough domain land left to support his own knights, was forced to ask for a return of part of each barony.[1]

The import and export duties were always an important source of revenue, as were the sales taxes in the commercial towns both on the coast and on the inland frontiers. A list of taxable merchandise is given in the *Assises de la Cour des Bourgeois*, chapters CCXLII– CCXLIII, and one hundred and eleven articles are listed. Rey added some eighteen articles more and Chalandon pointed out that the tariff scale, higher on goods produced in Syria than on those not found there, indicated a protective tariff policy,—though I do not feel that he proves his case.[2] It must be observed that the trade which went through the Syrian ports was largely in bulky goods and was never as profitable to the Jerusalemite treasury as the Egyptian trade in smaller articles of higher value was to the Egyptian government.

The mode of collecting the taxes at the port is familiar through the famous account of Ibn Djubair who described the *Dîwân* of Acre, with its Christian scribes writing in Arabic, with their gold and ebony inkstands and their 'quiet and courteous manner.'[3]

An anchorage tax of one silver mark was charged for the use of the port, but was often remitted in charters granting commercial privileges to favored communes.[4] In 1277 Bohemond VII of Antioch-Tripoli exempted the Venetians from the harbor tax but continued the tax on Venetian ships rented to others than Venetians.[5]

---

[1] Ernoul, p. 287; Mas Latrie, ii, 9, 1, 44–46.

[2] *Assisses*, ii, 173–82; Rey, *Colonies Franques*, p. 258. Heyd, *Histoire du Commerce du Levant*, i, 172, describes the inland customs offices on caravan routes.

F. Chalandon, *Histoire de la Première Croisade* (Paris, 1925), pp. 350–51. Olives paid 20% tax, ivory 12%, sugar only paid 5%. On the whole the list given in the *Assises* does not substantiate Chalandon's theory.

[3] Ibn Djubair (*R. H. C. Or.*, iii), p. 449. This passage is quoted in Dodu, Chalandon, and Rey, and is translated into English in D. C. Munro and G. C. Sellery, *Medieval Civilization* (2nd ed.; New York: Century, 1914), pp. 261–62.

[4] *Regesta*, doc. 606,—charter of Baldwin IV; *Liber Jurium*, i, doc. 569, *Regesta*, doc. 950,— charter of John d'Ibelin to Genoa; *Regesta*, doc. 282, Tafel-Thomas, i, 133–135,—charter of Renaud and Constance of Antioch to Venice lowering the harbor tax.

[5] *Regesta*, doc. 1412; Rey, *Recherches Géographiques et historiques sur la domination des Latins en Orient* (Paris, 1877), pp. 42–45.

On the inland frontiers taxes were collected from the caravans, and customs houses were found here as well as in the sea ports. On goods imported from Saracen lands the normal tax was one karouble per besant (i.e. one twenty-fourth).[1] Goods brought into Jerusalem were taxed at the David Gate, and as early as 1120 Baldwin II remitted the tax on corn, beans, and barley.[2] A tax of eight per cent was laid against goods re-exported without having been sold, though this was also frequently remitted to most favored nations. In 1130 Baldwin II remitted the tax at Acre on personal property of pilgrims valued at less than forty besants, and that on property of higher value if they would swear that it was not intended for sale in the city but only for personal use or transhipment.[3]

In addition to the import and export duties there were the sales and purchase taxes and the charges for the weighing and measuring of goods. The treaty of Bohemond VII with the Venetians in 1277, cited above, contains several provisions which throw considerable light on these charges. Bohemond grants the Venetians freedom of entrance, exit, sale and purchase within his dominions. But if there are two taxes leviable against the commodity,—that is both sale and purchase tax,—they shall pay the purchase tax but not the sale. Venetian goods sold by other than a Venetian shall not be tax exempt, nor may Venetian ships rented to others escape the harbor tax. All sales must be registered in the court of the *Fonde*. In 1192 Henry of Champagne exempted the Genoese from the charges in Tyre unless they brought in goods from Saracen lands in which case they paid the regular sales taxes.[4] In the case of most favored nations the charges for weighing and measuring were removed unless the work was done by the royal or seignorial agents and assessors in which case their services were paid for.[5] These sale and purchase taxes were levied against foreigners, natives, and Syrian Franks alike, and the sale of lands was taxed as well as that of merchandise.[6]

---

[1] *Assises*, ii, 175 ff.; Rey, *Colonies Franques*, pp. 259–61; Heyd, *op. cit.*, i, 172.

[2] Rozière, doc. 45; Fulcher, III, viii, 636–37; William Tyre, XII, xv, 534.

[3] *Assises*, ii, 174; *Liber Jurium*, i, doc. 569; *Regesta*, doc. 950; Rozière, doc. 46; *Regesta*, doc. 125.

[4] *Regesta*, doc. 707; *Liber Jurium*, i, doc. 405.

[5] Mas Latrie, ii, 51–56; *Regesta*, doc. 1037; *Liber Jurium*, i, doc. 693.

[6] *Assises Cour Bourg.*, xxxi, 36. The man who sold *censive* land (i.e. land burdened with

There was moreover a tax on pilgrims, and travellers other than merchants. Ibn Djubair mentions this tax, and a treaty of 1123 grants the Venetians freedom from taxation except for the tax on pilgrims whom they brought to the country.[1] Besides these domain and port revenues which the king had in common with all the great lords who were seised of cities, there were certain royal monopolies such as dyeing, tanning, fishing, working copper and other metals, which the king worked through his own agents or let out to concessionaires.[2]

Coinage was in general a royal monoply though shared with the great counts of Antioch, Tripoli and Edessa, and with many of the other barons. While Ibelin lists twenty-two fiefs which had the rights of '*court et coins et justice*'[3] it does not seem that many of the barons availed themselves of this right as Schlumberger can cite existing coins of only four of them,—Beirut, Sidon, Toron, and Tyre.[4] The Venetians maintained a mint in their commune at Tyre which issued many coins, but on the whole the royal coinage seems to have been prevalent. There is a passage in the *Livre au Roi*, which says that '*nul hom ne deit aver port, euvreneour ne monée labourant, fors li rois, par dreit ne par l'assize*',[5] and which makes the issuance of coins a crime punishable by loss of fief; but it is impossible to reconcile this statement with the coins in existance and with the

payments or services) paid a tax of one silver mark, while the purchaser paid three besants, which was one eighth the sales tax. There was no tax on the sale of non-censive land. The purchaser of a bourgeois house paid a tax of 1 besant 1 raboin (*Ibid.*, cccii, 224).

[1] *Regesta*, doc. 102; William Tyre, XII, xxv, 550; Ibn Djubair (*R. H. C. Or.*, iii), p. 447.

[2] Rey, *Colonies Franques*, pp. 261–62. The weighing and measuring in the market towns came under this head. Monopolies were a very common source of revenue in the Middle Ages. Alexis I had a monopoly of the Byzantine grain and wine trades. Albert Aix, II, xvi, 311, remarks that all the money which Alexis gave to the crusaders went back into his own treasury through his monopoly on the sale of wine, oil, and grain.

Benjamin of Tudela (edited by M. Komroff, *Contemporaries of Marco Polo* (New York: Boni and Liveright, 1928), pp. 268–79) tells of the Jews who had the monopoly on the dyeing industry, which they had purchased from the king of Jerusalem. He found Jews exercising this monopoly in Jaffa, Lydda, and Bethlehem. In Tyre and Antioch they also manufactured glass. See also C. Beazley, *The Dawn of Modern Geography* (London, 1897–1906), ii, 241.

[3] Ibelin, cclxx, 419–22.

[4] Schlumberger, *Numismatique*, pp. 108–129.

[5] *Livre au Roi*, xvi, 617. As issuance of '*fauce monée ou faus besans*' is mentioned as a special offence, the passage cited cannot refer to counterfeiting.

provision of the *Assises de la Cour de Bourgeois* which says that counterfeiting the coins of the king or any of his barons is punishable by death.[1] Were the kingdom of Jerusalem a more centralized state, it would be tempting to rely on the *Livre au Roi* and to see in Ibelin's phrase *coins* a right to collect fines in the private court like the English *sac and soc* but the extreme decentralization of the kingdom, and the existence of the baronial coins, show that coinage was a monoply enjoyed by others than the king himself.

One of the chief sources of revenue enjoyed by the kings of Jerusalem was the poll tax of one dinar and five karoubles levied on all Moslems. Nevertheless Ibn Djubair points out that Moslems lived in greater comfort under the Franks than in Moslem states, and prays 'may Allah preserve us from such a temptation' as preferring to live under the rule of the Infidel.[2] For the Moslems, being exempt from the ecclesiastical tithe, which weighed so heavily on all Christians, and from the royal tithe on all newly conquered lands, were the privileged class as far as taxation went. This light taxation of a large subject population is one of the few thoroughly intelligent policies pursued by the Latin kings of Jerusalem, but it so shocked Thoros of Armenia that he refused to send Armenians to settle in the sparsely populated lands around Jerusalem.[3]

In addition to the above revenues, which may be termed domainial, the king enjoyed, as chief feudal seignor, certain feudal revenues. He received the profits of the justice from both the High Court of the realm and the royal vicecomital courts of burgesses. The king does not seem to have collected the regular feudal aides which were common in the West except the aid for ransom. There is no mention of the *aide pur file marier* or the aid for knighting the eldest son.[4] Ransom was however an essential duty of the liegemen of

---

[1] *Assises Cour Bourg.*, ccxcii, 220.

[2] Ibn Djubair (*R. H. C. Or.*, iii), p. 448. Moslem farmers owned their farms and paid only a slight tax on fruits, a half of their harvest, and a poll tax.

[3] Ernoul, pp. 29–30; Beugnot, 'Mémoire sur la Régime des Terres', *B. E. C.* xv (1854–55), 424 ff..

This, however, kept satisfied a large Moslem population which might otherwise have rebelled and caused the earlier destruction of the state. The kings of Cyprus showed the same sense in refusing to enforce the demands of the Latin clergy on the Greek population of Cyprus.

[4] The *Assises de Romanie*, art. 23, permitted the prince to collect the *aide pur file marier* from his tenants by simple homage. But he was unable to impose any kind of tallage or aide without the consent of the vassals.

Jerusalem. Ibelin says that if sufficient ransom cannot be obtained from the regular grant of one besant per hundred, the vassal must sell his fief and take the money thus obtained to ransom his lord.[1] The liegemen were also obliged to come to the assistance of the king when he had contracted a debt for the needs of the country and could not meet its payment. In this case the king first placed certain liegemen as pledges for the debt and then called on all his vassals to contribute to the redemption of their fellow vassals, if necessary selling their fiefs to raise the money.[2]

To the king went the escheats and forfeitures declared in the *Haute Cour*. The forfeitures were the penalties imposed for certain crimes or felonies which are classified in the various books of the *Assises* into three groups: those for which forfeiture takes place for a year and a day; those which entail forfeiture for life but no attaint against the heirs; and finally those most severe crimes which call for perpetual attainder. Forfeiture for a year and a day resulted from lesser defaults of service; that for life from murder, failure to perform homage or military service, or for some such infraction of feudal fealty. The most serious cases, which brought perpetual forfeiture, were limited by the time of Ibelin to heresy, apostacy, treason, selling the fief contrary to the assise, and securing a fief through use of a forged charter.[3]

As a feudal lord the king had also in common with the other

---

[1] Ibelin, ccxlix, 397; *Livre au Roi*, vii, 611.

The history of the Latin states shows several conspicuous examples of the ransoming of a prince by the lieges: Baldwin II was ransomed in 1124; Bohemond I of Antioch in 1103; Bohemond III in 1165, Renaud de Châtillon in 1176,—for these two princes the Antiochenes raised a total sum of 220,000 dinars; and after Saladin's conquest Guy de Lusignan was ransomed by the surrender of Ascalon, and Humphrey de Toron by the surrender of Krak and Montreal.

[2] *Livre au Roi*, viii, 612. Liegemen were also required to serve on demand as hostages when the king was captured. (*Ibid.*, vii, 611.)

[3] Ibelin, clxxxiv, 287; cxc, 303–05; cxci, 305–06; *Livre au Roi*, xvi, 616–17; xlvi, 640; xx, 619. If the vassal is accused of murder and flees the realm, the fief is forfeited to the lord perpetually. Any vassal who refuses to serve as hostage for the king also forfeits his fief (*Ibid.*, vii, 611), and if a man leaves his fief and goes into the Saracen country without first recommending his fief to his lord, the lord may take possession of the fief, and, if the possessor does not return within a year and a day, may keep it though he must grant a dower to the vassal's wife or widow for her life. (*Ibid.*, xxii, 621.) See appendix for the law of treason and its penalities.

lords the rights of wardship and marriage. The *Livre au Roi* provides that a widowed liegewoman may remain unmarried for a year and a day after her lord's death, nor may her suzerain force her to marry within that time. At the end of that time, however, the lord shall give her her choice of three candidates whom he shall select for her. If she refuses to accept any one of the three she is forfeit of her fief. If she at any time marries without the consent of her lord she is forfeit, as is her husband. If a widow has minor children the lord may not declare her forfeit, but may take the bailliage for the children himself.[1]

The same rights were exercised over the heiresses of fiefs held from the crown; thus King Foulque married Constance of Antioch to Raymond of Poitiers. At Raymond's death Baldwin III, who had succeeded Foulque on the throne of Jerusalem, proposed several candidates to Constance, but she refused them all and Baldwin was unable to force her to accede. She chose Renaud de Châtillon, and Baldwin consented though Renaud was not one of the king's nominees. This case illustrates the right of the suzerain over the unmarried heiress and also over the widowed heiress, and also shows that in regard to the more powerful vassals the king could do nothing.[2]

The fines from the *Cour des Bourgeois* also augmented the royal treasury. The *Assises* of this court list cases with their fines and include such matters as damages in assault and battery where the defendant paid 100 besants to the court and 100 sous to the plaintiff; $67\frac{1}{2}$ sous were paid to the court for disregard of the royal ban and the same sum for giving false measure.[3]

---

[1] *Livre au Roi*, xxx–xxxii, 626–28. In the Morea the widow of a liegeman was free to marry whom she chose, save an enemy of her lord, upon payment of $\frac{1}{3}$ year's revenue of her fief. The widow of a tenant by simple homage had to have the lord's consent. (*Assises de Romanie*, art. 31.)

[2] William Tyre, XIV, ix, 618; XXII, xxvi, 802; Ernoul, p. 23; Schlumberger, *Renaud de Chatillon*, pp. 17–19.

Ernoul says that the king suggested Renaud. The whole affair was complicated by the fact that Constance was also the vassal of the Basileus Manuel, who tried to marry her to his nephew the Caesar John Roger Comnenus. Constance placed her county under Manuel's protection but none-the-less married without consulting him, after having refused his candidates. See also *Familles*, pp. 190–92.

[3] *Assises*, ii, 221–24. In cases of assault the fine was cut in half if the defendant was either a woman or a Syrian. An unsuccessful accusation cost the instigator seven sous.

The king had also the escheat of the possessions of anyone dying intestate within the realm, and the waiver of this right in favor of Italian communes was one of their most cherished privileges.[1]

Flotsam and jetsam and treasure trove were among the rights of the king which he enjoyed as lord of the fief. Guibert de Nogent tells a story of how King Baldwin I, when he had completely exhausted his revenues and could no longer retain his men, was saved from his dilemma by the discovery of a vast hoard of gold which had been sunk near Jaffa in the wreck of a Venetian ship.[2] The Venetians soon eliminated the possibility of a recurrence of this, and the treaties with the Venetians, Genoese, and Pisans regularly included among the privileges granted them the protection of shipwrecked mariners, and the surrender of any salvage from their wrecks to their consuls or baillies.[3]

Besides these regular sources of revenue, extra money was obtained in several more occasional ways. The spoils of war, ransom of prisoners, and the tribute from conquered cities (or tribute paid by cities to avert conquest) added materially to the resources of the early kings. Baldwin I collected fifty thousand besants in ransom of forty-five Damascene prisoners in 1101, and at the same time Ascalon, Caesarea, Acre, and Tyre bought peace.[4] Chalandon lists as series of payments made as tribute by cities, running from 1099, when Aleppo paid 12,000 dinars, to 1168, when Cairo paid 1,000,000.[5] After the last date the tribute largely ceased, and with the spread of Saladin's conquest the tribute flowed out from the Franks to the Moslems rather than in the reverse direction.[6]

---

[1] *Assises Cour Bourg.*, clxxxix, 127; cclxxiii, 206; *Liber Jurium*, i, doc. 8; *Regesta*, doc. 43.

[2] Guibert de Nogent, *Gesta Dei per Francos (R. H. C. Oc.*, iv), VII, xlvii, 259. The *Assises de Romanie*, art. 155, provide that if a freeman finds treasure on his own land he shall divide equally with the prince; if a freeman finds it on another's land, the finder, the prince, and owner of the land each gets a third. The discovery of treasure by a slave or serf goes to his owner or master, as though he found it.

[3] Tafel-Thomas, i, docs. 46, 55, 61, 68, pp. 102–03, 133–35, 148–49, 175–77; *Regesta*, docs. 197, 282, 434, 632. *Liber Jurium*, i, doc. 424; *Regesta*, doc. 753. Mas Latrie, ii, 39; *Regesta*, doc. 912.

[4] Albert Aix, VII, li–liii, 541–42.

[5] Chalandon, *Première Croisade*, p. 357.

[6] Until the fourteenth century when the Cypriots collected tribute from the cities of Anatolia.

On several occasions money was obtained through gift; or a princess brought with her a rich dower, as when Baldwin I received a large fortune with the countess of Sicily, and when in 1158 Manuel Comnenus gave a dower of 100,000 gold pieces with his niece Theodora on her nuptials with Baldwin III.[1] But the kings had further occasional sources of supply. In 1187 Guy de Lusignan raised an army with the money and treasure which Henry II of England had sent to Jerusalem, when he had planned a crusade as penance for the murder of Becket. The treasuries of the Orders were often called upon to meet the needs of the kingdom, and the incident of the seizure of the Templars' hoard by Joinville is a familiar story which well illustrates the treatment accorded the Orders, though in this particular case the money was used by the crusading king of France rather than by the monarch of Jerusalem.[2] Gifts were made and legacies were left to the crusading kingdom as well as to the Orders and to the Church, a notable example being the bequest of Philip Augustus.[3]

In times of special emergency taxes were also levied and special aids taken. In 1166 Amaury summoned a meeting of his whole curia at Neapolis to vote a levy for the campaign against Syracon in Egypt. If the Latin text of William of Tyre can be accepted at its face value, this meeting included commoners as well as nobles, and a tenth of all movables was voted from everyone. William says:

curiam apud Neapolim convocat generalem: ubi praesentibus domino patriarcha, archiepiscopis, episcopis, et aliis ecclesiarum praelatis, principibus et populo, necessitates regni docet ex ordine, omnium suppliciter implorans auxilium. Decretum est ergo, et communi voto susceptum, ut omnes generaliter, nemine excepto, ad regni subsidium, universarum rerum mobilium decimas darent.[4]

From the wording of this passage it might be possible to infer that the whole community voted a general tax but that this was not the case is proven by the phraseology of the *Eracles*, the contemporary

[1] William Tyre, XI, xxi, 488–89; XVIII, xxii, 857–58.
[2] Joinville (ed. De Wailly: Paris: Firmin Didot, 1874, in 4to), LXXV, ccclxxx–xv, 208–10.
[3] *Eracles*, pp. 356–57; D. L. *Cartulaire*, doc. 1755.
[4] William Tyre, XIX, xiii, 903.

Old French version of William's history, which limits the tax to those who did not serve in the army, thus reducing it merely to a strictly feudal assessment exacted from the tenants of the king. The Old French text says:

manda un parlement à Naples où furent assemblé li baron et li prelat de la terre . . . et fu acordé que tuit cil qui n'iroient avec lui en l'ost li donroient la disme de toz leur meubles qu'il avoeint où qu'il fussent; ce promistrent et clerc et lai, et le tindrent bien.[1]

The *nemine excepto* of the Latin text must therefore be taken to mean that no franchise or immunity could prevail against this aid.

In February 1183 was levied in Jerusalem a tax which was unique in the history of the realm to that time, and which was in many respects unique at the time in the history of Europe, for it is the first *national tax* of which there is any record in the feudal period, and antedates the celebrated Saladin tithe of Henry II by five years. Of this tax Cartellieri says, '*Allem Anschein nach gab sie aber im Abendlande zu einer neuen allgemeinen Besteuerung Anlass*', and points out the features of this tax which were repeated in the levies of 1184 in France and England;[2] and Röhricht refers to it as '*eine ausserordentliche Steuer*'.[3]

William of Tyre describes this tax at great length, quoting the decree establishing it in full.[4]

A general council of the realm was held in February 1183 at Jerusalem to organize the defense against Saladin.[5] It was decided '*post multas deliberationum partes*' that a census should be taken throughout the kingdom and a tax should be collected '*de communi omnium principum, tam ecclesiasticorum quam seculairum, et de assensu universae plebis regni*'. The tax rate was established as one (gold)

---

[1] *R. H. C. Occ.*, i, part ii, 904.

[2] A. Cartellieri, *Philipp II August*, ii, *Der Kreuzzug* (Leipsic and Paris, 1906), p. 16.

[3] Röhricht, p. 402. He terms the levy of 1166 merely 'Beistand' (*Ibid.* p. 322), thus classing the earlier tax as a purely feudal aid and emphasizing the unusual character of the tax of 1183.

[4] William Tyre, XXII, xxiii, 1109–12. As William was one of the most important custodians of the tax he may have had a more personal interest in it, but he shows that he considered it extraordinary and worthy of considerable attention.

[5] William says 1182; Röhricht, pp. 402–03, corrects it to 1183. See also Cartellieri, *op. cit.*, p. 14, and Kingsford in *E. H. R.*, xi (1896), 146.

besant on every hundred of property and debts, and two on every hundred of income for churches, monasteries, barons, and their vassals. Mercenary soldiers paid one besant per hundred on revenue. Lords of casales paid one besant for every hearth in their possession, which they should collect themselves from their peasants apportioning it fairly among them. Free men who had not one hundred besants in property or revenue should pay one besant hearth tax, and if they could not pay one besant were to pay a half a besant or a raboin.[1] The tax was to be universal and apply to everyone alike.

Hoc autem debent observare in his omnibus, qui habent valens centum byzantiorum, cujuscumque linguae, cujuscumque nationis, cujuscumque fidei, non habita differentia sexus; sed sive sint viri, sive feminae, omnes indifferenter huic legi subjacebunt.

This included Christians, Moslems, and Jews; Greeks, Italians, Franks, and Syrians; and the unfree peasantry were provided for by the provision that their lords should pay for them, while the poorer free were scaled and taxed according to their paying power.

The people assessed and declared the value of their own possessions and four men were elected in each district (*civitas*) to hear the declarations and collect the tax. They were sworn to keep secret the information thus obtained and not to reveal the wealth or poverty of anyone. The money collected in each district was placed in a sack and sealed, and each sack was marked with the name of the district. The country was divided into two divisions and all the money was brought into the two central treasuries of Jerusalem and Acre. All the divisions from Haïfa south returned to Jerusalem, those north as far as Beirut to Acre. At these cities were kept chests for the reception of the money, the chest at Jerusalem being kept in the Holy Sepulchre, that at Acre in the cathedral church. Each chest was to have three locks and three keys. The keys of the southern chest were confided to the patriarch, the prior of the Holy Sepulchre, and the third to the castellan of Jerusalem and the four sworn assessors of the city. The keys of the Acre chest were kept by the archbishop of Tyre (William), Count Joscelin the seneschal, and the four assessors

---

[1] This proves that the besants meant are gold besants as the raboin was worth a third or a fourth of a gold besant.

of Acre.[1] The money was turned in by the collectors in the presence of the keepers of the keys and each sack was carefully marked and placed in the chest. This money could be spent only for the defense of the kingdom and not for any ordinary expenses. During the time of this special tax all ordinary taxes and aids were suspended.

This special tax bulks large in the history of taxation for here for the first time the people are found assessing their own property. The idea of taxation of personal property was not new; personal goods had been taxed in England in 1166 in Henry II's tax for the benefit of the Holy Land.[2] The taxation of 1184 in England and France merely carried out this same principle. But not until the famous Saladin tithe of 1188 is there any western tax for the collection of which the people evaluated their own property.[3] In discussing the Saladin tithe Bridrey says: *'C'est justement à l'occasion des croisades que se présente la première idée d'un impôt, c'est-à-dire un somme d'une taxe générale, levée sur tous dans un intérêt commun'*,[4] and to this might be added that the mode of collecting this came also from the crusading states.

From the above it may be readily seen that the kingdom of Jerusalem was comparatively rich in resources, but nevertheless it was almost continually bankrupt and the kings were in debt and often insolvent. Constant demands were made for help from western

---

[1] This was a popular method of securing valuables in the Middle Ages. Compare with this the chest with three locks and keys in which were kept the *Lettres du Sépulcre* (*Assises*, i, 25–26), and that containing the crown of the kingdom. (*Eracles*, pp. 28–29.)

In 1166 the tax for the relief of the Holy Land which was collected in England was kept in chests in the churches, the three keys of each chest being kept by the priest and two honest men of the parish. (Gervaise of Canterbury (ed. W. Stubbs; *Rolls Series*: London, 1879), i, 199).

[2] Text in Gervaise of Canterbury, i, 198–99. Full discussion in Cartellieri, *op. cit.*, pp. 7–9.

[3] Text in Stubbs, *Select Charters of English Constitutional History* (9th ed.; Oxford: Clarendon Press, 1921), pp. 188–89 (from Benedict of Peterboro and Roger of Hovedon). English translation in G. B. Adams and H. M. Stephens, *Select Documents of English Constitutional History* (New York: Macmillan, 1901 *et seq.*), pp. 27–28. See Cartellieri, *op. cit.*, p. 59 ff..

[4] E. Bridrey, *La Condition Juridique des Croisées*, (Paris, 1901), pp. 67–71. Bridrey says further: 'À la différence des précédents la dime saladine offre le caractère d'un impôt général frappant toutes les classes de la société féodale. Elle présente aussi cet intérêt d'avoir été criée uniquement pour la croisade, tandis que les autres ne sont que des adaptions plus ou moins heureuses des taxes existantes.'

This statement seems hardly justified in view of the tax of 1166 which was to apply to *'clerici, comites, barones, vavasores, milites, cives, burgenses, rustici'*. (Gervaise, i, 198.)

Europe, and though much was sent, the kingdom never managed to meet expenses. The reason for this was that the heavy military establishment and the necessity for constant defensive measures kept the kings poor. The great prosperity of the kings of Cyprus in the fourteenth century shows what the kingdom of Jerusalem might have enjoyed had it been less exposed to attack, and had it not been forced to bend every effort to bolster up a long and militarily indefensible frontier. Further, much of the profits from the extensive commerce which took place in the Syrian towns was lost to the kings by virtue of the widespread immunities and exemptions which they granted to the western trading nations, though, as this was equally true in Cyprus, it must take second place after the expenses of defense and the general economic insecurity due to incessant 'war and rumors of war'.

BOOK III

SOME POLITICAL RELATIONSHIPS OF THE KINGS OF JERUSALEM

CHAPTER 9

THE RELATIONS OF THE KINGS OF JERUSALEM WITH THE PRINCES OF ANTIOCH AND THE COUNTS OF TRIPOLI AND EDESSA

'*L A TIERE de Triple ne d'Antioce n'est mie dou roiaume*', said Ernoul in describing the lands of the kingdom of Jerusalem;[1] and in truth the principality of Antioch and the counties of Edessa and Tripoli never were a real part of the kingdom, but were rather allied states which recognized the primacy of the kings of Jerusalem. The Middle Ages expressed it feudally and termed it suzerainty; modern phraseology would term it hegemony. William of Tyre clearly recognized the lack of unity within the kingdom when he said, '*Orientalis enim Latinorum tota regio quatuor principatibus erat distincta.*'[2] The desire of each state to expand caused much trouble, according to the archbishop. In another passage he remarked that the affairs of the '*regni Orientalis*' were going well and that it was enjoying peace though Edessa was lost and Antioch was being devastated by the enemy, thus clearly omitting these territories from the realm.[3]

If among the barons of the principality of Jerusalem the king was *primus inter pares*, in respect to the great counts (and throughout this section the term counts will be used to include the princes of Antioch) he was hardly even that. Certainly Bohemond I never recognized either Godfrey or Baldwin I as in any respect his superior. Prutz maintains that while ideally subordinate to the king, as lord of the Holy City, the counts were not his vassals and were not obligated to the duties inherent in vassalage.[4]

---

[1] Ernoul, p. 27.
[2] William Tyre, XVI, xxix, 754–55.
[3] William Tyre, XVII, xiii, 779.
[4] H. Prutz, *Kulturgeschichte*, p. 161: 'Gelegentlich werden sie geradezu als zwei 'Reiche' bezeichnet. Auch sind der Fürst von Antiochien und die Grafen von Tripolis und von Edessa

Occasionally the king did exercise some influence and control over the counts, and it would seem that under stronger kings in Jerusalem and under weaker counts the king did secure the recognition of his suzerainty; but it is necessary to examine the history of the relations of the various Outremer states with each other to determine how far and under what circumstances the king was able to assert his primacy and preëminence. The *Assises de Jérusalem* are silent in regard to this question, for they contain only the laws of the principality of Jerusalem. Yet this is in itself an eloquent fact, for it shows that the counties were not under the laws of Jerusalem, and that the essential unit in the governmental organization was not the kingdom but the county. Antioch had her own *Assises*, which, while generally based on those of Jerusalem, differed in detail; and the *Haute Cour* of Antioch was the supreme body there as was that of Jerusalem in the principality of Jerusalem. Politically Armenia was hardly more independent of Jerusalem than was Antioch.

In the first period of the kingdom Tripoli was more a part of the principality of Jerusalem than it was in the later period. Until the union of Tripoli with Antioch, which occurred in 1201 under Bohemond IV, Tripoli was a fief of Jerusalem and occupied a position, legally as geographically, midway between the practically independent Antioch on the north and the fiefs south of the Nahr-el-Kalb which were directly dependent upon the king of Jerusalem, such as Galilee, Jaffa, and Montreal.

Generally speaking, the relations of the kings with the counts fall under various heads:—recognition of suzerainty by the counts, as shown by their swearing allegiance and taking homage; the right of the king to act as bailli of the county during a minority or the absence of the count, though, as will be seen, the kings did not exercise this right save upon the invitation of the knights of the county; coöperation in war, though the counties enjoyed freedom in foreign affairs, alliances, and treaties; and miscellaneous privileges, such as

---

dem König von Jerusalem zwar vermöge des Ehrenvorranges, der diesem als Herrn der heiligen Stadt zusteht, ideell untergeordnet, aber sie sind nicht seine Vasallen und nicht zu den Leistungen verpflichtet, welche einem Vasallen dem Lehnsherrn gegenüber obliegen'.

Dodu, pp. 85–86, grants a greater *legal* power but admits that it was not enforceable.

wardship for minors and marriage for heiresses, and the occasional confirmation of grants and charters.

It must be borne in mind that the dependence of the counties on the kings was directly proportional to the danger of attack from Saracen or Greek, the strength of the kings in Jerusalem, and the ability of the county to fend for itself. Bohemond I of Antioch knew no secular suzerain until after his defeat in 1108, when he was compelled to become the vassal of the Emperor Alexis. Raymond of Antioch, on the other hand, recognized both Jerusalem and Byzantium as his suzerains, though he referred to himself as prince '*Antiocheni regni*' and both he and Bohemond III dated their charters from the year of their reign.[1]

The great counts had their own grand officers and their courts were organized on the model of that of Jerusalem. Constables, seneschals, marshals, chancellors, and chamberlains of Antioch, Tripoli, and Edessa appear in the documents of the counties, and in the narratives of the chroniclers.[2] On the other hand the lords of Galilee, Jaffa, and Caesarea also had their own grand officers as did the patriarch and the Orders of the Temple and Hospital.[3]

Homage and fealty were personal contracts and depended for their value on the strength of the lord to enforce them and the good faith of the vassal to live up to them. The great counts were vassals of the kings of Jerusalem at best only as were the dukes of Normandy and Burgundy and the counts of Anjou and Flanders vassals of the Capetian kings, who, like the kings of Jerusalem, derived their chief strength not from their titular suzerainty over the others, but because they were lords of large counties themselves and were strong

---

[1] Charter of Raymond of 1140: Rozière, doc. 89; *Regesta*, doc. 194. Charters of Bohemond III: *Regesta*, docs. 424, 451, 493, 511, 523, 550, 555. See above under the discussion of chancery forms in the chapter on Grand Officers and Chancery, and Dodu, p. 102.

[2] Partial lists of these officers are to be found in Rey's Ducange, *Familles d'Outremer*, and in the appendix of this book.

[3] Under William de Buris, prince of Galilee, in 1121 were: Edric the seneschal, Frederick the constable, Gerard the marshal, and Serlo the chancellor. (Delaborde, docs. 10, 11; *Regesta*, docs. 92, 93.) In 1129 Richard the seneschal, and in 1131 Albert the chamberlain, and Baldwin the seneschal of Caesarea appear on charters. (*Regesta*, docs. 126, 139.) In 1133 Halelmus dapifer of Jaffa appears. (*Regesta*, doc. 147.)

in their own domain. Like the Flemish counts, the princes of Antioch were of divided allegiance, and sometimes recognized no tie binding them to their suzerain of Jerusalem.[1]

As both Antioch and Edessa were established before the kingdom of Jerusalem, the first rulers of these counties were naturally not bound in any way to the rulers of Jerusalem. In 1108 Bohemond recognized the suzerainty of Alexis Comnenus and received from him the investiture of the county of Antioch and adjacent territories as a fief.[2] He had already in 1100 recognized the suzerainty of the patriarch, when at the time of the election of Daimbert to the patriarchal See, Godfrey and Bohemond had both accepted their lands as fiefs from the patriarch. Daimbert later took occasion to remind Bohemond of his duties to the Papal See, whose representative he was.[3]

Edessa was independent during the rule of Baldwin I there, and there is no mention of his even having recognized the suzerainty of the patriarch as did Bohemond and Godfrey. When, however, in 1100, Baldwin became king of Jerusalem, he gave Edessa as a fief to Baldwin de Burg who held it as a vassal of the Jerusalemite king.[4] When Baldwin de Burg in turn succeeded to the throne of Jerusalem, he granted Edessa to his kinsman Joscelin de Courtney, who had done so much towards making him king in Jerusalem. Thereafter Edessa was regularly considered a fief held from the king of Jeru-

[1] Dodu, pp. 84–105; Beugnot, *Assises*, i, Introduction, 13 ff.; Prutz, *Kulturgeschichte*, p. 159.

[2] F. Dolger, *Regesten der Kaiserurkunden des Oströmischen Reiches* (Munich, 1925), ii, no. 1243; Anna Comnena, *Alexiade* (*R. H. C. Grec*, i), xiii, 170; F. Chalandon, *Essai sur la regne d'Alexis Ier Comnène* (Paris, 1900), p. 247; R. B. Yewdale, *Bohemond I, Prince of Antioch* (Princeton, 1924), pp. 127–31; Rey, 'Princes d'Antioche', *R. O. L.*, iv (1896), 333.

Bohemond denied completely the claim of Alexis to Antioch as under the agreement of 1097, claiming that Alexis had broken the terms of that agreement. He accepted the emperor as his suzerain by the treaty of 1108. The emperor's chrysobull is given in Anna Comnena. The most recent treatment of the subject is in A. C. Krey, 'A Neglected Passage of the *Gesta*', *Munro-Crusades*, pp. 57–78, and in Yewdale. Vasiliev, *History of the Byzantine Empire* (Madison, Wisconsin, 1929), ii, 57–60, has a very short treatment, based largely on Chalandon and Yewdale.

[3] Fulcher, III, xxxiv, 741–42; William Tyre, IX, xv, 387; *Regesta*, doc. 34; Yewdale, pp. 89–91; Röhricht, *Geschichte des Ersten Kreuzzuges*, p. 209.

[4] Albert Aix, VII, xxxi, 527; Fulcher, II, i, 353; *Chronologie*, no. 501.

salem, though with special rights.¹ Joscelin was, however, the vassal of the prince of Antioch and possibly of the Byzantine emperor as well as of the king of Jerusalem.²

Tripoli, which was not won until after the establishment of the kingdom, was from the beginning held as a fief from the king. In 1109, when the city was taken, Bertrand became the liegeman of King Baldwin for his lands.³ But feeling himself bound by the oath which Raymond of St Gilles had taken to the Emperor Alexis, Bertrand in 1111 swore personal allegiance to the basileus.⁴ In 1122 and again in 1131 Count Pons of Tripoli endeavored to renounce his allegiance to Jerusalem but on both occasions was defeated and forced to submit.⁵

There can be no doubt therefore that Tripoli and Edessa positively recognized the suzerainty of Jerusalem, and Antioch seemed sometimes to accept it, though allegiance was also owed by the counties to the Byzantine Empire; and the claims of the two suzerains were respected proportionately to their power at the moment.⁶

---

¹ William Tyre, XII, iv, 516–17; Rey, 'Princes d'Antioche', p. 350.

² F. Chalandon, *Jean et Manuel Comnène* (Paris, 1912), p. 124 and notes 1 and 2. William Tyre, XV, ii, 658, refers to the prince of Antioch as the lord of the count of Edessa.

³ William Tyre, XI, x, 469: *'factus est fidelitate manualiter exhibita domini regis homo ligius, unde et eius successores usque in praesentem diem regni Hierosolymorum idipsum tenentur exhibere'*.

By the agreement between Bertrand and William Jordan, Bertrand had become the vassal of Jerusalem and William the vassal of Antioch. (William Tyre, XI, ix, 466.) It was also agreed that if either should die without heirs the other was to inherit his estates. As William was killed shortly thereafter Bertrand presumably became the vassal of Antioch for Archas and Tortosa which he inherited from William.

⁴ Anna Comnena, *Alexiade*, xiv, 191–92; Chalandon, *Alexis*, pp. 252–53; Rey, 'Princes d' Antioche', p. 339.

Alexis demanded Antioch from Tancred at the death of Bohemond and was refused. Alexis then appealed to Bertrand and Baldwin de Burg, who agreed to help him against Tancred; but Baldwin of Jerusalem supported Tancred, and Alexis and his allies were unsuccessful.

⁵ Fulcher, III, xi, 646–48; Rey, *op. cit.*, pp. 351, 357–58; William Tyre, XII, xvii, 536, XIV, iv–v, 611–14. Schlumberger, *Numismatique*, p. 95, says that Pons' submission in 1122 was forced by his vassals who refused to support him against the king, and that Pons *'sollicité par ses barons et reconnaissant sa folie . . . consentit à se soumettre et à jurer de nouveau fidélité à son suzerain.'*

⁶ See my 'To What Extent was the Byzantine Empire the Suzerain of the Latin Crusading States', *Byzantion*, vii (1932).

The kings of Jerusalem were often baillies for one or another of the great counties during the captivity of the lord of the county or during a minority. But the bailliage seems to have been held as a result of invitation of the barons and people of the county rather than by any right derived from their legal relationship.

From 1119 to 1126 Baldwin was regent of Antioch for Bohemond II; and in 1126 Baldwin invested him with his lands, and presided while the liegemen of Antioch took their oaths of allegiance and homage to the new prince. The houses of Jerusalem and Antioch were bound together by the marriage of Bohemond to Alice, daughter of King Baldwin.[1] The regency of 1119–1126 was undertaken by the king at the request of the Antiochenes, as was that of 1131, when Bohemond II was killed and the county was left without a ruler. Alice, who wished to keep the county for herself, conspired to keep her father out of the county, but the barons of Antioch invited him to take control as regent for his granddaughter Constance, the daughter of Bohemond and Alice. Baldwin was successful in defeating the conspiracies of Alice, and the Antiochenes took their oaths to him as regent for Constance.[2] In the following August Baldwin died, and Alice allied herself with Pons of Tripoli and Joscelin of Edessa to secure the regency for herself, but the barons of Antioch summoned Foulque, who had succeeded his father-in-law on the throne of Jerusalem. Pons refused to allow Foulque to cross Tripoli on his way to Antioch, so the king went by sea and then returned to Tripoli and administered a severe defeat to his rebellious

---

[1] Fulcher, III, vii, 635, says that Baldwin ruled two kingdoms (*'duum regnorum possessorem'*); while William Tyre, XII, xii–xiv, 530–34, says that the people of Antioch gave him full power to govern *'sicut in regno habebat'*, clearly showing the distinct separation of Antioch from the kingdom. William further says that Baldwin was as careful of Antioch as if it had been his own country: *'licet regnum eius esset proprietas quam etiam ad successores suos jure posset transmittere; principatus vero, commissus.'* The actual administration and defense of Antioch were done after 1122 by Joscelin of Edessa, which, according to Rey ('Princes d' Antioche', p. 352–53), gave the counts of Edessa their claims over Antioch which caused so much trouble later.

For the investiture of Bohemond and his marriage to Alice, see: Fulcher, III, lxi, 820–22; William Tyre, XIII, xxi, 588–89; Rey, *op. cit.*, pp. 354–55.

The close relationship between the kings and princes of Antioch gave them claims to later bailliages, as the nearest relatives.

[2] William Tyre, XIII, xxvii, 598–601; Rey, pp. 356–67.

vassal. Returning to Antioch, he organized the government of the county at the request of the inhabitants, and appointed Renaud Mansoer, lord of Margat and constable of Antioch, his bailli when he returned to Jerusalem.[1] Charters of Foulque issued in 1133 and 1135 show him employing the titles *'rector ac baiulus Antiocheni principatus filieque Boamundi iunioris'* and *'baiulus et tutor Antiocheni principatus'*.[2]

As their princess grew older the barons of Antioch sought a husband for her and appealed to Foulque to advise and help them. The king suggested Raymond of Poitiers, who was at the court of Henry I of England, and brought him to Syria where he became the husband of Constance and the prince of Antioch in 1136. The emperor, John Comnenus, who considered that as suzerain of Antioch he should have been consulted in the selection of a husband for the princess, marched against the county. Meanwhile, Foulque had been besieged in Montferrand by Zenghi and Raymond had departed to assist his lord. John besieged Antioch, which was ill defended, and Raymond came back and negotiated a peace with the emperor whereby he recognized himself the vassal of Byzantium, and went so far in admitting the rights of the emperor over Antioch that he agreed to surrender the city to him if John could conquer and grant him as fiefs the districts of Aleppo, Hama, Sheizar, and Emesa (Homs). Further the Greek banner was to float from the citadel of Antioch and the emperor was to have free admittance into the city at any time.[3]

The year 1144 brought invasion, and Edessa was attacked and overrun by Zenghi. Count Joscelin appealed first to his suzerain of Antioch but Raymond refused help.[4] Joscelin then appealed to

---

[1] William Tyre, XIV, iv–v, 611–14; Rey, pp. 357–58.

[2] Rozière, docs. 85, 86; *Regesta*, docs 149, 157.

[3] William Tyre, XIV, ix, 618–19, xx–xxi, 635–38, xxiv, 641–42, xxx, 651–53; Rey, pp. 358–62; Chalandon, *Jean et Manuel*, pp. 122–34. Chalandon establishes that John based his claim to Antioch on the treaty of 1108. He offered aid and protection to Tripoli and Jerusalem in return for fealty and recognition of his overlordship at the same time, but his offer was refused. When in 1138 John made a triumphal processesion through Antioch, the prince of Antioch and the count of Edessa walked before him as marshals. (William Tyre, XV, iii, 658–60.)

[4] William Tyre, XVI, iv, 710. William uses the phrase *dominum suum* in reference to Raymond. The *Eracles* says *'cria merci . . . coume à son seingneur'*.

Queen Melissande of Jerusalem, who sent an army under Manasses, the constable, but the aid came too late to save the city. When the European crusaders came to the rescue of the Holy Land on the second crusade, the prince of Antioch tried to divert them from going on to Jerusalem and took no part in the conference at Acre which decided to attack Damascus. When, in 1151, Joscelin was captured and the Saracens overran the remaining portions of the county of Edessa, the Emperor Manuel offered to purchase the county from Beatrice, the wife of the captured count. Baldwin III was in Antioch at the time, and appeal was made to him, but he agreed to the cession of Edessa to Byzantium as it was apparent that the powers of the Frankish states were not enough to defend the county. Baldwin took control and carried out the transfer of the lands to the Greeks, preferring, says William of Tyre, that the disgrace of surrendering Christian lands to Nureddin should fall upon the Greeks and not upon the Franks. The Greeks entered into possession, but were very shortly after driven out by the forces of the atābeg.[1]

Meanwhile, in 1149, Constance of Antioch, widowed by the death of Raymond, and terrified by the advance of the Saracens, had placed herself and her county under the protection of the basileus. But the defense of the county was undertaken not by the emperor but by Baldwin III who took over the bailliage and commanded an army which came to the defense of the harassed state. Both suzerains saw that a husband must be found for Constance who could manage the affairs of Antioch, and both suggested candidates for her hand. The choice of Manuel was John Roger Comnenus, but Constance rejected his candidacy and was enthusiastically supported by her people who feared the increasing Greek control.[2] Baldwin III offered the princess her choice between Ivo de Mela, count of Soissons, Walter of Falconberg, who later became lord of Tiberias, and Ralph de Merle; but the princess rejected all three and declared that she would remain unwed. This resolution lasted until the charm of the bold and dashing Renaud de Châtillon won the approval of the

[1] William Tyre, XVII, xv–xvii, 783–89; Dodu, p. 94; Chalandon, *op. cit.*, pp. 424–26.
[2] Cinnamus (*R. H. C. Grec*, i), p. 268; Chalandon, pp. 426–27; Rey, p. 369.

princess and she decided to entrust the care of herself and her county to his inexperienced hands. When she decided to marry Renaud she sent to Baldwin for his consent but neglected to mention the matter to Manuel.[1] Renaud was quick, however, to recognize the suzerainty of Byzantium as well as that of Jerusalem, and in 1155 attacked Thoros of Armenia, in alliance with, and at the request of, the basileus, '*ut imperialibus deserviret mandatis*'.[2] When, however, Manuel failed to pay the expenses of the campaign as he had promised, Renaud turned against him and sought compensation by plundering Cyprus, then a dependency of the Empire. Manuel marched against his rebellious vassal and Renaud appealed to King Baldwin to assist him. But before the latter arrived, Renaud had gone to meet Manuel at Mamistra where he humiliated himself, and, garbed in rags, barefooted, and with a rope around his neck, threw himself at the mercy of the emperor. Manuel accepted his repentance and submission and granted him Antioch as a fief.[3] But Antioch was once again left undefended, when, in November 1160, Renaud was captured by Mejd-ed-Din in a foray near Aintab, and the Antiochenes again appealed to Baldwin. The king came to Antioch, took charge of the government, and, arranging for a weekly allowance for Constance, committed the management of the city and county to the Patriarch Amaury.[4] Four years later (1164) Bohemond III was attacked by Nureddin. Amaury of Jerusalem was at the time engaged in his Egyptian campaign against Syracon, and could not come to the aid of his vassal. Bohemond gathered an army and drove Nureddin back from Harenc but the Christian forces were destroyed and Nureddin captured Bohemond, Ray-

---

[1] William Tyre, XVII, xviii, 789–91, xxvi, 802–04; Chalandon, p. 435; Schlumberger, *Renaud du Châtillon*, p. 11.

[2] William Tyre, XVIII, x, 834–35.

[3] William Tyre, XVIII, xxiii, 860–61; Cinnamus (*R. H. C.*, *Grec*, i), p. 275 ff.; Schlumberger, *op. cit.*, pp. 72–93; Chalandon, pp. 439–49; Röhricht, pp. 298–99.

Manuel's willingness to accept Renaud's dramatic apology and penance was due probably to the fact that Amaury, Latin patriarch of Antioch, who had quarreled with Renaud, was conspiring to make Baldwin of Jerusalem prince of Antioch; and Manuel did not not care to see Antioch pass under the direct control of Jerusalem. Further Renaud agreed to the establishment in Antioch of a Greek Orthodox Metropolitan.

[4] William Tyre, XVIII, xxviii–xxx, 868–74; Röhricht, p. 305; Schlumberger, *Renaud*, p. 115 ff.. In 1163 Bohemond III succeeded to the throne of Antioch on the death of his mother.

mond of Tripoli, Calmann duke of Mamistra, Hugh de Lusignan, and many others.[1] Word was at once sent to Amaury appealing for help; and in the meantime the patriarch took control, organizing the defense, rationing the food supply, and endeavoring to stave off famine. Manuel Comnenus offered assistance, but the aid of the Greeks seemed to the Franks no less destructive than the attacks of the Saracens, and they appealed to France to save them in their hour of peril. Geoffrey Fulcher, procurator of the Templars, wrote Louis VII saying that unless help was sent at once Antioch must fall,—either to Nureddin or Manuel. *'Ne exspectetis hinc alios nuncios, quia, Rege et magistro absentibus, non audemus dimittere probos homines in hoc arcto'*:—with this simple yet eloquent statement ended the appeal.[2]

The help came from Jerusalem. Amaury, returned from Egypt, heard the news from Antioch, and, joining to himself the count of Flanders who had come to the East with a considerable force some time before, hurried to Antioch. In January 1165 he wrote Louis VII from Antioch explaining the sad condition of affairs there. Negotiations were at once begun for the ransom of Bohemond, and he was released on promise to pay 100,000 dinars and supply hostages for the payment. The money was given by the emperor, who had shortly before married Marie, Bohemond's sister.[3] For a time after this Byzantium and the Frankish states drew closer together, and an era of good feeling set in, marked by closer relations between both Antioch and Jerusalem and the basileus.

But while Antioch was again ruled by her own prince, Tripoli was

---

[1] William Tyre, XIX, ix, 895–97. More detailed accounts are to be found in a series of letters sent to Louis VII of France asking for aid:—letters of Geoffrey Fulcher, Templar; Amaury, patriarch of Antioch; Amaury, king of Jerusalem (*R. H. Fr.*, xvi, 60–63, 79; *Regesta*, docs. 403, 404, 405, 411).

The letter of the patriarch says that Bohemond was made governor of Jerusalem when Amaury went to Egypt: *'nobis et novo Principi nostro cognato suo Boamundo illius Raimundi Principis filio, in reditum usque suam tam regni sui quam et terrae commiserat curam'*.

[2] Letter of Geoffrey Fulcher to Louis VII: *R. H. Fr.*, xvi, 62–3; Migne, *P. L.*, clv, 1279–80.

[3] William Tyre, XIX, xi, 900–02; Letter of Amaury of Jerusalem to Louis VII:—*R. H. Fr.*, xvi, 79; *Regesta*, doc. 411. William suggests that Nureddin released Bohemond because he feared that otherwise King Amaury would himself become bailli of Antioch, or would appoint a bailli who would be more dangerous to the Saracens than was the inexperienced Bohemond. Renaud de Châtillon, who had been captured four years before, remained in the prisons of Aleppo twelve years more, while Bohemond was released almost at once.

without its count, and King Amaury took over the bailliage of the county from 1164 to 1171. In 1168 the king confirmed a grant made to the Amalfitans by Raymond, and in 1170 issued a charter to the Hospitallers, granting certain lands in Tripoli, and guaranteeing Raymond's acceptance of the grant when he should be released and return to his county. In issuing this charter Amaury styled himself *'Tripolis comitatum procurans.'*[1]

The above instances illustrate the activity of the king of Jerusalem as a regent or bailli over the great counties. But it should be observed that the kings usually became baillies by the invitation of the barons of the county, especially in Antioch. The king did not force himself on the county, nor were the people obliged to call on him. What power he had in this respect was due rather to his own ability, and to the prestige accruing to him as ruler of the largest of the states in the federation which was the kingdom. If the examples given above come from the early reigns, it is because the later weak kings almost never interfered in the politics of the principalities, and Antioch became virtually independent of the Jerusalemite monarch. The bailliage was on several occasions offered to others than the king. When Bohemond I was captured in 1101 the Antiochenes called in Tancred to govern them without consulting the king on the matter at all.[2] In 1104 Tancred was again made bailli of Antioch, this time by the appointment of Bohemond, who entrusted the county to him when he went to Italy. At the same time Tancred was bailli of Edessa, having been appointed to that position by the Edessans and Bohemond.[3] Towards the end of the kingdom, when Tripoli and Antioch had been united under a single prince, we find Lucie,

---

[1] Charter of 1168:—Camera, i, 203–04; *Regesta*, doc. 453. This was only the normal confirmation which the suzerain might always make. Raymond's grant was in 1163:—Camera, i, 202–03; *Regesta*, doc. 380. The charter to the Hospital is found in: D. L. *Cartulaire*, doc. 411; *Regesta*, doc, 477. The king promised to assist the Hospital if Raymond tried to get the lands back from them. Raymond confirmed the grant, however, and there was no trouble. (D. L. *Cartulaire*, doc. 467; *Regesta*, doc. 519.)

[2] Fulcher, II, vii, 392–93; *Chronologie*, nos. 538, 542, 546.

[3] Albert Aix, IX, xli, 616; Raoul de Caen (*R. H. C. Occ.*, iii), cli, 712; Fulcher, II, xxvi, 465–67; William Tyre, X, xxx, 447; Mathew of Edessa (*R. H. C. Arm.*, i), p. 73; Kemal ed Din (Röhricht, *Beiträge zur Geschichte der Kreuzzüge* (Berlin, 1874), i), p. 232; *Chronologie*, nos. 723, 728; A. A. Beaumont, 'Albert of Aachen and the County of Edessa', *Munro-Crusades*, pp. 126–28. The western chroniclers all say that Tancred was asked by the Edessans to govern them, but the oriental agree that he was appointed by Bohemond.

the mother of Bohemond VI, exercising the regency for her son in 1251; and in 1274 Sibylle, the dowager countess, ruled as regent for her son Bohemond VII, against the protests of Hugh III, king of Jerusalem and Cyprus, who claimed the bailliage as the cousin and closest male relative of the prince.[1]

It has been seen already that the regency for minors was governed by rules of succession, and the kings could sometimes claim the regency as the closest relative. It can hardly be said that the counties admitted the right of the king to act as bailli through any right which he had as king and suzerain. It was as a strong neighbor and ally, and sometimes as the legal regent by birth, that the king was asked to assume the regency or bailliage.

As regards foreign affairs, war, and the making of alliances and treaties, the counties were completely sovereign as far as the king was concerned. They were not obliged to obtain his assent to any treaties they might make, nor were they at all bound by the foreign relations of the kingdom of Jerusalem. A very few examples will suffice, for the fact is well known, and a glance at Röhricht's *Regesta* or his *Geschichte des Königreiches Jerusalem* is sufficient to show the freedom with which the great counts made treaties and alliances and declared war without consulting the king. In 1103 Bohemond I made an alliance with Melek Ghazi; Raymond of Antioch refused to coöperate in the attack on Damascus in 1148; Raymond of Tripoli allied with Saladin in 1186, after having been at war with him, and carried on a guerilla naval war with Byzantium when his sister was rejected by Manuel. Bohemond le Borgne of Tripoli sought assistance from Aleppo as well as from Henry of Champagne when his father was captured by Leo of Armenia;[2] and Renaud of Antioch had, as has been indicated, fought both Armenia and Byzantium. When the great counts coöperated on campaigns against a common enemy, it was as allies, and not because they were bound to serve together. Ibelin, in enumerating the military resources of the kingdom, does not even suggest that any service was due from any of the great counties outside of the principality. The counties were outside of the realm as far as military service was concerned, and when

---

[1] *Eracles*, p. 466; Mas Latrie, *Histoire de Chypre*, i, 450.
[2] Ernoul, p. 322; Rey, p. 385.

the king wished to assist them, he had to appeal to the generosity and public spirit of his vassals as he could not compel them to serve outside of the kingdom. Albert of Aix tells how Baldwin I appealed to his vassals of Jerusalem to go with him to the aid of Edessa, and it is obvious from the tone of the appeal that the Jerusalemites were under no obligation to go, but that the king urged them to perform this extra service to help their fellows in Edessa. Albert adds that they voluntarily prepared for the expedition.[1] Nor need the men of the counties serve in wars of the king of Jerusalem; when called upon for aid by the kings, they often did serve but it was not required, and when service was given, it was rather as allies than as vassals. Some instances of aid rendered the kings by Antioch are:—that given by Roger to Baldwin II in 1118; that which Bohemond II gave against Damascus in 1130; that of Raymond against Damascus in 1140; and that of Bohemond III at Hattin. On the other hand, they were free to refuse aid, as Raymond did in 1148, and did not consider themselves at all bound to help the kings. An exception might seem to be the case of Raymond III of Tripoli, who was made commander of the army of Jerusalem in 1183, but Raymond was lord of Tiberias and prince of Galilee in Jerusalem and had already acted as regent for Baldwin IV, holding the regency as closest relative of the king.[2]

The counties could be at peace with a power with which the kingdom was at war and vice-versa. Thus Raymond of Tripoli, who was at truce with Saladin kept his county neutral in the conflict which preceded the defeat at Hattin in 1187; throughout Saladin's war against Jerusalem, Tripoli was technically at peace with the Saracens, though the count, as a baron of Jerusalem, was fighting in the Christian army.[3]

The various rulers often sheltered, and even honored, refugees from their neighbor counties; and Baldwin I received Joscelin de Courtney when Baldwin de Burg drove him from Edessa in 1113,

---

[1] Albert Aix, XI, xviii–xix, 671. In describing the army which went to relieve Antioch in 1110 Albert shows that it was composed of various contingents under allied leaders, of whom King Baldwin was one (XI, xl, 682–83).

[2] William Tyre, XXII, xxx, 1130; Rey, 'Princes d'Antioche', and Röhricht, *passim*.

[3] *Eracles*, pp. 37–40.

and even granted him the fief of Tiberias which made him one of the greatest lords of the kingdom.[1] In 1186, when Baldwin of Rama refused to recognize Guy de Lusignan as king of Jerusalem, he went to Antioch where he was welcomed by Bohemond III, who bestowed upon him large estates.[2] In 1198 Ralph of Tiberias, driven from the kingdom for his supposed attempt to murder Amaury II, took refuge in Tripoli. In 1242 Lothaire Filanger, the imperialist commander at Tyre, when he was driven from his city by the Cypriots, fled to Antioch and was there received by Bohemond V with much honor.[3]

It was in the court of the king that disputes between the great counts were occasionally settled, but here it was a case of the king arbitrating between his peers rather than a lord summoning his unruly vassals into his court. In 1109 Baldwin de Burg and Tancred made up their differences in the court of Baldwin I;[4] in 1127 Baldwin II mediated between Bohemond II and Joscelin of Edessa;[5] and in 1195 Henry of Champagne made peace between Bohemond III and Leo of Armenia.[6] Yet the king did not always enforce his arbitration on the contesting counts, and the struggles of the princes of Antioch with the Armenians and with the Knights Hospitallers went on without any interference on the part of the king. There was no matter here of a legal right to try the suits and quarrels of vassals; it was merely that the king could sometimes get himself accepted as mediator.

On occasion the king was called upon to ratify and confirm the grants and charters of one or another of the counts. This was to give added security to the grant, and the confirmation of the Pope was also often secured. When Richard of England was in Palestine he

---

[1] William Tyre, XI, xxii, 489–92.
[2] Ernoul, p. 139. Baldwin appears on charters of Bohemond as among the knights of Antioch. (*Regesta*, doc. 649.)
[3] *Gestes*, par. 231; *Eracles*, p. 230.
[4] Albert Aix, XI, xxii, 673–74.
[5] William Tyre, XIII, xxii, 590.
[6] Ernoul, pp. 319–21. By this treaty Bohemond became the vassal of Leo for lands which he had taken from him, and at the same time quitted the Armenian of his fealty to Antioch, which he had, until that time, owed.

confirmed grants made by Syrian Frankish barons.[1] An interesting interchange of confirmations is that of Baldwin II and Joscelin of Edessa. Baldwin confirmed Joscelin's charter to the Hospitallers, while the count confirmed grants made by the king to that Order in the county of Edessa.[2]

The action of the king could not bind the count, nor could his approval make valid an action of a vassal of one of the counts, if the count had not himself given his consent. Thus, in 1210, Bohemond IV of Antioch-Tripoli tried and disseised Renaud of Nefin for marrying, without his consent, Isabelle the heiress of Gybelcar. Renaud had obtained the consent of King Amaury II, of Leo of Armenia, and of Eudes and Ralph of Tiberias, but not that of Bohemond. Renaud refused to come to court when Bohemond summoned him and a war broke out between them. After some initial successes, Renaud was defeated, and Gybelcar was surrendered to Bohemond as ransom for Renaud, who then fled to Cyprus.[3]

Not only did the counts not obey and follow the king, they often even threatened him, and there were times when a combination of Antioch and Tripoli might have seemed fatal to Jerusalem. In 1180 Baldwin IV feared that Bohemond III and Raymond of Tripoli were coming to drive him from his realm when he heard that they were coming together to Jerusalem.[4]

After the loss of the city of Jerusalem, in the second period of the kingdom, the principality of Antioch-Tripoli was as important and as strong as that of Jerusalem, and the lords of the two states were acknowledged equals, the prince of Antioch at one time claiming the regency over Jerusalem. In the later thirteenth century the kingship had so declined, however, that little remained to it of what power it had held formerly; and the entire country was controlled by the baronial oligarchy. But, in the earlier period, when kingship in

---

[1] *Regesta,* doc. 706; Müller, pp. 58–59. Richard confirmed the privileges of the Pisans granted them by King Guy. Richard also procured the grant of a charter to the Genoese by Guy. (*Regesta,* doc. 702; *Liber Jurium,* i, doc. 392.)

[2] D. L. *Cartulaire,* docs. 104, 137; *Regesta,* docs. 151, 206.

[3] *Eracles,* pp. 314–15.

[4] William Tyre, XXII, i, 1062–63. Baldwin hastened to strengthen his position by marrying his sister Sibylle to Guy de Lusignan.

Jerusalem was active and alive, the king was never more than theoretical suzerain over the counts; and, when the counties seemed to acknowledge the preëminence of the kings, it was because the kings were strong enough personally to enforce their primacy over their weaker neighbors. Further it was as rulers of the largest of the states which made up the kingdom, and as lords of the Holy Places, that the kings of Jerusalem had precedence over the other rulers of the Outremer states.

CHAPTER 10

THE RELATIONS OF THE KINGS OF JERUSALEM WITH THE CHURCH

'*L E REI dou roiaume de Jerusalem ne tient son roiaume que de Dieu*' wrote Ibelin.[1] It was true that Jerusalem recognized no secular suzerain. But the kingdom had been founded by armies raised and directed by the Pope, and their guiding policy throughout the crusade and even till the establishment of the kingdom was that laid down by Urban II, who saw in Jerusalem a state governed by the Apostolic See, a living proof in the East of the greatness and power of the Roman Church. The Hildebrandine Papacy aimed at world domination, and this Latin kingdom in the Holy Land, with a Latin patriarch in the See of Jerusalem, was a signal triumph for papal policy; and the successors of Urban had no intention of losing the initial advantages which had been gained by the Church in fathering the crusade.[2]

The crusaders had been, in fact as in name, soldiers of the Cross, enlisted under ecclesiastical supervision by preachers of the crusade commissioned by the Pope, and protected, as long as they were engaged on God's business, by the privileges and immunities of the Church.[3] They were already, as it were, vassals of the Church, soldiers enlisted in the Church's army in the great war of Christian-

[1] Ibelin, vi, 29. Dodu, p. 336, applies this quotation, erroneously I believe, to show that the Church had control over the crown and to argue that the king was not king until consecrated by the Church. I think that this is no more than a statement of the temporal sovereignty of the kings of Jerusalem. The *Établissements de St Louis* (ed. P. Viollet: *Soc. His. Fr.*; Paris, 1881), ii, par. 83, p. 135, says: '*li rois ne tient de nului fors de Dieu et de lui*', and this is said in proof of the fact that there is no appeal from the king's court. Certainly France did not recognize the temporal power of the Papacy; and Ibelin's statement is, like that in the *Établissements*, an assertion of the sovereignty of Jerusalem, rather than a statement of ecclesiastical prerogative. A. J. Carlyle, *History of Medieval Political Theory* (London, 1903–28), v, 359–60, cites Jerusalem as not recognizing spiritual as superior to temporal power.

[2] F. Duncalf, 'The Pope's Plan for the First Crusade,' *Munro-Crusades*, pp. 44–56; W. Norden, *Das Papsttum und Byzanz* (Berlin, 1903), pp. 46–47.

[3] A. Luchaire, *Innocent III*, iv, *La Question d'Orient* (Paris, 1911), pp. 3–6; E. Bridrey, *La Condition Juridique des Croisés* (Paris, 1900).

ity against Islam, and the direction of the army was but naturally assumed by the head of the Church, Christ's vicar on earth.

Duke Godfrey, elected first ruler of the new kingdom, recognized this claim of the Church to dominion over his realm and refused the title of king, assuming that of Baron and Defender of the Holy Sepulchre; and both Godfrey and Bohemond of Antioch performed homage to the Patriarch Daimbert as the papal representative, receiving their lands from him as fiefs held from the Church.[1]

The patriarch was at the head of affairs almost as much as was the king, and there was all too much truth in Ibelin's statement that:—'*Il y a ou reiaume de Jerusalem deus chiefs seignors, l'un esperituel, et l'autre temporel: le patriarche de Jerusalem est le seignor esperituel, et le rei dou reiaume de Jerusalem le seignor temporel doudit reiaume*'.[2]

Conflicts inevitably arose between the two powers. The Church of Hildebrand and Urban II, as represented by Daimbert, aimed at nothing less than the creation of a state of the Church in Palestine; and the patriarchate of Daimbert reflected in the East the familiar story of struggle of *sacerdotium* against *regnum*. Yewdale has shown that the patriarch aimed at using Bohemond and Tancred as foils against the power of the house of Bouillon, and that Bohemond supported Daimbert in a desire to obtain a valid title to his rule in Antioch.[3] The alliance of Baldwin I and Arnulf of Chocques was motivated by a mutual opposition to the Pisan Daimbert, who represented the extreme of ecclesiastical ambition. The story how Daimbert sought to prevent Baldwin's accession to the throne, and of the subsequent difficulties which developed between them, has been repeatedly told, and can be found in Fulcher, Albert of Aix, William of Tyre, and in the more recent works of Röhricht, Dodu, Mas Latrie, Hagenmeyer, and Hampel.[4] The election of Arnulf in 1112 closed this period of conflict, and the patriarch did not attempt to reassert

[1] *Chronologie*, no. 455; William Tyre, IX, xv, 387; Fulcher, III, xxxiv, 741–42; R. B. Yewdale, *Bohemond I of Antioch* (Princeton, 1924), pp. 89–91.

[2] Ibelin, cclx, 415; Dodu, p. 331; W. Jacobs, *Patriarch Gerold von Jerusalem* (Aix la Chapelle, 1905), p. 5.

[3] Yewdale, *Bohemond I*, pp. 89–91.

[4] E. Hampel, *Untersuchungen über das lateinische Patriarchat von Jerusalem . . . bis zum Tode des Patriarchen Arnulf* (Breslau, 1899).

his supremacy thereafter save for the short patriarchate of Stephen from 1128 to 1130. The kings performed homage to the patriarch for their lands and sought confirmation of their title from the Pope, but the patriarchs were in themselves no more than the primates of the Church within the kingdom and were in no wise rulers of the state.[1]

The policy of the Popes, which undoubtedly did much to restrain the ambitions of the patriarchs, was to keep a balance between the two powers and to keep both dependent upon Rome. The king was the vassal of the Papacy and must preserve the respect he owed the Church, but the patriarch had likewise to remember that he was subject to the Apostolic See and must not be allowed to become so powerful that he would aim at independence and endeavor to set up the See of Jerusalem in opposition to that of Rome. The immensely wealthy Jerusalemite patriarchate, endowed as it was with lands and enriched by gifts from all countries of Europe, might, with its apostolic tradition and the sacredness which attached to it as the See of the Holy City, have become a serious rival to Rome. The Popes were careful to keep the patriarchs always in their place and to discourage them when they threatened to become too aggressive. Grants of immunity from the diocesian jurisdiction to the religious Orders and the great abbeys of Palestine were useful checks on the power of the patriarch, and kept the Outremer clergy in direct dependence upon the Papacy.[2] Furthermore the secular power in the kingdom received papal support as long as it recognized the suzerainty of the Church. By placing themselves under the protection of the Papacy and recognizing a theoretical dependence thereon, the kings of Jerusalem secured in practice freedom from papal interference and a benevolent guardianship of their interests, which assisted them with men and money in time of need and otherwise left them rather much alone. The Popes were always interested

---

[1] Paschal II confirmed Baldwin I, and Honorius II confirmed Baldwin II. Honorius said in his confirmation: 'Nos vero . . . regnum Ierosolimitanum cum dignitate a predecessore nostre felicis memorie, papae Pascali, antecessori tuo, regi Balduino, atque Ierosolimitane ecclesie iuste discretionis moderamine tandem concessa apostolica tibi auctoritate concedimus.' (Rozière, doc. 15; *Regesta*, doc. 122; Jaffé, *Regesta Pontificum*, no. 7314.)

[2] For this point of view concerning the papal attitude towards the patriarchs, the author is indebted to the suggestion advanced by Dr. August C. Krey.

in the preservation of the Latin states in the East, and when danger menaced them, new crusades were preached, new armies sent out, special tithes were collected for the defense of the Holy Places, and special dispensations were offered to those who would settle in the crusading states. It is not the purpose of this chapter to trace the relations of the various Popes in the twelfth and thirteenth centuries with the rulers of Outremer; nor is such a chapter necessary in a study of Jerusalem more than in that of any other Christian state in the same period; the crusading states were hardly more subject to papal intervention than were those of Spain, much less so than those of Italy.

The affairs of the great religio-military Orders, the Templars and Hospitallers, who were under the especial protection of the Papacy as were many of the religious houses in Palestine, led the supreme pontiffs to intervene not infrequently in Jerusalem. Not only the kings, but the patriarch and diocesan bishops as well, had cause to resent the immunities granted these Orders and exempt establishments, who kept their own representatives at Rome and who refused to acknowledge any jurisdiction save that of the Papal Curia.[1] The long struggle between the Hospitallers and Bohemond IV and V of Antioch-Tripoli which lasted intermittently from 1217 to 1241 involved the Pope as the defender of the Order on more than one occasion. When Bohemond IV attacked the castles and possessions of the Hospital in Tripoli the Knights appealed to Pope Honorius III, who in 1226 wrote to the archbishops of Caesarea and Nicosia to see that justice was done, and authorized the Knights forcibly to regain possession of their properties. In 1230 Gregory IX excommunicated Bohemond, who had refused to yield to the Knights, with the result that the prince submitted to the patriarch's arbitration and paid damages to the Hospital.[2] But when Bohemond V succeeded to the principality he reopened the war against the Knights, seizing their fief of Maraclea, and the affair dragged on for eight

---

[1] A. C. Krey, 'The International State of the Middle Ages', *A. H. R.*, xxviii (1922), 9–10.

[2] Letters and bulls of Honorius III of 1226–1230: D. L. *Cartulaire*, docs. 1834, 1837, 1955, 1965. Final accord: *Ibid.*, 1999, 2000, 2001, 2002. The story is told in Delaville Le Roulx, *Les Hospitaliers en Terre Sainte* (Paris, 1904), p. 173 *et seq.*. It was settled by the Knights selling the lands to Bohemond who paid them damages and a fixed revenue from Antioch and Tripoli.

years until it was settled by the Knights selling the disputed lands to
the prince in return for annuities derived from the revenues of the
prince's cities.¹ The Pope was active throughout this affair trying to
reëstablish peace and appointing arbiters. One letter is of especial
interest: it is an epistle from Gregory to the Knights forbidding them
to ally themselves with the heretic Moslem sect of the Assassins
whom the Knights were evidently stirring up against Bohemond.²

The Popes were also called upon to guard the interests of the
Italian communes, whose privileges as accorded by treaties were
often disregarded; and a long series of papal letters show the assistance which was afforded Italians, especially the Genoese, who were
under special papal protection. The most important cases are those
of the Genoese vs. King Amaury I and his successors, and Genoa vs.
the Embriaci of Gibelet. In the first case Amaury was accused by
the Genoese of taking away and melting down the inscription in
letters of gold in the Holy Sepulchre which enumerated the privileges of the Genoese in Jerusalem. Alexander III wrote to Amaury
in 1167 demanding the restoration of the inscription; the king ig-
nored the papal order and in 1186 Urban III was still writing to the
Masters of the Temple and Hospital, and various prelates to force the
king to make the desired restoration.³ In the same year four letters
from Urban III order Hugh Embriaco of Gibelet of pay the rental
for which he held the fief of Gibelet from the Genoese.⁴ The conquests
of Saladin put an end to both these disputes. On occasion the Pope
interfered in a purely private matter; Alexander IV wrote intervening in behalf of a certain Raymond who appealed to Rome that he
had been disinherited of the constableship of Tripoli by Bohemond
VI;⁵ and in 1251 Innocent IV was putting pressure on the abbot

¹ The papal letters and documents concerning this affair are given in D. L. *Cartulaire*, docs.
2071, 2094, 2149, 2150, 2184, 2280. The case is mentioned in Rey, 'Princes d'Antioche',
R. O. L., iv, 389–400, and Delaville Le Roulx, *Hospitaliers*, pp. 174–89.

² D. L. *Cartulaire*, doc. 2149.

³ *Liber Jurium*, i, docs. 254, 255, 322, 345, 346, 347, 348, 349, 350; *Regesta*, doc. 438.

⁴ *Liber Jurium*, i, docs. 351, 352, 353, 354. Alexander III had written to Hugh of Gibelet
as early as 1179. (*Ibid.*, 321.)

⁵ J. Sbaralea, *Bullarum Franciscarum* (Rome, 1759–68), ii, 18–19; Potthast, *Regesta Pontificum*, no. 15713; *Regesta*, doc. 1224a. Raymond argued that the constableship had been
given to another heir whose legitimacy was doubtful wherefore he appealed his case on the
point of legitimacy in the church court.

and monks of St Saba at Alexandria to sell their house in Acre to the Genoese for a fair price.[1]

Appeal to the Roman Curia was common from Jerusalem as from any other country in the thirteenth century, and cases of all sorts were carried to Rome. Nor was there any law in Outremer forbidding such an appeal to Rome from the courts of the kingdom. The *Haute Cour* was supreme in those matters of which it took cognizance and recognized no appeal from its decisions to any court, but appeals from the church courts of the kingdom were common, and a long series of bishops, patriarchs, secular and regular clergy, and nobles journeyed to Rome in search of justice. On occasion appeal was lodged at Rome from a decision given in the *Haute Cour*, though this was never accepted as legal in Jerusalem. Marie of Antioch carried her case to the Papacy when she was defeated by Hugh III in the *Haute Cour*. The barons of course refused to recognize this appeal and Hugh ruled uncontestedly, but when he abandoned Acre in 1278, the bailli of Charles of Anjou, to whom Marie had sold out her claims to the throne, was accepted in Acre. This whole case has more to do with politics than law, for Charles' occupation was an invasion, and the Templars and others who accepted the Angevin rule were already *de facto* in revolt against Hugh.[2]

On the whole Jerusalem may be said to have been far more free of papal interference and control than her position as a vassal state of the Papacy would lead one to expect. But the head of the Church within the country was the patriarch and the relations of the kings with the patriarchs were not always of the best. During the first three reigns the patriarchs were inclined to assert themselves and demand temporal power and Daimbert and Stephen caused serious trouble, but after the death of Stephen in 1130 no patriarch seriously questioned the royal sovereignty and the patriarchs of the late twelfth and thirteenth centuries, while they often meddled in poli-

---

[1] *Liber Jurium*, i, docs. 818, 819.

[2] *Gestes*, par. 375; *Eracles*, pp. 475–76; *Assises*, ii, 416–19; and see chapter 4 above. The Papal Curia gave no decision in the case, which was carried to the Council of Lyons, also without getting a decision. The Pope did, however, negotiate the sale of Marie's claims to Charles of Anjou and gave letters and credentials to his baillies when they went to Syria.

tics as did Heraclius and Gerold, coöperated with the kings rather
than opposed them.[1]

More pertinent to this study are the powers which the king exercised over the clergy, and those which the patriarch had over the
king and nobles.

The king received his crown from the hands of the patriarch.
Ibelin says that he should be crowned in Jerusalem if the Christians
have it, and by the patriarch if there is one in the country. Jerusalem lacking, the coronation should take place at Tyre, and if the
patriarch cannot officiate it should be done by the archbishop of
Tyre. At his coronation the king swears to defend the Church and
preserve her rights, privileges, and properties, and the patriarch
promises to aid the king against all men and things—save Holy
Church and his Order.[2]

'*Dans le royaume de Jérusalem le sacre faisait le roi en confirmant
l'élection féodale*', says Dodu, '*L'élu des barons n'était validé qu'après
avoir reçu la sanction de l'Église*'.[3] While this may have been true
as regards the earliest kings, it certainly did not hold for the later
ones; and Ibelin specifically says that the patriarch announces that
he is crowning the *legitimate* heir. After the principle of heredity had
been accepted, the coronation added ecclesiastical sanction to the
king and invested him with that semi-religious character which was
an attribute of mediaeval kingship, but it was not needed to make him
king. Frederick II was king of Jerusalem and was recognized as such
by the barons, but he crowned himself and the Church did not recog-

---

[1] Dodu, pp. 358–60, gives a picture of the relations of king and patriarch drawn altogether
from the first thirty years of the kingdom and showing the two powers in constant and bitter
conflict. This is of course an untrue view of the situation as it presents but a single phase and
by no means the larger aspect.

J. Longnon, *Les Français d'Outremer* (Paris: Perrin, 1929), p. 121, lists the pretentions of
the Church as the first cause for the weakness of the state,—following Dodu,—and pp. 134
and 154 blames the Church for not assisting the Kings.

[2] Ibelin, vi–vii, 29–31. Baldwin I and II were both crowned by the patriarch in Bethlehem,
thereafter the coronations took place in Jerusalem or Tyre. Compare this oath of the patriarch with that to which the English clergy were forced to agree under the *Constitutions of
Clarendon*, article xii. (Stubbs, *Select Charters of English Constitutional History*, (9th ed.,
Oxford, 1921), p. 166.)

[3] Dodu, pp. 335–36.

nize him. The Popes withheld their sanction of his assumption of the royal title until 1231, and at the coronation ceremony in Jerusalem no ecclesiastic was present as Frederick was at the time excommunicate, and Jerusalem was placed under the interdict the day following the coronation. Yet Frederick was none the less king.[1] As another case may be cited Guy de Lusignan who received his crown from the hands of Sibylle, his wife, who had previously been crowned by the Patriarch Heraclius.[2]

If Guy's title was challenged later, it was not because he had not been legally made king, but because he ruled in virtue of his wife, and after her death the barons considered that the throne passed to her sister, and did not remain with her husband.

But the patriarch could, and did, exercise considerable power within the kingdom. The degree depended largely upon the personality and ability of the individual patriarch, and men like Daimbert, Warmund, Heraclius, and Gerold were of the first importance in the councils of the realm and in the practical administration thereof. In 1124 Warmund acted as regent for the kingdom during the captivity of Baldwin II and, *'vicem domini regis obtinens'*, directed the siege of Tyre.[3] Previously, in conjunction with William de Buris, he had signed a treaty with the Venetians and had assisted the constable in the government of the realm. Throughout his entire tenure of the patriarchate (1118–1128) he played a leading rôle in politics. A similar case is that of Amaury, patriarch of Antioch, who was bailli in place of King Amaury in 1160 when the king held the bailliage of Antioch, and who in 1164 took command of the city, organized the defense, and managed the affairs of the county while Bohemond III was a captive.[4] In 1105 Evremar, patriarch of Jerusalem, raised a force of an hundred and fifty men to help Baldwin I at Rama; and in 1132 Patriarch William led an expedition out from Jerusalem, in the absence of King Foulque, and built the

---

[1] Letter of Herman von Salza, Master of the Teutonic Knights:—*M. G. H. Epis. XIII Saec.*, i, doc. 383, p. 299; *Regesta*, doc. 1000; Jacobs, *Patriarch Gerold*, p. 33 ff..

[2] Ernoul, pp. 133–35.

[3] William Tyre, XIII, vi, 563.

[4] Geoffrey Fulcher to Louis VII, *R. H. Fr.*, xvi, 62–63; *Regesta*, doc. 404; William Tyre, XVIII, xxx, 872.

castle Arnald on the road to Ascalon.[1] It was Heraclius who, after Hattin in 1187, made Balian d'Ibelin stay in Jerusalem to organize the defense of the city, and who, when further resistance was useless, negotiated the terms of the surrender with Saladin.[2] In 1232 when the *Frarie de St André* was organizing itself against Frederick II, Patriarch Gerold was one of the leaders; and the commune of Antioch was organized under the auspices of the Patriarch Amaury.[3]

As the religious head of the state the patriarch obviously had considerable prestige and weight in the councils of the realm. He was one of the most influential members of the *Haute Cour* and Ibelin names him as one who must be consulted when the laws and assises were to be revised.[4] His assent was necessary to the validity of treaties, and the clergy refused to accept Frederick II's treaty with Egypt until he should get the approval of Gerold, although the assent of the baronage had been obtained.[5]

But if the patriarch had an important place in secular affairs, the king, on the other hand, exercised considerable influence in ecclesiastical matters, particularly in the election of bishops and in making appointments to ecclesiastical benefices. The king's rights in the election of the patriarch seem to have been unquestioned, though the defeated candidates had a habit of appealing to Rome against his selection. Ernoul says that when the patriarch died the canons of the Holy Sepulchre selected two men as candidates and that the king chose between them, and that this was the accepted practice of the kingdom. Thus it was that Baldwin IV chose Heraclius over William of Tyre, for Heraclius was supported by the queen mother.[6] Arnulf in one of his charters styles himself '*a rege, clero et populo in pastorem*

---

[1] Fulcher, II, xxxi, 492–94; Albert Aix, IX, xlix, 622; William Tyre, XIV, viii, 617; *Chronologie*, no. 753.

[2] *Eracles*, pp. 69–70.

[3] *Eracles*, pp. 395, 313–14; Jacobs, *Patriarch Gerold*, pp. 50–51; Rey, 'Princes d'Antioche', *R. O. L.*, iv, 384–85.

[4] Ibelin, iii, 24.

[5] Jacobs, *Patriarch Gerold*, pp. 29–30. Four barons assented on behalf of the liegemen of Jerusalem. Gerold was both patriarch and papal legate, which gave him increased influence.

[6] Ernoul, pp. 83–84. Ernoul explains this on the precedent of the Apostles who, when they wished to fill the vacancy in their number caused by the treason and suicide of Judas, chose between two, Joseph and Mathias; wherefore the selection should always be between

electus', clearly placing the king first and showing the royal control over the election.[1] The king's consent was customary for the validity of the election of the local bishops; in referring to his own election as archbishop of Tyre, William says, '*Consonante cleri et populi voto, regis quoque, ut moris est, conveniente assensu*'.[2]

While Dodu oversteps the mark in his assertion that the struggles of the patriarchs with the kings did much to ruin the kingdom of Jerusalem, it cannot be denied that Jerusalem was, numerically at least, a priest-ridden state, and that in some ways the Church formed a decided liability. This was particularly true in respect to military service, for the Church supplied far too few soldiers in proportion to the amount of land it held. Ibelin lists the sergeants owed by the various churches and abbeys, which, be it noted, were only to be given in time of particular stress; and the list shows that the Church gave very little in service for what it possessed in acreage.[3] The Holy Sepulchre for all the lands it held supplied only 500 sergeants. Yet it must be remembered that while the local churches supplied few soldiers, the Church as a whole supplied many, for the most important source of military strength in the Latin states was in the Orders which were chartered by the Papacy, and the members of which served as militant ecclesiastics. Further, extra soldiers were often obtained from the Church. Baldwin I in 1101 forced Daimbert to assume the responsibility for the payment of thirty knights, but, says Albert who tells the story, the patriarch paid them very poorly.[4]

Some idea of the holdings of the Church can be easily obtained from glancing through the documents in Röhricht's *Regesta*, Roziére's *Cartulaire du St Sépulcre*, or Delaborde's cartulary of the Abbey of Josaphat. William of Tyre contributes an enlightening detail when he says that when Eustache Grenier married the niece

---

two candidates. This practice was current in Cyprus where the king chose from two candidates presented to him by the chapter of Santa Sophia of Nicosia, when there was a vacancy for the archbishopric. In 1213 Innocent III wrote to Cyprus demanding that this practice be stopped. (Migne, *Patrologia Latina*, ccxvi, 733; Potthast, *Regesta Pontificum*, no. 4646.)

[1] Rozière, doc. 25; *Regesta*, doc. 75.

[2] William Tyre, XXI, ix, 1020.

[3] Ibelin, cclxxii, 426-27.

[4] Albert Aix, VII, lviii-lxi, 545-47. Baldwin only got the money by threatening the patriarch and by the good offices of the papal legate.

of the Patriarch Arnulf, he was given the lands of the church at Jericho which produced an annual revenue of 5000 gold besants.[1] The early sovereigns were lavish in their grants to the Church. Later, poverty caused them to give much less, and in the thirteenth century the Church and the Orders paid for almost all they acquired. Queen Melissande was perhaps the most generous donor to religious houses;—the later kings sold or gave very sparingly.[2]

Because of such enormous grants the Church soon acquired a disproportionate amount of land, and Jerusalem was one of the earliest of the feudal states to legislate against the gift or sale of land to ecclesiastics or churches. The *Livre au Roi*, the oldest of the surviving collections of Jerusalemite laws, provides that the king may not sell or give any castles to either the Saracens or the Church. Nor may any individual sell his fief to the Church, or to any religious Order.[3] In discussing lepers, the *Livre* says that the leper must go to St Lazare, his wife must enter a convent,—and his fief goes to his nearest relative. If the fief passes through the wife she may claim it but she may not give it to her convent. If a fief passes by inheritance to a woman who is a nun, she may claim it and should be invested with it, and should then invest one of her relatives who could serve for the fief. Bourgeois tenements might be inherited by nuns and while they could not be given to the convent, they could be sold and the money received from the sale given to the Order.[4]

In the thirteenth century, the law became less severe and less dogmatic, and Philip de Novare says merely that the king shall not lose any homage or service through the gift, exchange, or sale of lands to the Church.[5] Ibelin goes into the matter with more detail than Novare. He draws a clear distinction between sale or gift of lands to the Church with the consent of the lord, and without it. If a man gives or sells his lands to the Church without his lord's consent, the lord may confiscate the lands at once without compen-

[1] William Tyre, XI, xv, 479.

[2] Delaborde, *Chartes de la Terre Sainte*, Introduction, 2–3; William Tyre, XV, xxvi, 699–700, says that Melissande gave the convent at Bethany the whole city of Jericho.

[3] *Livre au Roi*, i, 607, xlv, 640.

[4] *Ibid.*, xlii–xliii, 636–38.

[5] Novare, lvi, 530.

sation to the Church; if on the other hand, the sale has been made with his consent, he has only the right to purchase the land back from the Church within a year and a day for the price paid by the Church.[1] The *Clef des Assises* merely reaffirms the rule that the fief of any one who becomes a monk reverts at once to the nearest relative.[2]

These laws clearly recognize the prevailing practice of granting and selling lands to the Church. They merely endeavor to retard the process somewhat, and Ibelin's laws involve no penalty for the man who sells with his lord's consent. Only if he does it without the approval of the lord does he become liable. The aim of this prescription was not to prohibit the sale of fiefs to the Church, but to assure the lord of his rights, and to secure to him that he should not lose service or aids through the passing of land into *mortmain* without his consent. That the laws of Jerusalem were not fundamentally hostile to the acquisition of property by the Church is attested by the article of the *Assises de la Cour des Bourgeois* which provides that if a man or woman has entered Holy Orders and dies intestate the Order shall receive the possessions of the deceased. It may be assumed that the '*tout canque ces ont*' which may be inherited thus by the Church refers only to movable goods and not to lands, but the law does not specify. This law is extremely unusual in assuming the right of monks and nuns to dispose of property by testament—a practice not tolerated in any other country.[3]

On the other hand, there is a strict prohibition against the purchase by any layman of any Church vessels, ornaments, chalices, or sacred utensils,—for these should not be in private and profane hands. The purchaser thereof loses the article and the price paid as well.[4]

Furthermore if the Church held lands for which it did inadequate service, it had a grievance in the refusal or reluctance of the laity to

---

[1] Ibelin, ccxxxiv bis, 372, ccxlix, 399.

[2] *Clef des Assises*, cxc, 593. The *Assises de Romanie*, arts. 25, 96, provide that only the prince can give lands to the Church in perpetuity. Anyone can give without his lord's consent,—but it can be only a grant for life and reverts at the donor's death.

[3] *Assises Cour Bourg.*, clxxxix, 127. The provisions of the law in case monks die intestate imply their right to make wills.

[4] *Ibid.*, xxxviii, 40.

pay the tithes which were its legal due. This was the source of especial difficulty in Cyprus, where the nobles obstinately refused to pay, and Pelagius the legate, Patriarch Gerold, and Pope Gregory IX himself complained at length of their neglect of this obligation.[1]

Jerusalem was not cursed with any important conflict over the demarcation of ecclesiastical and secular jurisdiction. The church courts in the kingdom were powerful, but remarkably little information has come to us concerning them. Within their jurisdiction they included the persons of ecclesiastics, and all cases relating to ecclesiastical property, also all those matters which came essentially under the canon law rather than the secular. The *Clef des Assises* lists the matters belonging to the Church's jurisdiction as matters of the Faith, marriage, and testament.[2] The *Assises de la Cour des Bourgeois* more specifically mention churchmen and church property, heresy, adultery, and cases between husband and wife except treason and murder, which latter are always reserved for the royal court.[3]

In general the competence of the ecclesiastical courts in Jerusalem was greater than in France, where adultery and all cases relating to fiefs were tried in the civil courts. The French church courts had no such competence over laity as had those of Jerusalem, and only perjury, which was tried by the secular courts in Jerusalem, was tried in the church courts in France. In England, while frankalmoin lands were amenable to the church courts, any cases of lay fiefs were tried in the secular courts.[4]

In cases of conflict between the civil and ecclesiastical jurisdictions the king's viscount and the jurors went into the church court and sat with the ecclesiastical judges in hearing the case.[5]

Members of the Orders,—Temple, Hospital, and Teutonic Knights,—were not privileged to claim full ecclesiastical immunity

[1] Though an agreement on the matter was reached in 1220 and revised and renewed in 1222, the Cypriots refused to abide by it, and the Popes and legates vainly tried to bring them to obedience. (Mas Latrie, iii, 612–14, 619–22, 631, 633–36, 641–42.)

[2] *Clef des Assises*, ix, 579. A. J. Carlyle, *History of Medieval Political Theory*, v, 360, thinks that the accepted maxim that custom should prevail against laws, decrees, or decretals indicates that in Jerusalem the feudal law was supreme over the canon.

[3] *Assises Cour Bourg.*, xiv, 27–28; clxxxi, 121; cclxxxix, 219.

[4] *Ibid.*, xxiii, 32; Dodu, pp. 325–28. Cf, *Constitutions of Clarendon*, article ix.

[5] *Assises Cour Bourg.*, xiv, 28; *Abrégé*, lxxii, 292. Cf, *Constitutions of Clarendon*, article iii.

and were subject to the lay courts, though in some respects they enjoyed an exempt position.[1] The competence of the church courts seems to have been well defined and well recognized in Jerusalem and we do not have any record of any considerable dispute over it, such as occurred in England.

On the whole we may sum up by saying that while the Church had a theoretical supremacy over the kingdom of Jerusalem, and while her privileges were extensive and her lands broad, Jerusalem was much better off in her relation with the Church than were most of the European states. For there was relatively little intervention by the Popes, and there was considerable assistance—both in men and money—supplied by the Church. And what Jerusalem lost through ecclesiastical exemptions, she gained—and more—from the assistance of the Orders and the support of the Papacy.[2]

[1] *Assises Cour Bourg.*, cxxix, 89, and note *c*. In general see D. Hayek, *Le Droit Franc en Syrie* (Paris, 1925), pp. 150–55.

[2] This was not the case in Cyprus where the Church constantly stirred up trouble with the Greek Orthodox natives through her efforts to subject them to the Latin rite and heirarchy. While in Jerusalem the Latin clergy were over the native sects, Armenian, Nestorian, Jacobite, *et al.*, there seems to have been little attempt to destroy their churches or to demand more than a nominal heirarchical subjection. See E. G. Rey, *Colonies Franques*, pp. 75–94, 273–74.

CHAPTER 11

THE RELATIONS OF THE KINGS OF JERUSALEM WITH THE RELIGIO-MILITARY ORDERS

AMONG the important groups in the crusading states whose relations with the kings must be here given attention are the great religio-military Orders, those semi-monastic, semi-chivalrous corporations which were among the most important factors in the life of the Outremer principalities and which played a rôle hardly less significant than that of the Mediterranean communes[1] Pope Gregory IX referred to the Orders of the Temple and Hospital in a letter to Frederick II in 1231 as *'sine quibus nequaquam posse creditur gubernari'*,[2] and in truth this hardly over-emphasizes the position of the Orders or the rôle they played in the governance and maintenance of the Frankish states.

Originally conceived for the purpose of ministering to the needs of pilgrims to the Holy Places, the three great Orders always retained some aspect of their initial purpose, and the Hospitallers in partic-

---

[1] This chapter makes no attempt to give a history of the Orders in the East, neither does it attempt to study the internal organization of the Orders. It aims merely to show the relations which the Orders of the Temple, Hospital, and Teutonic Knights had with the kings of Jerusalem. The lesser orders of St Thomas, St Lazare, Calatrava, and others, which were non-military or did not exist in Syria, have not been considered at all.

The standard works for the Hospitallers are those of J. Delaville Le Roulx, *Les Hospitaliers en Terre Sainte et à Chypre* (Paris, 1904), *Les Hospitaliers à Rhodes* (Paris, 1913), and his monumental cartulary. The old and voluminous *Histoire des Chevaliers . . . de Malthe*, by the Abbé de Vertot (Paris, 1726) has been wholly superseded and is now of interest only for its wealth of anecdote. The best work on the Templars has been done by Hans Prutz: *Kulturgeschichte der Kreuzzüge* (Berlin, 1883), *Die Geistlichen Ritterorden* (Berlin, 1908), *Geheimlehre und Geheimstatuten des Tempelherren-Ordens* (Berlin, 1879), and articles in the *Sitzungsberichte des Bayerische Akad. zum Wissenschaft*. The recent *Bibliographie de l'Ordre des Templiers*, by M. Dessubré (Paris; E. Nourry, 1928), lists printed works and manuscripts dealing with the Templars arranged by author and by country (and with the reference numbers of the Bibliothèque Nationale).

De Curzon, *La Règle du Temple* (*Soc. His. Fr.*, Paris, 1886), is the standard edition of the rule of the Templars, and contains a valuable introduction and notes.

[2] D. L. *Cartulaire*, doc. 1975.

ular never ceased, even after the kingdom of Jerusalem had long passed away, to maintain a hospital for the sick and needy in the Holy City. John of Würzburg, who visited the Holy Land in the decade from 1160 to 1170, remarks on the alms distributed by the Templars and Hospitallers, the latter of whom gives daily such alms 'that the whole sum total of its expenses can surely never be calculated even by the managers and stewards thereof.'[1] Theodorich, in 1171–1172, commented on the wealth, munificence, and charitable work of the Hospital, estimating the number of beds maintained for pilgrims at about a thousand,[2] a number which seemed probable, from the size of the buildings, to Felix Fabri who visited Jerusalem between 1480 and 1483.[3] Fabri's evidence is of interest as showing that the charitable work of the Hospital continued after the expulsion of the Franks from the Syrian mainland.

From Theodorich again is drawn a description of the services rendered by the Orders in protecting pilgrims who wished to bathe in the Jordan, where the Templars and the Hospitallers both kept patrols constantly on guard to protect the pilgrims during their pious ablutions.[4] Other references to the work of the Orders are to be found scattered through the writings of the pilgrims who visited the Holy Places during the period of Frankish control. But the Orders soon ceased to be primarily concerned with the services rendered to pilgrims, and the duty of fighting for and protecting the Holy Land became their true *raison d'être*. They were throughout most of the period of the Frankish control the most important single source of strength in the military establishment of the kingdom of Jerusalem, and their castles and garrisons were always to be found on the borders and in the most dangerous and strategic positions throughout the kingdom.

---

[1] John of Würzburg (*P. P. T. S.*, xiv), p. 44. John estimated the number of beds kept by the Hospital at 2000 as well as much food and alms distributed to others outside.

'Sometimes in the course of one day and night more than fifty are carried out dead while many other fresh ones keep continually arriving. What more can I say?' naïvely remarks the good traveler. What more indeed?

[2] Theodorich (*P. P. T. S.*, xvii), p. 22.

[3] Felix Fabri (*P. P. T. S.*, xx, part ii), p. 395. Upon arriving the pilgrim gave the warden of the Hospital two Venetian marks for which he was given free quarters, even for a year's stay.

[4] Theodorich, p. 48.

The Templars particularly were noted for their great prowess. 'In going (into battle) they are the first, in returning the last', writes an anonymous pilgrim in the thirteenth century, who describes how they fought in silence, to burst out in song when the battle has been won with the *Non Nobis Domine*![1] Their bravery was the subject of an eulogy by Jacques de Vitry who wrote in his exaggeratedly cumulative and repetitive style,—

Thus they became so terrible to the enemies of Christ's faith that one of them used to chase a thousand, and two of them ten thousand; and when they were called to arms they did not ask how many of the enemy there were, but where they were. They were lions at war, and gentle as lambs at home; in the field they were fierce soldiers, in church they were like hermits or monks; they were harsh and savage to the enemies of Christ, but kindly and gracious to Christians.[2]

In battle the members of the Orders occupied the most dangerous positions and were the first to charge and the last to retreat. In 1179 when the Christian host assembled to meet Saladin, Eudes de St Amand, the Master of the Temple, like an earlier Prince Rupert, led a charge of his Knights that by its sheer force so divided the Christian ranks that the battle was lost.[3] At Gaza in 1244 both the Masters of the Temple and Hospital were captured in the battle,[4] and at Damietta, on the fifth crusade, the Templars led the assault of the city.[5] Their enthusiasm for the war against Saladin which resulted in their attack upon the forces of El-Afdel at the battle of Nazareth and in the disastrous march to Hattin are well known to any student of the crusades. The execution of the Templars by Saladin after Hattin, when the rest of the prisoners, with the exception of Renaud de Châtillon, were spared, is a testimonial to their reputation as the most intransigeant enemies of Islam.[6] When Baldwin

---

[1] Anonymous Pilgrim (*P. P. T. S.*, xxiv), p. 30.

[2] Jacques de Vitry (*P. P. T. S.*, xxxi), p. 52.

[3] William Tyre, XXI, xxix, 1056–57. William says that it was due to the evil counsel of the Templars that the battle was lost.

[4] *Eracles*, pp. 429–30.

[5] *Eracles*, pp. 326–30.

[6] The incidents are familiar. A spirited account is to be found in English in S. Lane-Poole, *Saladin*. (London and N. Y.; Putnam, 1898.) Röhricht, p. 441, note 10, discusses the sources and estimates the number of Knights killed.

IV assembled his host at Ascalon in 1184 the only troops he had beyond some of his own vassals were the members of the Temple and Hospital, always ready, for war.[1] The magnificent but futile heroism of the Templars in the last desperate stand at Acre in 1291 has always remained a monument to the glory and valor of the Order.

Of especial value to the military defences of the kingdom were the great castles of the Orders which defended both the inland frontier and the coast, protecting the cities and keeping open the means of communication. Mighty Krak-des-Chevaliers (today Kalaat-el-Husn), the finest crusading castle in Syria and the chief inland stronghold of the Hospitallers, and Safita (Castel Blanc) of the Templars guarded the approaches from Homs protecting Tripoli and Tortosa; Belfort (Kalaat-es-Schekif) of the Templars, and Starkenberg (Montfort) of the Teutonic Knights guarded Tyre, Acre, and Sidon, from the east, commanding as they do the highlands whence signal fires could send warning of a foe approaching from the Saracen countries. Along the coast were the Hospitallers' castles of Margat (Markab) and Zibel, the Templars' strongholds at Archas and Athlit,—known then by the Frankish name of Chateau Pèlerin,—which, with the Templars' city of Tortosa were the last places to surrender after the fall of Acre in 1291. In addition to the castles, the Orders held fortified portions of cities, Tortosa, Acre, Gaza, Ascalon, Arsur, all being defended by citadels of the Knights.[2] In

---

[1] Ernoul, p. 42.

[2] Descriptions of the castles of the Orders are to be found in: 🖝 G. Rey, *Étude sur les Monuments de l'Architecture Militaire des Croisés en Syrie et dans l'Île de Chypre (Docs. Inéd.; Paris,* 1871); E. G. Rey, *Les Colonies Franques,* pp. 114–137; C. Enlart, *Les Monuments des Croisés dans le Royaume de Jérusalem* (Paris; Geuthner; 1925–28); P. Jacquot, *L'État des Alouites* (Beirut; Imprimerie Catholique, 1929).

The government of Syria and the Lebanon at Beirut issues a very interesting tourist map of Syria, showing the sites of crusading castles. Jacquot's book is an excellent guide book to the region between Tripoli and Latakaya, with good descriptions and illustrations of the castles included in the district.

According to Rey, the Templars held 18 fortresses, the Hospitallers 5, besides many other lands and fiefs. But the Hospitallers castles were on the whole larger than those of the Temple.

Gaza was granted to the Temple by Baldwin III in 1149 (William Tyre, XVII, xii, 778); Ascalon to the Hospital by Frederick II (*Regesta,* doc. 1112), but was reclaimed by John d'Ibelin of Jaffa in 1256 (*Regesta,* doc. 1245). Arsur was purchased by the Hospital in 1261 (*Regesta,* doc. 1313). Tortosa was acquired by the Temple, according to Jacquot in 1170 (*op. cit.,* p. 82),

these strongholds the members of the Orders kept their treasure, imprisoned captives, sheltered pilgrims and fugitives, and maintained garrisons ready for defense or attack.[1] In addition to the castles and towns which the Orders held in their own right they were often entrusted with the guard of royal castles, especially during a regency.[2]

The Orders also took over secular fiefs on several occasions, purchasing them from the lords who were no longer able to maintain their defence; it was in this way that the Hospital acquired the fiefs of Galilee in 1182 and Arsur in 1261,[3] the Teutonic Knights the seignory of Count Joscelin between 1220 and 1229,[4] and the Templars the fiefs of Belfort and Sidon in 1260.[5] An interesting case of this kind is the one cited by William of Tyre who tells how in 1156, the constable, Humphrey de Toron, unable longer to defend his fief of Baniâs, which was subject to Saracen attacks, surrendered half of it to the Hospitallers on condition that they would assume half the expenses of defending the entire fief. The Knights accepted the grant, but when they were defeated in an attempt to provision the city which was being besieged, returned their half to Humphrey leaving him the burden of trying to defend the whole.[6] Lands were often

but they had a settlement there at least by 1169 when an act was drawn up between the bishop of Valenia and the Templars of Tortosa (*Regesta*, doc. 462). In Acre, all three Orders held parts of the city, the Teutons holding a tower, the Hospitallers two gates. (Strehlke, doc. 35; D. L. *Cartulaire*, doc. 2612.) The possessions of the Templars cannot be definitely known, but in 1291 they defended their own part of the city.

[1] According to the *Eracles*, p. 169, it was in Margat that Richard of England had Isaac Comnenus of Cyprus and his family imprisoned. Ernoul, p. 273, says that the Templars imprisoned him, but tradition assigns his captivity to the Hospitallers' castle.

[2] As under the regency of Raymond of Tripoli for Baldwin V when the Orders were entrusted with the defence of the royal castles, (Ernoul, p. 116.). When the kings entrusted their castles to the Orders to guard they kept certain rights over them, as shown by the grant of Amaury II of a tower in Acre to the Teutons, wherein he reserves the right to demand the surrender to him of the tower in time of war if he so desires. (Strehlke, doc. 35. *Regesta*, doc. 744 omits the clause providing for the return on demand of the king.) Over the castles which the Knights themselves owned the king had no control, as evidenced by the attempt of Frederick II to occupy the Templars' castle of Chateau Pèlerin which was successfully resisted. (Rey, *Architecture Militaire*, p. 99.)

[3] D. L. *Cartulaire*, docs. 621, 645, 3047; *Regesta*, docs. 619, 618, 1313; *Eracles*, p. 446.

[4] Strehlke, docs. 52–54, 60, 63, 65, 67; *Regesta*, docs, 933–34, 978, 1002, 1011, 1013.

[5] *Regesta*, doc. 1319; *Eracles*, p. 445. For a discussion of the fiefs purchased by the Orders see Röhricht, p. 997.

[6] William Tyre, XVIII, xii, 837–39.

purchased or held as security for loans, the barons who held them
preferring to sell or mortgage part of their lands that they might have
sufficient funds to defend what remained to them.[1]

The Orders were, with the exception of the churches and monasteries, the largest landholders in the crusading states. A cursory
glance at the cartularies of the Hospitallers or Teutonic Knights will
suffice to show the great number of grants of land made to those
Orders; the possessions of the Templars were probably not less
extensive. Lands were acquired by conquest, purchase, and above all
by gift. Though the Orders supplied valuable military assistance to
the kingdom, they probably did not do more than serve for the lands
which they held, but for which they were legally exempt from service. For legally the passage of lands into the hands of the Orders
was *mortmain*; they were entirely independent of the king and the
feudal heirarchy, and, chartered by the Papacy and supported by
the Roman See, they were no more than ecclesiastical allies who
freely consented to assist the crown in its struggles with the enemies of Christ. When Frederick II demanded aid and service from
the Templars and Hospitallers, he was met by a refusal on the
grounds that he was under the ban of the Church, with the explanation that: '*Il est bien seu que nos somes establi par l'Iglise de Rome,
et à l'Iglise somes obedient.*'[2] Though the Knights were normally

---

[1] Among instances of the sale of lands may be cited:—the sale of Siletam with 103 tents of
Bedouins by Amaury, viscount of Neapolis, to the Hospital (D L. *Cartulaire*, doc. 550; *Regesta*,
doc. 562); the sale of Cafarlet to the Hospital by John of Caesarea, and the sale of Arames to
the Temple by John d'Ibelin in 1232 (*Eracles*, p. 398). Cases of the pledging of lands against
a debt are:—the pledging of Arsur for a debt of 4000 besants to the Hospital by Balian of Arsur (D. L. *Cartulaire*, doc. 3323; *Regesta*, doc. 1370); the pledging of a casale near Jerusalem
for a debt of 111 marks to the Teutons by Guy de Lusignan. (Strehlke, doc. 20; *Regesta*,
doc. 650.)

The Orders were sometimes made trustees for private estates, as in the case of Guy II of
Gibelet, who appointed the Hospital as the executor and trustee of his estate for his minor heirs.
(D. L. *Cartulaire*, doc. 3550; *Regesta*, doc. 1399a.)

As the banking activities of the Orders, especially the Temple, affect only incidentally the
kings of Jerusalem, no attempt is made in this chapter to consider this important and eventually disastrous aspect of their operations.

[2] *Eracles*, pp. 372–73. They consented to serve when the emperor proclaimed the ban
of the Church, omitting any mention of himself. The Teutonic Knights, under von Salza,
supported and served the emperor throughout his eastern campaigns.

most ready to assist the kings in any war against the Saracens, they always reserved the right to decide upon the justice of the war, and on several occasions refused to lend their support, as in 1168 when the Temple refused to participate in Amaury I's invasion of Egypt.[1]

They were equally independent in their treaty arrangements; in 1240 when the Temple allied with Damascus, the Hospital made a treaty with Egypt.[2] The Hospital enjoyed suzerainty over the emir of Hama;[3] the Temple was enriched for some years by the tribute of the Assassins.[4] Equal in strength to the greatest princes of Outremer, the Orders waged private wars upon the secular lords and upon each other. The Temple was at feud with Leo of Armenia over the possession of Gastin;[5] the Hospital carried on a long struggle against Bohemond IV and Bohemond V of Antioch-Tripoli[6] and quarreled with John d'Ibelin of Jaffa over the custody of Ascalon.[7] In 1233 the Temple and Hospital allied in a mutual struggle with

[1] William Tyre, XX, v, 949. The Templars claimed that they considered the invasion to be unjust; a more probable reason for their opposition is that the campaign was encouraged by the Hospital with which they were on bad terms.

[2] *Eracles*, pp. 419–20. Each refused to recognize the treaty of the other.

[3] When in 1233 the emir ceased to pay the tribute, the Hospitallers collected an army made up of knights from their own Order, the Temple, Antioch, Jerusalem, and Cyprus, and forced the emir back to his allegiance. (*Eracles*, pp. 403–04; Delaville LeRoulx, *Hospitaliers*, pp. 171–72.)

[4] William Tyre, XX, xxix, 997. When in 1172 the Old Man of the Mountain sent envoys to the king of Jerusalem to discuss the possibility of the conversion of the Assassins, the Templars, fearing to lose the tribute should the Assassins become Christians, murdered the envoys. Nor would they surrender the murderers to the king of Jerusalem for trial, but imposed light penalties on them in their own court. (William Tyre, XX, xxx, 998–99.) The Hospital allied with this sect in 1236 against the prince of Antioch, which brought down the censures of the Pope. (D. L. *Cartulaire*, doc. 2149.)

[5] *Eracles*, pp. 317–18. Gastin was a possession of the Temple which had been taken by Saladin, recovered from Saladin by Leo of Armenia, and claimed from Leo by the Templars. The Temple allied with Bohemond of Antioch against Leo and the Hospitallers.

[6] The struggle began with the support of Leo by the Hospital against the Templars and Bohemond. Throughout the war between Raymond Rupin and Bohemond, the Hospital supported Rupin. Later seizure of the Hospital's lands renewed the conflict, which lasted in all from 1217 to 1256, though the fighting was over by 1241. (Documents concerning this struggle are to be found in D. L. *Cartulaire*, docs. 1824, 1834, 1837, 1955, 1965, 1999, 2000–02, 2048, 2071, 2094, 2149, 2184, 2280, 2807; the best account is that in Delaville LeRoulx, *Hospitaliers*, pp. 148 ff., 173–75, 188–90.)

[7] D. L. *Cartulaire*, docs. 2810, 2816, 2817; *Regesta*, docs. 1247, 1249b, 1249c.

the commune of Marseilles;[1] in 1179, 1258, and 1262 they were bitterly quarreling with each other.[2]

Independent corporately of any authority save that of the Pope, the Knights as individuals claimed clerical immunity from any secular jurisdiction and maintained their right to be tried only in the courts of their own Orders. Though the *Assises de la Cour des Bourgeois* refused them full ecclesiastical immunities,[3] they were often able to defy royal justice and to adjudicate over their own members, as in the case of the murderers of the emissaries of the Assassins; though in 1166 King Amaury hanged twelve Templars guilty of surrendering a castle to the enemy.[4] This exemption was applied further to the field of taxation, the lands and goods of the Orders being exempt from lay taxation, though subject to clerical tithes.[5]

This semi-extraterritorial position as regarded the laws of the kingdom and their almost international character as protegés the Papacy made the Orders a further element of weakness in the organization of the Jerusalemite monarchy. In a country suffering from feudal decentralization the independence of the Orders added but another source of disunion. Nor was the military assistance which they afforded the king as allies always an unmitigated asset, for on more than one occasion the Knights were influential in precipitating wars which were not altogether successful. The Hospitallers urged

---

[1] D. L. *Cartulaire*, doc. 2067; *Regesta*, doc. 1046, give the document whereby the quarrel was settled by the mediation of Eudes de Montbéliard.

[2] The treaties settling these affairs are given in D. L. *Cartulaire*, docs. 558, 2902, 3028.

Other private wars and feuds in which the Hospital was involved include: the dispute with the Pisans over part of the wall of Acre (D. L. *Cartulaire*, doc. 3771; *Regesta*, doc. 1442a); the quarrel with the patriarch in 1154–55 (William Tyre, XVIII, iii–viii, 820–30); and the struggle in 1257 when the Hospital, Genoese, and Barcelonese allied against the Temple, Teutons, Venetians, Pisans, and Plaisance of Cyprus (*Rothelin Eracles*, p. 634). The Temple was the open enemy of the Lusignans and the supporter of Charles of Anjou; their opposition to Hugh III was the reason for his abandoning Acre. (*Gestes*, pars. 396, 435; *Eracles*, p. 474 ff.; Mas Latrie, i, 453; Röhricht, p. 975 ff.)

[3] *Assises Cour Bourg.*, cxxix, 89; D. Hayek, *Le Droit Franc en Syrie*, p. 154. The *Assises de Romanie*, par. 48, p. 194, say that some consider the Masters of the Hospital and the House of Mosteniza are to be considered judicially as clergy.

[4] William Tyre, XIX, xi, 902.

[5] In 1298 Pope Boniface VIII especially exempted the Latin clergy, the Templars, Hospitallers, and Teutonic Knights from the poll tax which he authorized King Henry II of Cyprus to levy on his subjects. (D. L. *Cartulaire*, doc. 4420.)

Amaury I on in his dream of conquest in Egypt; the Templars precipitated the war with Saladin in 1187 and counselled the fatal march to Hattin. In 1209 the Master of the Temple was instrumental in rejecting the offers for a renewal of the truce with Melek-el-Adel and in reopening hostilities; in 1219 at Damietta the Orders supported Pelagius in his refusal of the peace proposals of Melek-el-Kamel which had been accepted by the secular princes, thus causing the loss of all that had been gained.[1] In advising the refusal of peace offers and the continuance of war the Orders acted entirely in keeping with their fundamental *raison d'être*, which was war against the Infidel; but their insistence on the continuance of hostilities on some of these occasions resulted in considerable losses to the Christian cause. Theirs were the mistakes of over-enthusiasm common to militarists; the fault of Gerard de Ridefort in 1187 was the fault of Conrad von Hötzendorf and of Yanuškevich in 1914. Though they excelled in personal valor no glory in arms could compensate for their rashness in council.

But in attempting to estimate the rôle played by the Orders in the organization of the crusading states the final judgement must result in their favor. Like the Italian commercial communes their constant quarreling caused much trouble and reduced the unity so necessary to the state, but it may be safely said that the kings of Jerusalem profited from the Knights and that the Orders were among the main sources of strength to the kingdom. If they precipitated war, they were always ready to take their share of the burdens thereof. If they amassed huge treasures in land and goods, their wealth was always at the service of Christianity. If they fought among themselves, they fought first against the Moslem. Not more turbulent than the feudal barons, the members of the religio-military Orders supplied the most stable element in the military organization which preserved for almost two centuries on the eastern shore of the Mediterranean the feeble and decentralized feudal state which was the Latin kingdom of Jerusalem.

[1] *Eracles*, pp. 309, 342.

CHAPTER 12

THE RELATIONS OF THE KINGS OF JERUSALEM WITH THE ITALIAN AND PROVENÇAL COMMERCIAL COMMUNES

THAT the trade in eastern luxuries and other oriental commodities was one of the major results of the crusades has long been
an accepted fact and much has been written concerning the Levantine trade of the Italian cities and the effects thereof on the development, economically and politically, of the Italian towns. But little
has been done on that aspect of the problem which concerns the
effect of the Italian merchants on the Levantine countries, particularly the crusading states. If the eastern markets had a tremendous
effect on the Italian merchants, the merchants had no less effect on
the markets and on the countries in which they were located.
Though Heyd, Schaube, Rey, Prutz, and Byrne have all dealt with
aspects of the relations of the trading cities with the East, no study
of the institutions of Jerusalem would be complete without a special
chapter devoted to this subject; to place the Italian commercial
communes in their relation to the kingdom of Jerusalem may add
something to the knowledge already current on this most interesting
topic.[1]

The Latin kingdom of Jerusalem relied for its very existence
upon the maintenance of connections with western Europe. A seaboard community, it never had more than a foothold on the continent and was dependent upon, and largely supported by, the sea.
With the exception of Jerusalem and Neapolis, its chief cities were

---

[1] On the relations of the Italian communes with the East see in general: W. Heyd, *Histoire
du Commerce du Levant*, translated by Furcy Raynaud (Leipsic, 1885, reimpression 1923), i,
129–426; A. Schaube, *Handelsgeschichte der Romanischen Völker des Mittelmeergebiets* (Munich,
1906), pp. 190–223; E. G. Rey, *Les Colonies Franques de Syrie* (Paris, 1883), pp. 69–74; H.
Prutz, *Kulturgeschichte, der Kreuzzüge* (Berlin, 1883), pp. 376–393; and for Genoa in particular
see E. H. Byrne, 'The Genoese Colonies in Syria', *Munro-Crusades*, pp. 139–182, and 'Genoese
Trade with Syria in the Twelfth Century', *A. H. R.*, xxv (1919–20), 191–220; G. I. Bratianu,
Recherches sur le Commerce Gênois (Paris, 1929), pp. 42–61.

on or near the sea, and in the second period of its existence the kingdom was hardly more than a group of maritime cities. Acre, Tyre, Jaffa, Beirut, Sidon, Ascalon, Caesarea, and Haïfa in the principality of Jerusalem, Tripoli, Tortosa, Gibelet, Laodicea, and Port Saint Simeon in the northern counties, were all ports; and the lords of these cities were all in intimate contact with the merchants and governments of Venice, Genoa, Pisa, Marseilles, and the other western commercial cities.

From the very beginning of the crusades and the foundation of the crusading principalities the Italian cities played an important rôle, both in the initial conquest and in the subsequent development of the country. The services they rendered were paid for in every case with grants of privileges; and through series of charters, each granting a little more than the one before, the Italian communes gradually became powerful land- and concession- owners controlling the commerce of the ports in which they had depots. The baillies or consuls of the communes settled by the Italian cities in the East ranked among the greater lords of the kingdom and they often played important parts in the domestic affairs of the kingdom.

The first crusade was preached in Genoa by the bishops Hugh of Grenoble and William of Orange, and so responsive were the Genoese to their appeals that the first Genoese fleet of crusaders arrived in the East only a month after the crusading army had begun the siege of Antioch.[1] For the assistance which they rendered in the siege of Antioch the Genoese were granted by Bohemond a church, market, and thirty houses in the city, with privilege to trade there;[2] and it has been properly doubted if the impulse which brought them to the East was the pious desire to liberate the Holy Places from the hands of the Infidel. E. H. Byrne has observed, in commenting on this, that:

---

[1] Caffaro, *Liberatio Orientis* (ed. L. T. Belgrano in *Fonti per la Storia d'Italia*, xi), pp. 101–102.

[2] Hagenmeyer, *Chronologie*, no. 300; *Regesta*, docs. 12, 16; Caffaro, p. 109; Heyd, i, 134. Bohemond tried to make the Genoese at this time take an oath to assist him against all his enemies, but the Genoese excepted Raymond of St Gilles, against whom Bohemond particularly desired their assistance. The *Liber Jurium*, i, doc. 20, contains the renewal of this grant by Bohemond II in 1127.

From the religious and romantic impulse with which the Crusades began, the Genoese apparently were so free that to them the crusaders were merely men to be carried to the East 'certo naulo', maintained there by Genoese aid, in return for rewards and privileges of deep import!.[1]

Yet the siege of Jerusalem brought no special grant to Genoa, though the brothers Embriaco, who commanded the Genoese fleet, received considerable booty from the city and from the plunder taken at the battle of Ascalon.[2]

More extensive grants were obtained by the Genoese fleet which came to Syria in 1100. Tancred, regent of Antioch, renewed Bohemond's grants and promised lands in Laodicea and half the revenues there, lands and houses in Gibelet, and a third of the port revenues of Saint Simeon, in return for their services in capturing the coastal cities.[3] But they made no campaign and having accomplished nothing sailed south where they negotiated with Baldwin I a treaty whereby the king granted them a third of any city which they might help take; and in the campaign which followed they captured Arsur and Caesarea, in both of which they established themselves, besides gaining an immense plunder in spices.[4]

The fleet which came out in 1102 assisted Raymond of St Gilles to capture Tortosa, and that of 1104 helped him take Gibelet, of which they were granted a third.[5] In the latter year the Genoese also coöperated with Baldwin I in the capture of Acre, receiving in return a charter which gave them extensive privileges. The grants in Arsur and Caesarea were reaffirmed; a third of Acre together with a third of the revenues of the town, a street in Jerusalem and in Jaffa, and an additional revenue of 300 besants a year were granted, and they

[1] E. H. Byrne, 'Genoese Trade with Syria', A. H. R., xxv, 193.

[2] Caffaro, pp. 110–111.

[3] Chronologie, no. 580a; Regesta, doc. 35; Caffaro, pp. 113–14.

[4] Chronologie, nos. 559, 563, 567; Caffaro, Annales (Fonti, xi), pp. 5, 6, 9, Liberatio, pp. 117–118; Fulcher, II, viii–ix, 393–404. Caffaro says that Baldwin accepted the throne of Jerusalem only under the guarantee of Genoese help, and that he promised them a third of Jerusalem and Jaffa, and also of Arsur and Babylon if he could capture them. Fulcher says merely a third of all that they should help him take. William Tyre, X, xiv, 419–20, gives the treaty with these terms under the date of 1102. Caffaro says (p. 13) that the booty from Caesarea gave each of the Genoese 48 shillings Poitevin and two pounds of pepper. The chief bit of plunder was the Holy Cup which was taken to Genoa.

[5] Chronologie, nos. 631, 714; Caffaro, Annales, p. 14, Liberatio, pp. 118–120.

were promised a third of any city which they should help capture in the future. They were further promised security of person and goods throughout the realm, and the king renounced his rights over the property of Genoese who died within the realm intestate, promising to turn over to their compatriots the administration of their estates.[1] The text of this charter was engraved on stone in gold letters and was deposited in the Holy Sepulchre.

In 1109 the Genoese were back in the north, helping Bertrand of St Gilles, Raymond's heir, to capture Tripoli. For this they were promised a third of Tripoli itself, and all of Gibelet and Le Puy de Constable, together with promises of safety of life and limb and immunity from tribute throughout all of Bertrand's possession both in the East and West.[2] The bad faith of Bertrand prevented them ever getting any part of Tripoli, but they at once occupied Gibelet, granting the third already in their possession to Ansaldo Corso, and the two thirds recently acquired to Hugh Embriaco.[3] While Genoa got more than any other western state from the conquest, receiving concessions in every port of Outremer but Tyre, they were not alone in their acquisitions, and their allies the Pisans were also, but more slowly, securing possessions and concessions.[4] The Pisans had arrived too late for much of the actual fighting of the crusade, but they had helped Bohemond in his unsuccessful attack on Laodicea and had assisted in the fortification of Jerusalem and Jaffa. The leader of the Pisan fleet was Daimbert, the archbishop of Pisa and papal legate after the death of Adhelmar of Le Puy, who was elected patriarch of Jerusalem and who tried to enforce the rule of the Church

[1] *Chronologie*, nos. 720, 721, 722; *Liber Jurium*, i, doc. 8; *Regesta*, doc. 43; William Tyre, X, xxviii, 442; Caffaro, *Liberatione*, pp. 121–122. Caffaro says 600 besants instead of 300. This grant was confirmed by Baldwin in May 1105 in a general grant to the Genoese in which he confirmed all their possessions and privileges in Jerusalem, Antioch, Acre, Laodicea, St Simeon, Gibelet, Tortosa, Caesarea; and Arsur, which had been captured with their help. (*Liber Jurium*, i, doc. 9; *Regesta*, doc. 45.) At the time of this confirmation the Genoese swore to support Baldwin and never to act against him nor his honor, and they recognized his rights in Sidon. (*Liber Jurium*, i, doc. 10; *Regesta*, doc. 46.)

[2] *Liber Jurium*, i, docs. 11, 12; *Regesta*, doc. 55; Caffaro, *Libertione*, pp. 123–24. There were two treaties, one in June for Tripoli and one in August for St Gilles.

[3] Caffaro, p. 124; Byrne, 'Genoese Colonies', p. 147; Heyd, i, 149. They occupied Tripoli but Bertrand drove them out.

[4] Byrne, 'Genoese Trade', *A. H. R.*, xxv, 195.

over that of the state. Daimbert claimed high sovereignty for the patriarchate and secured from Godfrey recognition of his lordship over a quarter of Jaffa which the shrewd ecclesiastic turned into a Pisan colony.[1] In 1108 Tancred bought Pisan help in his campaign against Laodicea by granting them a quarter in Antioch and in Laodicea, and freedom of trade in both cities without payment of the ordinary dues and customs.[2] Yet the Pisan holdings and privileges were always small as compared with those of Genoa or of Venice.

Venice, destined to receive the greatest possessions and most liberal concessions granted to any of the Italian cities, took no active part in the first crusade.[3] The Venetians arrived in the East only after the capture of the Holy City, but they came in such numbers as to obtain greater concessions than those obtained by the Genoese and Pisans who had preceded them. In the summer of 1100 a Venetian fleet of two hundred vessels arrived in Palestine and sold their services to Duke Godfrey for the promised reward of a third of each city or town which they might help capture, and freedom of trade throughout the kingdom. Having agreed to assist Godfrey in his projected campaign against Haïfa and Acre, after his death in 1100 they carried on the war against Haïfa which they took the following August in conjunction with the troops of the patriarch. When Baldwin I ascended the throne he renewed Godfrey's treaty and continued its provisions for the duration of his own reign.[4] The Venetians were not able to take Acre at this time and it became the prize of the Genoese, who assisted Baldwin in his second siege.[5] In 1111, however, a

---

[1] William Tyre, IX, xvi, 388; Heyd, i, 145–6.

[2] Müller, p. 3; *Regesta*, doc. 53; Heyd, i, 145–6.

[3] M. da Canale, *Cronaca Veneta* (*Archivio Storico Italino*, viii, 1845), xiv, 294, tells of the first appearance of the Venetians in the crusading states:

'Voirs fu que li crestiens passerent la mer, et pristrent Acre et Ierusalem; mes les Venesiens n'estoient pas encore passes dela la mer; et lorsque il vindrent, il pristrent Caifas.   Et quant Monseignor li Evesque Henric Contarins, qui sire et chevetains estoit de l'ost des Venesiens, fu en saisine de Caifas, il dist as Venesiens: Seignors, puisque Dame Dieu nos a done ce chastel, faites les bien.   Ici vegnent trestuit li Venesiens, et vendent et achatent lor marchandies.'

[4] *Monachus Littorensis* (*R. H. C. Occ.*, v.), 272; *Regesta*, doc. 31; *Chronologie*, nos. 472, 478, 496; Tafel-Thomas, i, 64–65; Heyd, i, 137.   The treaty called for an equal division of lands to be taken in Tripoli should any be captured there.

[5] But the Venetians got part of Acre,—trading Haïfa which had been given them for a quarter in Acre, according to Canale. (*Cronaca*, pp. 294–96).

Venetian fleet helped the king in his conquest of Sidon and Beirut, and the charter granted after this expedition gave St Mark's and the doge a church, market, houses, and trading privileges in Acre, as well as privileges in Jerusalem.[1] Privileges of some sort were also obtained at an early date in the principality of Antioch by the Venetians, for the charter of Renaud and Constance in 1153 (the earliest grant to Venice by the princes of Antioch which has been preserved) mentions the privileges granted by Bohemond I, Tancred, and Bohemond II.[2] In Tripoli Count Pons, in 1117, piously granted a house to the Church of St Mark's in Venice for the benefit of the souls of Raymond, Bertrand, and his mother.[3]

But the great holdings of the Venetians in the early years of the kingdom were in Tyre. In 1118–19 Baldwin II sent to the West asking help from the Pope and from Venice, and in 1122 a fleet of two hundred ships sailed for Syria under the command of Dominico Michieli. After wintering at Corfu it went to Jaffa, where in the early months of 1123 it defeated a fleet from Ascalon which was besieging the city. In the meanwhile, Baldwin had been captured by the Saracens, and Warmund, the patriarch, and William de Buris, the constable, were governing the kingdom in his absence. The victory of the Venetians, together with a victory on land which the Franks had won shortly before, determined the Christians to take the offensive, and it was decided to attack Tyre, which was invested and captured.[4]

In his request for aid Baldwin had offered the Venetians extensive privileges, and the treaty which was drawn up between the Venetians and the barons of the *Haute Cour* granted Venice freedom of trade throughout the kingdom with total exemption from any taxation, except a fee to be paid if measuring or weighing of goods was

[1] Tafel-Thomas, i, docs. 30–34, pp. 66–75; Heyd, i, 142.

[2] Tafel-Thomas, i, docs. 27, 31, 42, 55; *Regesta*, doc. 282.

[3] Tafel-Thomas, i, doc. 36, pp. 76–77; *Regesta*, doc. 84.

[4] Canale gives a full and exciting account of the capture of Tyre in chapters xix–xxii, pp. 302–308, of his *Cronaca*. The Pope asked Venice to send aid to Jerusalem, and the Seignory sent out a fleet under Doge Dominico Michieli which took eleven Saracen ships and '*pristrent Scalone*'. After this feat they joined the Franks at the siege of Tyre, where to prove their good faith they grounded their ships, and joined the Franks in their camp. Letters from the sultan of Egypt promising aid to the Tyrians having been intercepted, the defenders of the city lost heart and surrendered. The Venetians, leaving a bailli in Tyre, came home by way of Greece where they plundered several towns.

done by royal agent, and a port tax on pilgrims. Further, in all cities which were then held or might be added to the kingdom, they were to receive a quarter with a church, bath, oven, and market, and in Jerusalem a quarter as extensive as that held by the king. In Tyre they were promised a third of the city and its revenues and an extra 300 besants, and a third of Ascalon should it also be taken. In each Venetian colony a Venetian court was granted which should settle all cases in which Venetians were involved except mixed cases in which a Venetian was plaintiff, which were reserved for the king's court. The crown further gave up all rights of *naufragium* as applied to Venetians, and goods salvaged from their wrecks were given into the custody of the officials of the Venetian commune. This treaty was guaranteed by the patriarch and the barons pledging themselves under oath that Baldwin would accept it, and that they would prevent anyone from ruling in Jerusalem who would not agree to its terms; wherefore of necessity Baldwin ratified it upon his release.[1]

Thus by 1124 the Venetians, Genoese, and Pisans were all well established in the cities of the kingdom of Jerusalem. By subsequent charters their privileges were extended and further properties were assigned to them.[2]

The Provençal cities also secured privileges, lands, and immunities in the East; Marseilles received its first charter from King Baldwin I in 1117 and a more complete grant from Foulque in 1136.[3] A grant of privileges to Marseilles issued by Conrad de Montferrat in 1187 included Montpellier, St Gilles, and Barcelona, which had hitherto been carrying on trade under the Marseillaise flag.[4]

---

[1] Tafel-Thomas, i, 84–89; *Regesta*, doc. 102; William Tyre, XII, xxii–xxv, 545–553; *Historia Ducum Veniticorum* (*M. G. H. SS.*, xiv), pp. 73–74; Canale, pp. 302–08; Heyd, i, 142–145.

The *Historia Ducum* says that after Tyre was taken the patriarch offered the Venetians two parts of the city but that they professed themselves satisfied with one: '*tertia tantum parte se contentos esse dicentes.*' The patriarch then gave them 100,000 gold pieces extra. When Baldwin ratified this treaty he inserted a clause which made the Venetians supply troops for the defense of the city in proportion to their share of the revenues.

[2] See appendix for list of grants made the various cities.

[3] *Regesta*, docs. 85, 163; Méry, *Histoire de Marseille*, i, 182; Heyd, i, 146–47. Raymond of St Gilles had granted St Victor of Marseilles a half of Gibelet when he should take it but the treaty had come to nothing. (*Regesta*, doc. 38; *Chronologie*, no. 686.)

[4] Méry, i, 190–92; *Regesta*, doc. 666.

The earliest grant to Montpellier alone which has been preserved is one of Frederick II in 1229.[1]

The Amalfitans received their first extant charter in 1163 from Bohemond III of Antioch, but a colony of them already existed in Antioch having been established there before the first crusade. There was also an Amalfitan colony in Acre, but beyond the grant of a cemetery to them by the bishop in 1161 no charters have been preserved.[2]

The status of these Italian and Provençal colonies depended on the rights conferred by the charters and ran all the way from the mere privilege to trade in the country without molestation to complete autonomy of administration and total exemption from payments of any kind. To the privileges which were granted for services in the conquest, further franchises were added by participation on one side or another in the disputes and rivalries between the princes of the Latin states. When Conrad de Montferrat and Guy de Lusignan were competing for the throne in 1190–1192 they sought the support of the Genoese and the Pisans by granting a series of charters which considerably increased the privileged position of both cities, until as a result Tyre and Acre were practically divided among the Italians.[3]

Similarly the Italians took part in the long struggle between Frederick II and the Outremer barons who supported the Ibelins and Alice of Cyprus. The Venetians and Genoese, true to their Guelph principles supported the anti-imperialists, while the Ghibelline Pisans allied with the emperor. In both cases the support of the Italians was secured by a series of charters conferring additional privileges.[4]

Another means of obtaining franchises in the East was by loaning

---

[1] E. Winkelmann, *Acta Imperii Inedita* (Innsbruck, 1880), i, doc. 302, p. 272; *Regesta*, doc. 1014.

[2] Camera, i, 200, 202; *Regesta*, docs. 372, 388; Heyd, i, 147–48.

[3] Strehlke, doc. 24; *Liber Jurium*, i, docs. 374, 375, 392, 401; *Regesta*, docs. 682, 691, 693, 702, 704: grants of courts and freedom from taxes to the Genoese. Grants to the Pisans are: Müller, pp. 26–40; *Regesta*, docs. 665, 667, 674, 675, 683, 684, 703. Conrad also granted a charter to Venice. (Tafel-Thomas, i, 212–15; *Regesta*, doc, 705.)

[4] *Regesta*, docs. 951, 957, 1037, 1049, 1114, 1116, *et al.*; Heyd, i, 340–44.

money to the ever impecunious kings, and it was in this way that Marseilles in particular gained its concessions.[1]

No attempt will be made here to enumerate or discuss in detail the various charters granted to each of the maritime cities; a list of these will be found in the appendices and further details are easily available in Heyd and Röhricht. From a study of these charters a few generalizations may be drawn regarding the kinds of privileges granted and the extraterritorial position of the citizens of the commercial colonies.

The normal grant made to the Italian cities was that of a special quarter in the city or even the grant of an entire third of the town. Acre, Tyre, and Tripoli were so divided among the Italians that very little could have remained to their lords. These quarters were organized as separate communes with their own officials, the members of each commune having one or more churches, a market, a bath, a mill, an oven, and in the larger ports also warehouses.[2] There, under the direction of their own officials, they unloaded their ships, exchanging the goods which they brought for the products of the Syrian cities or imports from inner Asia, which had been brought to the Syrian marts by Saracen traders. In the case of the most favored nation no charge was laid upon them, while from those less privileged a tariff of half or less of the regular rate was exacted.[3]

---

[1] Charter from Baldwin III in return for loan of 3000 besants needed for Ascalon campaign; charter of Amaury for loan of 2800 besants: Méry, i, 183–87; *Regesta*, docs. 276, 747. John de Brienne borrowed from the Genoese Luchino Corsali to whom he gave a charter, found in Röhricht, *Studien zur Geschichte des Fünften Kreuzzuges* (Innsbruck, 1891), pp. 69–70; *Regesta*, doc. 927.

[2] The Venetian bailli of Acre who ranked with the duke of Crete and the podesta of the colony at Constantinople, was one of the highest officers in the overseas service. The baillies in Antioch, Beirut, Tripoli, Laodicea, Aleppo, and Alexandria were all under his control. (H. Kretschmayr, *Geschichte von Venedig* (Gotha, 1905–20), ii, 25.)

[3] For example a charter of Bohemond VII of Antioch-Tripoli in 1277 granted the Venetians freedom of sale without tax save on copper. If any commodity had a double tax rating, i.e. paid both sale and purchase tax, the Venetians paid only one—the purchase tax, which was the lower of the two. Venetian goods sold by anyone other than a Venetian were liable to regular taxes, and the harbor tax was collected from Venetian ships which were rented or leased to non-Venetians. (*Regesta*, doc. 1412; Rey, *Recherches*, pp. 42–45.) Renaud and Constance granted a reduction from five percent to four percent on some goods and from seven to five percent on others and reduced the harbor tax. (*Regesta*, doc. 282; Tafel-Thomas, i, 133–35.) Bohemond III granted the Pisans a reduction of half of all dues and tariffs collected from merchants in Antioch. (*Regesta*, doc. 478; Müller, pp. 15–16.) These rates were further reduced

Anchorage was free, no charge was made for transhipped goods, and payment was exacted for weighing and measuring goods only if the king's assessors did the work.

In addition to these economic privileges the Italians were granted extraterritorial legal rights. In the port towns were the regular royal courts of the *Chaine* and the *Fonde* which dealt with maritime and market cases. The Italians were usually exempted from the jurisdiction of these courts by special provisions in the charters granted them, and were allowed to be under the jurisdiction of their own courts. All cases between citizens of the same commune were tried in the court of the consul or bailli of that commune, and only in cases where the plaintiff was an Italian and the defendant was a subject of the king of Jerusalem did civil suits involving Italians come into the royal court. This immunity extended to minor criminal cases, though the major crimes of treason, murder, rape, grand larceny, and all felonies involving life and limb were reserved for the royal courts.[1] A charter of Guy and Sibylle to Pisa in 1189 also reserved all pleas relating to fiefs, '*preterquam de feodis et assisiis et que ad feoda et assisias pertinent de quibus omnibus in dominiorum curia iudicentur,*'[2] and it would seem that when Italians accepted

by Bohemond IV. (*Regesta*, doc. 769; Müller, pp. 80–81.) In 1217 Guy de Gibelet reduced the sales taxes one half to Venetians. (*Regesta*, doc. 904; Tafel-Thomas, ii, 196–97). In 1232 Henry of Cyprus granted the Genoese freedom of trade without exactions save a charge for weighing and measuring wine, beans, barley, and other such commodities. The charge was a penny for every ten modi of weight or a penny for every ten besants worth of wine. (*Regesta*, doc. 1037; *Liber Jurium*, i, doc. 693.)

[1] This complete extraterritorial jurisdiction was usually gained gradually, and many charters attest its growth. In 1169 Bohemond III promised speedy justice in his courts to the Genoese; in 1189 he granted them their own court. (*Regesta*, docs. 471, 680.) Felonies were reserved for the lord's court; see charters of Amaury I to Pisa, Baldwin III to Pisa, Henry of Cyprus to Genoa, Bohemond VII to Venice. (*Regesta*, docs. 449, 322, 1037, 1412.) When John de Montfort of Tyre made peace with the Venetians in 1277 he granted them extremely liberal terms. Complete jurisdiction was granted them over all Venetians living in any part of Tyre, and over all inhabitants of the Venetian quarter whether they were Venetians, Syrians, or Franks, save only liegemen of the prince or burgesses of Tyre. If a Venetian offended a Tyrian the Venetian bailli made amends; if a Tyrian offended a Venetian, the prince of Tyre made amends to the Venetians. A tribunal appointed by the king of Jerusalem settled disputes, between the Venetian commune and the lord of Tyre. (Tafel-Thomas, iii, 150–59; *Regesta*, doc. 1413.)

[2] Müller, pp. 36–38; *Regesta*, doc. 683.

fiefs from Outremer lords, they became amenable to their lords' courts for their fiefs.

While from the modern point of view these extraterritorial immunities seem somewhat subversive of sovereignty, to the mediaeval mind which knew no theory of sovereignty, they were, like the early capitulations granted by the Ottoman sultans, desirable from the point of view of the king as well as of the Italians; for the royal court would not have to trouble itself with Venetian, Genoese, Pisan, and other laws and customs about which it knew little. While the major advantage lay with the communes, extraterritoriality was probably considered desirable by the kings also.

Security of goods in cases of shipwreck and death intestate while resident in the East was also guaranteed the Italians by provisions in their charters. The normal mediaeval custom was for the goods of ships wrecked on a coast to become the property of the lord of the coast, and the same was true of the possessions of foreigners dying intestate in any alien feudal community. While the various sea codes, such as the *Consulado del Mare*, the *Constitution Usus of Pisa*, the *Statutes of Ancona*, and the *Rhodian Sea Law*, all contained provisions to limit the rights of the lord under the law of wreck, granting him only a percentage of the goods salvaged, the crusading states were the first to grant complete safety of person and restoration of goods salvaged.[1] This abolition of the rights of *naufragium*, which was granted in the charters to the Italian commercial cities, was a decided incentive to trade and an important concession on the part of the lords of Outremer. The property of aliens dying intestate in Jerusalem was also protected by the charters, and was turned over to the bailli of the nearest commune of his nation to be administered.[2]

---

[1] W. Ashburner, *The Rhodian Sea Law* (Oxford, 1909), pp. ccxc–ccxciii; J. W. Thompson, *Economic and Social History of the Middle Ages* (N. Y.: Century, 1928), p. 581.

The *Assises de la Cour des Bourgeois*, xlix, 47, provide that the finder shall have half the goods salvaged and the lord of the fief the other half, but the treaties with the Italian cities grant them full restoration.

The *Assises*, like the *Consulado del Mare*, provide that goods on the bottom of the sea belong to the owner by whom they were lost. (*Assises Cour Bourg*, xlix, 47; Ashburner, *op. cit.*)

[2] Similar rights were conferred on foreigners of privileged nations in the Byzantine Empire, but in 1166 Manuel Comnenus claimed the inheritance of all foreigners dying intestate within his realms. (Heyd, i, 201–02.)

The property of these communes was further exempt from taxation. It is because of this that the *Assises de Jérusalem* prohibit the sale or gift of property to the communes as they do to the Church.[1] The communal corporation was as much the 'dead hand' as was the ecclesiastical, and the passage of lands into *mortmain* of any sort was to be prevented according to the *Assises*.[2]

Beyond the necessity of contributing to the defense of the city if attacked, the communes were not held responsible for services of any kind. The Italian merchant communes were never required to furnish troops for an aggressive campaign, and when they did so it was under a special treaty.[3] Special clauses in many of the charters provide that the citizens of foreign communes in the East shall not be held responsible for damages done by their countrymen abroad, or at least that the responsibility be limited. In 1199 Bohemond IV promised the Pisans in Tripoli a delay of three months before he would seize their persons as compensation or security for damages which might be inflicted upon him by the citizens of Pisa.[4]

Many of the Italians who came to the Latin East settled there, gave up their western affiliations, and, marrying the daughters of the Frankish lords or acquiring fiefs of their own, entered the ranks of the eastern nobility. Many more undoubtedly became burgesses in the eastern cities and went to make up their extremely hetero-

---

[1] *Assises*, i, 372, 399, ii, 255. A charter of Henry and Isabelle provides that if a Pisan holds a *burgensium*, i.e., land in the city held by burgage tenure and not part of the quarter assigned the commune, he must hold it as a subject of the king and must give up his special privileges. (*Regesta*, doc. 713; Müller, p. 60.) As with lands sold to the Church, the prohibition was against sale without the consent of the lord.

[2] For prohibitions of sale or grant to the Church see above p. 213 ff..

[3] Heyd, i, 157, says that the three knights from Tyre which must be supplied by the Venetians, mentioned in the list of knights which the various cities supply given in Ibelin, cclxxi, 425, were due by the commune under the terms of the revised treaty between Baldwin and Venice. But the Venetians were granted a third of the revenues and the treaty as amended said they supplied troops proportionately to their share of the revenues. I think that the three knights here referred to were probably due from lands held by the commune, outside of the quarter which they held, and that they owed the service for this extra fief which they held by knight service. Three knights certainly did not represent a third of the revenues. Beyond this one exceptional case, there is no indication of any service due by Venetians, Genoese, or Pisans in any Outremer city. Military service was occasionally demanded of the Italians in the Byzantine Empire.

[4] Müller, pp. 79–80; *Regesta*, doc, 758.

geneous population. The most famous case of Italians becoming prominent lords in Syria is that of the Embriaci who founded the house of Gibelet. In 1109 Bertrand of Tripoli had granted Gibelet to the Genoese in payment for their aid in his conquests. The republic granted two thirds of the city to Hugh Embriaco as a fief; and in 1154 the Genoese consuls granted a twenty-nine year lease on the entire city to William Embriaco, the son of Hugh, at the same time that they granted similar leases on their possessions in Acre and Antioch to Hugh II and Nicholas Embriaco, his brothers. At first the lords of Gibelet paid the rents for which they held their lands but Hugh III, the son of William, stopped paying, and in 1179 there began a series of letters from the Popes to the Outremer prelates and princes demanding that the lords of Gibelet pay the commune of Genoa that which was due it. The letters continued through 1186, then Gibelet was lost with the rest of the country during Saladin's invasion. When, after the third crusade, the lords of Gibelet regained their city, they held it in complete independence of the Genoese republic.[1] Another celebrated case is that of Plebanus the Pisan who purchased the hand of the heiress of Botron from Count Raymond of Tripoli, and who established himself as lord of Botron. He lost his fief and his liberty to Saladin, regained both, but died without male heirs.[2] Yet even these Italians who settled in the East and gave up their western citizenship conferred favors on their former fellow citizens. Daimbert, the patriarch, granted franchises to the Pisans; and the Embriaci made extensive grants to the Genoese, even while they refused to respect their suzerainty.

As a result of their privileged position and of their numbers, the

---

[1] *Liber Jurium*, i, docs. 11, 196, 197, 256, 321, 351–54; Heyd, i, 162–63; Byrne, 'Genoese Colonies,' p. 147 ff.. The Genoese branch of the family also held property in Syria in other cities. Benjamin of Tudela observed that Gibelet was governed by a committee of seven Genoese, of whom an Embriaco was always the chairman. (Komroff, *The Contemporaries of Marco Polo* (New York: Boni Liveright, 1928), p. 269.)

[2] *Brevis Regni Ierosolymitani Historia* in *Annales Ianuensis* (*Fonti per la Storia d'Italia*, xi), p. 138; Heyd, i, 321–22. The incident has special interest in that the defeated suitor for the hand of the heiress was Gerard de Ridefort who entered the Temple after the failure of his marital designs, became Grand Master, and was the persistent enemy and opponent of Count Raymond until his death at Hattin. Plebanus' daughter married Bohemond, a younger son of Bohemond III of Antioch, and Botron became a possession of this branch of the house of Antioch.

various Italian communes played an increasingly important part in the politics of the Latin states, and the wars which engaged the cities of Italy invariably affected their colonials. In his account of the fall of Acre, Ludolph von Suchem lays much of the blame for the loss of the city on the constant feuds which divided the Genoese and Venetians and prevented their coöperation against the common enemy.[1] Similar conditions were prevalent in the empire of Constantinople in the last critical days of its existence in 1453, and historians have commonly blamed the Italians for contributing to the weakness of the defense.

And the Italian colonists do seem to have been overly contentious. They quarreled with the kings, with the clergy, with the barons, and with the Orders, but especially with each other. Not always were they the aggressors however,—the papal support accorded the Genoese in their struggle with King Amaury and his successors from 1155 to 1187,[2] and that given the Venetians in their long conflict with the archbishops of Tyre,[3] would indicate that in both these cases the Italians were the injured parties. Nor are the Italians especially to be blamed that they took sides in the Imperial-Ibelin conflict or in the troubles of Conrad and Guy de Lusignan. But for their constant fighting among themselves the western merchant colonists are open to severe censure. Genoa, Venice, and Pisa

---

[1] *Discriptio* (*P. P. T. S.*, xxvi), pp. 54–61. Kretschmayr, ii, 26–28, blames the Venetians further for the fall of Jerusalem and the failure of the crusades in that they preferred the lucrative Saracen trade to helping Christians.

[2] King Amaury I, with the connivance of the clergy of the Holy Sepulchre, took down the plaque which stated the privileges of the Genoese,—probably for the gold which was in it. The Genoese appealed to Rome and the Popes Adrian IV, Alexander III, and Urban III wrote repeatedly to the kings, prelates, and chief barons demanding that the plaque be restored and the privileges of the Genoese be maintained. (*Liber Jurium*, i, docs. 254, 255, 322, 345, 346, 347, 348, 349, 350; *Regesta*,doc. 438; Caffaro, *Annales*, pp. 44–45.)

[3] *The Historia Ducum Veniticorum*, p. 91, says that in 1187 the archbishop usurped the privileges of the Venetians. A letter of 1200 from Innocent III announces that he has decided in favor of the Venetians in their quarrel with the archbishop, and six years later the Pope writes the archbishop to restore to the Venetians those things which he had taken from them. (Tafel-Thomas, i, 282–85; ii, 26–27.) In 1214, however, the Venetian bailli is still appealing to the Pope against the archbishop, and the case drags on until 1247 when the Pope finally took under his immediate protection the Venetian churches in Acre and Tyre. Even so, two years later the Pope wrote the archdeacon of Antioch to see that the Venetian churches were left unmolested. (Tafel-Thomas, ii, 174–75, 445–49.)

were rivals for the Levantine trade and were continuously at war in one or another theatre. There were troubles throughout the 13th century, Venice and Genoa allied against Pisa when the latter supported Frederick II; Pisa allied with Genoa against Venice, and later with Venice against Genoa. In 1238 peace was made between Venice and Genoa. Ten years later war broke out between the Genoese and Pisans in Acre, in which the Venetians were soon involved, and in which the Genoese were badly defeated.[1] The most serious conflict occurred, however, in the decade following 1255 when Venice and Genoa fought out the question of the commercial supremacy in Syria and the Aegean. It began in 1255 with the murder of a Genoese by a Venetian, followed by a Genoese attack on the Venetian quarter of Acre, and the expulsion of the Venetians from Tyre.[2] Then in 1257 Venice, having won Pisa to her alliance by the treaty of Modena, opened the attack on the Genoese colony at Acre. Both sides appealed to their home governments; both cities sent out war fleets to the East. The war became general and was fought out in Tyre and Acre, along the Syrian coast, and in the waters of Greece and Sicily. In the kingdom of Jerusalem it divided the country, the Genoese receiving the support of the Catalans, Anconitans, Hospitallers, and Philip de Montfort, lord of Tyre, while the Venetians were aided by the Pisans, Provençals, Templars, Teutonic Knights, the king of Cyprus, and most of the Outremer barons.[3]

---

[1] *Eracles*, p. 437; Heyd, i, 340 ff..

[2] The two chief sources for this war are the *Annales Ianuensis*, iv (*Fonti*, xiv), pp. 30–36, 55–56, 69; and the *Cronaca* of da Canale, pp. 452–630 (especially 452–476, 506–510, 542–550). The *Gestes*, pars. 268–290; *Eracles*, p. 443ff.; *Rothelin Eracles*, pp. 633–35; *Annales de Terre Sainte*, pp. 446–48, have short accounts.   The best secondary treatments are found in G. Caro, *Genua und die Mächte am Mittelmeer 1257–1311* (Halle, 1899), i, 28–43, 69–76, 158–170; S. Romanin, *Storia Documentata di Venezia* (Venice, 1853), ii, 265 *et seq.*; A. Weil, *The Navy of Venice* (London, 1910), pp. 154–183; F. C. Hodgson, *Venice in the 13th and 14th Centuries* (London, 1910), pp. 120–126; Kretschmayr, *op. cit.*, ii, 59–67; Röhricht, *Königreichs*, pp. 897–904, 923 *et seq.*; Heyd, i, 344–55; W. C. Hazlitt, *The Venetian Republic* (London, 1900), i, 365 ff..   The causes of the beginning of the conflict are variously told.   The seizure of St Saba by Marco Guistiniano in 1257 is the cause given by the eastern historians.   The *Annales Ianuensis* says that a Genoese was murdered by a Venetian and in revenge his compatriots attacked the Venetian quarter.   Canale says that the Genoese, though at truce with the Venetians, '*li firent outrage . . . et pristrent lor nes en traison*', and then goes on to relate the actions of Guistiniani and the coming of the Venetian fleet under Tiepolo.

[3] Canale, p. 460; *Annales Ianuensis*, iv (*Fonti*, xiv), pp. 35–36.

Acre, whence the Genoese were expelled, and Tyre became the opposing fortresses, and both were besieged and attacked on more than one occasion. While Genoa strained every nerve to win the supremacy, she was no match for the resources of Venice, and the Venetians emerged the victors as far as Syria was concerned, though they were not readmitted to Tyre until 1277.[1] But Genoa had been able to deal her rival a deadly blow in the course of the conflict by her alliance with Michael Paleologus and the consequent destruction of the Latin empire of Constantinople carrying with it the loss of much of the Venetian empire in the Aegean.[2]

The effect of the war on Syria was tremendously destructive. Over 20,000 men were killed at Acre in the first year of the war (1257–58) according to the *Rothelin Eracles*,[3] and the commerce and industry of both Tyre and Acre were destroyed. Pope Alexander IV, in demanding peace from the ambassadors of Venice, Genoa, and Pisa at Viterbo in 1258, pointed out to them the harm they were doing to Christianity by weakening the resources of the Syrian cities. '*Sachies, que votre guerre et votre male volentes est grant domaie a la Sainte Tere dela la mer, et a tote la crestiente*', he said,[4] and the attack which the Genoese and Tyrians made on Acre while Bibars was ravaging the countryside and threatening the city itself in 1267 certainly proved the truth of the Pope's statement, even if the Genoese were not, as some authorities have maintained, in direct alliance with the sultan.[5] It is the old familiar story of failure to unite and to bury mutual grievances in the face of an overwhelming danger, the story of 1187 before Hattin, the story of 1453 at Constantinople. The Italians were no worse offenders in this respect than were the nobles of the crusading states or the members of the military Orders. In 1289, when Benedetto Zaccaria came with a Genoese fleet to the relief of Tripoli he became involved in the civil war going on between the commune of the city and the Countess Lucie which destroyed the

---

[1] Tafel-Thomas, iii, 150–59, *Regesta*, doc. 1413, give the treaty of 1277.

[2] See in addition to the references given above in note 2, p. 240, C. Chapman, *Michel Paléologue* (Paris, 1926), pp. 41–45.

[3] *Rothelin Eracles*, p. 635.

[4] Canale, p. 476.

[5] Heyd, i, 353–54.

unity of the defense and made the city an easy prey to Kelaoun.[1] In the last hours of the kingdom, at Tripoli as at Acre, Venetians Genoese, and Pisans, Hospitallers and Templars finally united only when it was far too late in a desperate and heroic attempt to defend the cities; but the defenses had been too weakened, the command was too divided; against a strong army commanded by a general of ability they could not hope to stand.

Yet, if the Italians be blamed for a large share of those elements which caused internal weakness and accelerated the decline of the crusading states, they must be given credit for a great work in preserving them as long as they did last. Without their assistance the conquest of the coastal cities would have been impossible; without their keeping open the communications with the West, without the reinforcements which they constantly brought to the East, without the assistance rendered on many occasions, the maintenance of the Latin kingdom would have been extremely difficult; without the trade which they brought and the economic support which they provided, the wealth of the country would never have been developed; so that, while the Italian communes may have contributed to the decline at the end of the kingdom, they contributed no less to the greatness at the zenith, and while they contributed to weakness they were also in many ways the chief tower of strength which the struggling kingdom of Jerusalem possessed.

[1] *Annales Ianuensis* in *M. G. H. SS.*, xviii, 322–24; *Gestes,* pars. 468–79; Heyd, i, 356–58; Caro, *Genua,* ii, 120–133; Michaud, *Bibliothèque des Croisades* (Paris, 1829), iv, 561–64.

CONCLUSION

IN THE preceding chapters the institutions of the Latin kingdom of Jerusalem have been studied in more or less detail to obtain a picture of the administration and functions of a feudal monarch. It has been shown that the king was at all times merely the chief feudal seignor; that the High Court of the kingdom was superior to the king; that the monarch was always subject to the laws; that his military establishment and most of his financial resources were purely feudal; that the throne and the succession thereto was governed generally by the law of the fief; and that in his relations with his immediate inferiors, superiors, and allies, the king was at all times bound by the terms of feudal contracts.

It is for this reason that the institutions of Jerusalem are worthy of study; in no country of western Europe is such *pure feudalism* to be found for so extended a period of time as it is in the crusading states. In the West the encroachments of the royal power and the development of absolutisms modified and eventually destroyed the feudal states. In the East the feudal decentralization lasted throughout the life of the kingdom, and was largely responsible for its final destruction.

In estimating the effects of the various semi-autonomous groups within the kingdom with whom the monarch was in constant relations we have tried to show that while each one played an important rôle in building up and preserving the state, by the very fact that they were not under the direct control of the crown they increased that decentralization of authority and lack of unity of purpose which was the fundamental cause for the loss of the kingdom.

This volume attempts to give a picture of a pure feudal monarchy; there are available in English few works in which feudalism can be seen at work. Most of the studies of feudalism in English are studies of feudalism in England; Professor Haskins has given a thorough study of Norman feudalism, Professor Thompson of German, but in both of these cases, as in that of England, the feudalism has been so modified that it no longer can be considered a study of a purely feudal state. Norman institutions give us our best view of the centralization which was possible under feudalism, Jerusalemite show the decentralization which was inherent in feudalism before the organizing genius of the Normans set to work to alter it. The royal household in Jerusalem remains always largely a household; the chancery is always a rather simple affair with but few types of documents.

The first crusade, starting from Europe at a time when feudalism was nearest approaching its perfect form, carried with it the ideals of that feudal organization and transplanted them into the Levant. Ignoring the Byzantino-Saracenic institutions which already existed, save in the case of the financial administration (and here it should be noted Jerusalem made its greatest contribution to the advance of administration) and in the sphere of the government of the native population, the Frankish warriors established for themselves a state run on pure feudal principles. The renaissance of the twelfth century passed them by; they were living in the midst of a culture which was to influence the whole intellectual and social organization of western Europe but they were themselves unaffected by it. I do not think that the monarchs of Jerusalem were unaware of their position; the attempts of Amaury to modify feudalism prove that the kings would have liked to establish that centralization of government which was so needed in their country; but the feudal principles of government were too strongly imbedded. The barons of northern England were impotent to undo the administrative reforms of Henry II, the kings of Jerusalem were unable to overcome the essentially feudal character of their rule. That the kingdom of Cyprus produced a despot like Peter I shows that the western ideas of royal absolutism did not altogether fail to penetrate the East; that Peter was assassinated and his work undone by a coalition of barons intent on preserving their ancient rights and privileges shows that the feudalism of the first crusade was in the fourteenth century still too strong to be overthrown.

No attempt has been made in this study to examine the private law of the kingdom of Jerusalem; as stated in our preface the purpose of this book is merely to study the monarchy. The constitutional developments of the kingdom have been traced in the first section of this work; as there was no definite constitution this has been of necessity a rather difficult task, but it is hoped that what slight development there was has been brought out and that the differences between the first and second kingdoms have been shown. The study is all the more interesting that the purely feudal institutions of Jerusalemite monarchy are best studied as they existed in the thirteenth century, when western feudalism was dying:—that the ideal feudalism found in the writings of John d'Ibelin was contemporaneous with the 'Indian summer of feudalism' in France under the rule of St Louis.

Nor can one leave the study of the feudalism of Jerusalem without some speculation as to the stability of feudal institutions. It has been shown that the decentralization of the feudal organization weakened and in part precipitated the fall of the crusading states. Yet when one considers that they lasted for almost two centuries it must be admitted that there were in feudalism elements of strength; that the crusading states, menaced constantly from without by hostile powers, managed to exist as long as they did is the miracle. Would they have fared better under a different system of government? The weak kingdom of Jerusalem outlasted in point of time the strong Norman state of Sicily. The feudal constitution prevented in the East that absorption by the Empire which was fatal to the western kingdom. Who in 1185 could have foretold that Sicily, great in the glory of her fleet and her conquests under William II, would have fallen while the feeble kingdom of Jerusalem, threatened with destruction by the growth of the empire of Saladin, yet survived? The Latin kingdom was shorn of her provinces; city after city, fief after fief fell into the hands of the Moslems, but the kingdom still continued. Was not the very feudal character of the state in part responsible for its ability to sustain life in the dissected remains of what had been its body politic? Perhaps the barons of Outremer were wise; feudalism had been generated as a system for securing protection and some sort of government in adverse circumstances. Under feudalism the crusading states managed to keep alive. Can we say that the experiment failed altogether and that pure feudalism may not have been, in the circumstances, the most practical and permanent form of government?

APPENDICES

APPENDIX A

GENEALOGY OF THE KINGS OF JERUSALEM

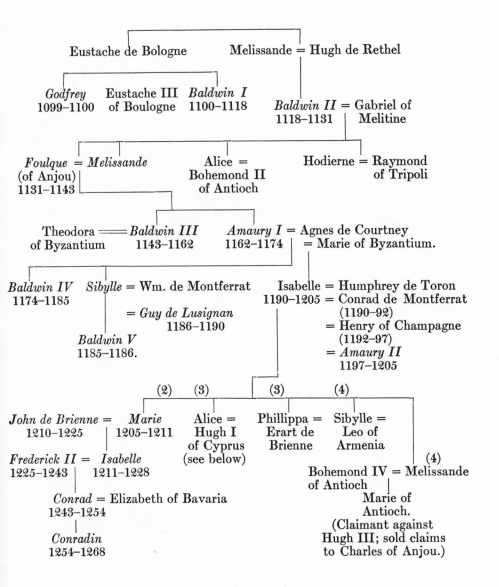

Eustache de Bologne   Melissande = Hugh de Rethel

Godfrey   Eustache III   *Baldwin I*
1099–1100   of Boulogne   1100–1118

Baldwin II = Gabriel of
1118–1131 | Melitine

Foulque = *Melissande*   Alice =   Hodierne = Raymond
(of Anjou)| Bohemond II   of Tripoli
1131–1143   of Antioch

Theodora ===== *Baldwin III*   *Amaury I* = Agnes de Courtney
of Byzantium   1143–1162   1162–1174 | = Marie of Byzantium.

Baldwin IV   *Sibylle* = Wm. de Montferrat   Isabelle = Humphrey de Toron
1174–1185   1190–1205 = Conrad de Montferrat
= *Guy de Lusignan*   (1190–92)
1186–1190   = Henry of Champagne
Baldwin V   (1192–97)
1185–1186.   = *Amaury II*
1197–1205

(2)   (3)   (3)   (4)

John de Brienne =   *Marie*   Alice =   Phillippa =   Sibylle =
1210–1225 | 1205–1211   Hugh I   Erart de   Leo of
of Cyprus   Brienne   Armenia
Frederick II =   *Isabelle*   (see below)   (4)
1225–1243 | 1211–1228   Bohemond IV = Melissande
of Antioch |
Conrad = Elizabeth of Bavaria   Marie of
1243–1254   Antioch.
(Claimant against
Conradin   Hugh III; sold claims
1254–1268   to Charles of Anjou.)

The Kings of Cyprus and Later Kings of Jerusalem

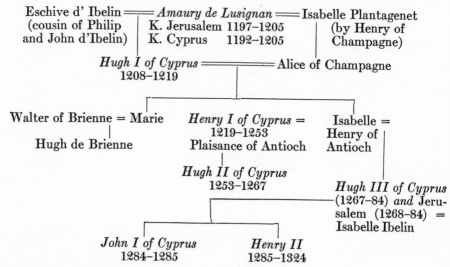

Eschive d' Ibelin ===== *Amaury de Lusignan* ===== Isabelle Plantagenet
(cousin of Philip | K. Jerusalem 1197–1205 | (by Henry of
and John d'Ibelin) | K. Cyprus   1192–1205 | Champagne)

Hugh I of Cyprus =========== Alice of Champagne
1208–1219

Walter of Brienne = Marie   *Henry I of Cyprus* =   Isabelle =
        | 1219–1253   Henry of |
   Hugh de Brienne   Plaisance of Antioch   Antioch |

                               Hugh II of Cyprus
                                   1253–1267   *Hugh III of Cyprus*
                                                          —(1267–84) *and* Jeru-
                                                           salem (1268–84) =
                                                           Isabelle Ibelin
              John I of Cyprus   *Henry II*
                  1284–1285   1285–1324

Note: The throne of Jerusalem definitely passed to the kings of Cyprus on the death of Conradin 1268, and Hugh III and his sons were kings of Jerusalem and Cyprus. Alice of Champagne had ruled in Jerusalem but without royal title.

APPENDIX B

MAJOR LINES OF THE HOUSE OF IBELIN

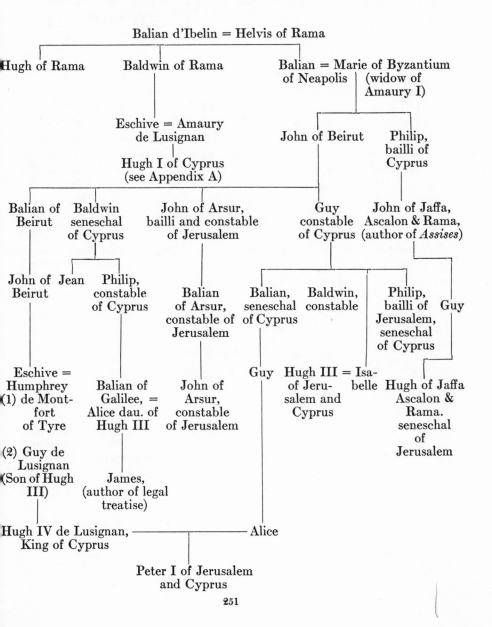

Balian d'Ibelin = Helvis of Rama

Hugh of Rama   Baldwin of Rama   Balian = Marie of Byzantium
of Neapolis (widow of Amaury I)

Eschive = Amaury de Lusignan   John of Beirut   Philip, bailli of Cyprus

Hugh I of Cyprus (see Appendix A)

Balian of Beirut   Baldwin seneschal of Cyprus   John of Arsur, bailli and constable of Jerusalem   Guy constable of Cyprus   John of Jaffa, Ascalon & Rama, (author of *Assises*)

John of Beirut   Jean   Philip, constable of Cyprus   Balian of Arsur, constable of Jerusalem   Balian, seneschal of Cyprus   Baldwin, constable   Philip, bailli of Jerusalem, seneschal of Cyprus   Guy

Eschive = Humphrey (1) de Montfort of Tyre   Balian of Galilee, = Alice dau. of Hugh III   John of Arsur, constable of Jerusalem   Guy   Hugh III = Isabelle of Jerusalem and Cyprus   Hugh of Jaffa Ascalon & Rama. seneschal of Jerusalem

(2) Guy de Lusignan (Son of Hugh III)   James, (author of legal treatise)

Hugh IV de Lusignan, King of Cyprus   Alice

Peter I of Jerusalem and Cyprus

251

APPENDIX C

LIST OF THE GRAND OFFICERS OF JERU-SALEM, CYPRUS, ANTIOCH AND TRIPOLI

(Note: This list is based on the lists given by E. G. Rey in his edition of Ducange, *Les Familles d'Outremer*, his *Sommaire du supplement aux Familles d' Outremer* (Chartres, 1881) and 'Les Dignitaires de la Principauté d'Antioche' (*Revue de l'Orient Latin, VIII (1901)*), the manuscript notes of Mas Latrie, B. N. *Nouvelles Acquisitions Françaises*, 6793, 6797, the review by C. Hopf of the *Familles* in the *Revue Critique*, ii (1870), pp. 223–241, and on the documents given in Röhricht's *Regesta Regni Hierosolymitani*. Names here published for the first time are italicized in this list. The dates given are derived from the documents in the *Regesta* for those not mentioned by Rey. In some cases the tenure of office has been extended beyond Rey's dates when documents in the *Regesta* show the person using his title at an earlier or later date than that given by Rey. As the dates give easy reference to the *Regesta*, we have not given further references except in cases where there is disagreement or room for doubt. Names listed by Ducange but rejected by Rey have been here omitted. All references to the *Regesta* are to documents rather than pages. Questionable names are enclosed in brackets.)

OFFICERS OF THE KINGDOM OF JERUSALEM

Seneschals or Dapifers

Hugh de St Omer, under Baldwin I.

Gervase, 1104.

Hugo Chostard, 1112.

[*Anscherius*, 1122? (He appears as seneschal on a charter of Baldwin of Jaffa and may not have been seneschal of the kingdom. *Regesta*, 100. On a charter of Baldwin of Jerusalem in the same year appears Anscherius de Mosteriolo without title. *Regesta*, 100a.)]

Isaac, 1149.

John, 1151. (Rey gives c. 1160 but the charter on which he appears is dated 1151 by Röhricht, *Regesta*, 273.)

Guy le Francois, 1164.

Miles de Planci, 1168–1171.

Ralph, 1176.

Joscelin III, count of Edessa, 1176–1190.

[Obertus Nepos, 1187–1192. (Under Conrad de Montferrat; may have been only personal.)]

Ralph of Tiberias, 1194–1220.

Raymond de Gibelet, 1240.

Baldwin d'Ibelin, 1256. (Regesta, 1250).

Geoffrey de Sargines, 1254?–1267? (The date 1254 is on the authority of the *Eracles* and is accepted by Rey. Geoffrey can only be dated on charters from 1258 to 1267 (*Regesta*, 1269–1350) as seneschal, although he appeared as bailli on a charter of 1269, in April of which he died.)

Robert de Cresque, 1269.

John de Grailly, 1272–1278. (*Gestes*, par 477, though he omitted his title on documents.)

Eudes Pelechin, 1277. (seneschal of Charles of Anjou.)

Philip d'Ibelin, under Henry II.

Constables

Simon, 1108–1115.

Hugh Caulis, 1120.

Eustache Grenier, 1123.

William de Buris, 1123. (Perhaps till 1141 as he was still alive then.)

Manasses, 1144–1151.

Humphrey de Toron, 1152–1179.

Amaury de Lusignan, 1181–1194; 1197.

John d'Ibelin, 1194–1200. (John traded the constableship for the fief of Beirut and the office was it seems returned to Amaury de Lusignan; but John appears with title in 1200.)

Walter de Montbéliard, 1206–1211.

Eudes de Montbéliard, 1220–1244. (Rey following the *Eracles* gives 1218, but Eudes signed without title until 1220. In March he signed without title, (*Regesta* 930.) in May with title. (*Regesta*, 934.))

Philip de Montfort, 1244.

John d'Ibelin of Arsur, 1251–1258.

William de Botron, 1258–1262. (*Gestes*, par. 296, gives 1258.)

Balian d'Ibelin of Arsur, 1268–1277.

John d'Ibelin of Arsur, 1272. (on authority of *Eracles*, 463.)

Richard de Neublans, 1277? (He was constable under St Severin. '*R- constabularium*' appears in a letter of 1277. (Regesta, 1424.))

[Simon de Montolif, constable in 1284, but it may have been of Cyprus. *Gestes*, par. 424.]

Baldwin d'Ibelin, c. 1286. (*'olim constabularii regni Hier'*. on charter of
   Henry II of 1286. (*Regesta*, 1461). Also *Gestes*, pars. 220–332.
   Röhricht's note page 381 of *Regesta*.)
Amaury de Lusignan, 1285–1300.

Marshals

Sado, 1125–1154.
Eudes de St Amand, 1155–1156. (gave up marshalship for viscounty of
   Jerusalem before 1160.)
Joscelin III, count of Edessa, 1156–1159.
William, 1159–1171.
Gerard de Pugi, 1169–1174 (and chamberlain 1174).
John, ante 1179. (*'tunc temporis merescalcus et camerarius regius'* on charter
   of 1179; *Regesta*, 582.)
Gerard de Ridefort, 1179. (*Regesta*, 587–588. Ducange lists him incor-
   rectly as seneschal.)
Walter Durus, 1185–1192. (under Conrad de Montferrat.)
Hugh Martin, 1191. (Rey says probably still marshal in 1195, but he fol-
   lowed Guy de Lusignan to Cyprus and was marshal of Cyprus in 1195,
   not of Jerusalem.)
Arnulf, 1193. (under Henry of Champagne.)
John, 1194–1200.
Aymar de Laron, 1206.
James de Dournai, 1211–1217.
Philip de Cossie, 1250.
Geoffrey de Sargines, 1254. (*Regesta*, 1221.)
John de Gibelet, 1261–1262.
William Canet, 1269–1273.
James Vidal, 1277. (under St Severin.).

Butlers

Winric, under Godfrey.
Gervais, 1107 (Hopf)
Paganus, 1120–1136.
Robert Crispin, 1145–1146.
Eudes de St Amand, 1164–1167.
Miles, 1185–1186.

Chamberlains[1]

Strabulon, personal chamberlain of Duke Godfrey.

[Geoffrey, personal chamberlain of Duke Godfrey.—Albert Aix, p. 526.]

Gerard, 1108–1115.

John, 1119–1128.

Ralph, 1129–1130.

John, 1136–1138.

Joscelin, 1138. (appears on same charter with John both signing as chamberlains; *Regesta*, 179.)

Miles, 1138.

Nicholas, 1150–1152.

Gauvain de la Roche, 1156.

Gerard de Pugi, 1169. (signs many other charters in the years 1161–1179 without title.)

Amaury de Lusignan, 1175–78.

John, ante 1179. (was also marshal *'tunc temporis,'* (*Regesta*, 582) he sold fief of Chamberlaine in 1179.)

Raymond, 1184.

Balian d'Ibelin of Jaffa, 1183–1185.

Thomas, 1190–1197. (*Regesta*, 698–736.)

Henry de Canelli, 1192. (chamberlain of Conrad de Montferrat; *Regesta*, 705.)

John, 1194. (*Regesta*, 717).

Rohard de Caïphas, 1201–1220.

Renaud de Caïphas, 1230–1232. (signs without title several acts from 1197 to 1234.)

John de Cossie, son and successor of above.

Philip de Cossie, 1250–1269, son and successor of John.

Chancellors

[Arnoul, archdeacon of St Sepulchre, under Baldwin I.]

Paganus, 1115–1128.

Amelinus, (Hemelin), 1130.

[*Franco*, 1133–1135. (appears as chancellor on charters of Foulque as bailli of Antioch; may not have been chancellor of kingdom. *Regesta*, 149–157.)]

Helias, 1136–1142.

Ralph, bishop of Bethlehem, 1146–1174.

[1] See Mas Latrie, 'La Fief de Chamberlaine',—*B. E. C.* xliii, pp. 644–52.

[Frederick, 1150. A charter of Melissande's is drawn up by *Frederici c...* *Regesta*, 262. Rey suggests that he was probably the chancellor of Melissande as regent.]

William, archbishop of Tyre, 1174–1183.

Lambert, 1177. (*Regesta*, 552. In 1176 he signed as chaplain on a charter which he drew up for Baldwin IV. *Regesta*, 537.)

Bandinus, 1188–1192. (chancellor of Conrad de Montferrat).

Peter, archdeacon of Lydda and bishop of Tripoli, 1185–1192.

Eudes, 1190. (chancellor of Conrad. *Regesta*, 691.)

Joscius, archbishop of Tyre, 1192–1200.

Ralph, dean of Acre, bishop of Sidon, 1206–1212.

Simon, archbishop of Tyre, 1226–1227.

Maregnan, before 1234, (mentioned as *quondam* chancellor.)

OFFICERS OF THE KINGDOM OF CYPRUS (XIII century)

Seneschals

Guy de Lusignan, son of Amaury, served under his father, 1195.

Amaury de Rivet, 1197–1210.

Baldwin d'Ibelin, 1246–1267.

Robert de Cresque, 1269.

Balian d'Ibelin, 1286–1302.

Constables

[Amaury de Lusignan, may have been constable before he became king.]

[John de Lusignan, son of Amaury, listed by Rey but questioned.]

Baldwin de Bethsan, 1195.

Walter of Beirut, lord of Caesarea, 1210–1229.

John d'Ibelin of Beirut, 1227–1229.

Balian d'Ibelin of Beirut, 1236–1239. (son of above).

Guy d'Ibelin, 1247. (son of John, brother of Balian.)

John d'Ibelin of Arsur, 1256.

[*Simon de Montolif*, 1284 (either Cyprus or Jerusalem.)]

Baldwin d'Ibelin, 1286.

Philip d'Ibelin, 1302.

Marshals

Hugh Martin, 1194–1196.

Renaud de Soissons, 1210–1217.

Adam de Gaures of Antioch.

John of Antioch, 1247. (succeeded his father Adam.)
Anceau.
William de Canet, 1269. (*Assises*, i, 414.)
Simon de Montolif, 1296.

Chamberlains

Amaury de Bethsan, 1218–1220.
Geoffrey le Tor, 1247.
Philip de Cossie, 1269. (*Assises*, i, 415.)
Walter of Antioch, 1286.

Chancellors

[*Peter*, bishop of Tripoli, was chancellor under Guy de Lusignan.—*Eracles*.]
Alan, archdeacon of Lydda and archbishop of Nicosia, 1195–1201.
Ralph archdeacon of Nicosia, 1217–1220.
Bonvassal d'Aude, canon of Nicosia, 1231–1248.
Peter, bishop of Paphos, 1269–1288.
Henry de Gibelet, archdeacon of Nicosia, 1291–1330.

GRAND OFFICERS OF THE PRINCIPALITY OF ANTIOCH

Seneschals

Eschivard de Sarmenia, 1149–1169.
Gervais de Sarmenia, 1181–1199.
Acharie de Sarmenia, 1216–1251.
Peter de Hazart, 1262.

Constables

Robert, 1098.
Richard, 1101–1114. (Rey suggests that he was merely titular.)
Adam, 1101–1114.
Rainauld Mansoer, 1126–1134.
Walter de Surdeval, 1134–1135.
Roger des Monts, 1140–1149.
Archembauld, 1153.
Geoffrey Jourdain, 1154.
Guiscard de l'Ile, 1170–1172.
Baldwin, 1174. (1175 according to Röhricht's dating: *Regesta*, 524.)
Rainald, 1179.
Ralph des Monts, 1186–1194.

Roger des Monts 1194–1216.
Robert Mancel, 1207–1219.
Simon Mancel, 1262.

Marshals

Raymond, 1140.
Guarin Malmuz, 1140–1160.
William Tirel, 1149–1169.
William de Cava, 1175–1186.
Bartholemew Tirel, 1186–1191.
Hugh Flauncurt, 1193 (1200?).
Thomas, 1200–1231.
[*Basil*, 1210, signs as marshal immediately after Robert Mancel and Roger
    des Monts on charter of Leo II in 1210.   May have been marshal of
    Armenia, or honorary marshal of Antioch. (*Regesta*, 843.)]
Bartholemew Tirel, 1262.

Butlers

Martin de Margat, 1140–1144.
Peter Salvarici, 1149.
William de Moci, 1169.
Paganus, 1210.
Julien le Jaune, 1216.

Chamberlains

Trigaud, 1138.
Basil, 1140.
Peter, 1151–1172.
William, 1163.
Raymond de Gibelet, 1174.
Oliver, 1179–1190.
Simon Burgevin, 1195.
Simon, 1215–1216. (Rey says this is a different person from the preceding.)

Chancellors

Walter, 1114–1122.
Ralph, 1127.
Franco, 1133–1135.
Eudes, 1140–1143.

John, 1149.
Walter, 1154.
Geoffrey, 1154–1155.
Bouchard, 1155.
Bernard, 1163–1170.
William, 1172.
John, 1177–1183.
Albert, archbishop of Tarsus, 1186–1200.
Alexander, 1193–1200. (Rey points out that Alexander was very probably the actual chancellor and Albert the titular, as he could not be always at court.)
John of Corbonio, 1203–1205. (*Regesta,* 792, 799, 807. Rey lists him as constable for these years but he clearly signs as chancellor.)
Jourdain, 1215–1216.
[John, ante 1225. (probably John of Corbonio.)]
Geoffrey, 1241.
William, 1262.

GRAND OFFICERS OF THE COUNTY OF TRIPOLI

Seneschals

Raymond, 1117.
Brunel, 1139–1143.

Constables

William Peter, 1106.
William Raymond, 1106. (Rey suggests that both of these were merely marshals of the camp.)
Roger, 1110–1117.
Silvius, 1139.
Rainier, 1140–1143.
Arnald de Crest, 1151–1155.
Hugh Sine Censu, 1161–1164.
Raymond de Gibelet, 1181–1183.
Osto, 1194.
Gerard of Ham, 1198–1217.
John, 1217, also marshal.
Thomas of Ham, 1227–1255.
William Farabel, 1277–1282.

Marshals

Falcrand, 1142–1145.
William de Lulen, 1151.
—— de *Monteprasto*, 1163. (*Regesta*, 380.)
Raymond, 1177–1179.
John, 1187–1217. (*Regesta*, 662–901. Also constable.)
John, 1241–1278. (*Regesta*, 1102–1425).

Chamberlains

Walter of Margat, 1137.
Rainald, 1139.
Albert, 1143.

Chancellors

Pons, archdeacon of St Paul, 1126.
Jotron, 1139–1143.
Peter, 1142–1145.
Alberic, 1163.
Mathew, 1174–1187.
[John 1202, is listed by Rey, but he was the chancellor of Bohemond IV
of Antioch-Tripoli and was probably the same as John of Corbonio
chancellor of Antioch at that time.]

APPENDIX D

CHARTERS AND TREATIES PERTAINING TO THE ITALIAN AND PROVENÇAL COMMUNES IN THE KINGDOM OF JERUSALEM

1. *Venice*

In the Kingdom of Jerusalem

1100, June: Godfrey de Bouillon grants the Venetians freedom of trade in the kingdom, with a church and market in all cities; a third of all cities which they helped capture, and all of Tripoli when it should be taken, in return for a tribute to be paid the duke. (*R. H. C. Occ.*, v, 272; Tafel-Thomas, i, doc. 28, pp. 164–65; *Regesta*, doc. 31; *Chronologie*, nos. 472, 478; Heyd, i, 136.)

1101–14: Confirmation of the above by Baldwin I. (Tafel-Thomas, i, doc. 30, p. 66; *Regesta*, doc. 31.)

1111: Baldwin I grants a quarter in Acre. (Tafel-Thomas, i, doc. 34, p. 75; Heyd, i, 142. The text of this treaty is lost and it is known only through the mention by Dandola. It may be the same as the above.)

1123: Warmund the patriarch and William de Buris, bailli of Jerusalem, in the absence of Baldwin II detained in the prison of Aleppo, make a treaty with Dominico Michieli whereby the Venetians receive a third of Tyre and Ascalon when they shall be taken, a quarter in Jerusalem as large as that held in domain by the king, and lands and revenues in Acre and all other cities of the realm, together with exemption from sales and purchase taxes in the ports and markets of the kingdom. (Tafel-Thomas, i, doc. 40, pp. 84–89; William Tyre, XII, xxv, 550–553; *Regesta*, doc. 102.)

1125, May: Baldwin II confirms treaty above, with minor emendations, whereby the Venetians are obliged to render military service for the lands held in Tyre. (Tafel-Thomas, i, doc. 41, pp. 90–94; *Regesta*, doc. 105; Heyd, i, 144.)

[1164, August: Charter of Vitalis Michieli granting to the Church of St Mark the revenue of 300 marks a year granted by Baldwin II and confiscated by Foulque. If the revenue can be recovered it shall go to the Church. (Tafel-Thomas, i, doc. 59, pp. 140–44; *Regesta*, doc. 402.)]

[1175, June: Charter of Sebastian Ziani granting to St Mark's the Venetian possessions in Tyre. (Tafel-Thomas, i, doc. 63, pp. 167–71; *Regesta*, doc. 526.)]

1192, May: Conrad de Monferrat confirms the Venetian privileges in Tyre. (Tafel-Thomas, i, doc. 76, pp. 212–15; *Regesta*, doc. 705.)

[1206, May: Vitalis Faletro grants the Seigneury of Venice his holdings in Tyre. (Tafel-Thomas, ii, doc. 166, pp. 11–13; *Regesta*, doc. 813.)]

1221, Dec.:   John d'Ibelin of Beirut grants freedom of trade and a court to the Venetians in Beirut. (Tafel-Thomas, ii, doc. 261, pp. 231–32; *Regesta*, doc. 951.)

1222, June: John d'Ibelin of Beirut extends the privileges above. (Tafel-Thomas, ii, doc. 262, pp. 232–34; *Regesta*, doc. 957.)

[1243–44:   Marsiglio Georgio, Venetian bailli in Acre enumerates the Venetian holdings and privileges in the kingdom of Jerusalem, principally in Tyre and Acre. (Tafel-Thomas, ii, docs. 299, 300, pp. 351–98; *Regesta*, docs. 1114, 1116.)]

1277, July: John de Montfort, lord of Tyre, restores to the Venetians their court, privileges, and possessions in Tyre, which he had confiscated during his war with them. (Tafel-Thomas, iii, doc. 369, pp. 150–59; *Regesta*, doc. 1413.)

In Antioch

1098–1099:   Charter of Bohemond I of which the text is lost. (Tafel-Thomas, i, doc. 27.)

1103–1112:   Charter of Tancred of which the text is lost. (Tafel-Thomas, i, doc. 31.)

1126–1131:   Charter of Bohemond II of which the text is lost. (Tafel-Thomas, i, doc. 42.)

1140, May: Charter of Raymond granting freedom of trade, reduced tariff, protection to shipwrecked Venetians, and granting the Venetians the right to be tried in the prince's court by their own law. (Tafel-Thomas, i, doc. 46, pp. 102–03; *Regesta*, doc. 197.)

1153, May: Charter of Renaud de Chatillon and Constance confirming the charters of Bohemond I, Tancred, Bohemond II, and Raymond, and further reducing the tariff. Further grants Venetians their own court in Antioch under their own magistrates. (Tafel-Thomas, i, doc., 55, pp. 133–35; *Regesta*, doc. 282.)

1167:   Charter of Bohemond III remitting half the taxes paid by merchants in Antioch, and confirming the court granted the Venetians. (Tafel-Thomas, i, doc. 61, pp. 148–49; *Regesta*, doc. 434.)

1183:   Bohemond III confirms all previous grants and concessions. (Tafel-Thomas, i, doc. 68, pp. 175–77; *Regesta*, doc. 632.)

1277, June: Bohemond VII grants freedom of sale in Antioch and Tripoli, with tax only on certain commodities and under certain conditions, and confirms the Venetian courts. (Rey, *Recherches*, pp. 42–45; *Regesta*, doc. 1412.)

In Tripoli

1117, Feb.:   Pons of Tripoli grants St Mark's a house in Tripoli. (Tafel-Thomas, i, doc. 36, pp. 76–77; *Regesta*, doc. 84.)

1217, Nov.:   Guy of Gibelet grants freedom of sale, etc. in Gibelet. (Tafel-Thomas, ii, doc. 250, pp. 196–97; *Regesta*, doc. 904.)

2. Genoa

In the Kingdom of Jerusalem

1101: Baldwin I grants a third of everything which the Genoese help capture. (Fulcher of Chartres, II, viii, 396–97; *Chronologie*, no. 559.)

1104: Baldwin I grants exemption from taxes; a third of Arsur, Caesarea, Acre, and whatever towns they may take together; a third of the port revenues of Acre; a street in Jerusalem and in Jaffa; and 300 besants revenue. (*Liber Jurium*, i, doc. 8; *Regesta*, doc. 43; *Chronologie*, no. 722.)

1105: Baldwin I confirms all previous grants to Genoese in Jerusalem, Antioch, Acre, Laodicea, Tortosa, Gibelet, Caesarea, Arsur, St Simeon. (*Liber Jurium*, i, doc. 9; *Regesta*, doc. 45.) Genoese take oath to Baldwin. (*Liber Jurium*, i, doc. 10; *Regesta*, doc. 46.)

[1154: Genoese consuls grant Hugh and Nicholas Embriaco the Genoese possessions in Acre on a 29 year lease for 1000 denarii a year. (*Liber Jurium*, i, doc. 198; *Regesta*, doc. 287.)]

[1155–1186: Letters from Popes Adrian IV (1155), Alexander III (1167), and Urban III (1186), to Kings Baldwin III, Amaury I, and Baldwin V, and to ecclesiastical and noble dignitaries, demanding the restoration of the privileges granted the Genoese, and the replacement of the inscription in gold letters stating them, which the kings of Jerusalem have destroyed. (*Liber Jurium*, i, docs., 254, 255, 322, 345, 346, 347, 348, 349, 350; *Regesta*, doc. 438; D. L. *Cartulaire*, doc. 793.)]

1187, July: Barons of the *Haute Cour* of Jerusalem grant Genoese freedom of trade and lands and a court in Tyre. (*Liber Jurium*, i, doc. 363; *Regesta*, doc. 659.)

1189, Sept.: Conrad de Montferrat grants Genoese a house in Tyre. (Strehlke, doc. 24; *Regesta*, doc. 682.)

1190, April: Further grants in Tyre by Conrad. (*Liber Jurium*, i, doc. 374; *Regesta*, doc. 691).

1190, May: Guy de Lusignan and Sibylle confirm privileges of Genoese in Acre. (*Liber Jurium*, i, doc. 375; *Regesta*, doc. 693.)

1190:   Richard of England promises the Genoese a third of all his conquests in the East. (*Liber Jurium*, i, docs. 381, 382.)

1190:   Philip Augustus of France promises freedom of trade, market, courts, etc. in all his possessions and conquests in the East, save those which Richard, his vassal, conquers. (*Liber Jurium*, i, doc. 384.)

1191, Oct.:   Guy de Lusignan confirms Genoese privileges at request of Richard. (*Liber Jurium*, i, doc. 392; *Regesta*, doc. 702.)

1192, April: Conrad de Montferrat and Isabelle of Jerusalem confirm privileges of Genoese, and grant court, lands, etc. at Acre; a third of the revenues of the port; and promise to restore the golden inscription. (*Liber Jurium*, i, doc. 401; *Regesta*, doc. 704.)

1192:   Henry of Champagne and Isabelle of Jerusalem confirm privileges and grant exemption from charges save on goods imported from Saracen countries; grant court at Tyre. (*Liber Jurium*, i, doc. 405; *Regesta*, doc. 707.)

1195, Sept.:   Henry of Champagne and Isabelle confirm grants in Tyre and grant court at Acre. (*Liber Jurium*, i, doc. 410; *Regesta*, doc. 724.)

[1219:   John de Brienne asks for an extension of the loan of 200 marks borrowed from Luchino Corsali of Genoa. (Röhricht, *Studien zur Geschichte des Fünften Kreuzzug*, pp. 69–70; *Regesta*, doc. 927.)]

1221, Nov.:   John d'Ibelin of Beirut grants freedom of trade, market, and court in Beirut. (*Liber Jurium*, i, doc. 569; *Regesta*, doc. 950.)

1223, May: John d'Ibelin confirms and renews the above. (*Liber Jurium*, i, doc. 585; *Regesta*, doc. 963.)

1234, Jan.:   Rohard II of Caïphas grants freedom to trade with reduced taxes in Caïphas (Haïfa). (*Liber Jurium*, i, doc. 718; *Regesta*, doc. 1050.)

[1249, July–Dec.: Genoese consuls enumerate possessions in Acre and Tyre. (*Archives Orient Latin*, ii, B, 215–24; *Regesta*, docs. 1182, 1184.)]

[1251:   Innocent IV writes ecclesiastics in the East to protect Genoese against molestation in Jerusalem, Antioch, and Tripoli. (*Liber Jurium*, i, docs. 795, 799, 800, 801, 818, 819.) He had taken Genoa under his protection in 1247. (*Liber Jurium*, i, docs. 779, 782.)]

In Antioch

1098, July 14:   Bohemond I grants Genoese a market with the Church of St John and thirty houses in Antioch. (*Regesta*, doc. 12; *Chronologie*, no. 300; Ughelli, *Italia Sacra* (Venice, 1717–22), iv. 846.)

1101:   Tancred, regent of Antioch, confirms the grant of Bohemond and grants the Church of St Lawrence of Genoa a third of the port revenues of St Simeon, and half those of Laodicea; a street and church in Laodicea, and lands in Gibelet when that shall be taken. (*Regesta*, doc. 35; *Chronologie*, no. 580a; Ughelli, iv, 847–48.)

1127, Dec.:   Bohemond II confirms the grant made by Bohemond. (*Liber Jurium*, i, doc. 20; *Regesta*, doc. 119.)

1144:   Raymond and Constance confirm the grants of Bohemond I, Tancred, and Bohemond II. (*Liber Jurium*, i, doc. 95; *Regesta*, doc. 228.)

1169:   Bohemond III confirms all existing privileges and promises the Genoese speedy justice in his courts. (*Liber Jurium*, i, doc. 276; *Regesta*, doc. 471.)

1189, April: Bohemond III grants the Genoese their own courts in Antioch, Laodicea, and Zibel. (*Regesta*, doc. 680; Röhricht, *Amalrich I*, p. 488.)

1190, Sep.:   Bohemond III grants freedom of trade without any taxes. (*Liber Jurium*, i, doc. 379; *Regesta*, doc. 695.)

1199, April: Bohemond III confirms the courts in Antioch and Laodicea. (*Liber Jurium*, i, doc. 424; *Regesta*, doc. 753.)

1216, Feb.: Raymond Rupin of Antioch, at court of Armenia, grants Genoese at Antioch free court and security. (*Liber Jurium*, i, doc. 516; *Regesta*, doc. 885.)

In Tripoli

1109, June: Bertrand grants the Genoese all of Gibelet, the chateau of Puy-le-Constable, and a third of Tripoli. (*Liber Jurium*, i, doc. 11; *Regesta*, doc. 55.)

[1154, Jan.: Genoese consuls grant 29 year lease on Genoese possessions in Antioch to Hugh and Nicholas Embriaco for 80 pounds a year. (*Liber Jurium*, i, doc. 196; *Regesta*, doc. 285.)]

[1154, Jan.: Genoese consuls grant a 29 year lease on Gibelet to William Embriaco for 270 besants a year to the commune, and ten to St Lawrence, and 100 besants for the investiture. (*Liber Jurium*, i, doc. 197; *Regesta*, doc. 286.)]

1168, Mar.: Hugh Embriaco, lord of Gibelet, grants freedom of trade without taxes to Genoese in Gibelet. (*Liber Jurium*, i, doc. 256; *Regesta*, doc. 445.)

[1179–86: Letters from Popes Alexander III and Urban III to Hugh de Gibelet, Raymond of Tripoli and eastern ecclesiastics demanding that Hugh of Gibelet pay the Genoese the rental due on his fief. (*Liber Jurium*, i, docs. 321, 351, 352, 353, 354; *Regesta*, doc. 580.)]

[1186: Letters of Pope Urban III to Raymond of Tripoli and the bishop of Tripoli to restore to the Genoese the third of Tripoli which had been promised them. (*Liber Jurium*, i, docs. 355, 356.)]

1205, July: Bohemond IV grants to Henry of Malta and the Genoese freedom of sale and a court in Tripoli in return for 3000 besants and two galleys with 300 men. (*Liber Jurium*, i, doc. 477; *Regesta*, doc. 807.)

In Cyprus

1218, July: Alice of Champagne grants freedom of sale without tax, and a court and lands in Nicosia and Famagusta. (*Liber Jurium*, i, doc. 544; Mas Latrie, ii, 39; *Regesta*, doc. 912.)

1232, June: Henry of Cyprus grants to the Genoese lands, courts, tax exemptions and protection throughout Cyprus. (*Liber Jurium*, i, doc. 693; Mas Latrie, ii, 51–56; *Regesta*, doc. 1037.)

1233, Dec.:   Henry I confirms Genoese in all privileges in Cyprus and Jerusalem, and signs an alliance. (Mas Latrie, ii, 56–58; *Regesta*, doc. 1049.)

1288:   Treaty of Henry II with Benedetto Zaccaria which was abrogated by Henry in 1292. (Mentioned in *Liber Jurium*, ii, doc. 111,—text not known.)

3. *Pisa*

(The Pisans had been established in Jaffa when part of that city was granted to Daimbert, the patriarch, who was formerly archbishop of Pisa, by Duke Godfrey.)

1118–1131:	Baldwin II grants the Pisans five houses in Tyre. (Müller, p. 7, note; Heyd, i, 150.)
1156, Nov.:	Baldwin III confirms the grant of Baldwin II and grants a court in Tyre. (Müller, doc. 5, pp. 6–7; *Regesta*, doc. 322.)
1157, June:	Amaury, count of Jaffa and Ascalon, grants half his rights in Jaffa to the Pisans. (Müller, doc. 6, p. 8; *Regesta*, doc. 324.)
1165:	Amaury I grants lands in Tyre. (Müller, doc. 9, p. 11; *Regesta*, doc. 412.)
1168:	Amaury I grants lands and court in Acre for assistance in siege of Alexandria. (Müller, doc. 11, p. 14; *Regesta*, doc. 449.)
1169, Sept.:	Amaury I grants freedom of trade in Egypt and courts in all cities that they shall capture there. (Müller, doc. 12, p. 15; *Regesta*, doc. 467.)
1182, Aug.:	Baldwin IV grants lands in Acre. (Müller, doc. 19, p. 23; *Regesta*, doc. 617.)
1187, Oct.:	Conrad de Montferrat confirms a charter of Raymond of Tripoli granting lands in Tyre. (Müller, doc. 23, pp. 26–28; *Regesta*, doc. 665.)
1187, Oct.:	Conrad grants privileges in Acre and Jaffa when they shall be recaptured. (Müller, docs. 24, 25, pp. 28–31; *Regesta*, docs. 667, 668.)
1188, May:	Conrad grants lands in Acre and Tyre. (Müller, docs. 27, 28, pp. 33–35; *Regesta*, docs. 674, 675.)
1189, Nov.:	Guy de Lusignan and Sibylle confirm grants by Raymond of Tripoli in Acre which Conrad had already confirmed. (Müller, doc. 31, pp. 36–38; *Regesta*, doc. 683.)

1189, Nov.:   Guy and Sibylle confirm Conrad's grants in Tyre. Müller, doc. 32, pp. 38–39; *Regesta*, doc. 684.)

1191:   Conrad and Isabelle confirm privileges in Tyre and throughout Jerusalem and Tripoli. (Müller, doc. 33, pp. 39–40; *Regesta*, doc. 703.)

1192:   Richard of England confirms Guy's charters. (Müller, doc. 35, pp. 58–59; *Regesta*, doc. 706.)

1193, April: Pope Celestine III confirms charters of Guy, Richard, and Conrad. (Müller, doc. 36, pp. 59–60; *Regesta*, doc. 711.)

1193, May: Henry of Champagne and Isabelle confirm grants of Amaury I and Baldwin IV and grant freedom of trade. (Müller, doc. 37, p. 60; *Regesta*, doc. 713.)

1195, Jan.:   Henry and Isabelle restore to Pisans their possessions in Acre which had been confiscated when Henry drove them out of the city. (Müller, doc. 40, pp. 65–66; *Regesta*, doc. 721; cf. *Gestes*, par. 53.)

1197, Oct.:   Henry grants freedom of trade. (Müller, doc. 45, p. 73; *Regesta*, doc. 735.)

1200, Oct.:   Theobald, bishop of Acre, grants Pisans the right to have their own church in Acre. (Müller, doc. 52, pp. 82–83; *Regesta*, doc. 775.)

1229, April: Three charters of Frederick II granting court in Jerusalem, restoring the possessions confiscated by Thomas of Acerra, his bailli, and granting privileges in Acre, Tyre, and Jaffa. (Müller, docs. 64, 65, 66, pp. 95–98; *Regesta*, docs. 1005, 1006, 1007.)

In Antioch

1108:   Tancred grants quarter in Antioch and Laodicea. (Müller, doc. 1, p. 3; *Regesta*, doc. 53.)

1154:   Raymond and Constance grant lands in Antioch and Laodicea. (Müller, doc. 4, p. 6; *Regesta*, doc. 292.)

1170:   Bohemond III confirms all privileges. (Müller, doc. 13, pp. 15–16; *Regesta*, doc. 478.)

1200: Bohemond IV confirms privileges granted by Constance and grants reduced tariff of one half the regular rates. (Müller, doc. 50, pp. 80–81; *Regesta*, doc. 769.)

1216, April: Raymond Rupin confirms grants of Bohemond and Constance. (Müller, doc. 58, pp. 90–91; *Regesta*, doc. 886.)

In Tripoli

1179, Aug.: Raymond III of Tripoli grants house in Tripoli. (Müller, doc. 15, pp. 17–18; *Regesta*, doc. 585.)

1182: Pisans purchase house in Tripoli. (Müller, doc. 20, p. 24; *Regesta*, doc. 621.)

1187, Aug.: Raymond III of Tripoli grants freedom of trade and a court. (Müller, doc. 22, pp. 25–26; *Regesta*, doc. 662.)

1194, Jan.: Bohemond (III?) of Antioch and Tripoli grants Pisan commune of Acre a third of the import revenues of Tripoli and freedom from taxes, in return for 500 besants. (Müller, doc. 39, p. 65; *Regesta*, doc. 718.)

1199, Aug.: Bohemond IV makes peace with Pisa on receipt of 9000 besants, and promises not to hold the Pisans of Tripoli responsible for damages done by their fellow-countrymen. (Müller, doc. 49, pp. 79–80; *Regesta*, doc. 758.)

1202, Mar.: Plebanus of Botron and Celia his wife grant Pisans freedom of trade without tax save a slight charge on grain. This was not to include Pisans resident in Botron or Tripoli. (Müller, doc. 53, pp. 83–84; *Regesta*, doc. 788.)

1233, Mar.: Bohemond V of Antioch-Tripoli confirms grants to Pisa made by Raymond of Tripoli, and by his father. (Müller, docs. 68–69, pp. 99–100; *Regesta*, docs. 1041–42.)

In Cyprus

1291, Oct.: Henry II grants commercial privileges and courts. (Müller, doc. 73, pp. 108–09; *Regesta*, doc. 1518.)

4. *Marseilles and Montpellier*

1103:

Raymond of St Gilles grants a half of Gibelet when it shall be taken to St Victor of Marseilles. (*Regesta*, doc. 38; *Chronologie*, no. 686.)

1117:

Baldwin I grants privileges to Marseilles. (*Regesta*, doc. 85).

1136, April:

Foulque and Melissande confirm privileges and grant 400 besants from the revenues of Jaffa. (Méry, i, 182; *Regesta*, doc. 163.)

1152, Sept.:

Baldwin III grants church and quarter in Jerusalem and freedom from tax in all maritime cities for 3000 besants. (Méry, i, 183–84; *Regesta*, doc. 276.)

1163:

Ralph, bishop of Bethelehem, grants house in Acre, and casale, for 1211 besants. (*Regesta*, doc. 386; Rey, *Recherches*, pp. 18–19.)

1187, Oct.:

Conrad de Montferrat grants trade, market, and court in Tyre to Marseilles, Montpellier, St Gilles, and Barcelona. (Méry, i, 190–92; *Regesta*, doc. 666.)

1190, Oct.:

Guy de Lusignan and Sibylle grant court and freedom of trade without taxes in Acre. (Méry, i, 194; *Regesta*, doc. 697.)

1198, Oct.:

Amaury II and Isabelle confirm privileges and grant freedom of trade without tax, and a casale in Cyprus for the 2800 besants which the Marseillais gave them. (Méry, i, 85–89; Mas Latrie, ii, 24; *Regesta*, doc. 747.)

1212, Jan.:

John de Brienne confirms possessions and privileges of Marseillais in Acre. (Méry, i, 226; *Regesta*, doc. 855.)

1223, Sept.:

John d'Ibelin of Beirut grants freedom of trade and sale without tax in Beirut. (Méry, i, 287–89; *Regesta*, doc. 965.)

1229, April:

Frederick II grants freedom of trade and equality with Marseilles to Montpellier, whose merchants had until this time come in Marseillaise ships. (Winkelmann, *Acta Imperii Inedita*, i, doc. 302; *Regesta*, doc. 1014.)

1236, Mar.: Henry of Cyprus grants reduced tariffs to Marseilles and Montpellier in Cyprus. (Méry, i, 419–24; *Regesta*, doc. 1071.)

1243, Feb.: Bohemond V of Antioch-Tripoli grants privileges to Montpellier. (*Regesta*, doc. 1110; Germain, *Histoire de la Commune de Montpellier*, (Montpellier, 1851), ii, 513–15.)

1268–1271: Confirmations by Pope Clement IV of grants of Guy, Amaury, and Baldwin III. (Méry-Guindon, v, 73.)

1284: Charles of Anjou confirms the privileges of Marseilles in Acre. (Méry-Guindon, v. 73.)

4. *Amalfii*

1161:   William, bishop of Acre, grants lands for a cemetery to the Amalfitans settled in Acre. (Camera, i, 200; *Regesta*, doc. 372.)

1163, June: Raymond of Tripoli confirms the Amalfitans in certain possessions in Laodicea for 1200 besants, a case concerning this having been brought into his court. (Camera, i, 202–03; *Regesta*, doc. 380.)

1163:   Bohemond III of Antioch grants privileges and lands in Laodicea for 1300 besants. (Camera, i, 202; *Regesta*, doc. 388.

1168, Oct.   Amaury I confirms grants of Raymond of Tripoli. (Camera, i, 203–04; *Regesta*, doc. 453.)

1190, April: Guy de Lusignan and Sibylle grant Amalfitans a court and privileges in Acre, placing them on an equality with the Genoese, Pisans, and Venetians. (Camera, i, 201; *Regesta*, doc. 690.)

5. *Trani, Ancona, Siena*

1196, May: Amaury of Cyprus grants freedom of trade to Trani. Mas Latrie, ii, 30: *Regesta*, doc. 729.)

1257, Aug.: John d'Ibelin, bailli of Jersualem, confirms the Anconitans in their possession of a church, market, etc. in Acre. (Paoli, i, 157–61; *Regesta*, doc. 1259.)

1268, July: Conrad II grants Siennese trading privileges in Acre and the East as well as in Sicily and Italy. (Müller, doc. 70, pp. 100–101, *Regesta*, doc. 1360.)

APPENDIX E

NOTE ON THE LAW OF TREASON IN THE ASSISES OF JERUSALEM

Apparent treason, murder, and homicide were three crimes according to the laws of Jerusalem for which trial by battle was necessary.[1] And as befitted the most serious crimes the penalty inflicted upon those convicted of treason was that of hanging, with attainder and perpetual forfeiture for the heirs.[2] Yet while the mode of trial and the penalties were always fixed, the exact definition of treason was less surely known and varied somewhat between the early law of Baldwin II and the final treatise of John d'Ibelin. The *Livre au Roi*, which contains the law of Baldwin II, does not at any place define treason.[3] It lists in chapter XVI the crimes and offenses for which the fiefs of the culprit were forever forfeit, and among these are to be found those which undoubtedly were considered as treasonable acts. Twelve crimes are listed:—1) a vassal taking arms against the lord; 2) giving judgment against the lord (*'fait justice contre son seignor'*); 3) making false coins or monies; 4) poisoning the lord, his wife, or his children; 5) the making by a vassal of a port for ships or a road into *paienime* (Saracen countries) which will increase the value of his own land and reduce that of his lords; 6) a vassal making his own coins; 7) entrance by force of Saracens into possession of land for which he owes the lord service, if done without the consent of the lord or the approval of the court; 8) raising his villains against the lord and coming against him with armed force; 9) abandoning his fief and becoming a Moslem; 10) desertion of his lord in battle; 11) refusal to obey a reasonable command of the lord; 12) sale or surrender to the Saracens of a castle or town or lands without the consent of the lord. Not all of these are treasonable offenses but by the law of Baldwin II all were punished with the same penalty of perpetual forfeiture. And from them the later law of treason took its start.

Treason in the thirteenth century, when Philip de Novare and John d'Ibelin wrote, was divided into two distinct parts—apparent and non-apparent. For apparent treason the only mode of trial was by battle and if the person accused of it refused to present himself for trial his life was

---

[1] Ibelin, lxxxi, 129.

[2] Ibelin, cxc, 303–05; cxcii, 307–10.

[3] *Livre au Roi*, xvi, 616–17: '*Et tout ce est raison par dreit et par l'assise et par l'establissement dou roi Bauduin segont, à cuy Dés pardoint'*.

forfeit and his fiefs reverted to the lord.[1] Treason non-apparent was not recognized as a plea before the court and could only be fought out at the request of both parties and with the consent of the lord. But after the gages had been given and accepted by the lord, the battle took place by the will of all three parties and no one of them could prevent it.[2] '*Traïzon . . .*' says Novare, '*en ceste y a moult soutil plait,*' and the defendant must endeavor to show that what seems to be treason apparent is really treason non-apparent if he is not desirous of clearing his name by combat. 'And many assert that treason is not apparent if he who did it does not avow it, or if it is not proven by witness or by battle.'[3] Further the defendant can challenge the witness (they were not witnesses of fact but rather supporters of the plaintiff somewhat akin to the German compurgators, though not the same) and if the witness refuses to prove his words with his body, the plaintiff cannot force a battle on the defendant. Novare defines as evident *traïzon apparant*: 'when the lord has been betrayed apparently in anything, either of a fortress which he has lost or of evil counsel which has been discovered; or of his body if he has been hindered going or coming about his business; or if he has been attacked at night; or if he has received any manner of damage in which it seems apparent that he has been betrayed.'[4] Ibelin does not attempt a definition of treason but does cite specifically the crimes which are considered as treason apparent. They are: 1) the surrender or sale of a castle to the enemy; 2) attack upon the lord, either by armed men who waylay him on the road or who enter into his house, which can be shown to have been done by the defendant; 3) the capture of the wife, daughter, sister, or mother of the lord; 4) the murder of his father, son, or brother; 5) refusal to assist in securing the lord's ransom. Ibelin's discussion is elaborate and considerably more detailed than the simple enumeration of the crimes given in the *Livre au Roi*. Battle is

---

[1] Novare, xiv, 487–88; Ibelin, lxxxi, 129, xcviii, 160–62.

[2] Ibelin, xcv–xcvi, 155–58; *Clef des Assises,* cxxi, 588; Novare, xiv, 488. But the lord may refuse to accept the gages of battle and prohibit the fight as it was not required by law; '*car bataille de traïson ne peut estre par esgart ne par conoissance de court ne par assise, se la traïson n'est aparant*'. (p. 156.)

[3] '*Et plusiors dient que traïson n'est apparant se celui qui la fait ne le conoist, ou se elle n'est provée par garens ou par bataille*'. (Novare, xiv, 487.) Beugnot notes that it would be rather difficult to establish the plea if the accused had to be persuaded of it.

[4] '*Quant le seignor a esté trahi aparaument d'aucune choze, ou de fortrese qu'il a pardue, ou de conseill qui ait esté descourvert; ou de son cors qui a esté encombré, alant et venant en ses besoingnes; ou assailli nuitancré; ou se il a receu aucune maniere de damage, en quei il semble apparammed qu'il ait esté trahi*'. (Novare, xiv, 487.)

however necessary that treason be proved against the defendant.[1] To this list of crimes which are clearly treason, Ibelin adds others for which the penalty is forfeiture of the fief for all time. Besides the specifically enumerated treasonable crimes, conviction of treason by battle and failure to appear when accused of treason, perpetual forfeiture was entailed by: heresy; laying hands on, or coming in arms against, the lord; surrender of a castle as long as there was enough to eat and drink; betrayal of the lord and deserting him in battle; purchasing his death; an illegal sale of the fief.[2] This list compared with that of *Livre au Roi* shows that the concept of treason had crystallized considerably in the period between the compilation of the two works. Of the earlier list the murder of the lord or his family and sale of a castle to the enemy have become definitely treason. The other offenses are somewhat elaborated and in some cases altered slightly; they still remain cases where forfeiture was the penalty, though it did not imply the hanging which accompanied treason. To come in arms against the lord was not treason so long as it was done openly, but if he was attacked from ambush or surprised in his own home the act was one of treason.

Against the accusation of treason apparent, the defendant could only offer to prove his innocence by battle, unless, following the suggestions offered by Novare, he could turn the accusation from treason apparent to treason non-apparent. In the latter case battle was optional unless the lord refused to allow it, and it was rather a matter of preventing too frequent battles than of forcing the parties to appeal to this form of the *Iudicium Dei*. 'Car le plus de ceaus qui sont apelé dient que il deffendront volontiers de lor cors contre celui de l'apelor', says Novare. Under this charge of treason non-apparent, the plaintiff could accuse the defendant that he had falsely, disloyally, and treasonably wounded, assailed, maltreated, and injured him, without proper defiance, and the offense was aggravated if it was at night.[3] Novare stands between the *Livre au Roi* and Ibelin. His definitions are rather more vague than those of his great pupil and show a transition stage in the development of the idea of treason. In Ibelin's treatise treasonable acts are definitely marked off from lesser offenses.

---

[1] Ibelin, xcvii, 158–60. The plaintiff may demand battle on these grounds, and if the defendant does not appear he is guilty. Ibelin, ccxlix, 398, declares refusal to assist in ransoming the lord to be *traïson aparant*.

[2] Ibelin, cxc, 303–05.

[3] 'Quant aucuns a esté naffré ou assailli ou malmené, ou damagé d'aucune grant choze, il peut . . . dire que il li a ce fait fausement et desloiaument, en traïzon, sans deffiance et nuitancré, se ce fu du nuit'. (Novare, xiv, 487–88.)

The procedure in cases of treason is interesting. The plaintiff accuses the defendant of treason apparent and offers to prove his charges with his body. If the defendant is not present at the court three members of the court are sent to summon him. The first, representing the lord, presents the summons, and the other two, representing the court, witness that the summons was delivered. If the defendant does not appear at court on the date fixed by the summons he is declared guilty and attainted. If he comes, he immediately asks for counsel, and denies word for word the charges of the plaintiff. If he wishes to fight he offers his body in proof of his innocence, and offers his gage to the lord who accepts it as he had previously accepted the gage of the plaintiff. The court then sets the place and conditions of the battle, which was to take place forty days after the day on which the gages were accepted. They also regulated the arms to be borne by the contestants, but they must be knightly weapons. We have already seen that the defendant '*qu'il n'a talent de combatre*' could endeavor to change the charge and avoid the battle. If however the battle is agreed upon, both parties are required to appear and fight. If the defendant loses, he is hanged and his heirs attainted. His fief reverts to his lord, nor may his heirs ever hope to recover it.[1] Several interesting cases of treason are found in the history of Cyprus in the thirteenth century, reported in the *Mémoires de Philippe de Novare*. In 1225 a knight named William de la Tour, having been attacked, charged Gauvain de Chenchi of treasonable attack upon him. The gages were given and received in the High Court and the battle fixed. The peace which was made after the battle was a hard one for Gauvain, who felt that William had had the support of the Ibelins who governed Cyprus at the time. While Novare does not say, one infers from his account, that the battle was indecisive, for Gauvain was free to go to the court of Frederick II.

In 1233 Henry of Cyprus charged of treason Amaury Barlais, Amaury de Bethsan, and Hugh de Gibelet, and they were declared forfeit and outlawed ('*deshérité et fortjugié en cors et en avoir*'). As they did not appear for trial the confiscation was proclaimed. This charge was not in accord with the law as later stated by Ibelin for their rebellion was an open one. The penalty of confiscation was of course merited in any case but technically the charge of treason did not conform with the law, unless it was brought on the grounds that they sold the king's castles to the enemy. A more clear case is that of Martin Rousseau, a captain of sergeants, who during the siege of Kyrenia conspired with the enemy to kill the leaders of the Cypriots.

---

[1] The best account of the procedure in treason trials is in Ibelin, xcviii, 160–62. Novare has a shorter account.

The treason was discovered and the case was administered by Philip de Novare himself. Rousseau and some accomplices were hanged by order of the court.[1]

In the thirteenth century as today, practice modified the law. Ibelin states a clear theory and law of treason. The actual cases which are recorded seldom conform to the law in all their details. Yet there are several points of interest in the Outremer law of treason:—it was restricted, and treason apparent was limited to a very few cases (and these could not always to be proven to fall under this head); treason was carefully differentiated from rebellion in law if not in fact, and the latter was not the serious crime the former was; treason had to be *done*,—desiring to encompass the death of the monarch was altogether outside the competence of the law of treason.

[1] *Gestes des Chiprois*, par. 199. Novare does not mention any trial by battle for Rousseau or his accomplices. While Rousseau was himself a commoner, one of his fellows was a liegeman of the king. But the state of war and the conclusive evidence justified a more speedy decision of the case than the normal procedure would afford.

APPENDIX F
NOTE ON THE SOURCES

The sources of the crusades and of the crusading states have probably been subjected to as intensive criticism as those of any field of mediaeval history. Since the initial work of Von Seybel the narrative sources have been the subject of study, and the relative merits of William of Tyre, Fulcher of Chartres, Albert of Aix, and the historians of the crusades have been discussed by several generations of scholars. The only thing that can be attempted in here discussing the sources of this work is to show why certain materials have been used in preference to others, and to call attention to some few lesser known sources. A thorough discussion of the sources which Dodu used is to be found in the introduction of his *Histoire des Institutions Monarchiques*, and little can be here added to his description of the materials which he employed.

The *Assises de Jérusalem* provided, of course, the basis for the entire work. While these are amply described by Dodu, the recent researches of Maurice Grandclaude, whose *Étude critique sur les Livres des Assises de Jérusalem* appeared in 1923, have completely altered the older conception of the relation of the various volumes of the *Assises* to each other and have corrected the misapprehensions under which Beugnot and Dodu labored as to the dates of compilation of at least two of the texts. The *Assises de la Cour des Bourgeois*, which were dated by Beugnot as around 1187 before the city of Jerusalem had fallen to Saladin, have been shown to have been compiled between 1229 and 1244 when the city was for the second time in the Frankish possession. The *Livre au Roi*, on the other hand, which Beugnot dated as between 1271 and 1291 and thought to be a supplement to the book of Ibelin, has been shown by Grandclaude to have been compiled between 1197 and 1205 under the rule of Amaury and Isabelle, and to be the oldest of all the Outremer texts. This obviously enhances the value of the *Livre au Roi* as it makes it the work which can best claim to represent the older customs of the first kingdom. Throughout this study the provisions of the later books of the *Assises*,—Ibelin, Novare, the *Assises de la Cour des Bourgeois*, and the other thirteenth century compilations—have been used to illustrate only the conditions in the second kingdom, and only the *Livre au Roi* has been used in reference to the first kingdom, and even then the occurrences of the last quarter of the century have caused modifications of the earlier law which are reflected in the *Livre* and which necessitate caution

281

in applying it to the first period of the kingdom. Much valuable information for comparison has been derived from the *Assises d'Antioche* and from the *Assises de Romanie*, the codes of Antioch and the Morea which were deeply influenced by the laws of Jerusalem.

Among the chroniclers and narrative historians, while first place must be accorded to William of Tyre, much valuable material has been obtained from the *Gestes de Chiprois*, especially the center portion which is the *Mémoires de Philippe de Novare*. This source was apparently unknown to Dodu, who knew it only through the later Italian chronicle of Amadi, though the *Gestes* had been published by G. Raynaud for the Société de l'Orient Latin in 1887. This is, in the opinion of the author, the most valuable single source for the affairs of Jerusalem and Cyprus in the thirteenth century, and has consequently been used as the chief narrative account with which to check the statements of the *Assises* for the second period of the kingdom. The history of Ernoul and the *Livre d'Eracles*, the continuators of William of Tyre, have also been laid under heavy contribution for the events of the thirteenth century, but in cases of conflict with the *Gestes*, the account of the latter has been followed.

The Arabic historians offered little to this study. Ibn Djubair, Usamah, and Beha-ed-Din supplied some bits of information, but on the whole the Arabs were concerned with the crusading states only in their foreign affairs, which have not been considered in this work at all, and knew very little of the internal organization of the kingdom.

It is in the use of documentary materials that this study differs most widely from that of Dodu. As has been stated in the preface, Dodu unfortunately wrote before the publication of R. Röhricht's *Regesta Regni Hierosolymitani* and so was without the benefit of the *Regesta* as a guide to documentary sources. This may in part explain Dodu's neglect of the wealth of material which is to be found in the documents of the Venetian, Genoese, Pisan, and other Italian and Provençal communes, as found in the collections of Tafel and Thomas, the *Liber Jurium Ianunesis*, Müller, Camera, Méry, et al.. The ecclesiastical documents edited by Rozière, Delaborde, and Beugnot were used by Dodu, and while he used Strehlke for the Teutonic Knights he was forced to rely on the old edition of Paoli for the documents of the Hospitallers, which have since been edited so splendidly by Delaville Le Roulx, and of the Templars, on whose cartulary a beginning was made by the Marquis d'Albon.

The editions which have been used in this study are cited in the table of abbreviations, or, in the case of less frequently cited materials, the bibliographical information has been supplied on the first occasion when the work was cited in each chapter.

INDEX

(This Index does not include Introduction, Appendices, or citations of authorities in notes.)